THE ARAB LANDS UNDER OTTOMAN RULE, 1516–1800

A History of the Near East
General Editor: Professor P. M. Holt

THE ARAB LANDS UNDER OTTOMAN RULE, 1516–1800

JANE HATHAWAY
WITH CONTRIBUTIONS BY
KARL K. BARBIR

PEARSON
Longman

Harlow, England • London • New York • Boston • San Francisco • Toronto
Sydney • Tokyo • Singapore • Hong Kong • Seoul • Taipei • New Delhi
Cape Town • Madrid • Mexico City • Amsterdam • Munich • Paris • Milan

PEARSON EDUCATION LIMITED

Edinburgh Gate
Harlow CM20 2JE
United Kingdom
Tel: +44 (0)1279 623623
Fax: +44 (0)1279 431059
Website: www.pearsoned.co.uk

First edition published in Great Britain in 2008

© Pearson Education Limited 2008

The rights of Jane Hathaway and Karl Barbir to be identified as authors
of this work have been asserted by them in accordance with the Copyright,
Designs and Patents Act 1988.

ISBN: 978-0-582-41899-8

British Library Cataloguing in Publication Data
A CIP catalogue record for this book can be obtained from the British Library

10 9 8 7 6 5 4 3 2 1
12 11 10 09 08

Set in 10.5/13pt Galliard by 35
Printed in Malaysia (CTP-VVP)

The Publisher's policy is to use paper manufactured from sustainable forests.

Dedicated to the memory of
Professor P. M. Holt

CONTENTS

CONTENTS

ACKNOWLEDGEMENTS

This book has been a very long time in preparation, and it seems that the more time passes, the more debts of gratitude I accrue. First and foremost, I owe a tremendous debt to Professor Peter Holt for recommending me for this project. One of my great regrets is that he did not live to see the publication of this book, which is dedicated to his memory. I sincerely hope that his confidence was not misplaced. I am also deeply grateful to the editors at Addison Wesley Longman/ Pearson Education for their patience and to my friend and colleague Professor Colin Heywood, who read the entire manuscript and made numerous valuable suggestions. Thanks, also, to Professor Karl K. Barbir, who read drafts of the Introduction and Chapters 1–6 and made a number of useful suggestions, many of which I have incorporated into the text.

Much of the book's conceptualization, as well as a draft of the Introduction, was accomplished at the Institute for Advanced Study in Princeton, New Jersey, where I was a fellow of the School of Historical Studies during winter and spring 2000. I thank my fellow fellows and the permanent members of the School of Historical Studies for their comments on a presentation I gave based on the Introduction. I am likewise grateful to the M. Münir Ertegün Foundation for Turkish Studies in the Department of Near Eastern Studies, Princeton University, and above all Professor M. Şükrü Hanioğlu, for allowing me to serve as Ertegün Visiting Professor of Turkish Studies in spring 2003; the course on the Ottoman Arab provinces which I taught in that capacity helped me to shape the main part of the book's text.

Reaching back a bit farther in time, I should like to thank Professors Abraham Marcus and Cemal Kafadar, my MA and PhD advisors, respectively. During the lengthy process of revision, I turned again and again to notes and outlines from their courses. Naturally, responsibility for any errors is entirely mine, not least because too many years have passed since I took my postgraduate degrees to hold my advisors responsible for my own shortcomings! At Ohio State, my colleagues Cynthia Brokaw and Stephen F. Dale, as well as PhD candidate Lisa Balabanlılar, helpfully recommended secondary sources on the Qing and Mughal empires for comparative purposes. Mr Chris Aldridge and Mr Mitchell

Shelton of the Harvey Goldberg Program for Excellence in Teaching in Ohio State's History Department were instrumental in preparing the maps and illustrations for this book.

Finally, my heartfelt thanks to Beshir and Stella, and to my husband, Robert Simkins, for bearing with this project for all these years.

NOTE ON TRANSLITERATION AND DATES

Transliteration – that is, the rendering in Roman letters of words in languages that do not employ the Roman alphabet – is a challenge, particularly when two Middle Eastern languages with very different sound systems, in this case Arabic and Ottoman Turkish, are involved. I have retained distinctive Turkish letters apart from c, ç and ş, which I feared general English-speaking audiences would find simply too alien and which I have therefore replaced with j, ch and sh, respectively. In the case of modern Turkish titles cited in the Bibliographical Essay, however, it has proven impossible to forgo these letters. Here is an equivalency guide to the Turkish letters:

c = j
ç = ch
ğ = soft 'g,' as in French *espagnol*
ı ≈ u, as in 'put'
ö ≈ ur, as in 'hurt,' or French œ
ş = sh
ü ≈ u, as in 'mute,' or French u.

Apart from a few Arabic titles in the Bibliographical Essay, I have avoided indicating long vowels in Arabic or Ottoman Turkish. Where these do occur, they have the following equivalents:

ā ≈ a, as in 'ah'
ī = ee, as in 'weed'
ū = oo, as in 'too'.

Otherwise, a, i and u in Arabic words and names should be regarded as sounding like slightly shorter equivalents of the long vowels listed above.

In a few cases, as well, I have found it necessary to employ a superscript 'c' (') for the Arabic letter *ayn*, a guttural sound that does not exist in English, and a forward apostrophe (') for the Arabic glottal stop, or *hamza*. Apart from certain Arabic titles cited in the Bibliographical Essay, I do this only to separate vowels that would otherwise form a diphthong, as in al-Kha'in, 'the Traitor,' or to differentiate certain

Arabic names from their English homonyms, e.g. Fakhr al-Din Ma'n instead of Fakhr al-Din Man.

Where the Arabic definite article, *al-*, is concerned, I render it *al-* in all cases, without signifying the elision with the following consonant that often occurs (e.g. 'al-Din' in 'Fakhr al-Din' should properly be pronounced 'ad-DEEN'). My purpose here is to keep the function of the *al-* particle as clear as possible, and thereby to avoid making Arabic names seem unnecessarily complicated or unfathomable. Readers familiar with Arabic will make the necessary mental adjustment themselves.

A question closely related to transliteration choices is which form of Muslim proper names to employ: Arabic or Turkish. I have opted for Turkish forms in the case of Ottoman officials and most provincial notables, and Arabic forms in the case of figures from early Islamic history, provincial ulema and Bedouin tribal leaders.

Finally, terms that can be found in English dictionaries, such as 'emir,' 'mamluk,' 'reaya,' 'Sufi' and 'ulema,' retain the spellings found there.

Dates are given according to the Gregorian calendar and identified where necessary as Common Era (CE, equivalent to AD) or Before the Common Era (BCE, equivalent to BC).

LIST OF FIGURES

Publisher's acknowledgements

We are grateful to the following for permission to reproduce copyright material:

Figure 2.1: Istanbul University Rare Works Library; Figures 3.1, 5.1 and 7.2 Topkapı Palace Museum, Istanbul; Figure 5.3: Professor André Raymond; Figure 6.1: Gary Otte/Aga Khan Trust for Culture.

In some instances we have been unable to trace the owners of copyright material, and we would appreciate any information that would enable us to do so.

LIST OF MAPS

1. Expansion of the Ottoman Empire, c.1300–1590.

Source: Adapted from Halil Inalcik, *The Ottoman Empire: The Classical Age, 1300–1600*, trans. Norman Itzkowiitz and Colin Imber (London: Weidenfeld and Nicolson, 1973; paperback London: Phoenix Press, 2000), pp. 24–25

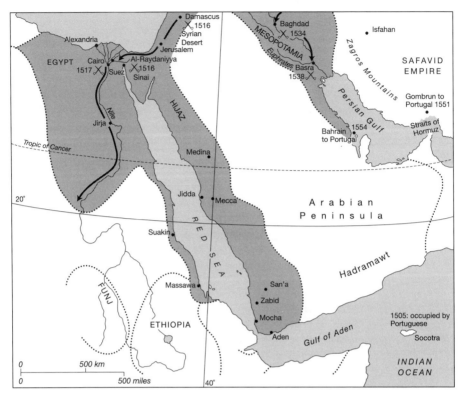

2. Egypt, the Arabian peninsula and the Persian Gulf region, *c.*1550. Arrows denote the route of Ottoman conquest.
Source: Adapted from *The Prentice Hall Atlas of World History* (Upper Saddle River, NJ: Pearson Education/Prentice Hall, 2005), p. 75

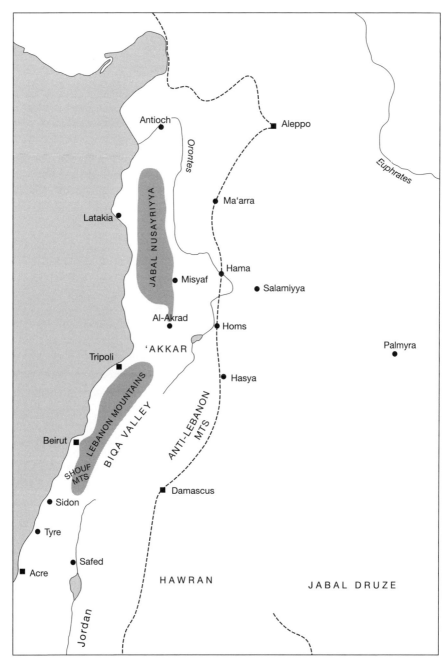

3. The northern and central parts of Ottoman Syria.
Source: Adapted from Dick Douwes, *The Ottomans in Syria: A History of Justice and Oppression* (London: I.B. Tauris, 2000), p. 12

REWRITING ARAB HISTORY, 1516–1800

To every student of Arab history, Peter M. Holt's magisterial survey *Egypt and the Fertile Crescent: A Political History, 1516–1922* is indispensable. First published forty years ago, the book provides a straightforward political narrative of developments in Egypt, Greater Syria (including what are now Lebanon, Jordan, Israel and the Palestinian Authority), Iraq, the Arabian peninsula and Yemen from the time of the Ottoman conquest of the Arab lands to the end of World War I. For sheer factual completeness, it is still a valuable reference tool.

P.M. Holt was for many years professor in the University of London's School of Oriental and African Studies. He started out in the civil service of Sudan's British administration and in the 1950s prepared the ground for the study of modern Sudanese political history. In the late 1950s and early 1960s he moved on to lay the foundations for the study of Egypt during the Ottoman period. The *Bulletin of the School of Oriental and African Studies* during those years became a showcase for his work, publishing one pathbreaking article after another on Ottoman Egypt's political elites. *Egypt and the Fertile Crescent* is, in many respects, the culmination of this phase of his scholarly career.

There is no escaping the fact, however, that *Egypt and the Fertile Crescent* is now forty years old. Longmans, Green and Company, the predecessor of Addison Wesley Longman, brought out the British edition in 1966, quickly followed by Cornell University Press's paperback edition. In recent years, Addison Wesley Longman and its successor, Pearson Education, have begun publishing a new series surveying Middle Eastern, Ottoman and African history. The present work was conceived as an updated version of *Egypt and the Fertile Crescent* which would take its place alongside these recently published surveys. This book's scope, however, is somewhat more modest than that of *Egypt and the Fertile Crescent*, encompassing Egypt, Greater Syria, Iraq, the Arabian peninsula and Yemen from 1516 only to 1800, the conventional dividing line between the

· 1 ·

early modern and modern periods in the region. Furthermore, as will soon become apparent, the book covers a somewhat different range of topics, including, in addition to political events, social, economic, religious and demographic issues. It attempts to do justice to *Egypt and the Fertile Crescent* while at the same time taking account of the innovative work that has been done in the past four decades on the Arab provinces of the Ottoman Empire. This introductory chapter furnishes some idea of the issues this book addresses and how it both builds upon and departs from its predecessor.

Why *The Arab Lands under Ottoman Rule*?

The present work's title, *The Arab Lands under Ottoman Rule*, stands in obvious contrast to that of Holt's book, *Egypt and the Fertile Crescent*, which, self-consciously or not, makes no reference to the Ottoman Empire or, on the other hand, to Arabs. While the author does not provide a rationale for this choice, the title is a modern-day geographical descriptor of the region surveyed. It may also aim to accommodate Egypt's arguable separation from the empire in the nineteenth century, first as a semi-autonomous polity under Mehmed (or Muhammad) Ali Pasha and his descendants, then, after 1882, under British occupation and protectorate. Before the 1980s, historians did not conventionally regard nineteenth-century Egypt as Ottoman, although that viewpoint has become dominant in the years since.

The Arab lands and geography

Otherwise, neither title is unproblematic with regard to geographical scope and appropriateness to the period under study. 'Fertile Crescent', a term whose meanings will be explored in Chapter 1, stems from Biblical scholarship and thus might be construed as an Orientalist label. It was not, in any case, a term the Ottomans themselves employed to refer to the Arab provinces of their empire. On the other hand, they did not use 'Arab provinces' either. To be sure, Ottoman narrative sources convey a sense of Syria and Iraq as Asiatic provinces in contradistinction to the empire's European provinces. In this context, they were closely linked to Anatolia, the peninsula that comprises the bulk of modern-day Turkey. This consideration in turn makes the term 'Arab lands' problematic since it seems to incorporate the boundary demarcation between the current Republic of Turkey and the Arab nation-states to its south. This was not necessarily a boundary the Ottomans recognized. Likewise, various parts of what is now Iraq spent sizeable portions of the Ottoman era under the political control of the rulers of Iran; in this light, the Iran/Iraq border seems as artificial to a survey of the Ottoman provinces as the south-eastern border of Turkey. Egypt, for its part, enjoyed symbiotic commercial relationships with the North African provinces to its west and, to the south, with Sudan and Ethiopia; thus, despite its historical territorial integrity, its borders are equally questionable as limits to an historical survey. The same could be said even of southern Iraq and Yemen, both of which cultivated commercial ties to India.

The Arab lands and nationalist historiographies

The adjective 'Arab' is equally problematic outside the realm of geography. As will be detailed in Chapter 1, 'Arab' during the period 1516–1800 usually referred to either a Bedouin nomad or a sub-Saharan African; it had few, if any, of its modern-day ethnic, regional or linguistic connotations. Even if we conform to the modern-day definition of the term, the population of the territories in question was by no means entirely Arab or even Arabic-speaking during the Ottoman period. As Chapter 1 will point out, sizeable populations of Kurds, Armenians, Turcomans and Persians inhabited these lands even before the Ottoman conquest, while Ottoman administrative practices resulted in an influx of Greeks, Bosnians, Hungarians, Albanians, Anatolians of various kinds, and members of various populations from East Africa and the Caucasus.

In this book, 'Arab lands' serves chiefly as a geographical term, to indicate in broad strokes the territory covered. Like Holt's book, however, the present volume does not adhere strictly to these geographical limits at all times but acknowledges the territory's indispensable links to surrounding regions. Admittedly, though, 'the Arab lands' is comprehensible to a general readership because it obviously corresponds to the present-day nation-states that identify themselves as Arab. This in turn reflects the inordinate influence modern nation-state boundaries have had on the historiography of the Ottoman provinces, to the extent that studies spanning the borders of more than one province are extremely rare. Until the last quarter century or so, it was the norm for even a scholarly history of a given province to proceed teleologically, as if the nation-state were the foreordained outcome of the historical process.

Similarly, old-school nationalist histories habitually presented the first three centuries of Ottoman rule in the Arab lands as a demoralizing prelude to the European-style reforms and nascent nationalisms of the nineteenth century, which eventually enabled the future nation-states to 'throw off the Turkish yoke'. Perhaps in part for this reason, a disproportionate number of historians of the Ottoman Arab provinces are orientated towards the nineteenth century, and some of them frame the realities of the earlier period as preparation for nineteenth-century developments. This approach is, frankly, distorted. The developments of the preceding three centuries have importance in their own right; their study need not be justified by reference to the modern period, nor should they be evaluated in terms of nineteenth-century criteria.

By the same token, this book rejects the conventional nationalist portrayal of the nearly three hundred years between the Ottoman conquest of the Arab lands and 1800 as little more than an oppressive occupation which contributed little to what was essentially an undiluted Arab culture. The Ottoman context is critical to an understanding of political, social and economic developments during this period. Holt was fully aware of this Ottoman context: both *Egypt and the Fertile Crescent* and his numerous micro-studies of Ottoman Egypt display a striking sensitivity to it, despite his unfamiliarity with Ottoman Turkish sources. In partial tribute to Holt's example, acknowledgement of the Ottoman milieu in which these societies existed during the premodern period is now routine in scholarly publications. Notwithstanding, as will be pointed out below, more subtle threats have emerged to this rapprochement with the Ottoman reality.

The Arab lands and Islam

Readers will not have failed to notice that neither *Egypt and the Fertile Crescent* nor the title of the present book evokes Islam, even though many inhabitants of the Arab lands before 1800 would have identified more readily with the Muslim, or at least Sunni, community than they would have done with an ethnic or even a linguistic group. Holt published *Egypt and the Fertile Crescent* at the height of the Cold War and during the heyday of Arab nationalism, when the roots of nationalist movements and modern nation-states were much on the minds of policy-makers who dealt with the Middle East. Only a few years earlier, Bernard Lewis had published the first edition of *The Emergence of Modern Turkey*. Today, when extremist strains of Islam are regarded as a far more potent force than nationalism in the Middle East, one sees comparatively few general histories of the Arabs; the last major such work in English was the late Albert Hourani's *A History of the Arab Peoples* in 1991. In contrast, histories, or at least assessments, of Islam and of the Middle East have become far more common. Yet, as Chapter 1 will explain, 'Middle East' is a quite recent coinage which had no meaning for the Ottomans. And while the Ottoman Empire was officially Sunni Muslim, substantial numbers of Ottoman subjects, even in the Arab provinces, were non-Muslims who deserve space in the historical narrative. Moreover, while religion was extremely important in Ottoman provincial society, it took many more forms and served many more purposes, each shaped by the specific social context within which it emerged, than could be suggested by a single generic reference to 'Islam'.

In summary, there is no wholly satisfying manner of framing the topic of the present book. However, *The Arab Lands under Ottoman Rule* comes closest to reflecting the dramatic changes in scholarly approaches to these territories in the past four decades.

Sources for the study of the Ottoman Arab lands

One reason the historiographical landscape has changed so dramatically since the publication of *Egypt and the Fertile Crescent* is the much broader range of historical sources now available to scholars. Holt based his account of the Ottoman Arab lands almost entirely on narrative sources in Arabic, chiefly annalistic chronicles and biographical dictionaries. The political elites who dominate these sources likewise dominate the narrative of *Egypt and the Fertile Crescent*. On the other hand, *Egypt and the Fertile Crescent* does not devote significant attention to high-ranking Muslim scholar-officials (ulema) or wealthy merchants, even though these figures are well represented in certain widely available chronicles. Clearly, then, sources alone do not determine the kind of history a scholar writes. However, they can impose limits to historical enquiry or, on the other hand, bolster pre-existing attitudes.

Holt did not exploit the wealth of Ottoman documents available in Turkey's archives, which, at the time *Egypt and the Fertile Crescent* was published, had been open to scholars for just over a decade. These documents – sultanic orders, complaints to the sultan from provincial officials, tax registers, military pay registers – offer sometimes revelatory insights into the fiscal and institutional underpinnings of Ottoman provincial administration, as well as the relations of provincial personnel with the imperial government and with their counterparts in other provinces. They can prove critical to reconstruction of the Ottoman context of provincial societies.

On the other hand, the exploitation of provincial archival sources has revolutionized the study of provincial social history in the last forty years. The registers of the Muslim law courts have been particularly valuable in uncovering the history of non-elites, notably middling merchants, artisans and peasants. Such a register consists of transcriptions, often abbreviated, of cases involving a wide range of issues, including commercial partnerships, property disputes, the witnessing of various transactions, marriage and divorce, inheritance, and estate disposition, as well as criminal cases, such as theft of money or property, adjudicated according to Islamic law (*sharia*). In the Arab provinces, these registers were kept in Arabic rather than in Ottoman Turkish. A noteworthy feature of the court registers is their social inclusiveness; everyone from the provincial governor and the most powerful grandees and religious officials to humble craftsmen and farmers from the countryside had recourse to the Muslim courts, as did an astonishing number of non-Muslims. Court cases can shed light on issues as varied as the class composition of urban neighbourhoods, the rural economy, and the status of women and non-Muslims. Documents registered in the courts, notably estate inventories and the foundation deeds for pious endowments, can likewise reveal details of material culture, intellectual trends, and modes of religious observance.

In combination, these central and provincial archival sources, along with the considerably broader spectrum of local chronicles now available and judiciously chosen foreign observers' accounts, can support a nuanced and multifaceted interpretation of provincial culture. Happily, the past twenty-five years have seen a steady proliferation of monographic studies of the Arab provinces employing both central and provincial sources and perspectives.

Ironically, however, the much greater array of locally produced Arabic sources has bolstered a resurgence of the old Arab nationalist historiography, albeit in more sophisticated theoretical trappings. Typical of this approach is an insistence on the 'authenticity' of purely Arabic sources as reflecting the reality of the 'indigenous' population; as a corollary, Ottoman Turkish sources originating with the central government are ignored, or in a few cases dismissed, as reflecting nothing more than the agenda of the administrative elite in a distant imperial capital. A closely related attitude holds that locally produced sources offer the only clues to non-elites whereas only the elite are represented in sources emanating from Istanbul. Since non-elites are implicitly equated with Arabs and elites with Turks, the effect of this mindset is to resurrect the old mutually exclusive nationalist categories of 'Arab' and 'Turk' in the name of authenticity and historiographical populism. In addition, the laudable goal of allowing non-elites a voice is too often used as an excuse for ignoring the Ottoman context of provincial societies. The result is sloppy scholarship which, ironically, denies these non-elites agency by portraying them as hermetically sealed within their provincial borders when, in fact, many of them could and did forge commercial and patronage links to populations in other provinces and in the imperial capital.

Nothing in the history of the Arab provinces themselves warrants this artificial polarization of the field between 'Arabists' and 'Turcologists', which seems to have far more to do with present-day nation-state and academic politics than it does with the provinces themselves. Furthermore, it is a disservice to the scholarship that Holt pioneered. Regardless of what sources historians of the Arab provinces are able to or choose to employ, they must take the Ottoman context into account. This, of course, implies having a thorough knowledge of the Ottoman context, including developments at the imperial centre and in other provinces.

Indeed, it is clearer today than ever before that we simply cannot understand the history of the Arab lands between 1516 and World War I without a thorough understanding of Ottoman history and institutions. This means more than just a parade of governors and judges imposed upon a supposedly supine indigenous population. It means acknowledgement and appreciation of the manner in which the Arab lands were incorporated into the Ottoman system politically, militarily, agriculturally, fiscally, commercially, socially and even artistically. Four hundred years is too lengthy a period to label an 'occupation'. Although the Arab provinces were not settler colonies of the Ottoman centre – that is to say, they were not colonized by masses of immigrants from the central lands – they both absorbed and contributed to the population of Ottoman officials of various kinds. Soldiers dispatched to one or another province from Istanbul might remain there, for example, while families indigenous to the Arab provinces might join the ranks of Ottoman provincial governors. Nor did the Arab lands retain their previous administrative, fiscal, educational and architectural structures beneath a thin Ottoman veneer. In fact, a broad cultural synthesis emerged that we might call not simply Ottoman-Arab but Ottoman provincial, so as not to preclude comparison and exchange with the Ottoman Empire's non-Arab – that is, Anatolian and Balkan – provinces. This book tries to reflect this synthesis by providing an account of the Arab provinces' history which integrates central and provincial elements.

'Decline' and decentralization

Quite apart from the exploitation of an array of new sources, scholarship on the Ottoman Arab provinces has profited from several key reconceptualizations within the broader Ottoman field. At the same time, certain problematic concepts remain dominant in Ottoman studies, thus hindering the development of a truly integrative provincial historiography.

One of the most momentous changes to have occurred in Ottoman studies since the publication of *Egypt and the Fertile Crescent* is the deconstruction of the so-called 'Ottoman decline thesis' – that is, the notion that towards the end of the sixteenth century, following the reign of Sultan Süleyman I (1520–66), the empire entered a lengthy decline from which it never truly recovered, despite heroic attempts at westernizing reforms in the nineteenth century. Over the last twenty years or so, as Chapter 4 will point out, historians of the Ottoman Empire have rejected the narrative of decline in favour of one of crisis and adaptation: after weathering a wrenching economic and demographic crisis in the late sixteenth and early seventeenth centuries, the Ottoman Empire adjusted its character from that of a military conquest state to that of a territorially more stable, bureaucratic state whose chief concern was no longer conquering new territories but extracting revenue from the territories it already controlled while shoring up its image as the bastion of Sunni Islam.

So far as the Arab provinces were concerned, the chief hallmark of this 'crisis and adaptation' was increasingly decentralized rule. Decentralization, however, has its own paradigmatic narrative which is, in its own way, as problematic as that of decline. As younger and weaker sultans took the throne from the turn of the seventeenth century, according to this narrative, the Ottoman central authority's hold on the provinces loosened. Meanwhile, with the waning of imperial expansion, provincial governors were less and less frequently seasoned warriors with solid provincial experience, and more and more the products of palace patronage networks. Their terms of office, furthermore, tended to shrink from several years to a year or even less. This resulted in a lack of continuity in provincial policies; at the same time, the short-term governor had little incentive to improve conditions within the province and every incentive to milk the province for maximum tax revenues. To fill the vacuum left by the central authority's negligence and to counter the governors' rapacity, powerful 'local notable' families and households emerged. These notables, or *ayan*, the subject of Chapter 5, would come to exercise near-hegemony in many Ottoman provinces by the late eighteenth century.

As Chapters 4 and 5 will attempt to demonstrate, the problem with the conventional narrative of decentralization is that it is too pat. It implies a neat dichotomy between Ottoman officials and local notables that did not, in fact, exist. Many 'local notables' cultivated strong ties to powerful figures within the palace, taking advantage of what we might call 'decentralization at the centre' – that is, the emergence of multiple competing interest groups within the palace itself – to acquire room to manoeuvre on the local scene. At the same time, figures in the central government continued to patronize provincial clients, often through specially commissioned agents (singular *wakil* in Arabic, *vekil* in Turkish) on the spot. The Chief Eunuch of the imperial harem, for example, had a permanent agent stationed in Egypt long before the eunuch himself retired to that province. In short, exchanges between centre and province continued, if in somewhat altered form, after the sixteenth century, and the boundary between central and local jurisdiction remained fluid. Moreover, the degree of decentralization and the complexion of 'local notables' varied from one province to another, and even from one district to another. In the mountains of Lebanon, for instance, the Ottomans had employed locally entrenched tribal families as proxies since their conquest of these territories in 1516; several of these families are discussed in Chapters 4 and 8. The Ottomans were careful, however, to play competing families off against each other and to shift their patronage whenever a particular family threatened to amass a formidable power base. In regions with less intimidating geography, such as Egypt and southern Syria, in contrast, entrenched local notable families and households emerged only in the eighteenth century for reasons that will be discussed in Chapter 5.

The conventional historiography equates this decentralization with weakness at the centre, thus imputing an inherently negative character to decentralization, and holds that imperial weakness enabled the rise of local elites who would ultimately lead certain of the Arab provinces, notably Egypt, to virtual autonomy. What such an interpretation ignores, however, is the fact that decentralization proved a viable, although admittedly far from perfect, administrative strategy for the Ottomans for over two hundred years. Inability to conceive of decentralization as the end-product of a series of rational choices on the part of both central and provincial actors stems from the overarching perception of the process as an unstoppable force that somehow transcends both individual actions and societal factors. On the other hand, misapprehension of the utility of decentralization results in part from a misunderstanding of the political culture of the Ottoman Arab provinces. This book attempts to remedy this misunderstanding to the extent possible in a general survey.

State and society

The centre–provincial dichotomy discussed above can also be detected in the tension between state and society that looms large in current Ottomanist scholarship, both 'central' and 'provincial'. The Ottoman government, large, unwieldy, dispersed and, above all, changeable as it was, is frequently referred to collectively in this scholarship as 'the state', while those subjects who were not somehow connected to the government are termed 'society'. To some degree, this division is coloured by the classic Ottoman distinction between *askeri* (literally, 'military'), meaning the tax-exempt elite, including all government officials, members of the armed forces, and high-ranking Muslim scholar-officials, or ulema; and *reaya* (literally, 'flock'), including peasants, nomads, merchants and craftspeople. Otherwise, the 'state' and 'society' categories seem unmanageably broad, the divisions between them impossibly vague. By the late eighteenth century, the state could be understood to encompass the sultan and all palace pages, the approximately 1,000 scribes of the central bureaucracy, the grand vizier and his consultative council, 150,000 imperial Janissaries and, on the provincial scene, myriad scribes, clerks and judges. Limitations to the boundaries of the state can seem arbitrary. If we attribute all government policy to the grand vizier, for example, we are guilty of ignoring, at the very least, the sultan's mother and the Chief Harem Eunuch, who may have been instrumental in choosing the grand vizier or, on the other hand, may have opposed him. If we attribute all policies to the decision-makers in Istanbul, we deny agency to governors, military commanders, judges and a host of others in the provinces.

In extreme, but by no means anomalous, cases, the scholarship reduces these individuals and interest groups to a monolithic entity with objectives, motivations and desires that somehow transcend the sum of its parts. In this scheme of things, 'society' is implicitly oppositional, if not antagonistic, to the state: the victim, the acted-upon, the taxed, the exploited. There is a natural temptation to identify the exploiting state anachronistically with 'the Turk' and to identify the exploited 'society' with the Arab, Armenian or Balkan populations – assuming, of course, that these ethno-linguistic labels are themselves self-explanatory and unproblematic.

These oppositional categories are highly misleading. To begin with, both state and society were in constant flux, absorbing and ejecting individuals and groups every day. Both were also inextricably intertwined, so that a government minister, or vizier, for example, operated within a web of relationships: to his household, neighbourhood, market, mosque, taxpayers and so on. This fluid reality has led a few scholars to employ the terminology of discourse theory when describing the state–society relationship: the demarcation line between state and society was discursively constructed and was constantly being contested and negotiated. For example, a case brought before a Muslim law court might constitute a form of discourse through which the dividing line was tested, called into question, reaffirmed or subtly altered. The plaintiff might be a peasant from a small rural village who sought to demonstrate that the official in, say, Cairo who farmed his village's taxes – that is, who bought the revenue collection rights from the government, in a process to be described in Chapter 4 – extorted absurdly high taxes from the villagers. The tax-farmer was an agent of the state, but he might also be a regional figure whose various agents and clients mediated between him and the village population. Indeed, the peasant now bringing a case against him might have been one of his clients. The case would be presided over by another agent of the state, the judge, or *qadi*, in this case probably the judge in the neighbourhood of Cairo where the tax-farmer lived and where the peasant or his appointed representative would have been obliged to come. Yet the judge himself might have started out as a resident of the peasant's village who came to Cairo, studied at al-Azhar university, then obtained an official judgeship. Ultimately, the case might result in a reallocation of state revenues – that is, the taxes paid by the peasant – or in the revocation and reassignment of the tax farmer's collection rights. In short, while we cannot utterly abandon the notion of a boundary between state and society, we must admit that it was fluid and permeable.

At the same time, both state and society were diffuse and often driven by internal tensions. This is fairly obvious where society is concerned, far less so in the case of the state. But as the Ottoman Empire expanded, as the corps of palace personnel grew, as the state payrolls (particularly those of the military regiments) lengthened, competing interest groups formed within the state apparatus – again, the process of decentralization at the centre. By the seventeenth century, sultans competed with their mothers, concubines, daughters and sons-in-law, as well as with the palace eunuchs, the grand viziers and the commanders of the imperial Janissaries, for influence; any or all of these figures could interact separately or in concert with figures in the Ottoman provinces, many of whom had started their own careers in the palace or were the offspring or clients of people who had done so. The well-known Ottoman courtier and traveller Evliya Chelebi, writing in the late seventeenth century, sums it up nicely:

> They say the fish stinks from the head; it is well-known that this is the root of rebellion. . . . In Sultan Selim's time [Selim II, r. 1566–74],[1] when a vizier became governor of Egypt, he was given 3,000 gold pieces in travel money from the sultan's treasury and was sent off with the injunction, 'Egypt is God's trust; administer it with justice and equity.' That vizier would come to Egypt and govern it according to the law (*kanun*), sending the sultan a gift of 12,000 gold pieces every year, free of any other taxes. But nowadays, to be appointed to Egypt, the viziers have to pay 1,500 purses in bribes to the sultan, the

grand vizier, his lieutenant, the sultan's mother, the sultan's favourite concubines, the princes and their lieutenants, the Chief Black Eunuch, the Chief
White Eunuch, the other eunuchs, the chief jurisconsult, the chief judge, the
molla (*mufti*, or chief jurisconsult) of Istanbul, the viziers of the sultan's council, the financial officers, and 110 other people in charge of various affairs.[2]

One aim of this book is to show that Ottoman administration of the
Arab provinces changed provincial society while provincial society
changed the Ottoman 'state'. A governor appointed to a province
brought with him a large entourage of men and women from the palace
and from his household in Istanbul or in the province where he had
most recently served. Many of these officials joined or started households in this new province, injecting their own clients into the provincial economy and political culture, or forming ties with households
and individuals already locally ensconced. True, the rate of this sort
of 'injection' did not remain constant throughout the period covered
in this book. Considerably more transplantations of personnel from the
imperial centre occurred during the sixteenth and seventeenth centuries
than in the eighteenth. Still, the process never entirely ceased. By the
same token, local military and political elites might attach themselves to
the governor or to some other officer in the provincial administration
and by this means acquire ties to the imperial palace, or to the administration of another province.

Local notables and localization

This revisionist view of 'state and society' can, in turn, lead to a
revisionist appraisal of the social group labelled *ayan* in provincial
chronicles and Muslim law court records. As Chapter 5 will explain, much
scholarship, following the lead of Albert Hourani, has interpreted *ayan*
to refer to local Arabophone military administrators who, along with ulema
and certain other of the provincial sociopolitical elite, served as intermediaries between the provincial population at large and the Ottoman
administration. Yet the sources cited above, to say nothing of Ottoman
documents, are not necessarily consistent in their usage of the label *ayan*,
leading one to suspect that it was a flexible term that could carry
different meanings in different contexts, and that the boundaries of
ayan membership, rather like those of *askeri* or *reaya* membership, were
constantly contested. As Chapter 5 will emphasize, this more flexible
definition of *ayan* allows us to subsume a considerably larger group
of people under this rubric: in particular, the problematic and diffuse
category of *localized* elites. Someone in this category might be a member of a governor's entourage who remained in the province when the

governor departed, attracted clients, purchased military slaves (mamluks) and other slaves, built a mansion in a fashionable quarter of the provincial capital, and endowed pious foundations. He might be a soldier assigned from Istanbul to one of the provincial garrisons who worked his way up the regimental hierarchy, then established his own household. He might be a harem eunuch exiled from Istanbul to Cairo on his deposition, as became standard practice beginning in the mid-seventeenth century, who likewise built up a household and acquired enterprises in Cairo and throughout Egypt's subprovinces. *She* might be a Georgian concubine purchased by one of the district governors within a province, who out-lived her husband, married his senior client and joined his household, then built up her own parallel female household, consisting in large part of her own female slaves. And, of course, a notable could still be a mem-ber of the ulema or a military strongman native to the province.

Households

As the context within which provincial notables operated, the household, to be discussed in Chapters 4 and 5, itself offers an alternative frame-work within which to view their activity while at the same time avoid-ing the pitfalls of attempting a rigid definition of who were *ayan* and who were not. The household was, first and foremost, a social, economic, political and often military structure which served as an arena for patronage. It did not necessarily originate in a kinship group, although a family, even a nuclear family, could form the core of a household. Rather, the household consisted of a network of patron–client ties. In provincial political culture, being a patron or client was arguably more important than one's ethnicity or one's status as slave or free. The household might be centred in an actual house (*bayt* in Arabic, *hane* or *kapı* in Turkish), but it could also take shape in a military barracks or in a fairly modest dwelling. Such were the origins of some of the most influential provin-cial households, covered in Chapter 5.

The hegemony of households in provincial political culture is an observable phenomenon throughout the Ottoman Empire beginning in the latter part of the sixteenth century. The ultimate model for these households was, of course, the sultan's household in Istanbul's Topkapı Palace. Viziers who had risen through the ranks of the palace pages often received governorships of provinces; once installed in the provincial cap-itals, they attracted clients and emulated the sultan's household on a smaller scale. Eventually, this trend spread throughout the Ottoman provinces; in the Arab provinces, it was facilitated by the pre-existing example of the elite households of pre-Ottoman regimes. The households of the

Mamluk sultanate, which had ruled Egypt, Syria, the western Arabian peninsula, and parts of south-eastern Anatolia before the Ottoman conquest, were one such model – but only one. In Syria and Iraq, as well as south-eastern Anatolia, households also drew on the legacies of smaller regional potentates, some of which retained elements of household paradigms going back to Tamerlane, the Mongols and earlier Turkic regimes. In summary, the political culture of households ultimately drew on the collective political traditions of the Turco-Iranian military patronage states that had dominated the Middle East throughout the Middle Ages. It would be very difficult, if not impossible, to sort out exactly which influences came from which regimes. At the same time, the influence of the imperial palace as a model should not be under-estimated. The provincial elites were constantly reminded of the palace by officials appointed to the provinces from Istanbul and by their own trips to Istanbul to present petitions or deliver revenues.

Yet the household was by no means limited to the military and administrative echelons. High-ranking Muslim scholar-officials, or ulema, and long-distance merchants might also establish households; through commerce and marriage, furthermore, they often cultivated links with military-administrative households. Indeed, an attractive historiographical feature of the household is that it accommodates both the military and administrative cadres, including those transplanted from Istanbul and other locales, and indigenous elements, including merchants and ulema. Non-elites could also participate in household-based political culture, either by becoming clients of elite household heads or by heading their own rudimentary households, as the example of soldiers forming households in the barracks and in modest dwellings suggests. In short, the household served as a bridge between elites and non-elites. Nor was founding or joining a household the only mode of participation. A household was an intricate economic operation which distributed food, clothing, cash and luxury goods to its members, who in turn might redistribute them to their own nascent households, to their neighbourhoods or even, through charitable foundations, to the poor.

Households and localization

In fact, the household provided a conduit for acculturation and localization of the disparate collection of men and women from outside the Arab provinces who participated in provincial political culture. Although we know little about specific training programmes along the lines of the Mamluk sultanate's barracks schools, we find occasional hints in chronicles and Muslim court records of the sorts of cultural stimuli to which recruits to Ottoman-era households were exposed. The highest military and administrative grandees, as well as ascendant merchants, appear to have had access to a solid Sunni Muslim education, as indicated by the libraries which some of them endowed containing classic works of Muslim jurisprudence (*fiqh*) and commentaries thereon; works on mysticism, grammar, logic, medicine and history can also occasionally be found in such collections. Some of these libraries are discussed in Chapters 5 and 6. Certain grandees commissioned poetry extolling their own courtly and/or military virtues; in this, they were unquestionably taking a cue from palace culture. In such a milieu, a raw recruit from the Caucasus or a *devshirme* boy – that is, a recruit from among the Christian peasants of Anatolia and the Balkans – who had arrived with the previous governor's entourage could construct a new Ottoman provincial identity predicated on his membership of his patron's household and ties to other members of that household.

The role of popular folklore in this process of acculturation and identity formation is a subject scholars have only recently begun to explore; it seems likely, however, that provincial history, as reimagined by household members themselves, was transmitted through popular epics such as the tales of the herculean hero of Arabic literature, Antar, or the epic of Sultan Baybars, founder of the Mamluk sultanate and victor over Mongol invaders during the thirteenth century; these are considered in Chapter 7 in connection with the culture of the coffeehouse. Male household members would have heard such tales either in the coffeehouses, which many of them frequented, or within the house or barracks itself; women would conceivably have heard such tales in the harem.

Localization was not necessarily equivalent to Arabization, however. If, for example, a mamluk, or elite military slave, from the Caucasus steeped himself in Muslim doctrine, participated in a mystical brotherhood, memorized tales of Antar, and perhaps opened a shop in the bazaar, he was presumably localized. But what if he never learned to speak fluent Arabic, as did most of the artisans and merchants in the bazaar? What if, as was the case with certain Janissaries in Cairo during the seventeenth century, he purchased a small house and opened a shop in a quarter dominated by Anatolian soldiers, where only Turkish was spoken? Was learning Ottoman Turkish, a language radically different from those of the Caucasus, part of a Caucasian mamluk's localization, even in an Arab province? Such considerations suggest that localization, too, was a fluid and contested process; at any given time, large numbers of people would be at different stages in different processes of localization.

The loyalties resulting from localization would likewise differ. This was a pre-nationalist era; still, various forms of territorial or regional loyalty to a certain province, district or city are easily discernible among a wide array of Ottoman subjects. Loyalty to a particular household, faction or regiment was arguably equally common. Membership of the Janissary corps provided entrée to a military and commercial culture with an extraordinarily long institutional memory and entrenched institutional traditions. Bonds and identification between Janissaries in Istanbul and those in the provinces, despite differences in composition and function, have been underestimated in secondary scholarship. Meanwhile, Janissary infiltration of the artisan guilds, and the purchase by artisans of places in the regiment so as to avoid taxes, provided a bond between the military and civilian populations, and arguably a link between the elite and the non-elite.

Artisans

As a consideration of the household makes clear, individuals are most effectively studied in the social frameworks within which they operated. For members of the elite, this approach is useful; for artisans, peasants and tribespeople, it is almost unavoidable since the individual at these levels of society is very difficult to access in the available sources. To some degree, even these decidedly non-elite groups could be incorporated into households. The lower-ranking Janissaries who opened shops in Cairo, as noted above, may well have grouped themselves in rudimentary households modelled on the regimental hierarchies with which they were familiar. Likewise, as Chapter 8 will point out, a network of financial and commercial obligations could tie a rural population to an urban notable household. Nevertheless, other kinds of structures played a larger role in the social experiences of these groups.

For artisans, discussed in Chapter 7, craft organizations, not unlike guilds, were the key source of group solidarity. Quasi-mystical artisanal brotherhoods had existed in Islamic societies since the Middle Ages, even if corporate guilds in the European sense, with a rigid hierarchy and well-defined collective legal rights and interests, did not exist. Known as *futuwwa* (literally, 'young manhood') organizations, these bodies produced manuals laying down rules of craft organization and describing initiation rites and communal lore; such manuals as have survived can thus serve as valuable guides to artisanal culture. Meanwhile, Muslim court records, including estate inventories registered in the courts, have shed much-needed light on artisans' fiscal arrangements, material wealth and general lifestyle, as the seminal work of André Raymond has shown. The Ottoman government, much more than its medieval predecessors, used these professional structures as a means of controlling the marketplace. In some cities, the judge of the local Muslim law court took an active role in setting prices and choosing guild leaders, as the Muslim court registers demonstrate. Market inspectors' manuals likewise contain detailed guidelines on quality control.

Rural populations

The vast majority of the Ottoman Empire's subjects, in the Arab provinces as in Anatolia and the Balkans, lived in the countryside, outside cities and towns. Yet Arab provincial history still tends to be dominated by the provincial and/or regional capitals, where, after all, the bulk of the chronicles were composed and where the major administrative and religious functionaries, including Muslim court judges, were based. Since the publication of *Egypt and the Fertile Crescent*, notwithstanding, judicious exploitation of the kinds of material discussed in the section on sources above has helped to add rural populations to the historical narrative. (The fruits of some of these efforts will be explored in Chapter 8.) Ottoman tax registers detail the number of family-based households and the economic resources in particular villages, as well as the grandees, often urban-based, who controlled village tax farms. Individual peasants and their concerns and grievances, however, are to be found almost solely in the Muslim court registers. Truly integrative scholarship, showing the links between land tenure and urban enterprises, between urban and rural elites, and between urban-based notable households and the peasantry, is still in its infancy. Still, promising recent studies have analysed networks of towns and villages in Ottoman Palestine, as well as the phenomenon of urban-based military officers purchasing tax farms in the countryside around Damascus.

Even more difficult to access than the peasantry are the Bedouin, Turcoman and Kurdish tribal populations, some of them nomadic or semi-nomadic, even though they played major roles in premodern Ottoman provincial history. For obvious reasons, they tend to be underrepresented in Muslim court records; chronicles mention them, but sometimes almost formulaically. As a result, the influence of these tribes on provincial economies and political culture has been systematically underrated. Over the past four decades, a number of more general works on individual Arab provinces have included discussions of key tribal elements, while a few scholars have contributed detailed micro-analyses of specific tribes; their results will inform the section of Chapter 8 dealing with tribes. Turcoman and Kurdish tribes have received considerably less attention than Arab Bedouin, despite the important economic and military functions they fulfilled in the Ottoman Arab provinces during the premodern era. Turcoman tribesmen, for example, were a key element in the armies of the rebellious emir Fakhr al-Din Ma'n in early seventeenth-century Lebanon, to be discussed in Chapter 4.

Movement of tribal populations had an enormous impact on provincial economies and political culture, as certain tribes displaced others and took advantage of new sources of wealth, notably life-tenure tax farms. Tracing these changes, however, requires moving beyond the conventional nation-state boundaries that still circumscribe most scholarship on the Ottoman Arab provinces; thus, studies of this topic are still rare. Nonetheless, even single-province studies which take into account the annual pilgrimage to Mecca devote attention to tribal shifts that affected the transport of pilgrims and goods, for example the eighteenth-century paramountcy in the Syrian Desert of the Anaza Bedouin, who received a stipend from the Ottoman treasury in return for escorting the Damascus pilgrimage caravan. In Upper Egypt, meanwhile, the enormous Hawwara confederation, originally a Berber population from North Africa, became regional power brokers by acquiring the tax farms of villages that produced grain for Mecca and Medina. These tribal shifts did not occur in isolation but involved a whole network of patronage ties between the various tribes and provincial administrators at various levels. In short, the activities of the tribes cannot be separated from the overall political and economic circumstances of the Arab provinces.

Marginal populations

It will be obvious how much more inclusive Ottoman historiography has become in the past forty years, even though the activities of some social groups are difficult to document. Of all the various groups covered in the present work, doubtless the most challenging to include are what we might call marginal groups, such as members of religious minorities, women, slaves and the floating population of unemployed beggars, thieves, prostitutes and assorted other 'street people'. Yet the past few decades have seen valiant attempts to uncover their experiences, which will be reviewed in Chapter 9.

Women

The explosion of interest in women's history which began in the 1970s quickly spawned a series of pioneering works on women in various Muslim societies. Recent years have seen a steady flow of publications on women in the Ottoman Empire, including the Arab provinces. In addition to studies focusing specifically on women, more general histories are beginning to incorporate women as integral players in the making of Ottoman Arab history. Like elite men, elite women are much more visible in narrative and archival sources than their lower-class counterparts; however, the registers of the Muslim law courts provide an invaluable window onto the lives of lower-class women, both Muslim and non-Muslim. Even so, the premodern period is woefully under-represented among historical studies of Ottoman women relative to the nineteenth and early twentieth centuries, for by the latter period women had become dramatically more visible and audible through the advent of print journalism, including a healthy corpus of women's magazines, to say nothing of the invention of photography and a fledgling movement for women's education and rights. As in the case of merchants and artisans, furthermore, a hazard of this type of historical writing is the neglect of the Ottoman – and to some extent even the provincial political – context in the rush to bring women's roles and experiences in the Arab provinces to light.

Non-Muslims

Much the same situation prevails in the case of non-Muslim populations in the Ottoman provinces. These consisted primarily of Rabbinic Jews and various Christian sects; the different groups will be enumerated in Chapter 1 while their circumstances under Ottoman rule will be discussed in Chapter 9. An additional challenge specific to non-Muslim populations, however, is the vexing question of tolerance *versus* persecution. Until quite recently, an entire non-Muslim community's status during a particular period was commonly summed up according to how many times the group was violently attacked or how often the standard catalogue of sartorial and behavioural restrictions was imposed. By these standards, most non-Muslims enjoyed a fair degree of tolerance throughout the Ottoman era in comparison with the experiences of religious minorities in other Muslim empires and in Christian Europe. Yet historians of Ottoman Jewish communities in particular feel a growing dissatisfaction with the habit of reducing a minority religious group's experience to the presence or absence of persecution, preferring instead to analyse these populations in the context of other collectivities – class, neighbourhood, profession, city or town – of which they were a part. Once again, Muslim court records provide evidence of both minority activity – for non-Muslims frequented the Muslim courts for a wide variety of transactions – and a broader social context. They are, however, complemented by popular literature, sultanic decrees, and decrees of provincial governors.

Critical changes occurred both within and among the non-Muslim communities of the Arab provinces during the period covered by this book. In the early sixteenth century, the Jewish communities of the Arab lands were still absorbing the wave of Sephardic immigrants who had been expelled from Spain in 1492. By the end of that century, the deepening economic and demographic crisis had contributed to a hardening of attitudes towards non-Muslims throughout Ottoman society. In the late seventeenth century, Jewish communities throughout the Ottoman Empire were profoundly shaken by the appearance and conversion to Islam of the messianic figure Sabbatai Sevi, whose influence has until recently been severely downplayed in the scholarly literature. In the eighteenth century, finally, the European powers began to use non-Muslim merchants, particularly Orthodox Christians, in the Arab provinces as intermediaries with local markets, often granting honorary citizenship to these agents. Largely as a result of French and Vatican pressure, many Orthodox agents recognized the Pope, spawning a new Syrian Catholic sect. As will be noted in Chapter 9, Syrian Catholic merchants became a highly visible presence throughout the ports of the eastern Mediterranean during this period, arguably contributing to European commercial penetration of the region.

Shiites

In addition to the non-Muslim populations, we should not forget the large Twelver Shiite populations of Iraq and Lebanon or the Zaydi and Ismaili Shiites of Yemen. Research on Shiites under Sunni Ottoman rule has been extremely sparse, apart from studies of Twelver Shiite elements in eastern Anatolia who supported the emergent Safavid empire in Iran in the early sixteenth century. The Zaydis of Yemen have received attention because they rebelled against Ottoman rule almost continuously, ultimately forcing the Ottomans out of Yemen entirely in the 1630s, as will be noted in Chapter 4. Yet virtually no studies exist of Ottoman attempts to co-opt Zaydi and, even more so, Ismaili populations during their near-century of rule over Yemen. Equally scarce are works dealing with Twelver Shiite populations co-existing with Sunnis in Greater Syria and Iraq. Twelvers are not well represented in conventional sources, including Muslim law court registers, in part because of their own policy of public dissimulation, in part because of official Ottoman refusal to recognize non-Sunni Muslims as separate communities. Nonetheless, a few studies have recently appeared that attempt to show how Twelver Shiites were integrated into provincial commercial life, rather than treating them as oppositional figures.

'People without history'

Doubtless the most marginal of these marginal populations are the social outcasts or 'misfits' mentioned at the beginning of this section: beggars, prostitutes, thieves, the physically and mentally disabled. Apart from the seventeenth-century traveller Evliya Chelebi's rather fanciful depictions of certain of them processing as 'guilds', noted in Chapter 7, these groups are virtually unrepresented in the sources at our disposal. And yet even these 'people without history'[3] have become a focus of historical enquiry. Even if the voices of these people cannot always be recovered, the careful study of court records, along with the application of architectural history and archaeology, has contributed to a new appreciation of the residential milieus and material culture of these elements. Meanwhile, a growing body of work on charity and poor relief, exploiting the deeds of pious foundations for soup kitchens and hospitals, is bringing increased visibility to the institutions set up to accommodate them, which will be surveyed towards the end of Chapter 9.

Non-elite slaves

If there is a population more marginal, or at least more poorly represented, than the populations just discussed, it would be the substantial number of non-elite slaves, most of them from East Africa, most female, and most employed as domestic servants of one kind or another. Regrettably, although they were part of virtually every substantial household in the Ottoman Arab provinces and many less substantial ones as well, there is next to no trace of these people, apart from a rare mention here and there in provincial chronicles and Muslim law court records, before the nineteenth century, when the bureaucracy of the modernizing state kept more efficient records on runaways, illegitimate children born to slaves, and the like. The most the historian can do, as Chapter 9 will attest, is to compile information on the African slave trade and slave trade routes, and extrapolate from nineteenth-century conditions.

Conclusion

Clearly, writing a history of the Ottoman Arab provinces is a far different proposition today from what it was in 1966. A far broader spectrum of social groups must be included; meanwhile, new conceptualizations of Ottoman history and of the Arab provinces' place in that history must be taken into account. On the other hand, we cannot hope to equal Holt's attention to political detail.

In addition, the Ottoman Empire's interactions with the rest of the world deserve attention. The period from 1516–1800 was one of steadily increasing contact with Europe: regular warfare with the Habsburg Empire, Venice and Russia combined with burgeoning commercial and diplomatic exchanges with France and England above all. In the spirit of anti-declinism, these contacts must be presented as two-way encounters rather than as a litany of Ottoman inadequacy in the face of a rising West. One way to balance these highly charged encounters with Europe is to consider the Arab provinces' encounters with polities outside Europe, notably with India, sub-Saharan Africa and China.

In pursuing this agenda, notwithstanding, the present study hopes to build on the remarkably solid foundations laid by *Egypt and the Fertile Crescent*. Ultimately, it aims to reflect the changing face of Ottoman provincial historiography while serving as a complement to its illustrious predecessor.

Notes

1. Although Selim I (r. 1512–20) conquered Egypt, there was only one Ottoman governor of that province during his lifetime: Khayrbay, the former Mamluk governor of Aleppo (see Chapters 2–3).
2. Evliya Chelebi, *Seyahatname*, 10 vols (Istanbul, 1966), X, p. 721 (my translation).
3. The term was coined by the late Eric Wolf, author of *Europe and the People Without History* (Berkeley, CA, 1982).

chapter one

LAND AND PEOPLES

Regions and nomenclature

The Ottoman Empire encompassed territories on three continents: Europe, Asia and Africa. This book's focus, the Arab provinces of the empire, occupied a region roughly half the size of the United States. Although these provinces were located in the region commonly known today as the Middle East, that term was not applied to these territories until relatively recently. Inhabitants of the provinces in question, like many residents of these same regions today, did recognize a distinction between the Arab 'West' (*Maghrib* in Arabic) – that is, those parts of North Africa comprising present-day Libya, Tunisia, Algeria and Morocco but excluding Egypt – and the Arab 'East' (*Mashriq*), encompassing Egypt, the Arabian peninsula, and present-day Syria, Lebanon, Israel and the Palestinian territories, Jordan and Iraq.

In the nineteenth century, western Europeans began to use the term Near East to refer to the eastern Mediterranean region and Anatolia (known to the ancient Greeks and Romans as Asia Minor), the peninsula comprising most of present-day Turkey; these territories were 'near' in relation to Europe and, of all the Ottoman lands, were most intensively in contact with Europe. The term Middle East, meanwhile, was coined in 1902 by the American admiral Alfred Thayer Mahan to designate the lands between the Mediterranean Sea and India; this term, then, encompassed a substantially larger territory than that conventionally designated by 'Near East'. The meaning of 'Middle East' has broadened still further over the years, so that today it subsumes the original meanings of both Near and Middle East. Today, in fact, 'Near East' is often used in an academic context to refer to Egypt, Anatolia and the eastern Mediterranean only as they existed in antiquity. In some cases, 'Middle East' can even include North Africa, although North Africa is usually regarded as falling outside the Middle East, strictly speaking.

Within the territory covered by the Ottoman Arab provinces, we can identify two major regions: Egypt and the Fertile Crescent, not coincidentally the title of P. M. Holt's famous book. Egypt corresponds more or less exactly to the modern-day country of that name. Indeed, Egypt is the only country in the modern Middle East which has historically retained its territorial integrity. This is because Egypt is an almost completely flat land in which the vast majority of settlement occurs along the Nile River, which forms a long, fertile strip down the country. Accordingly, the flow of the Nile determines the chief territorial division within Egypt: between Lower Egypt – that is, the lower courses of the Nile – extending from Cairo to where the Nile empties into the Mediterranean Sea, and Upper Egypt, extending southward from Cairo to the borders of Sudan. In approximately 3500 BCE, the first Pharaoh united Lower and Upper Egypt, which have formed a single civilizational and political unit ever since. Agricultural cultivation in Egypt until the very recent past has depended on the annual Nile flood. Channelling the Nile waters through irrigation channels is critical to successful agriculture. Maintaining these channels would prove a continual struggle for Ottoman governors of Egypt and various other provincial authorities.

The Fertile Crescent, a term coined in the nineteenth century by European scholars of the Bible, is essentially the crescent of land extending between the Nile and the Tigris-Euphrates river valleys although, strictly speaking, it does not include the Nile valley. The fertility in question is of two kinds. The eastern Fertile Crescent, roughly equivalent to modern Iraq, depends, like Egypt, on river floods: specifically, the flooding of the Tigris and Euphrates rivers. In contrast to the Nile flood, floods along the Tigris and Euphrates have historically proven irregular and unmanageable. Devastating floods pervade the history of Baghdad, constructed in 762 CE as the new capital of the Abbasid dynasty, who claimed leadership of the Muslim community as descendants of the Prophet Muhammad's uncle Abbas. Some of these floods damaged the capital irreparably. To exploit the rivers, the various rulers of the region developed a complex system of irrigation canals which arguably required a highly centralized government to maintain them.

The western Fertile Crescent, roughly equivalent to Greater Syria, which includes modern-day Syria, Lebanon, Jordan, Israel and the Palestinian Authority, has historically relied not on river-fed irrigation but on rain for its water. This fact, plus the region's relatively inaccessible terrain – hilly to mountainous, especially in Lebanon and Syria – helps to explain why the region has tended to resist complete incorporation into centralized empires.

Geographical features

Deserts

The image many non-specialists have of the Middle East and North Africa is of a region that is predominantly desert. Although this impression is somewhat misleading, as will be explained below, the region does boast several very impressive deserts. Largest and grandest is the Sahara, which has historically separated the Muslim peoples of northern Africa, including Egypt, from the populations south of the desert, who consist largely of Christians and animists, or worshippers of spirits in nature. (Islam did, however, penetrate to sub-Saharan Africa during the Middle Ages, and substantial Muslim populations are found there.) More central to the territory covered by this book is the Arabian Desert, which covers most of the Arabian peninsula, with the notable exception of Yemen, and its extension, the Syrian Desert, which stretches north into southern Syria, eastern Jordan and western Iraq. The Sinai desert separates Egypt from the eastern Mediterranean littoral while serving as a continental divide between Africa and Asia.

The desert was hard put to support any lifestyle but nomadic herding. We might immediately think romantically of camel caravans in the desert. These there were, certainly, but there were also nomadic herders of sheep, goats, donkeys and mules. Nor did all nomads live in the desert; the Turkic nomads who would give rise to the Ottoman Empire originally inhabited the grassy steppes of Central Asia. Within the territory covered by this book, semi-nomadic Kurds and Turkic nomads commonly known as Turcomans lived in the mountainous regions of Lebanon, Syria and northern Iraq, as well as south-eastern Anatolia and western Iran. Mountainous Yemen, meanwhile, was home to semi-nomadic Arab tribesmen while a small population of Arabic-speaking nomads inhabited the only slightly less mountainous terrain of the Hadramawt, today the region encompassing south-eastern Yemen and western Oman. The largest nomadic and semi-nomadic populations inhabiting this territory, however, were the Arab Bedouin who dwelt in the Arabian, Syrian and Sinai deserts, as well as in various parts of Egypt, desert and otherwise. All these nomads were of necessity closely connected with the towns and the settled agriculturists who lived in and around the towns. On the other hand, a certain rivalry developed between the centres of settled civilization and the realm of the nomad, particularly in times of economic and political crisis. The boundary and the friction between 'the desert and the sown' form a recurring theme in Middle Eastern history.

River systems

Notwithstanding the high visibility of deserts, the Middle East breaks down regionally according to its river systems, which supply the arid region with the bulk of its water and which historically have tended to attract its highest concentrations of population. The Middle East boasts two of the world's greatest river systems, the Tigris-Euphrates and the Nile, two of the earliest sites of settled agriculture in the world and, consequently, seats of two of humankind's most ancient civilizations.

The German Orientalist Bertold Spuler once wrote that from antiquity to the Ottoman conquest of Egypt in 1517, Mesopotamia and the Nile valley belonged, with only rare exceptions, to separate political entities.[1] The Ottoman Empire was one of the few empires in history to rule the lands of these two river valleys – that is, Egypt and Iraq – simultaneously. As we shall see, the Ottomans struggled to keep Iraq out of the hands of the rulers of Iran and to keep Egypt from acquiring too great a degree of autonomy from the Ottoman central authority.

Mountains

Many readers' image of the Middle East will not include mountains. Notwithstanding, the region is home to several impressive ranges, three of which lie at least partially in the Arab lands that are the subject of this book. The largest of these are the Zagros Mountains, a major chain extending through western Iran and northern Iraq, and the Taurus Mountains, which run across southern Anatolia to what is now the border region of Turkey, Iraq and Iran. Smaller ranges run through much of Syria and Lebanon. The Jabal al-Nusayriyya range runs north–south through western Syria, parallel to the coastal plain. The Jabal Druze range (recently renamed the Jabal Arab) and the Anti-Lebanon Mountains are located in south-western Syria, the former near the border with Jordan, the latter near the Lebanese border. Across the Bekaa Valley in Lebanon, the Lebanon Mountains provide much of that country's dramatic landscape. To the south and east of Beirut lie the Shouf Mountains, technically a branch of the Lebanon chain.

Several of the nomadic populations noted above roamed these mountains during the Ottoman era. Kurds were – and are – found in both the Zagros and Taurus ranges, while Turcomans inhabited the eastern portions of the Taurus range. Mountains could also serve as refuges to members of religious and ethnic minorities. High in Iraq's Zagros range lived members of the tiny Kurdish Yazidi sect. Nusayris, also known as Alawis, inhabited the Jabal al-Nusayriyya, while Druze lived in the Jabal Druze to the south, as well as in Lebanon's Shouf Mountains, which were also home to Arab Christians of both the Orthodox and Maronite sects. (All these faiths are discussed below.)

Of the Turcomans living in the eastern Taurus Mountains, a number were Twelver, or Imami, Shiites who provided military might for the Safavid dynasty, which conquered Iran at the beginning of the sixteenth century. Before their collapse in 1722, the Safavids waged numerous campaigns against the Ottomans; these had a profound effect on the Arab lands, above all Iraq, where much of the fighting took place.

Peoples

At the time of the Ottoman conquest of the Arab lands, the Middle East was inhabited by peoples most of whom fall into one of four modern ethno-linguistic categories: Arabs, Persians, Kurds and Turks. These categories tend to confuse religious, ethnic, linguistic and biological identities, making a historical perspective on these peoples somewhat problematic. Nonetheless, they are useful as a means of description, though it is important to remain aware of variations in their meaning over time. Before the nineteenth century, people seldom identified themselves with any of these groups but rather defined themselves as members of a religious community, inhabitants of a city or region, or some combination of these.

Arabs

Before the advent of Islam in the early seventh century CE, Arabs lived in the Arabian peninsula and along the caravan routes that extended from the peninsula into Syria and Iraq. As a result of the Muslim conquest of the Middle East, their numbers in the region increased exponentially. During the Ottoman period, the word 'Arab' did not have the ethno-national connotations it does today but instead was a somewhat derogatory term used by speakers of both Arabic and Ottoman Turkish to refer to a nomadic or semi-nomadic inhabitant of the desert or the rural hinterlands of towns. (In Ottoman Turkish, furthermore, 'Arab' also frequently connoted a sub-Saharan African.) On the other hand, cities, towns and villages in the Ottoman Arab provinces were inhabited by Arabic speakers who tended to identify themselves by their places of residence and/or by the confessional communities to which they belonged.

Persians

Persians have inhabited Iran since approximately 1500 BCE History's three great Persian empires, extending from the sixth century BCE to the Muslim conquests of the seventh century CE, encompassed Iraq as well. In the centuries following the Muslim conquests, however, the Persians of Iraq became assimilated to the growing Arabic-speaking population. By the Ottoman era, Persian-speaking populations in the regions covered by this book were largely limited to southern Iraq, above all Najaf and Karbala, sites of the tombs of Ali ibn Abi Talib and his son Husayn, respectively, and therefore Shia Islam's holiest cities. Because of the impact on the Arab lands of Ottoman antagonism towards Shiite Iran, however, Iran's overwhelmingly Persian population should not be discounted in the history of the Ottoman Arab provinces. Indeed, the presence of Persians in southern Iraq resulted largely from Shiite immigration to the region from Iran during sporadic periods of Safavid rule in the region. The two shrine cities were powerful attractions for these immigrants.

Kurds

The term 'Kurd' appears to have been used since antiquity to refer very broadly to a population that speaks an Indo-European language related to Persian and inhabits the mountains of south-eastern Anatolia, north-eastern Syria, northern Iraq and western Iran. The Ottomans used the term in a similarly loose sense. During the Ottoman period, many Kurdish populations were nomadic or semi-nomadic.

Turks

As for Turks, they were not a significant presence in the Middle East until the ninth century CE, when Turkish tribes in Central Asia, under pressure from a centralizing Chinese government, began to migrate west. In the eleventh century, a huge Turkish tribal confederation known as the Oghuz crossed the Oxus, or Amu Darya, River, which now separates Turkmenistan from Uzbekistan, and Afghanistan from Uzbekistan and Tajikistan, and swept through the heartland of what was then the empire of the Abbasids. Led by the Seljuk family, the Oghuz took control of the Abbasid capital of Baghdad in 1055. They did not depose the Abbasid caliph, however, but recognized him as the supreme religious authority in Sunni Islam while the Seljuk ruler, who took the title *sultan*, derived from an Arabic word for 'power' or 'authority', wielded political and military power. In the late eleventh century, a Seljuk offshoot founded a state in Anatolia with its capital at the ancient Byzantine city of Iconium, which under Turkish influence came to be called Konya. Because of this state's location in former Byzantine, or Roman, territory, its rulers are commonly known as the Seljuks of Rum.

Until the nineteenth century, 'Turk,' like 'Arab', was a somewhat pejorative term for a member of a rural and, often, tribal population, with the added sense of rough and uncultured. Nomadic and semi-nomadic Turkic populations, who inhabited parts of northern Iraq, Syria and Lebanon, as well as eastern Anatolia and north-western Iran, during the Ottoman era, are typically called Turcomans in English. Meanwhile, speakers of Arabic and Ottoman Turkish tended to refer to Ottomans from the empire's core lands in Anatolia and the eastern Balkans as Rumis, the adjectival form of Rum.

Other ethno-linguistic groups

Apart from these four major groups, the Arab lands counted significant populations of Armenian Christians, primarily in the cities of Greater Syria, above all Damascus, Aleppo and Jerusalem. In addition, Berbers, the indigenous population of North Africa, could be found among the semi-nomadic tribes of Upper Egypt, although they were far more numerous in what are now Tunisia, Algeria and Morocco. The Hawwara, a tribal confederation that would come to dominate Upper Egypt in the eighteenth century, were Arabized Berbers who had migrated into Egypt sometime in the thirteenth century.

The Ottoman Empire itself would greatly increase the ethnic diversity of the Arab lands, stationing soldiers from Anatolia and the Balkans in Arab cities and towns while appointing officials from these regions to Arab provincial posts.

Religious minorities

Although the population of the Arab Middle East had been predominantly Muslim since about the tenth century CE, when a steady wave of voluntary conversions to Islam becomes noticeable, the region under the Ottomans contained significant populations of non-Muslims, as well as Shiites. Several of these populations will be examined in more detail in Chapter 9. Here, we will briefly survey the wide variety of minority religious groups.

Christians

As part of the Byzantine Empire, Egypt and the eastern Mediterranean littoral acquired large numbers of Christians in the centuries after the Byzantine emperor Constantine (r. 306–37) made Christianity the empire's official religion. Following the pivotal Council of Chalcedon in 451, most Byzantine Christians adopted the Council's ruling that Jesus Christ possesses two separate natures, divine and human. Christians adhering to this view are known as Diphysites; today, their ranks include the vast majority of the world's Christians, Orthodox, Roman Catholic and Protestant alike. The Egyptian church, however, defied the Council of Chalcedon, insisting that Christ's nature was one and inseparable; for this, Egyptian Christians, who came to be known as Copts, an appellation related to 'Egypt', suffered persecution by the Byzantines. Although another Monophysite church emerged in Syria, the Copts remained the world's largest Monophysite sect and one of the largest Christian populations in the Arab lands.

Even before the Council of Chalcedon, the Christian bishops in the city of Antioch, located in the border area between Syria and Anatolia, were insistently Monophysite; the Syrian Orthodox church which they spearheaded, sometimes known as the Jacobite church after a proselytizing sixth-century bishop, has remained so to this day. Antioch's Monophysitism prompted a dissenting priest known as John Maron (a local term for 'lord') to flee with his followers to the mountains of Lebanon. Followers of this priest, who died in roughly 410, came to be known as Maronites; they continue to be an important segment of Lebanon's population. The Maronites acquired their own patriarch in the late seventh century, when they were cut off from the Byzantine patriarch in Constantinople by the early Muslim conquests. After aiding the Crusaders, however, they reconciled with the Vatican in 1182.

Following the schism between the Greek and Roman Churches in 1054, the overwhelming majority of Christians in Greater Syria, as well as those in Anatolia, remained loyal to the Greek Church, which today is commonly called the Orthodox Church. To this day, significant populations of Orthodox Christians remain in Syria, Lebanon, Israel and the Palestinian territories. These lands are also home to smaller, but not insignificant, numbers of Armenian Christians, who follow their own Diphysite rite.

In Ottoman Iraq lived remnants of the ancient Nestorian church, a sect espousing extreme Diphysitism which takes its name from John Nestorius, a monk of Antioch who became patriarch of Constantinople from 428–31. In fact, this sect, also known as Assyrians, have roots reaching back to at least the third century in south-eastern Anatolia and in Iraq. Nestorian Christians were patronized by the Sasanian empire, which ruled Iraq and Iran before the Muslim conquests, and held influential offices in the Abbasid administration. By the Ottoman period, however, their numbers and influence had dwindled.

Under the Ottomans, Christian merchants played important roles in trade within and among the Arab provinces. In addition, Armenians were particularly active in the overland trade with Iran and India. During the eighteenth century, as France and Britain became increasingly important commercial forces in the region, more and more Christian merchants engaged in trade with Europe as well. In Egypt, Copts served the Ottoman governors and the provincial grandees as financial officers.

Jews

Most cities in the Arab lands were home to small populations of Jews. At the time of the Ottoman conquest of these territories in 1516–17, most resident Jews were Arabic-speakers known as Mustarabs ('Arabized'). But during these very years, the Arab lands were absorbing the influx of Jews expelled from Spain following the Catholic conquest of Granada and Spain's consequent reunification under Christian rule in 1492. These Spanish-speaking Sephardic Jews quickly came to dominate Jewish communities throughout the Ottoman Empire. While Christians of all sects were as likely to live in rural villages as in cities, Jews tended to be urban-dwellers. In the Arab lands, Sephardic Jews of some substance served in the financial administrations of various provinces and worked as merchants, bankers and physicians. Jews of the lower classes were disproportionately represented in textile manufacture, particularly dyeing.

Shiites

Small but occasionally problematic populations of Shiite Muslims lived under Ottoman rule. These included members of all three surviving sub-sects of Shiism: Twelvers, or Imamis; Ismailis; and Zaydis. Although all Shiites believe that Ali should have succeeded the Prophet Muhammad directly as leader of the Muslim community and that the community leader, or imam in Shiite parlance, must be a descendant of Ali, Twelvers, Ismailis and Zaydis differ in the specific lines of imams they recognize. Twelvers and Ismailis concur on the first six imams but disagree as to which son of the sixth imam, who died in 765 CE, continued the line. The Ismailis' appellation derives from their recognition of Ismail, the sixth imam's eldest son, as the rightful seventh imam (for which reason they are also sometimes called Seveners). Ismail in turn, they hold, passed the imamate to his son Muhammad, who, however, went into hiding from the Abbasids and died at an early age, perhaps in his twenties. Many Ismailis believed that he had entered an occulted state and would return at the end of time; a large proportion, however, came to regard the Fatimid caliphs, who in the tenth century established an anti-Abbasid counter-caliphate, as living imams. From their capital at Cairo, the Fatimids ruled Egypt, Syria and the Holy Cities of Mecca and Medina from 969–1171. By the Ottoman period, however, the leader of the one branch of Ismailism that continued to recognize a living imam was located in Iran while the chief missionaries of the two strands of the other main branch could be found in Yemen and India.

Twelvers contend that the line of imams continued through the youngest son of the sixth Shiite imam. The twelfth imam of this line, who disappeared when he was a very small child, is, they believe, in occultation and will return at the end of days as a messianic figure.

Zaydi Shiites take their name from a great-grandson of Ali who rebelled against the Umayyad caliphs in 740 CE and whom they initially regarded as the fifth imam (they are occasionally labelled Fivers as a result). Ultimately, however, the Zaydis came to recognize as imam any descendant of Ali's elder son Hasan – or, more rarely, a descendant of his younger son Husayn – who was learned in Islam and who could defend the community.

Twelver Shiites

Since the Ottomans were officially Sunni and since most of the Arab provinces had had Sunni majorities even before the Ottoman conquest, Twelver Shiites living under Ottoman rule constituted a religious minority, and one regarded with more suspicion than virtually any other minority as a consequence of the Ottomans' ongoing conflict with the Safavids of Iran. Shiites had constituted a significant presence in southern Iraq since the early Islamic period, owing to the concentration of followers of Ali ibn Abi Talib there and the presence in the cities of Najaf and Karbala, respectively, of the tombs of Ali and his son Husayn. Arab Shiites were an important component of the population of those two cities and, to a lesser extent, of the port of Basra. They also inhabited the extensive marshes at the confluence of the Tigris and Euphrates rivers, although mass conversion of the marsh Arabs to Shiism apparently did not occur before the late eighteenth century. As a result of sporadic Safavid occupation of the region, furthermore, as noted above, Persian Shiites could also be found in the shrine cities, in particular Karbala.

Outside southern Iraq, Twelver Shiites were relatively rare in major urban centres, although Aleppo in northern Syria did boast a prominent family of Shiite *ashraf*, or descendants of the Prophet Muhammad. In the countryside of southern Lebanon, however, lived a large population of Arab Shiite peasants, known collectively as Matawila.

Ismaili and Zaydi Shiites

Yemen, which the Ottomans ruled for only a century (1538–1636) during the period covered by this book, was the only Ottoman province inhabited by significant populations of Ismaili and Zaydi Shiites. Yemen's Ismaili population dates from the heyday of the Fatimid caliphate; during these years, a sympathetic Ismaili dynasty, the Sulayhids, took control of Yemen. Following the collapse of the Sulayhids at the end of the twelfth century, Ismailis concentrated in the central highland regions of Yemen, where coffee was grown beginning in the fifteenth century, as well as farther north.

Zaydi Shiism, the smallest of the three surviving Shiite subsects, was established in Yemen in the late ninth century, when the imam Yahya al-Hadi migrated there from Medina. The Zaydi stronghold has always been mountainous northern Yemen. In contrast to Twelver and Ismaili Shiism, Zaydism posits an imam who is not only present in the community but defends the community, militarily if necessary. Perhaps for this reason, the Ottomans faced near-constant Zaydi rebellions during their century of rule over Yemen. It was a massive and prolonged Zaydi revolt that forced the Ottomans out of Yemen altogether during the 1630s. Yemen's Ismailis, on the other hand, were divided in their political tendencies during the Ottoman period, as will be noted in Chapter 3. Most appear to have remained quietist, but some actively collaborated with the Ottomans while others joined Zaydi-led rebellions. Even after the Ottoman ouster, furthermore, merchants and administrators in Egypt continued to nurture relations with Ismaili coffee cultivators, who transported their beans to the Red Sea coast for shipment to Egypt, from where coffee was transshipped to the rest of the empire and to Europe.

Alawis and Druze

The mountains of Syria and Lebanon, like those of Yemen, offered a haven to religious minorities. Two mountain ranges in Syria are named after the members of sects loosely related to Shia Islam. In western Syria, the Jabal al-Nusayriyya takes it name from the Nusayris, also known as Alawis, a sect which, while not doctrinally Shiite, holds Ali ibn Abi Talib in special reverence. Likewise, the Jabal Druze, to the south, along with Lebanon's Shouf Mountains, were home to members of the Druze sect, an offshoot of Ismaili Shiism which recognizes the Fatimid caliph al-Hakim (r. 996–1021) as a divinity. While the Alawis appear to have been relatively quiescent under Ottoman rule, the Druze, under the chieftain Fakhr al-Din Ma'n II, launched a major rebellion, lasting several years, during the early seventeenth century which was quashed only by an Ottoman expeditionary force.

Yazidis

Although most of the Kurds of the Zagros and Taurus Mountains were
Sunni Muslims, as were the Ottomans, the Zagros were also home to
Kurds of the tiny, much maligned Yazidi faith. At the core of Yazidism,
an ancient religion influenced to some degree by Zoroastrianism, is the
worship of powerful angels; because one of these angels bears the name
Iblis, a Muslim appellation for Satan, the religion has sometimes been
labelled devil-worship.

Like earlier Muslim rulers, the Ottomans tended to allow their non-
Muslim, and even their non-Sunni Muslim, subjects a fair degree of
autonomy so long as they remained obedient and paid their taxes. Non-
Muslims and Shiites alike were obliged to observe restraint in their
religious rituals; the degree of this restraint varied according to time and
circumstance. The Ottoman central and provincial administrations employed
non-Muslims in various positions, largely financial, while patronizing non-
Muslim merchants, bankers, medical practitioners and money-lenders.
Which groups the central and provincial governments favoured tended
to vary with the times; during the eighteenth century in particular, the
empire's relations with various European powers often had a bearing on
the patronage enjoyed by different minority populations.

Conclusion

Throughout its history, then, the Middle East has been a region of great
demographic diversity, some of which corresponds to its geographic
diversity. Demographic flux has also characterized the region, with
new populations sweeping in periodically from different directions. The
major population movements in the Common Era have come from the
Arabian peninsula and from the Central Asian steppe. The Ottomans themselves ostensibly had their roots in one of the Central Asian migrations,
as did the Mongols, whose invasion of the Middle East in the thirteenth
century created the conditions for the Ottomans' rise.

Note

1. Bertold Spuler, *A History of the Muslim World*, I: *The Age of the Caliphs*, trans.
   F.R.C. Bagley (Princeton, NJ, 1994; paperback reissue of 1960 edn), p. 72.

chapter two

THE OTTOMAN CONQUEST
OF THE ARAB LANDS

The rise of the Ottomans

By the time the Mongols sacked Baghdad in 1258, burning the city and murdering the Abbasid royal family, much of Anatolia was already a Mongol protectorate. Following a military rout in 1243 by the Mongol regime which had occupied Russia in the 1230s, the Seljuks of Rum had sued for peace and become Mongol vassals. In 1256, they were attacked by a Mongol noble acting on behalf of the Mongol horde that had recently entered Iran. Crushed again, the Seljuks were allowed to survive under a Mongol protectorate; in this drastically weakened form, they lingered until the early fourteenth century.

Otherwise, Mongol control in Anatolia remained fairly loose. A few autonomous Mongol princelings existed alongside the remnant of the Seljuks of Rum and a number of Turkish political entities, descendants of tribes that had been pushed westward by the Mongol advance. These Turkish entities included two expansionist regional powers, Karaman and Germiyan, in central Anatolia and, in the west of Anatolia, a number of smaller principalities, or emirates (from Arabic *amir* or *emir*, 'prince'). The emirates were toughened by border warfare with the waning Byzantine Empire and with the Latin Crusaders, who occupied Constantinople from 1204–61, while maintaining ambivalent relationships with the larger Turkish states to the east. One of these emirates, in the north-west of Anatolia, was ruled by a tribal chieftain known as Osman, and it is from his principality that the Ottoman Empire sprang.

During the fourteenth century, the fledgling Ottoman principality took advantage of Byzantine weakness to the west and the turmoil wrought by the Mongols to the east to expand into the Balkans and across Anatolia. This expansion continued, with only a temporary setback by the Central Asian Turkic conqueror Timur (known in Europe as Tamerlane) in the early fifteenth century, and culminated in Sultan Mehmed II's ('the

Conqueror', r. 1451–81) conquest of the Byzantine capital of Constantinople in 1453. Thus, some 1120 years after the emperor Constantine the Great had moved the Roman capital to Constantinople, and after centuries of Byzantine resistance to the attacks of various earlier Muslim dynasties, the Ottomans finally brought the ancient empire to an end.

The Mamluk sultanate (1250–1517)

In *Memoirs of a Janissary*, his engaging account of his service in a Janissary auxiliary unit after being captured by Mehmed II's army, the sometime Serbian foot soldier Konstantin Mihalowicz has the Conqueror declaring, 'I would march to attack the Zoldan, but I fear God, lest I besmirch the holy cities.'[1] The 'Zoldan' in question was the Mamluk sultan, ruler of a venerable Sunni Muslim empire which had held Egypt, Syria, south-eastern Anatolia and, yes, the Holy Cities of Mecca and Medina since 1250. If the Ottomans indeed wished to rule the Holy Cities, they would have to overcome the Mamluk sultanate first.

The Mamluks were a very distinctive regime. They started out as Turkish elite slaves (mamluks, from the Arabic word for 'owned') of the Ayyubid dynasty, founded in 1171 by Salah al-Din Yusuf ibn Ayyub, who was known to Europeans as Saladin. The Kurdish client of the Seljuk provincial governor of northern Iraq and Syria, Saladin served as a military commander for the Ismaili Shiite Fatimid caliphs in their struggle with the Crusaders but ultimately displaced the Fatimids and took control of their empire. Mamluks formed the backbone of the Ayyubid armies; a Mamluk force halted the Mongol advance into Syria in 1260. By this time, they had already largely displaced the Ayyubids as rulers of Egypt and Syria, much as the Ayyubids had displaced the Fatimids. An Abbasid prince who had escaped the carnage of the Mongol sack of Baghdad was welcomed at the Mamluk court and made a sort of shadow-caliph; if nothing else, he and his descendants legitimized the Mamluk regime. The Mamluks were not a dynasty; instead, each sultan was a freed slave. He would almost always try to pass the throne along to his son (if he had one), but in most cases the other Mamluk commanders, known as emirs, proved too powerful, and one of them assumed rule. Thus, the regime most closely resembled an oligarchy in which authority belonged to the elite of Mamluk emirs.

The Mamluks were, of course, aware of the rise and expansion of the Ottomans to their north. In October 1453, a Mamluk chronicle records the arrival of an ambassador from the Ottomans with news of the conquest of Constantinople the previous May.[2] As the Ottomans expanded into south-eastern Anatolia in the wake of this momentous conquest, they confronted the Mamluks and their vassals, a Turkic dynasty known as the Dulkadiroğlu ('Sons of Dulkadir'), who ruled a swathe of territory in the vicinity of the Taurus Mountains. Sultan Bayezid II (r. 1481–1512), son of Mehmed the Conqueror, fought a series of wars with the Mamluks in this region during the late fifteenth century. In the end, these conflicts proved largely inconclusive, and the Mamluks and Ottomans maintained a rough balance of power.

At the beginning of the sixteenth century, however, two new threats sprang up to both the Ottomans and Mamluks that would upset this balance. In the east, a new Shiite Muslim power, the Safavids, conquered Iran and Iraq. In the south, the Portuguese sailed into the Indian Ocean and menaced the Mamluks in the Red Sea, endangering the Muslim Holy Cities of Mecca and Medina at one point. These two new challenges would be major factors in the eventual Ottoman conquest of the Mamluk sultanate.

The Safavids

The Safavids were originally a Turcoman dynasty of adherents to a mystical, or Sufi, brotherhood known as the Safavid order after its founder, Shaykh Safi al-Din (1252–1334), who flourished in Iranian Azerbaijan during the fourteenth century. In the fifteenth century, the family embraced a militant form of Twelver, or Imami, Shiism and began actively proselytizing in neighbouring eastern Anatolia. Towards the end of that century, under the charismatic chieftain Shah Ismail, the Safavids conquered Iraq and Iran from the Sunni Turcoman dynasty known as the Akkoyunlu (White Sheep). Shah Ismail and his descendants made Twelver Shiism the official religion of their domains and exerted prodigious efforts to establish it among the masses of their subjects. As a result, Twelver Shiism became the majority faith of Iran and remains so to this day. Iraq's ancient Shiite population, meanwhile, was augmented.

As Shiite proselytizers with a devoted following in eastern Anatolia, the Safavids posed a major threat to the Ottomans. When Sultan Selim I (r. 1512–20) came to the throne, he launched an aggressive attempt to stop the Safavid expansion, including persecuting and executing Ottoman subjects in eastern Anatolia who seemed to harbour Safavid sympathies. Indeed, the struggle with the Safavids arguably helped to define the Ottomans as guardians of Sunni Islam. In 1514, Selim dealt the Safavids a major blow at Chaldiran, near Lake Van in eastern Anatolia; in the aftermath of this victory, he conquered south-eastern

Anatolia, including the territory of the Mamluks' Dulkadiroğlu vassals, and what is now northern Iraq. As a result of his conquests and those of his son and successor, Süleyman I, in Iranian Azerbaijan and in central and southern Iraq, the Ottomans acquired a lengthy land border with the Safavids, along which the two rival empires would engage in a series of conflicts until the collapse of the Safavids in the early eighteenth century. During this period, the Ottoman-Safavid frontier shifted dramatically, as will be noted in subsequent chapters. Southern Iraq, as home to the Shiite shrine cities, was especially coveted by the Safavids.

Selim I suspected that the Mamluks, although they were Sunnis themselves, might try to forge an alliance with the Safavids in order to counter the Ottomans, whose expansion seemed unstoppable. In the wake of Chaldiran, Shah Ismail and the Mamluk sultan Qansuh al-Ghuri (r. 1501–16) had forged what amounted to a defensive pact whereby, in the event of another Ottoman attack on the Safavids, Mamluk troops would move into Syria to threaten the Ottomans' southern flank. Some scholars speculate that the fear of a Mamluk-Safavid alliance was what triggered Selim's attack on the Mamluks.

The Portuguese

However, there is another possibility also. In 1498, Portuguese navigators, led by Vasco da Gama, succeeded in sailing around the Cape of Good Hope to reach the Indian Ocean. This feat provided them with a route to India, with its spices and jewels, which bypassed the Ottomans, but it also made them a threat to the Muslim powers that bordered the Indian Ocean, the East African coast, the Red Sea and the Arabian Sea – including the Mamluks.

There is reason to believe, incidentally, that the Ottomans were aware of the European voyages of discovery, not only around Africa but also to the New World, and even contemplated joining the race for transatlantic expansion. Particularly telling in this respect is the *Book of Naval Matters* (*Kitab-i Bahriyye*), compiled in the late fifteenth century by the future Ottoman admiral Piri Reis; copies of this work prepared after the author's death even included maps of the American coastline. On the more fanciful side, a story recounted by the seventeenth-century Ottoman traveller Evliya Chelebi has Sultan Bayezid II pointedly refusing to venture into the Atlantic, insisting that the Ottomans' destiny lay in the Mediterranean. In any event, it was Muslim domination of the eastern Mediterranean and the Red Sea, to say nothing of the overland routes through Asia, that prompted the Portuguese to seek an alternative route to India.

In the early sixteenth century, the Portuguese launched a series of naval attacks on Yemen and on the Red Sea islands off the Yemeni coast. The Mamluks, who had never had a particularly effective navy, appealed to the Ottomans for help, and in 1509 a joint Mamluk–Ottoman naval force confronted the Portuguese. This effort resulted in a curious situation in which the coast of Yemen was, for a number of years, run by Ottoman naval commanders, even though it was not formally part of the Ottoman Empire. The possibility now existed that the Portuguese would take the Holy Cities of Mecca and Medina, an eventuality that would be intolerable to all Muslim powers. It is thus conceivable that Mamluk inefficacy against the Portuguese played into Selim I's decision to attack the Mamluks.

Conquest of the Mamluks

In June 1516, Selim I pitched his campaign tent at Üsküdar, on the Asian side of the Bosphorus. As this gesture was the customary way for the ruler to indicate the direction of his campaign, the population of Istanbul knew that Selim was planning a campaign in Asia rather than in Europe. The question now for Selim was which Asian power to attack: the Safavids or the Mamluks? He marched east as far as south-eastern Anatolia, then turned south towards Syria, so that it was now clear that he was going to attack the Mamluks.

Learning of Selim's trajectory, the Mamluk sultan Qansuh al-Ghuri, who had already advanced into Syria in keeping with his agreement with Shah Ismail, hurried north to confront the Ottomans. The two armies met in August 1516 at a site known as Marj Dabiq near the present Turkish-Syrian border, probably just on the Syrian side. According to the story the Egyptian chroniclers tell of the ensuing battle, the Ottomans 'unfairly' deployed cannon and muskets rather than trying to beat the Mamluks at their own game, namely, horsemanship. In fact, al-Ghuri had tried desperately to introduce cannon and firearms into his armies, but they had been scorned as messy and ignoble by the Mamluk emirs; in addition, his cannon were far more primitive than those the Ottomans had at their disposal. Regardless, the Ottomans proved superior at the cavalry charges which were the essence of medieval Turco-Iranian warfare; in this respect, they *did* beat the Mamluks at their own game. At the critical moment, moreover, Khayrbay, the Mamluk governor of Aleppo, who was commanding one of the Mamluk flanks, defected to Selim with his troops. The Ottoman victory required roughly one hour. As for Qansuh al-Ghuri, who in 1516 was some seventy-five years old, 'he fell to the ground unconscious', according to one Egyptian chronicle,[3] probably as a result of some kind of seizure or stroke. His body was never found, and popular tales soon sprang up claiming that spirits, or *jinn*, had absconded with it.

Proceeding southward from the battlefield, Selim reached Aleppo within days; there, the population opened the city gates to him. Damascus had to be taken by force, but taken it was the following October. This left Egypt, where Selim and his army arrived in January 1517. In Cairo, the Mamluk emirs had named a new sultan, Tumanbay, from among their ranks. Tumanbay confronted Selim at Raydaniyya, just outside Cairo, but was defeated in a matter of hours. After two more attempts to defeat Selim militarily, he fled into the Lower Egyptian countryside, where he was finally betrayed by the Bedouin among whom he was trying to hide. He was brought to Cairo and hanged, after which his head was displayed on the ramparts of Bab Zuwayla, the southern gate of the original Fatimid city of Cairo, for many weeks.

By April 1517, Selim had put an end to the Mamluk sultanate. He stayed in Cairo for several more months, then went back to Istanbul. No other Ottoman sultan would visit Egypt again for nearly 350 years.

Süleyman I's conquest of Iraq

Central and southern Iraq, as well as Yemen, would be conquered under Selim's son, Süleyman I. His reign also saw the addition to the Ottoman Empire of the coastal plains of what are now Libya, Tunisia and Algeria. Morocco was the one North African territory in which the Ottomans never succeeded in establishing a permanent foothold, despite a brief occupation of the eastern part in the late sixteenth century.

Süleyman wished to secure Iraq from Safavid influence. The Safavids could use their territory in central and southern Iraq as a base for spreading propaganda and encouraging unrest in the recently conquered Ottoman holdings in the north, as well as in Syria and southern Anatolia. Meanwhile, the Portuguese remained a threat in the Indian Ocean and had even taken a strategic point on the Straits of Hormuz, where the Indian Ocean joins the Persian Gulf. There was a distinct possibility that the Safavids might ally with the Portuguese against the Ottomans, using the Persian Gulf and the port of Basra to link up with them.

At the same time, the continuing struggle against the Safavids in Iraq and north-western Iran drew Ottoman attention, men and materiel away from the European front against the Habsburg Empire, which was unquestionably the enemy on which Süleyman wished to concentrate, far more so than his father. The Habsburgs themselves were at the height of their powers in the early sixteenth century. Benefitting from the marriage alliances of his grandparents, Süleyman's arch-rival, the Habsburg emperor Charles V (r. 1519–56), ruled not only the Habsburg core lands in central Europe but also Spain, the Netherlands, parts of Italy and a burgeoning American empire.

In 1534, therefore, Süleyman set out on what was known in Ottoman Turkish as the 'campaign of the two Iraqs'. His goal was really to conquer both 'Arab Iraq', roughly equivalent to the modern country of Iraq south of Mosul, and 'Persian Iraq', equivalent to much of Iran; in other words, he wished to wipe out the Safavids altogether. He did not succeed in this goal, but he did take over all of Arab Iraq and even a bit of north-western Iran, including Tabriz, the principal city of Iranian Azerbaijan and the Safavid capital. He was accompanied on the campaign by the sixteenth-century Ottoman equivalent of the wartime photographer: a man known to us as Matrakchı Nasuh, who produced a series of 'city-scapes' of all the towns where the Ottoman army halted, beginning with Istanbul and continuing all the way to Tabriz. These scenes, taken together, illustrate the Ottoman line of control, in other words the boundary with the Safavids.

In 1555, Süleyman signed a peace treaty with Shah Ismail's son, Shah Tahmasp (r. 1524–76), ending Ottoman–Safavid hostilities for the time being and allowing Süleyman to devote his attention to the conflict with the Habsburgs, which would occupy him for the next eleven years, until his death from illness while on campaign in Hungary in 1566. As a token of good faith, Shah Tahmasp sent Süleyman a magnificent illuminated manuscript of the great tenth-century Iranian epic, the *Shahname*, prepared by the finest miniaturists and calligraphers in the Safavid royal atelier. This manuscript is world-famous today as the Houghton *Shahname*, named after the wealthy American collector who for many years owned the work.

Yemen

In 1538, only four years after the campaign of the two Iraqs, one of Süleyman's admirals took over Yemen for the Ottomans. Yemen's status had been rather anomalous ever since the series of anti-Portuguese naval campaigns, described above, in which the Ottomans had assisted the Mamluks. These campaigns often centred on Yemen, situated as it was at the southern edge of the Red Sea, a clear jumping-off point to the Portuguese strongholds on the African and Indian coasts. Having established fortified trading posts all along the coasts of eastern Africa and western India, the Portuguese wished to secure the route

Figure 2.1 Matrakchı Nasuh's depiction of Baghdad.
Source: Naṣūḥü's-Silāḥī (Matrakçı), *Beyān-i menāzil-i sefer-i 'Irākeyn-i Sulṭān Süleymān Ḫān.* Istanbul University Library, MS T. 5964, folio 47b

in-between, which meant the Persian Gulf and the southern Arabian coast. The Mamluks had taken political control of most of coastal Yemen from a local Arab dynasty in 1515, but, as a result of these joint naval efforts with the Ottomans, Ottoman naval officers were now running coastal Yemen de facto even though Yemen was not a formal part of the Ottoman Empire. These naval officers were very much a law unto themselves.

Once Selim I had conquered Egypt, Yemen's status quickly became problematic. Egypt had historically wielded great influence over the lowland and coastal portions of Yemen, and now these territories were clearly a critical point of defence against Portuguese aspirations in the Red Sea. The early Ottoman governors of Egypt occasionally found themselves sending troops to Yemen to ward off the Portuguese, as well as the Zaydi Shiite tribes in Yemen's northern highlands, and even occasionally fighting the Portuguese in the Indian Ocean.

Finally, in 1538, the Hungarian eunuch admiral Süleyman Pasha took formal control of Yemen as part of an extended Ottoman campaign against the Portuguese. Süleyman Pasha acquired a reputation as a particularly brutal and ruthless commander, and an unappealing human being in general. As one British India Office functionary described him some three centuries later, 'He was about eighty years of age, . . . short and stout, and so hideous, and of so savage a disposition, as to have resembled a beast rather than a man.'[4] He bestowed a robe of honour upon the ruler of the southern port of Aden, a member of the local Arab dynasty displaced in other locales by the Mamluks, then summarily executed him; he then pursued the Portuguese admiral all the way to the coast of India. There, the local Indian princes who had requested Ottoman aid against the Portuguese, hearing of Süleyman's treatment of the Yemeni ruler, remained unwilling to join his cause. The anti-Portuguese campaign ended inconclusively, and Süleyman returned to Yemen. But Yemen was now an Ottoman province with its own governor, often a former or future governor of Egypt.

Between 1549 and 1552, Yemen was governed by Özdemir Pasha, a nephew of the defeated Mamluk sultan Qansuh al-Ghuri who had entered Ottoman service after Selim I's conquest of Egypt. He participated in Süleyman Pasha's conquest of Yemen and remained there as an emir until his appointment as governor. Following his service in Yemen, Özdemir led an expedition for Sultan Süleyman which conquered a swathe of territory encompassing much of present-day Sudan and coastal Ethiopia. These new conquests were incorporated in 1555 as the province of Habesh, the Ottoman term for Ethiopia.

North Africa

The conquests of what are now Libya, Tunisia and Algeria ran parallel to that of Yemen in that they were accomplished largely by naval commanders acting on their own. As in Yemen, these commanders typically ended up governing the provinces they conquered. And in the same way that Yemen and southern Iraq served as front lines in the struggle against the Portuguese in the Indian Ocean, so the North African coast suffered Spanish naval incursions throughout the sixteenth century. In 1580, Habsburg Spain absorbed the Portuguese crown following the death of the heirless Portuguese king, a nephew of Spain's Philip II, in 1578 at the Battle of Alcázar in Morocco, a confrontation known in western Europe as the Battle of the Three Kings inasmuch as it resulted in the deaths not only of the Portuguese monarch but also of two rival claimants to the Moroccan throne, one of whom had solicited Portuguese support. With Spain and Portugal united, the possibility loomed of a consolidated anti-Ottoman effort in both the Mediterranean and the Indian Ocean. Ironically, however, the Habsburgs neglected the Portuguese outposts, allowing the Dutch, themselves still under Habsburg rule, to seize them by the time Portugal reverted to an independent monarchy in 1640.

Conclusion

The conquest of the Mamluk sultanate propelled the Ottoman sultan Selim I into the position of chief representative of Sunni Islam on the face of the earth. Süleyman I reinforced this position with his campaigns against the Safavids in Iraq and Iran, and against the Portuguese in the Red Sea and Indian Ocean. The conquests of Egypt, Syria, Iraq, Yemen and North Africa gave the Ottoman Empire a much larger Muslim population than it had previously had. It was no longer a predominantly Balkan empire with a largely Christian population. With the conquest of the Mamluk sultanate, furthermore, had come control of the Holy Cities of Mecca and Medina, and responsibility for the massive pilgrim caravans that left Cairo and Damascus each year. Thus the Ottoman sultan replaced the Mamluk sultan as 'custodian of the two Holy Cities', reinforcing the newly found Ottoman identity of guardians of Sunni Islam. Nevertheless, the empire remained a complex collection of ethnicities and religions.

Notes

1. Konstantin Mihalowicz, *Memoirs of a Janissary*, trans. Benjamin Stolz, historical commentary and notes by Svat Soucek (Ann Arbor, MI, 1975), p. 115.
2. Abu al-Mahasin Yusuf ibn Taghri Birdi, *History of Egypt, 1382–1469 A.D.*, part VI: *1453–1461 A.D.*, trans. William Popper (Berkeley, CA, 1960), pp. 38–9.
3. Ahmad ibn Zunbul al-Rammal, *Wāqiʿat al-Sulṭān al-Ghawrī maʿa Salīm al-ʿUthmānī* (*The Incident of Sultan al-Ghuri with Selim the Ottoman*), ed. Abd al-Munam Amir (Cairo, 1997), p. 36 (my translation).
4. Robert L. Playfair, *A History of Arabia Felix or Yemen* (Amsterdam and St Leonards-on-Sea, East Sussex, 1970; reprint of 1859 edn), p. 101.

chapter three

THE ORGANIZATION OF THE OTTOMAN PROVINCIAL ADMINISTRATION

Relations with the conquered population

The Ottomans did not storm into their newly conquered territories, whether formerly Byzantine, formerly Mamluk, formerly Safavid, or formerly Habsburg, and force the conquered population who were not already Sunni Muslim to choose between conversion and death. Only a few conquering Muslim armies in history have ever taken such action. On the contrary, the Ottomans generally did not proselytize; they allowed the conquered non-Muslim populations to continue practising their religions and handling their own community affairs so long as they remained obedient to the Ottoman state and paid a poll tax, to be discussed in Chapter 9, levied on adult male heads of household.

In parts of the Arab lands formerly ruled by the Mamluk sultanate – that is, Syria, Egypt, the western Arabian peninsula, and the coastal regions of Yemen – much of the population was Sunni Muslim already. The Ottomans differed from the Mamluks, however, in espousing the Hanafi legal rite of Sunni Islam as their official rite. During the early centuries of Islam, as law and theology began to take shape, different modes of extracting legal decisions emerged among legal scholars who placed varying degrees of emphasis on the sources of Islamic law: the Quran, the sayings of the Prophet Muhammad, community consensus, logical analogy, and independent rational interpretation. Of these modes or rites, four have survived among Sunni Muslims: the Hanafi rite, the Shafii, the Maliki and the Hanbali. They differ from one another most noticeably in details of ritual observance and interpretations of personal status concerns, such as divorce and inheritance. Since at least the eleventh century, the rites have broken down along regional lines also. The Hanafi rite was adopted by most rulers among the Seljuk Turks, who invaded Iran and Iraq during that century (see Chapter 1), even though it was not the rite of all members of the Seljuk administration.

The Seljuks of Rum were likewise Hanafi, as were virtually all of the Turkish emirates of western Anatolia and the Mamluk sultans themselves. The Ottomans distinguished themselves from these regimes, however, in making Hanafism their empire's official rite, meaning that all religious officials appointed from Istanbul had to be Hanafi.

The Ottomans' promotion of Hanafism did not mean, however, that they tried to win 'converts' to Hanafism; Sunni Muslims adhering to other rites continued to follow those rites, although it was acceptable to turn to a different rite for specific purposes, such as obtaining a more favourable ruling in an inheritance or divorce case. This was no small consideration in the Arab provinces. Whereas the Muslim population of Anatolia was almost entirely Hanafi owing to the espousal of Hanafism by the region's pre-Ottoman rulers, while Muslims in south-eastern Europe were Hanafi by virtue of the Ottomans' own influence, significant non-Hanafi populations existed in the Arab lands. Shafiis predominated in Lower Egypt and in the Kurdish regions of northern Iraq; Malikis formed the majority in Upper Egypt. Syria, meanwhile, was home to Shafiis and small numbers of Hanbalis, as well as Hanafis.

Yemen was rather a special case because of the sectarian divisions among its Muslim population. The lowland and coastal regions were inhabited by a Sunni population belonging to the Shafii legal rite, which had spread there via Red Sea merchants from Lower Egypt, where that rite still predominates. The Shafiis, by and large, tended to support Ottoman rule. Inhabitants of the northern highlands were largely Zaydi Shiites, members of the smallest of the three surviving subsects of Shia Islam (see Chapter 1). Because the Zaydi imam was a living presence who actively defended his community, in contrast to the hidden imams of the Twelvers and Ismailis, the Zaydis posed a constant threat of rebellion against Ottoman rule. Northern Yemen's mountainous topography aided them when they did rebel. The Ottomans put down a major Zaydi rebellion in the 1560s and were expelled from Yemen by another rebellious Zaydi imam in the 1630s, to return only in 1872. Meanwhile, the central highlands were the domain of Ismaili Shiites, who were, so to speak, a political wild card. By and large, they accepted Ottoman rule, but when a Zaydi imam mounted a promising rebellion, certain of the Ismailis might throw in their lot with him. Others remained quietist or emigrated to India.

In the regions which had fallen under their control, the Safavids had made concerted efforts to spread Twelver Shiism, notably by implementing the Shiite call to prayer (distinguished from its Sunni counterpart by the addition of the line 'Come to the best of works') in cities and towns, and by encouraging public commemoration of anniversaries significant to Shiites, particularly the martyrdom of Ali's younger son Husayn and the occasion on which, according to Shiite belief, the Prophet designated Ali his successor as leader of the Muslim community. Consequently, in the Safavid territories which they occupied in Iraq and north-western Iran, the Ottomans encountered a sizeable Shiite population. Although they did not compel this population to renounce Shiism, the Ottoman authorities refused to recognize the Shiites as a separate religious community from Sunnis, and repressed these public commemorations to varying degrees throughout their rule.

Administrative subdivisions

Like the earliest Muslim caliphs before them, the Ottomans appointed military governors to administer the newly conquered provinces. These governors carried the title *pasha*, a word of Persian origin. Normally, a governor would be a member of the sultan's household, trained in the palace in Istanbul and sent out to the province; from the late sixteenth century, however, it was not uncommon for governors to belong to the households of high ministers (viziers) in the sultan's ruling council. Each province was governed according to an administrative hierarchy. The province as a whole was known in Ottoman Turkish as a *vilayet* (*wilaya* in Arabic), and the pasha who governed it was known either as *vali/ wali* or as *beylerbeyi*, literally, 'the bey of beys'. A bey was a lower-level official who governed a district within the province; each province was made up of a number of districts. Each district, corresponding roughly to an English or American county, was known by the Turkish term *sanjak* or the Arabic *liwa* (*liva* in Turkish pronunciation), literally, 'flag', referring to the flag symbolizing Ottoman authority. Thus, a district governor was referred to as a *sanjak beyi* or, alternatively, as a *mir liwa*, 'prince/commander of the flag'.

Süleyman I had official law codes drawn up for all the territories, Arab or otherwise, which he or his father had conquered. Each of these codes is known as a *kanunname*, literally, 'book of law', *kanun* (from the Greek 'canon') referring to law formulated by the sultan or his representatives, supplemental to Islamic law, or *sharia*, which governed personal and civil status matters. The *kanunname* of Egypt, for example, is made up of several chapters, or divisions, explaining the administrative hierarchy: the governor of Egypt, the subprovinces and their administrators, the regiments of Ottoman soldiery stationed in the province and, most importantly, the different kinds of taxes for which the province is liable. Attached to the *kanunname* of each province at the time of an area's incorporation into the Ottoman Empire, and kept in the court of the chief judge, was a cadastral survey – that is, a census of the households in each village – showing the various villages and the amount of land each village farmed. On this basis, taxes were assessed and collected. Unfortunately for both historians and Ottoman administrators, these surveys were seldom updated after the sixteenth century.

For taxation purposes, the population of the Ottoman Empire was divided into two large and rather nebulous categories: *askeri* (literally, 'military'), the upper echelon who were exempt from taxes, and *reaya* (literally, 'flock'), the lower, tax-paying echelon. The *askeri* included not only all members of the armed forces but also government officials, regardless of whether their roles were military or not, and the ulema. The reaya comprised peasants, artisans and merchants, Muslim and non-Muslim alike, no matter how wealthy or influential. In Ottoman political philosophy, as it developed between the rise of the empire and the sixteenth century, these were not simply fiscal categories but represented the underpinnings of the state. The *askeri* enabled the sultan to rule and the state to function. On the other hand, the sultan was bound to protect the reaya; in return, they filled the state coffers. Maintaining a strict boundary between the two status groups was an ideal of Ottoman statecraft, not least because a large proportion of tax-paying reaya among the sultan's subjects meant a healthy revenue base. Fiscal and social dislocation occurred when large numbers of reaya achieved *askeri* standing, and thus tax exemption, by, for example, buying their way onto the military payrolls. As we shall see in the next chapter, this began to happen with alarming frequency at the beginning of the seventeenth century.

Land tenure

To understand how taxes were collected, it is essential to understand the Ottoman system of land tenure. Before the conquest of the Arab provinces, most of the Ottoman territories were divided into estates known as *timar*s, which had been employed as a means of supporting cavalry forces since at least the reign of Orhan, the second Ottoman sultan (*c.*1324–62). Under this system, an Ottoman cavalryman would be settled on a plot of land. He would raise horsemen for the sultan's army on this land and pay for their equipment by collecting the peasants' taxes. This system maintained the Ottoman armies while keeping the land under cultivation. It also tied the *timar*-holders, or timariots, to the state since the *timar* was granted by the sultan and his bureaucracy; the timariot did not own the land but controlled the right to its revenue, which could be taken away or redistributed by the state. The state actually owned the land. Although this system shared features with late Byzantine and Sasanian modes of land tenure, it nevertheless allowed the Ottomans to conform to the principles of Islamic law, which maintains that the ruler holds sovereign rights to the land (a concept known in Arabic as *riqaba* and in Ottoman Turkish as *rekabet*) and its natural resources. This helps to explain why the governments of modern Middle Eastern countries that were once part of the Ottoman Empire control oil and other natural resources located within their national boundaries. Peasants had rights on the land, as well, namely, a share of the crop, conceptualized as usufruct: 'use of the fruit'.

When the Arab provinces were conquered, Greater Syria and the province of Mosul in what is now northern Iraq were put under the *timar* system. Egypt, Baghdad, Basra, Yemen and North Africa, however, were not. The *timar* system was by this time growing somewhat obsolete, in any case, since its essential purpose was to provide cavalry for the army. Yet with the spread of gunpowder weapons, cavalry became less and less important while gun-toting infantry and artillery grew more and more important. Rather than raising horsemen on plots of land, these infantry troops received salaries, in cash and provisions, from the imperial or, in the case of Egypt, the provincial treasury. Meanwhile, the governor of each of these provinces was required to remit a lump sum as tribute, drawn from tax revenues, to the imperial treasury each year. As a partial result, a new form of post-*timar* administration was instituted in Egypt. Initially, the Ottoman central authority attempted to collect taxes directly by appointing administrators known as *emins* (*amin* in the Arabic singular) from Istanbul who came to Egypt for a year and made the rounds of the villages, collecting taxes.

Outside Egypt, the *timar* system by the mid-seventeenth century was swiftly giving way to tax-farming, which around the same time displaced the *emin* system in Egypt as well. Tax-farming was a system of delegated tax collection which had been in use in one form or another in various parts of the Muslim world since at least the ninth century. According to this system, a grandee in Egypt, for example, bid at auction for the right to collect the taxes of a given village or district, or of an urban operation such as port customs. The amount he bid and the price he paid if successful were based on the amount of taxes he expected to collect. Any amount he actually collected above the purchase price he kept as profit. Obviously, such a system entailed a substantial potential for abuse if a tax-farmer or his agent oppressed the peasantry so as to maximize tax revenues. Nonetheless, tax-farming remained an effective, if far from perfect, system of delegated revenue collection until well into the nineteenth century.

The nature of Ottoman rule in Egypt

A word is in order on the nature of Ottoman rule in Egypt in view of the fact that Ottoman Egypt's relationship to its Mamluk past is a rather vexed topic. After defeating the last Mamluk sultan, Tumanbay, as described in the preceding chapter, Sultan Selim I appointed Khayrbay, the former Mamluk governor of Aleppo whose defection had hastened Selim's victory, as the first Ottoman governor of Egypt. Following Khayrbay's five-year tenure, which ended with his death in 1522, governors of Egypt were dispatched from Istanbul until the early nineteenth century. In this respect, Egypt's governors were technically no different from those of the other Arab provinces, at least before the nineteenth century. Notwithstanding, by the terms of Egypt's *kanunname*, which was promulgated in 1525 by Ibrahim Pasha, grand vizier of Sultan Süleyman I, the governor did have certain responsibilities and privileges that differentiated him from other provincial governors. Like the Ottoman grand vizier, he presided over a permanent administrative council, or *divan* (*diwan* in Arabic), which met four times per week; in other provinces, the *divan* met only when the governor chose to call it into session. He was also in charge of a provincial treasury which functioned independently of the imperial treasury in Istanbul.

Apart from the role of the governor and the seven regiments of Ottoman soldiery stationed in Egypt under the terms of the *kanunname*, the conventional wisdom regarding the administration of Egypt under the Ottomans is that the Ottomans left much of the old Mamluk regime in place and the Mamluks themselves ultimately 'returned' to 'rule' Egypt under a thin Ottoman veneer by the early seventeenth century. Such an interpretation is inaccurate. True, Selim I did allow former Mamluk emirs who swore loyalty to him and to Khayrbay to join the Ottoman administration. However, he, followed by Süleyman I, altered the province's land tenure system and administrative structure, as noted above.

What has perhaps confused historians regarding Egypt is that mamluks – military slaves – had come to be employed in Egypt's army and administration by the end of the sixteenth century as Ottoman officials and, eventually, provincial grandees began to purchase them from the Caucasus. By the seventeenth century, this had become fairly common practice throughout the Ottoman Empire, so that men from Circassia in what is now southern Russia, Georgia and Abkhazia (the north-western portion of the modern republic of Georgia) served regularly as grand viziers and governors of major provinces. The conquest of the Mamluk sultanate had given the Ottomans their first major exposure to this pool of manpower, and they did not hesitate to exploit it, in the first instance alongside the *devshirme*, that is, the system of 'collecting' Christian boys from among the Ottoman subjects of the Balkans and Anatolia, converting them to Islam, and training them for either palace service or the Janissary corps. (Ottoman chroniclers further confuse the issue by occasionally referring to *devshirme* recruits as mamluks, even though this is technically incorrect.) Whereas the *devshirme* fell into disuse in the seventeenth century, mamluks from the Caucasus remained a key source of manpower for the Ottoman Empire until well into the nineteenth century. In parallel fashion, large numbers of female slaves were purchased from the Caucasus for the imperial harem and those of provincial governors and grandees.

This employment of Caucasian mamluks, while it obviously had a precedent in the usages of the Mamluk sultanate, must be regarded as an Ottoman phenomenon. Moreover, it had little or no bearing on the pattern of Ottoman administration in Egypt. True, this administration, like Ottoman administration of other provinces, did draw on certain Mamluk sultanate antecedents in the same way that it drew on Seljuk, Abbasid, Byzantine and Sasanian antecedents. But it did not constitute a revival of the Mamluk sultanate; such an interpretation is clearly anachronistic.

Early challenges to Ottoman rule

These, then, were the administrative structures that were put in place in the Arab provinces early in the sixteenth century by the two sultans who conquered these territories: Selim I and his son and successor, Süleyman I. They were not in all cases accepted without challenge, however. Before Ottoman rule in Egypt and Syria had been consolidated and codified, there were several attempts to resurrect the old Mamluk regime, or at least to throw off Ottoman rule. In Yemen, meanwhile, the Ottomans faced a near-constant threat of rebellion by the Zaydi imams of the northern highlands.

Janbirdi al-Ghazali

What may be most remarkable about Khayrbay, the first governor of Egypt after the Ottoman conquest, is that he remained steadfastly loyal to Sultan Selim, then to Sultan Süleyman. The fact that Selim had removed him from his old base in northern Syria – a bit of foresight for which Selim almost never receives credit – may have contributed to his fealty.

Not all former Mamluk administrators incorporated into the Ottoman regime shared this loyalty, however. In 1520, following Selim I's death,

Janbirdi al-Ghazali, the governor of Damascus, rebelled and attempted to seize all of Syria. Janbirdi had governed the western district of Hama for the Mamluk sultan Qansuh al-Ghuri and had been appointed to Damascus only a few weeks before Selim took the city by force – in contrast to Aleppo, which, as noted in Chapter 2, surrendered peacefully. By this time, Janbirdi had abandoned his post and gone over to the Ottomans. Perhaps in recognition of his support and of his success in restraining southern Syria's restless tribal populations, Selim reconfirmed him as governor of Damascus, allowing a continuation of the Mamluk land tenure system combined with administration by tribal proxies of certain rural districts. For the rest of Selim's reign, Janbirdi remained vigilant against the tribes.

On Selim's death in October 1520, however, Janbirdi rebelled, removing the district governors whom Selim had appointed in southern Syria and Lebanon and refusing to insert the name of the twenty-six-year-old Süleyman I in the Friday sermon. Of the new sultan, he allegedly scoffed, 'This boy doesn't have the strength to do anything [like his father]. I don't think he'll last a year in power.'[1] He then besieged Aleppo, only to be outlasted by the Ottoman governor of that city. Retreating to Damascus, he declared himself 'sultan of the Two Holy Sanctuaries', referring to the Mamluk sultanate's custodianship of Mecca and Medina, a duty and privilege now very consciously stressed by the Ottoman sultans. In February of the following year, Janbirdi was killed in fighting with the Ottoman punitive expedition that had been sent to retake Damascus. A thoroughly Ottoman administration, including *timar*s, was subsequently imposed on all of Syria.

Janım and Inal Beys

Similar rebellions by former Mamluk officials followed the death of Khayrbay, the governor of Egypt, in 1522. Sultan Süleyman, no doubt mindful of what had recently occurred in Syria, appointed his brother-in-law, Mustafa Pasha, governor of Egypt. At this, Janım Bey al-Sayfi and Inal Bey, Mamluk emirs who since the Ottoman conquest of Egypt had governed two of Egypt's subprovinces, rebelled in early 1523 and, with an army composed largely of Bedouin tribesmen, advanced into the eastern Nile Delta. There, they hoped to rally other remnants of the old Mamluk order and overthrow the Ottoman regime. When Inal executed the envoy whom Mustafa Pasha had sent to him, Mustafa sent a punitive expedition. While Janım died in the fighting, Inal fled towards Gaza and was never seen again.

Figure 3.1 Death of Janbirdi al-Ghazali, from the *Süleymanname*, the official history of Süleyman I's reign.
Source: Topkapı Palace Library Museum, MS H. 1517, folio 63b

Ahmed Pasha 'al-Kha'in'

Scarcely a year after Janım's and Inal's revolt had been quashed, however, Ottoman control over Egypt faced a far more serious challenge from the provincial governor himself. This was Ahmed Pasha, a member of

Selim I's household whom Süleyman appointed to Egypt in 1523. Accounts vary as to his origin, background and motives. A pervasive claim, particularly in chronicles produced in Egypt, is that he was Circassian and for that reason felt an ethnic bond with the late Mamluk sultans and sought to resurrect their regime. Some central Ottoman sources, in contrast, insist that he was Greek, which seems marginally more plausible given the prevalence of Greek *devshirme* recruits at Selim's court, although mamluks from the Caucasus were not unheard of at the imperial court even at this early date. What does seem improbable is that a product of the Ottoman palace, and particularly of Selim's household, would sympathize with the Mamluk sultanate to the extent of trying to recreate it. On the other hand, he had been passed over for the grand vizierate in favour of Süleyman's childhood friend and close confidant Ibrahim Pasha, and this may have bred intense resentment of a young, still relatively untried ruler who would so readily turn his back on his father's coterie. He perhaps regarded Egypt as a site where he could assert independent authority without regard for the wishes of Süleyman and his favourite. Intent on amassing the capital to support an autonomous regime, he confiscated the wealth and property of provincial officials and levied extraordinary taxes on Egypt's peasantry and non-Muslim populations.

In many respects, the story of Ahmed Pasha's rebellion is one of an autonomy-minded vizier *versus* the long arm of the imperial household. Ahmed had been accompanied to Egypt by Janım Bey al-Hamzawi, the nephew of former governor Khayrbay, who had served as an intermediary between Istanbul and Cairo on numerous occasions and led a contingent of garrison soldiers from Egypt in Süleyman's 1522 conquest of Rhodes. Ahmed Pasha was clearly suspicious of Janım, whom he imprisoned, and of the commander of Egypt's Janissary regiment, which at the time functioned as an extension of the sultan's authority in the province. He went so far as to have the Janissary commander executed, after which he rebelled openly, declaring himself sultan of Egypt and ordering his name inserted in the Friday sermon in place of that of the Ottoman sultan. He also ordered the director of Egypt's mint, a Sephardic Jewish merchant named Abraham Castro, to mint coins bearing Ahmed's name in place of Süleyman's. At that, Castro fled to Istanbul.

Ahmed Pasha managed to wrest Cairo's citadel from the Janissaries in early 1524, only to find himself under attack by Janım al-Hamzawi, who, in a famous anecdote recounted in several local chronicles, besieged the bathhouse in which Ahmed Pasha had just had half of his head shaved. 'The attack prevented him from having the second half shaved', as one chronicler laconically puts it,[2] and he fled, semi-bald, across the bathhouse roof. He eventually reached the eastern Nile Delta, where Janım al-Sayfi and Inal had made their stand a year earlier, and rallied the Bedouin of the region to his aid, only to have them abandon him when they learned that Janım al-Hamzawi was approaching with an expeditionary force, backed up by a thousand Janissaries dispatched from the imperial capital. Ahmed Pasha fled again but was captured and executed in early March 1524. He went down in Ottoman annals, both central and provincial, as Ahmed Pasha 'al-Kha'in', 'the Traitor' (Hain Ahmed Pasha in the Turkish form of the expression).

Although some sources speculate that Ahmed Pasha may have been in league with the Shiite Safavids, the aftermath of his rebellion can nonetheless be read as the codification of Ottoman rule in the former Mamluk territories and, at the same time, as the consolidation of Süleyman's power. A year after confronting this challenge to his authority, Süleyman sent his grand vizier, Ibrahim Pasha, to Egypt to regularize the province's administration. The result was the *kanunname* of Egypt, which formally established the province's political, fiscal and legal infrastructure, in the process stipulating the governor's duties and limitations. This, then, was what the historian Leslie Peirce has termed an 'imperializing moment', much like Süleyman's Ottomanization of Syria's administration in the wake of Janbirdi al-Ghazali's revolt, and his Ottomanization in the 1530s and 1540s of the territories conquered by his father from the Mamluks and Safavids in south-eastern Anatolia and northern Iraq. In Egypt, nonetheless, the impact of Süleyman's inner circle looms particularly large. Ahmed Pasha was preceded in Egypt by Mustafa Pasha, Süleyman's brother-in-law (and Selim's last grand vizier), and succeeded by Ibrahim Pasha, the sultanic favourite who had won the post that Ahmed Pasha coveted. In a sense, Süleyman's response to this rebellion was calculated to demonstrate that he was sultan in his own right.

Imam al-Mutahhar's rebellion in Yemen

By contrast, the Zaydi Shiite rebellion which led to the 'second conquest of Yemen' in 1567–8 occurred in the years immediately following Süleyman's death and may have been triggered in part by his demise, although the Zaydis had been a volatile element ever since the formal Ottoman acquisition of Yemen in 1538. Zaydi doctrine, as noted in Chapter 1, calls for a living, active imam who defends the community militarily, if necessary. This religious impulse, combined with the Zaydis' 700-year domination of Yemen's northern highlands, made the Zaydis a constant threat to Ottoman control of the province. Every

Ottoman governor could expect to spend part of his time ordering or heading expeditions into the highlands to battle one imam or another.

In addition, Imam al-Mutahhar ibn Sharaf al-Din's cataclysmic rebellion followed an administrative innovation in 1566: the division of the province into two units, each with its own governor. A pasha appointed from Istanbul governed the northern highlands, now known as 'Sanaa', after the highland capital, while one of Egypt's beys governed the southern coastal region, known variously as 'Yemen' and 'Tiha'im' (the plural of Tihama, the name denoting the coastal plain). This division was no doubt designed to bring the highlands under firmer Ottoman control. But it may also have reflected the commercial policies of the powerful grand vizier Sokollu Mehmed Pasha, who served Süleyman I and his two immediate successors, Selim II (r. 1566–74) and Murad III (r. 1574–95), before his assassination in 1579. As recent research has shown, Sokollu sought to tax the Indian spices and Yemeni coffee that were shipped through the Red Sea to Egypt.

Perhaps in response to these growing pressures, al-Mutahhar declared full-scale *jihad* in late 1566, plunging two successive Ottoman governors into a brutal year-long struggle. Scores, if not hundreds, of Ottoman soldiers fled the province to escape the death sentence to which service in the highlands often amounted. Fighting in their own territory, al-Mutahhar's tribal followers racked up victory after victory while Ottoman casualties from both battle and disease, to say nothing of desertions to the imam, mounted. Little wonder that Ottoman chroniclers of this conflict attack al-Mutahhar with unusual vehemence, calling him 'bastard', 'wretched little Shiite', and other choice epithets. 'The heretics who follow him are an obstinate sect', claims one.[3] By late 1567, the Zaydis had broken out of their highland retreat and were advancing on the critical coffee port of Mocha. At this point, grand vizier Sokollu Mehmed sent two massive expeditionary forces to surround al-Mutahhar. The commander of the land force, the legendary admiral Koja Sinan Pasha, fought al-Mutahhar to a stalemate, so that the imam was finally obliged to agree to a truce.

Following this extremely costly and draining struggle to retain Yemen, Sokollu restored Yemen's status as a single administrative unit. As for al-Mutahhar, he died of a stomach ailment in 1572. His five sons then struggled against each other until the Ottoman governor exiled them to Anatolia so as to keep the peace. Nonetheless, one son, Ibrahim, apparently acted as a spy for the Ottomans, no doubt reporting on rival lines of Zaydi imams. Rather ironically, it was a rival, indeed enemy, line of imams who would ultimately force the Ottomans out of Yemen completely some sixty years later.

Clearly, al-Mutahhar's rebellion was not of the same kind as the rebellions of former Mamluk officials in Syria and Egypt or even as the revolt of Ahmed Pasha al-Kha'in in Egypt. In many respects, it was the culmination of an ingrained pattern of Zaydi resistance against whatever power attempted to hold sway over the strategic coastlands. At the same time, however, the revolt responded to fundamental administrative changes that were no less transformative, in their own way, than the initial Ottoman conquest had been. In that sense, it bears comparison with the mass rebellion, described in the next chapter, of Jelali governors against the reforms of the Köprülü grand viziers nearly a century later. The Ottoman sources' stress on al-Mutahhar's radicalized brand of Zaydi Shiism, moreover, underlines the role of defender of Sunni Islam that the Ottomans had assumed in the wake of Selim's struggles with the Safavids and that is likewise visible in the accusations of Safavid sympathies levelled against Ahmed Pasha al-Kha'in. At the least, the struggle to restrain al-Mutahhar demonstrated how far Ottoman administration had been stretched under Süleyman. In Yemen, it had arguably reached its limits.

Despite these isolated, though by no means insignificant, challenges to Ottoman rule in the decades following the conquest of the Arab lands, the Ottoman administrative framework stood the provinces in good stead until the last years of the sixteenth century. During the following century, however, empire-wide fiscal and demographic crises would set the stage for provincial decentralization, which is the subject of the next chapter.

Notes

1. Ibn Zunbul, *Wāqi'at al-Sulṭān al-Ghawrī*, p. 190 (my translation).
2. Muhammad Abd al-Muti al-Ishaqi, *Kitāb akhbār al-uwal fī man taṣarrafa fī Miṣr min arbāb al-duwal* (*Acts of the Most Prominent: The Men of State who Administered Egypt*) (Bulaq, Egypt, 1887), p. 153 (my translation).
3. Rumuzi, *Tārīḫ-i fetḥ-i Yemen* (*History of the Conquest of Yemen*), Topkapı Palace Library (Istanbul), MS Revan 1297, f. 34r (my translation).

chapter four

CRISIS AND CHANGE IN THE SEVENTEENTH CENTURY

The 'decline' paradigm

During the reign of Sultan Süleyman I (1520–66), the Ottoman Empire reached its greatest territorial extent: from the borders of Morocco in the west to north-western Iran in the east, from Hungary in the north to Ethiopia in the south. Observers have conventionally labelled Süleyman's reign the golden age of the Ottoman Empire: the empire was still victorious on the battlefield; meanwhile, its institutions had reached full development. For the latter reason, it is also known among historians of the empire as the empire's classical age. Süleyman himself was mythologized both by Europeans, who knew him as 'the Magnificent', and by Ottomans, among whom he was known as Kanuni, the 'Lawgiver' (from *kanun*, the name applied to sultanic law), a sobriquet clearly reminiscent of the Biblical and Quranic King Solomon.

By the end of the sixteenth century, however, military expansion had faltered, corruption had infiltrated Ottoman institutions, and the empire was beset with financial difficulties. This post-Süleymanic era has been widely regarded as the era of the Ottoman Empire's decline; according to the conventional wisdom, this decline lasted from shortly after Süleyman's death in 1566 straight through to the adoption of European-style reforms in the nineteenth century, or even to the end of the empire after World War I. Seldom does an empire last for three hundred years, yet the Ottomans are supposed to have had the luxury of declining for such a lengthy span of time. Nowadays, most Ottomanists have cast aside the decline paradigm and prefer to frame the seventeenth century as one when the empire was changing direction from a military conquest state to a bureaucratic state more focused on shoring up its religious institutions, retaining control of the territories it still ruled, and collecting taxes from these territories.

Why did modern scholarship cling to the decline paradigm for so long? One reason is that Ottoman intellectuals of the late sixteenth century and later believed that the empire was indeed in decline, and they wrote about their concerns. Ironically, treatises on decline and what to do about it made up part of the great literary output of the post-Süleymanic Ottoman Empire. Many among the current generation of Ottomanists would contend that these writers simply failed to adapt to the changing nature of the empire. They found themselves left behind and, in some cases, dismissed from their jobs; therefore, they complained.

A disproportionate amount of Ottoman 'decline literature' comes from the pens of bureaucrats employed in the Ottoman Empire's finance ministry, which was in charge of assessing and collecting taxes and making land allotments, including *timar*s. Finance ministry employees were the first to observe that taxes were going uncollected, that provincial governors were squeezing the peasants for revenue, and that *timar*s were being awarded in exchange for bribes while tax-farming spread. They also had access to the pay registers of the Janissary corps, from which they could tell that the regiment was no longer the exclusive preserve of *devshirme* recruits and that the Janissaries, originally celibates, were now marrying, having families, and even enrolling their families on the regimental payrolls, a practice that accounts for the decline writers' complaints about women and children appearing in the registers.

In addition, Janissaries were pursuing activities other than soldiering. The Ottoman army was not a professional army in the modern sense; thus, while the Janissaries lived in barracks, they did not train year-round. Moreover, the wave of inflation that began in the late sixteenth century (to be discussed below) put enormous pressure on Janissaries to find other sources of income with which to supplement their fixed stipends from the imperial and provincial treasuries. By the seventeenth century, in consequence, it was not unusual for a Janissary to open a shop in the marketplace. 'I gazed upon the army; it's a market, a bazaar', goes a Janissary song from seventeenth-century Algiers. '. . . Your soldiers are jam-sellers, sour-milk vendors. . . . Your soldiers are grocers. . . . You must know this, my Padishah [sultan].'[1] More insidious was the practice of so-called 'protection' (Arabic *himaya*, Turkish *himayet*) whereby a group of Janissaries would barge into a shop, place the insignia of their particular division on the wall, and inform the shopkeeper that he was now under Janissary protection – that is, that the shop was now in business for the Janissary corps. This practice was part of a larger web of Janissary connections to the craft guilds (discussed in Chapter 7), which enabled Janissaries to enter the crafts while craftsmen entered the regiments. Neither group was likely to do much actual fighting. Instead, they would typically send hired proxies: for example, Bedouin or Turcoman tribesmen, townsmen of various descriptions, or even the basest riff-raff.

To their denunciations of all these developments, the bureaucrats in the finance ministry added their personal complaints. The writings of Mustafa Ali, a finance ministry official during the reign of Murad III (r. 1574–95), are typical in this regard. Although he served as chief financial officer of Egypt and governor of the critical Arabian port of Jidda, he never achieved his ultimate goal, which was to be appointed grand vizier. His bitterness comes through in a series of brilliant works, including one memorable 'decline poem' in which every stanza ends, 'No pleasure can there be at the banquet of this world. / The cup of Fate is filled with poison to the brim.'[2] His experience became increasingly common among government employees during succeeding centuries. Although the bureaucracy swelled, it could not keep pace with the pool of trained scribes vying for government positions. Under these circumstances, every bureaucrat could expect to be rotated out of office and to spend a few years unemployed at intervals throughout his career. Cut-throat competition grew rife as many bureaucrats failed to achieve promotion despite every conceivable effort. Such career frustrations magnified the threat these bureaucrats felt from the changes occurring in Ottoman administration.

The classic works of Ottoman decline writing follow an ancient genre of advice literature, often called the Mirror for Princes genre, dating back at least to the Sasanian Empire, which ruled Iran and Iraq for some four centuries before the Muslim conquests of the seventh century CE. A typical Ottoman Mirror for Princes took the form of a treatise addressed to the sultan, recommending the reforms he should undertake to halt the decline; clearly, the decline writers sought to correct, not subvert or overturn, the Ottoman system. Their suggested reforms usually included rectifying administrative practices by eliminating bribe-taking and office-selling in favour of promotion solely by merit, and cleaning up the government payroll so that only those performing real service received government salaries. Reforming the military was likewise a key proposal: ensuring that the Janissaries were not allowed to marry, to engage in commerce, or to add their relatives or cronies to the regimental payroll; and seeing that the timariot cavalry administered their land grants properly, treated the peasants justly so that they practised productive agriculture rather than fleeing the land, and supplied the proper number of soldiers to the imperial army. The sultan was repeatedly urged to halt tax-farming and the abuses that tended to accompany it. Behind all these suggestions lay the premise that, if the sultan governed according to the *sharia*, he would ensure a just, and therefore prosperous, empire.

This tradition of Ottoman decline literature lasted almost as long as the alleged decline itself, continuing sporadically until the introduction of western-style reforms in the nineteenth century. The wellspring of this literature remained the finance ministry, and the basic recommendations remained the same: prune bloated government payrolls; revive merito-cracy; stop the distribution of posts to friends and relatives; ensure that the military is really trained to fight. In short, self-criticism became an intellectual tradition in the Ottoman Empire, linked to the tradition whereby intellectuals, many of whom were government functionaries, debated history in what amounted to reading circles. Indeed, the first tentative attempts at westernizing reform at the end of the eighteenth century would result from a series of reform memoranda, very much in the decline literature tradition, prepared by Ottoman administrators in response to mounting military defeats by European powers.

The crisis of the seventeenth century

The decline paradigm resulted not only from decline literature but from a very real crisis that gripped the Ottoman Empire in the late sixteenth century and lasted well into the following century. Most Ottomanists today, however, assert that the empire's adaptation to this crisis by the end of the seventeenth century enabled it to survive for over two hundred years more. Thus, they prefer a paradigm of 'crisis and adaptation' to outmoded declinism.

The crisis in question was economic, demographic and military, and resulted from a variety of factors. Modern-day historians of the Ottoman Empire have tended to stress three above all: inflation, overpopulation and the spread of firearms among the peasantry. Yet these fundamental factors contributed to others, notably discontent among the Ottoman soldiery, which played an undeniable role in the crisis.

Inflation and debasement

The influx of silver from Habsburg Spain's colonies in Peru and Mexico into first European, then Ottoman territory exacerbated an existing inflationary trend, itself part of a series of long-term socio-economic changes, others of which will be examined below. Between 1550 and 1600, prices of some commodities rose as much as 400 per cent, and this following a lengthy period of relative stability. In response, coin counterfeiters and even the official mints in some Ottoman provinces began issuing debased currency, that is, currency in which the volume of precious metal was sharply reduced, replaced by less valuable metals such as copper. In the absence of an international silver or gold standard, debasement reduced the real value of the Ottoman silver currency, known as the *akche*, often Europeanized to asper. As a result, the purchasing power of those on fixed incomes from the state, notably Janissaries and other troops, dropped precipitously; in addition, payment of their salaries was more and more frequently delinquent. Not surprisingly, soldiery revolts, particularly among the Janissaries in Istanbul, became increasingly common.

Soldiery revolts

Uprisings by soldiers spread into the Arab provinces, too, in the last years of the sixteenth century. In Egypt, disgruntled troops deposed an Ottoman governor for the first time in 1586, setting an ominous precedent. Unrest in Egypt tended to centre on the three cavalry regiments, who were not *timar*-holders but simply salaried troops. Because they were the lowest-paid of the seven regiments of Ottoman soldiery stationed in the province, they were especially vulnerable to the effects of inflation on their incomes. Yet they could not easily augment their incomes by opening shops, as the Janissaries could, because their service regularly took them into the countryside. Customary gifts and exactions, some of questionable legality, were therefore indispensable supplements to their salaries. In 1604, when the newly arrived governor Ibrahim Pasha refused them the governor's customary accession gift to the soldiery, cavalry troops attacked his camp; the following year, they killed him. Some five years later, after the governor Mehmed Pasha abolished an extortionate fee that rural cavalry troops collected from the peasantry, the troops attempted to stage a revolution, even naming their own sultan. The threat posed by this insurrection comes across in provincial chroniclers' descriptions of the rebels, whom they label 'Kharijites', referring to an heretical sect of early Islam. Faced with nothing short of the overthrow of Ottoman rule in the empire's largest province, Mehmed Pasha responded with merciless force, crushing the rebels militarily, executing their ringleaders and those who had tried to flee, and sending the rest, in chains, to Yemen. These achievements earned him the sobriquet *Kul Kıran*, 'Breaker of the *Kul*', referring to soldiers and other 'servants of the sultan'.

Population pressure, firearms and mercenaries

In the countryside of Anatolia, overpopulation was a problem because the rural populace had boomed during the prosperous and expansionist years of the sixteenth century. With the onset of inflation, peasants found themselves unable to market their crops profitably or to buy the provisions they needed from towns. Likewise, *timar*-holders faced growing difficulties in equipping cavalry troops. Such hardships triggered a flow of population out of the countryside and into the cities.

This dislocation coincided with the costly Long War (1593–1606) against the Habsburgs, which ended in stalemate. In this series of battle-field confrontations, the Habsburgs and Ottomans alike relied as never before on gun-bearing infantry. Consequently, both empires supplemented their regular armies with ever-increasing numbers of mercenaries. In the Ottoman case, the timariot cavalry and the Janissary infantry were rein-forced by thousands of armed Anatolian peasants, many of whom had, in any case, fled the land as a result of the economic crisis. Once a given confrontation drew to a close, these peasants would return to the countryside with their firearms. With farming and herding rendered unprofitable or even unsustainable by inflation, many turned to brigandage. The resulting waves of lawlessness throughout Anatolia at the close of the sixteenth century have come to be known as the Jelali Rebellions after Shaykh Jelal, leader of an unrelated pro-Safavid uprising in central and eastern Anatolia in 1519. Terrorized and economically devastated by the chaos, which followed on the already ruinous inflation, agriculturalists fled the land en masse in what came to be known as the Great Flight.

Peasant mercenaries who had returned from the battlefield could also offer their services to provincial governors, both in Anatolia and in the Arab provinces, who were beginning to amass their own private armies. In short, mercenaries, typically known as *sekban*s, were in the Ottoman armies to stay. From the period of the Long War to the very first European-style reforms at the end of the eighteenth century, they would form an important component of the Ottoman military.

*Kul*s and Osman II

Within the imperial household in Topkapı Palace, the imperial Janissaries and the various bodies of palace troops had become, by 1600, an entrenched interest group. Such a 'servant of the sultan' was known as a *kul* (literally, 'slave', the root of the English 'coolie'), a flexible term that could apply to military forces and officials in the sultan's service anywhere in the Ottoman Empire, including the disgruntled cavalry troops who rebelled in Egypt in 1609. In the early seventeenth century, however, the term *kul* usually designated a soldier or functionary recruited through the *devshirme* and often trained in the palace, as some of the Egyptian soldiers may, in fact, have been. *Kul* elements were roundly denounced by early decline writers for failing to perform necessary military duty while demanding larger and larger gifts and more and more privileges from the sultan. Matters came to a head during the brief reign of Sultan Osman II (1618–22), who attempted to reassert his control over the imperial household by curtailing the *kuls'* influence and lost his life for his pains.

Osman II, the son of Ahmed I, came to the throne at the tender age of fourteen and appears to have been heavily influenced by the Chief Eunuch of the imperial harem, with whom, in mid-1622, he conceived a scheme of supplementing the *kul* forces with an army composed of mercenaries recruited from the empire's Asian provinces. He even considered moving the capital from Istanbul, which had become the bastion of the *kul*s, to a city in the Asian provinces: Bursa, Damascus, perhaps even Cairo. Not surprisingly, the *kul*s felt threatened by this move, even though these mercenary troops were to supplement, not replace, them. The young sultan was deposed by *kul*-friendly elements and ultimately strangled on the orders of the new grand vizier. His uncle Mustafa was escorted out of the harem, where crown princes were raised by the seventeenth century, and enthroned.

This did not end the matter, however. Some governors in the provinces believed that Osman had taken a necessary step; they had no intention of allowing the *kul*s and Sultan Mustafa to ride roughshod over them. The governors of Erzurum and Diyarbakır in eastern Anatolia rebelled against Mustafa and, with their own armies of mercenaries recruited from Anatolia and the Caucasus, began marching towards Istanbul. The first to rebel, and the more famous, was Abaza Mehmed Pasha, the governor of Erzurum in north-eastern Anatolia. The sobriquet 'Abaza' signifies that he was from Abkhazia, today a region in northwestern Georgia. As such, he was part of a wave of Abkhazian mamluks, or elite military slaves, who entered Ottoman government service in the seventeenth century, including the father of the patron of the famous seventeenth-century traveller Evliya Chelebi. The sultan's chancery dispatched flurries of orders demanding that the rebels desist, then ultimately sent out a punitive expedition, which, according to court chronicles, mysteriously 'failed to encounter' the rebel forces. In short, the crisis was defused through inaction. Only years later was Abaza suppressed by Sultan Murad IV.

*Kul*s, however, continued to be major power brokers in the imperial capital until the reforms of the Köprülü grand viziers in the late seventeenth century. Evidence suggests, moreover, that a '*kul* problem' had also emerged in Egypt in the early years of the century. Mehmed Pasha, the Ottoman governor who in 1609 put down the massive cavalry rebellion described above, also investigated the assassination of his pre-decessor, Ibrahim Pasha. He suspected that some role had been played by the twenty-four *sanjak beyi*s of Egypt, for 'the *sipahi*s would not have killed him without the knowledge of the *sanjak*s'.[3] These beys were, like Egypt's cavalry troops, salaried functionaries, as opposed to *timar*-holders; while some of them governed Egypt's subprovinces and were thus parallel in function to the *sanjak beyi*s of other Ottoman provinces, others were based in Cairo. In the early seventeenth century, most of the beys were one-time *devshirme* recruits, or the sons of such recruits, who had been promoted from the two elite infantry regiments attached to the governor's council, or *divan*. Most had come to Egypt from Istanbul and seemed intent on turning Cairo into a *kul* stronghold, much like the capital. Mehmed Pasha expelled thirteen beys from Cairo, thus decimating the beys' strength in the provincial capital. His '*Kul*-Breaker' sobriquet, while it probably referred primarily to his thorough-going humiliation of Egypt's cavalry troops, may have extended to his punishment of the beys. It was perhaps because Cairo's *kul* problem had been resolved that Sultan Osman II considered the city a candidate for imperial capital.

The East–West dichotomy

As the example of the rebellious Abkhazian governor in Anatolia shows, Asiatic mercenaries and Caucasian mamluks by the seventeenth century represented a clear alternative to the *kul*s recruited through the *devshirme*. Following the conquest of the Arab provinces between 1516 and 1538, the Ottoman authorities began to exploit the pool of military slaves used by the Mamluk sultanate and the Safavid empire, namely, the Caucasus region. Mamluks from the Caucasus were brought into Topkapı Palace in Istanbul and ultimately into the households of influential viziers and provincial governors, who might themselves be emancipated Caucasian mamluks like Abaza Mehmed Pasha. In either milieu, they created friction with the 'traditional' pool of Ottoman man- and woman-power, namely, the Balkan and Anatolian populations who were prime candidates for the *devshirme*.

Antagonism between 'westerners' from the Balkans and western Anatolia and 'eastern' Caucasians was not always a given; loyalty to sultan or patron could override ethnic and regional differences. None-theless, this East–West antagonism was a factor in the political culture of the Ottoman Arab provinces during the seventeenth century. In Greater Syria, as will become apparent presently, it exacerbated the long-standing rivalry between 'northern', or Qaysi, and 'southern', or Yemeni, Arab tribal blocs. In Egypt, it seems to have lain behind the appearance during the seventeenth century of two tenacious rival political/military factions, to be discussed below.

Janissary hegemony in the Arab provinces

In the Arab provinces, tension between *kul*s and mercenaries, as well as East–West antagonism, fed into a broader pattern in which provincial governors with mercenary armies confronted the officers of the regiments of Ottoman troops garrisoned in the provincial capitals. Janissaries figured prominently among the garrison troops, but they were supplemented by other, usually smaller, regiments that had different functions. Egypt was unique among the Arab provinces in hosting seven regiments. During the sixteenth century, the officers of these regiments were almost without exception *kul*s; by the seventeenth century, *kul*s were still a major presence among regimental officers, but they were increasingly joined by sons of *kul*s, locals who had bought their way into the regiments, and even mercenaries who had relocated from other parts of the Ottoman Empire.

Janissaries in the Arab provincial capitals served as guards, often called Mustahfizan, a term that literally means 'protectors', as in protectors of urban defences. They were housed in the citadel, where the province's governor was based. Because they were based in the capital cities, they had easy access to urban markets, where, as in Istanbul, they opened shops and coerced existing craftsmen to pay them protection money. In coastal and riverain cities, such as Cairo, they often monopolized port customs as well. By the seventeenth century, Janissaries were a powerful force in the urban life of most of the Arab provinces and had even begun to acquire tax farms in the countryside. In Egypt, they controlled the lion's share of the increasingly lucrative trade through the Red Sea in coffee from the Yemeni port of Mocha. These relatively secure sources of wealth allowed Janissary and other regimental officers to build households that could ultimately rival the household of the governor. One Janissary officer, Mustafa al-Kazdağlı, who apparently came to Egypt from western Anatolia sometime around 1640, began to amass a fortune in coffee-related revenues that would, in the eighteenth century, propel the household which he founded into dominance of Egypt. The regiments themselves provided a ready source of household members for whom membership of an officer's household was an extension of the pre-existing regimental hierarchy.

The Janissaries garrisoned in Damascus collected hefty fees on the overland trade entering the ancient city, which had been a commercial hub for millennia. As Damascus enjoyed strong commercial links to Aleppo, some 350 kilometres to the north, the Damascus Janissaries towards the end of the sixteenth century infiltrated Aleppo also, hoping to profit from that city's rich caravan trade with Anatolia, Basra and Iran. The Damascene Janissaries came to dominate Aleppo politically until 1602, when the Ottoman governor combined with a local Kurdish chieftain to drive them from the city, as described below.

In the Iraqi provinces, the common pattern of Janissaries augmenting their salaries with ambitious commercial ventures combined with the risks and opportunities presented by the region's status as a frontier zone abutting the enemy Safavid empire. The Safavid threat meant that soldiery revolts must be put down at all costs; however, it also meant that rebels could look to the Safavids for support. The most serious example of this tendency involves a Janissary officer named Bakr, who served as Baghdad's *subashı*, or chief of police, in the early seventeenth century. Around 1620, he amassed a following among the men of his regiment and became the de facto regional strongman. To counter him, the governor of Baghdad, Yusuf Pasha, combined with the commander of the Azeban regiment, a somewhat smaller infantry unit based, like the Janissaries, in Baghdad's citadel. Baghdad's Janissaries and Azeban were rivals, much as the two regiments would be in Cairo early in the following century. Yusuf Pasha and the Azeban planned to attack Bakr and his followers when they returned to Baghdad from a punitive expedition against one of central Iraq's many Arab tribes. Bakr learned of the plot in advance, however, and besieged the city on his return, killing Yusuf Pasha and the Azeban commander in the process.

When the youthful sultan Osman II ordered his governor of Diyarbakır, Hafiz Ahmed Pasha, to retake Baghdad, Bakr Subashı appealed to the Safavids for aid. The great Safavid Shah Abbas I (r. 1588–1629) sent an army to Baghdad, at which Hafiz Ahmed Pasha withdrew, naming Bakr governor of Baghdad. Bakr attempted to renew his allegiance to the Ottoman sultan, but the Safavids occupied the city and executed him. Baghdad remained in Safavid hands until 1638, when Sultan Murad IV led a massive expedition to reconquer it. Even after its restoration to Ottoman control, however, Janissaries continued to play a dominant role in the city's economy and political culture for much of the rest of the seventeenth century.

In Basra, the fabled port city at the confluence of the Tigris and Euphrates rivers, the Ottoman governor in the 1590s actually sold his office to a Janissary scribe and local grandee who went by the pregnant name Afrasiyab. The name, alluding as it does to the arch-enemy of Iran in the Persian national epic, the *Shahname*, all but marked Afrasiyab as an enemy of the Safavids. Perhaps to compound this impression, he claimed descent from the Great Seljuks, the staunchly Sunni Turkic dynasty that had occupied Iran and Iraq in the eleventh century (see Chapter 1). The fabricated Seljuk genealogy, moreover, gave him a regional legitimacy that complemented his de facto recognition by the Ottoman sultan. Afrasiyab founded a dynasty which governed Basra until 1668, when his grandson, Hüseyin Pasha, was ousted by the governor of Baghdad.

Jelali governors and their equivalents

These provincial governors who led punitive expeditions against the provincial Janissary bosses were not simply extensions of the sultan's authority. Inevitably, each of them accumulated his own following in parallel to the sultan's entourage. Such a following consisted of clients bound to the governor by ties of patronage; they might be aides; slaves, including mamluks; mercenaries; and the governor's own wives and concubines. Together, they made up the governor's household. This sort of household is visible as early as the reign of Süleyman I, when powerful viziers who belonged to the sultan's ruling council, or *divan*, such as the grand vizier and the chief financial officer, or *defterdar*, presided over large retinues that were housed in their own palatial residences. Süleyman I's influential grand vizier Ibrahim Pasha (term 1524–36) was an early founder of one of these 'vizier and pasha households', as one scholar has labelled them.

A vizier such as Hafız Ahmed Pasha would, in the course of his career, be appointed governor of several different Ottoman provinces. In that case, he would transfer his household to the provinces concerned, augmenting it as he deemed fit with mercenary troops and local personnel. In broad terms, the households of these governors represented a diversion of political influence and economic resources from the imperial capital to the Ottoman provinces.

In addition, provincial governors had begun to come not out of Topkapı Palace but out of the households of viziers, who trained up their own clients just as the sultan nurtured his palace pages. Unable to order their own *devshirme*, however, the viziers attracted followers from among existing palace pages, purchased their own slaves from the Caucasus, and hired mercenaries. Thus, these households not only embodied the tension between the imperial capital and the provinces but also the East–West dichotomy noted above since many of their members were 'easterners' from the Caucasus and eastern Anatolia, as opposed to the 'westerners' who still dominated Topkapı Palace. The overriding loyalty of these men – and women, too – might well be to the vizier who headed the household, rather than to the sultan. This made it all the easier for a provincial governor to contemplate rebellion if he disagreed vehemently with the sultan's policies or wished simply to carve out his own sphere of influence.

By the reign of Osman II (1618–22), provincial governors with their own mercenary armies, such as Abaza Mehmed Pasha, the governor of Erzurum who marched on Istanbul following Osman's murder, represented a threat of rebellion similar to that of the Jelalis a few decades earlier. In fact, rebellious provincial governors in the seventeenth century were often termed 'Jelali governors'.

Fakhr al-Din Ma'n II

Jelali governors emerged not only in Anatolia but in the Arab provinces as well, where their private armies often included tribesmen and peasants native to the region. In Lebanon and Syria in the early years of the seventeenth century, the Ottomans confronted a particularly troublesome figure known as Fakhr al-Din Ma'n. Fakhr al-Din belonged to the region's Druze population: descendants of Ismaili Muslims who had split from the Fatimid caliphate in the eleventh century after asserting the divinity of the caliph al-Hakim (r. 996–1021 CE) (see Chapter 1). (By the Ottoman period, the Druze were no longer considered Muslim at all.) Although the Ma'n family had lived in the Lebanese mountains since before Sultan Selim I's conquest of the region, Fakhr al-Din fits the pattern of the Jelali governor, despite the efforts of Lebanese nationalists to portray his regime as a forerunner of the modern Lebanese state.

In mountainous territories that were difficult to control, notably Lebanon and the Kurdish regions of northern Iraq and south-eastern Anatolia, the Ottomans had recourse to notable or princely families, many of whom had been ensconced in these lands long before they fell under Ottoman rule. The Ma'ns were one of these families. Fakhr al-Din's grandfather, also named Fakhr al-Din and therefore known to historians as Fakhr al-Din I, submitted to Selim I and received the right to collect taxes from Lebanon's peasantry.

As the economic crisis of the late sixteenth and early seventeenth centuries deepened, mercenaries became more widely available throughout the Ottoman provinces. In Lebanon, they were often hard-pressed Turcoman, Kurdish and Arab tribesmen of various loyalties. Like the rebellious provincial governors, Fakhr al-Din II gathered an army of mercenaries, making particular use of Arab and Turcoman tribesmen, and attempted to carve out a bailiwick for himself in the mountains of Lebanon and in neighbouring parts of Syria and Palestine. This brought him into conflict with the Ottoman governor of Damascus, who used Fakhr al-Din's regional tribal opponents against him.

In so doing, the governor was able to take advantage of the ancient antagonism between Qaysi, or 'northern', Arabs and Yemeni, or 'southern', Arabs, briefly noted above. The division dates to the pre-Islamic era, when the language and cultural traditions of Yemen were markedly different from those of the nomadic and semi-nomadic tribesmen farther north in the Arabian peninsula. By the time Islam emerged, descendants of Yemenis were dispersed throughout the peninsula. Both Qaysi and Yemeni tribesmen joined the early Muslim armies; as the early Islamic conquests rapidly spread, they dispersed throughout the Middle East. Over the centuries, the rivalry metamorphosed into an entrenched factional conflict in which the original geographical distinctions lost all meaning. By the Ottoman period, Qaysi–Yemeni tension was limited largely to Lebanon and Palestine; in these regions, however, it continued well into the twentieth century. As the Ma'ns were Qaysis, the governor of Damascus joined up with Yusuf Pasha Sayfa, the scion of a Yemeni family who had been appointed governor of the northern Lebanese district of Tripoli in 1579.

At his lowest ebb, in 1613, Fakhr al-Din fled to the protection of the duke of Tuscany in northern Italy. Tuscany had a huge stake in the commerce in luxury goods that came through Damascus via the western Arabian peninsula and along the old Silk Road through Aleppo; the duke had signed a commercial treaty with Fakhr al-Din in 1608. Fakhr al-Din spent the next five years in the Tuscan port of Livorno (Leghorn) and in the city of Messina in Sicily, part of the Spanish Habsburg possessions. When he returned to Lebanon, however, he faced the same situation: confrontation with the governor of Damascus combined with competition with regional rivals, including Yusuf Pasha Sayfa. Moreover, the Ottoman central authority had, in 1614, created the province of Sidon to administer southern Lebanon and northern Palestine directly, thus potentially threatening Fakhr al-Din's ability to operate autonomously. But in 1623, Fakhr al-Din defeated the governor of Damascus in battle and took him prisoner, forcing him to recognize Fakhr al-Din's regional hegemony. Two years later, the aged Yusuf Pasha Sayfa died, and the young sultan Murad IV issued a decree confirming Fakhr al-Din's control of Lebanon.

Later in his reign, Murad IV was less tolerant of Jelali governors and their equivalents. In 1638, he marched to retake Baghdad from the Safavids, who had recaptured it from the Ottomans under their greatest shah, Abbas I (r. 1588–1629), in 1623. To secure the route to Iraq, Murad ordered his governor of Damascus to eliminate Fakhr al-Din, which he did. Fakhr al-Din and his sons were taken captive to Istanbul and later executed, except for one son who entered palace service.

Ali Pasha Janbulad

A similar situation unfolded during these same years in the Syria-Anatolia border region, where the Ottomans had appointed a local Kurdish chieftain, Hüseyin Janbulad, governor of his home district of Kilis, today in south-eastern Turkey. In the early 1600s, Hüseyin Pasha Janbulad allied with the Ottoman governor of Aleppo against the Janissaries of Damascus, who, as noted above, had infiltrated the Aleppine economy. Having driven them from the city, the two pashas replaced them with local elements. Hüseyin Pasha succeeded to the governorship of Aleppo himself, only to be executed in 1605 for failing to heed a summons to join a campaign against the Safavids. His death inspired his nephew, Ali Pasha Janbulad, to rebel against the new governor of Aleppo with the assistance of other disgruntled governors in the region; he even allied himself with Fakhr al-Din Ma'n II. Ultimately, he and his army of tribal mercenaries were defeated by the grand vizier Kuyuju Murad Pasha, a noted suppressor of the Jelali Rebellions, in 1607. Although it has long been thought that a descendant of Ali Pasha Janbulad migrated with his clan in the early 1630s to Lebanon under Fakhr al-Din Ma'n's protection, and that this uprooted Kurdish clan supplied the root of the Druze Jumblatt clan prominent in Lebanon today, recent scholarship has suggested that the Lebanese Jumblatts descend from an entrenched Arab Druze clan who had been enemies of Fakhr al-Din Ma'n.

In general terms, the economic and demographic crises of the late sixteenth and early seventeenth centuries, combined with the empowerment of Greater Syria's tribal mountain populations during the Long War, encouraged regional tribal grandees such as Fakhr al-Din and the Kurdish Janbulads to expand their influence from within the Ottoman administrative hierarchy, making use of mercenary armies composed largely of tribesmen from the area. In this effort, however, they clashed not only with rival regional elements but also with the palace-trained personnel traditionally appointed to top administrative posts, particularly the major provincial governorships. Like the 'easterners' from the Caucasus, these regional grandees posed a threat to the *devshirme* recruits and other 'western' elements who had traditionally dominated imperial strategy.

The Faqari and Qasimi factions in Egypt

This East–West split informed the political culture of Egypt during the seventeenth century no less than it did that of Greater Syria, as becomes clear from a consideration of two politico-military factions which appeared in Egypt early in the century. Accounts of the factions' origins are vague and laden with myth and legend, typically attributing their emergence to the Ottoman conquest of Egypt by Sultan Selim I. Scholarship on Ottoman Egypt has tended to equate the Faqari and Qasimi factions with the multiple factions of the Mamluk sultanate, each of which centred on a particular sultan and comprised his personal mamluks and other followers. The two seventeenth-century factions, however, differed fundamentally from the Mamluk-era factions in their relentless bilateralism – no third faction ever presented itself – and in their greater social inclusiveness. Whereas the Mamluk-era factions were, by and large, restricted to the military-administrative class, the Faqaris and Qasimis encompassed urban artisan guilds and even tapped into an older division among Egypt's Bedouin, who were divided into two loose tribal blocs known as Sa'd and Haram. As one early eighteenth-century chronicler puts it, 'The people of Egypt from ancient times were in two factions, soldiers and Bedouin and peasants: white flag and red flag . . . until the administration of the House of Osman, . . . [when they became] Faqari-Sa'd and Qasimi-Haram.'[4] Intriguingly, the factional origin myths recounted by other eighteenth-century Egyptian chroniclers associate Haram and Sa'd, respectively, with the Qays and Yemen, or 'northern' and 'southern' Arabs – the same dichotomy that permeated Ottoman Lebanon and Palestine, as noted above.

The two factions appear to have coalesced during the Ottomans' long, tortuous and ultimately futile struggle to hold Yemen in the face of a prolonged rebellion by a new line of Zaydi imams (see below). In fact, the Qasimi faction almost certainly took its name from Qasim Bey, commander of an expedition to Yemen in 1631. Mamluks from the Caucasus recruited for service in Yemen appear to have formed the core of the fledgling Qasimi faction while a corresponding cadre of Rumis – 'westerners' from western Anatolia and the European provinces of the empire – seem to have comprised the rank-and-file of the early Faqari faction. By the 1640s, a pattern had emerged whereby a rank-and-file of mercenaries – Rumi 'westerners' in the case of the Faqaris; 'eastern' Asiatics of various descriptions, including Bedouin tribesmen, Arabophone locals, and deserters from the Safavid and Uzbek armies, in the case of the Qasimis – were commanded by regimental officers and *sanjak beyi*s of Caucasian mamluk origin.

The first confrontation between the Faqari and Qasimi factions erupted during the 1640s, when two ostensibly Qasimi beys, Qansuh and Memi, attempted to take the lucrative and influential positions of pilgrimage commander and governor of the grain-rich Upper Egyptian superprovince of Jirja from two ostensibly Faqari beys, respectively, Rıdvan and Ali. This power play coincided with, and was almost certainly related to, an order from the Ottoman governor of Egypt to expel all the *awlad al-Arab*, or 'sons of the Arabs', from the seven regiments of Ottoman soldiery stationed in Egypt. Although this term has been interpreted by several scholars as referring to members of Egypt's 'native' Arab population, it seems actually to have been a far more generic term for members of populations who were *not* Rumi – that is, who were 'Asiatics', or 'easterners', as opposed to 'westerners' from western Anatolia and the Balkans. The two rival pairs of beys drew their private military forces from among the seven regiments, which had been infiltrated by mercenary clients of regimental officers and beys. Whereas Rıdvan and Ali Beys employed Rumi mercenaries, Qansuh and Memi appear to have favoured these *awlad al-Arab*. Ultimately, Rıdvan and Ali prevailed while Qansuh and Memi were executed on the sultan's orders.

In Egypt, East–West antagonism dovetailed with a competition among the higher echelons of beys and regimental officers for control of key positions and the revenues that went with them. In the seventeenth century, the province's two most lucrative and influential administrative positions were those of pilgrimage commander and governor of Jirja, the enormous Upper Egyptian subprovince which functioned as the breadbasket not only of Egypt itself but also of the Holy Cities, to which its grain was transported during the annual pilgrimage. The governor of this province and the pilgrimage commander could forge a formidable power alliance capable of deriving spectacular profits from pilgrimage-related commerce. Hence, it comes as no surprise that in Egypt the 'Jelali governor' pattern in the seventeenth century concerned the governor of Jirja.

Mehmed Bey, governor of Jirja in Egypt

The governors of Egypt's subprovinces assumed roles parallel to those of provincial governors elsewhere in the empire. This was particularly true of the governor of Jirja, which in the seventeenth century rivalled Cairo as a locus of power. Under Ali Bey, Jirja and much of Upper Egypt seem to have become a sphere of influence of the Faqari faction. Ali Bey was, in fact, the first grandee to assume the sobriquet 'Faqari', which in all probability derived from his use of the sort of Ottoman battle flag frequently employed by the Janissaries, emblazoned with the image of the early Islamic caliph Ali ibn Abi Talib's double-bladed sword Dhu'l-Faqar. At the height of the conflict between Ali and his partner Rıdvan Bey, on the one hand, and Qansuh and Memi, on the other, Ali advanced on Cairo with an army of nearly 4,000 Rumi mercenaries, who succeeded in intimidating the Ottoman governor into withdrawing his support from Qansuh and Memi, triggering the pair's downfall. On Ali's death in 1653, the governorship of Jirja passed to his protégé and former mamluk Mehmed Bey, who in the late 1650s rebelled outright against the Ottoman governor and led his own mercenary army towards Cairo. In 1659, however, the governor led a major expedition to Jirja to put down Mehmed Bey's revolt. 'This poor one has seen many military processions, but such a magnificent army was unique,' recalls an obviously biased Turcophone chronicler of Egypt, who, significantly, refers to Mehmed Bey as 'Jelali Mehmed' in recognition of the parallel between the bey of Jirja and the contemporary Jelali governors of Anatolia and northern Syria. As if to underline this point, he interrupts his account of the fighting to report the arrival of news that 'Jelali' Hasan Pasha, the rebellious governor of Aleppo (see below), had been defeated and executed.[5]

The loss of Yemen

While Syria, Iraq and Egypt during the seventeenth century served as arenas for ambitious power-brokers from the ranks of the provincial and subprovincial governors and regimental officers, Yemen slipped from Ottoman rule entirely. As noted in the preceding chapter, the Zaydi Shiite population in the northern highlands were prone to rebel against the Ottomans. The sons of the imam al-Mutahhar, whose revolt in the 1560s had led to the 'second Ottoman conquest' of the province, were exiled to Anatolia so that al-Mutahhar's descendants would pose no threat to the Ottoman administration in Yemen. In 1598, however, a new Zaydi dynasty was founded by the imam al-Qasim Mansur, who resuscitated the anti-Ottoman *jihad*. For decades, Ottoman governors of Yemen struggled to contain the Qasimis, relying on special expeditionary forces recruited largely from Egypt. Qasim Bey, namesake of Egypt's Qasimi faction, led one of these expeditions, as noted above. (Though the Egyptian faction and the Yemeni dynasty had the same name, there does not appear to have been any direct connection between them.) Finally, in the early 1630s, al-Qasim's son and successor, al-Muayyad Billah Muhammad, systematically drove the Ottomans from the major towns of the southern coastal plain. By the time the imam's army besieged the last remaining Ottoman forces in the Red Sea port of Mocha, the Ottoman central authority had apparently elected to let Yemen go. While his men were killed in battle, died of disease, or deserted to the imam, the Ottoman commander sent envoys to warn the governor of Egypt that 'if three or four thousand foot soldiers and musketeers . . . are not sent, the port of Mocha, too, will slip from our hands and fall under enemy rule', yet 'however much they pleaded, not a word was heard'.[6] In 1636, the commander and his surviving 100 men finally evacuated Mocha on an Indian merchant vessel, leaving Yemen to the Qasimis.

The Köprülü reforms

By the time Mehmed Bey, the governor of Jirja in Upper Egypt, rebelled, a new element had entered the Ottoman central administration that would have a profound effect on the pattern of provincial rebellions. This was the Köprülü family of grand viziers. They were an Albanian family founded by Köprülü Mehmed Pasha, a palace functionary who, contrary to all expectations, was appointed grand vizier in 1656 on the urging of the young Sultan Mehmed IV's mother. He was, by all accounts, a hard-bitten old man who held no brief for either the *kul*s or the rebellious provincial governors. He began to crack down on both, mainly by the traditional means of reform advocated by the decline writers: pruning bloated payrolls and making new appointments. These appointments were, however, from his own sizeable household and extended not only to provincial governors but to the top of the palace hierarchy, including Chief Eunuchs, *defterdar*s and top religious officials.

The existing provincial governors recognized a threat in the Köprülü reforms. In 1658, another Abkhazian provincial governor rebelled: Abaza Hasan Pasha, governor of Aleppo. He forged a united front of fifteen provincial and district governors in Syria and south-eastern Anatolia for one massive anti-Köprülü rebellion; the plan was for the governors' mercenary armies to converge on the central Anatolian city of Konya. The fact that Köprülü Mehmed Pasha was Albanian, and therefore 'western', while Abaza Hasan and other governors in the region were from the Caucasus, and therefore 'eastern', was, naturally, not insignificant even though the Köprülüs were not tools of the palace *kul*s.

Köprülü Mehmed sent a punitive expedition under the governor of Diyarbakır, Murtaza Pasha, to crush the rebellion, yet this formidable military force was ambushed and routed by the rebels while passing through western Anatolia. The following winter, nonetheless, Murtaza Pasha, who had regrouped at Aleppo, managed to harass the rebels until they agreed to a truce. Arriving in Aleppo to negotiate terms, Abaza Hasan and his fellow rebel governors dined regally with Murtaza Pasha, after which their host rose to perform the ablution before the night prayer. At this signal, his men 'grabbed their swords and daggers, and [cut] their polluted skins to pieces . . .'.[7] This episode only strengthened Köprülü Mehmed's determination to exercise total control over the provincial administration.

Köprülü Mehmed Pasha was succeeded as grand vizier by his son, Köprülü Fazıl Ahmed Pasha, who, as grand vizier from 1661–76, put the definitive Köprülü stamp on the administration of the entire empire. His strategy was essentially to replace competing vizier and pasha households with the Köprülü household. For example, he sent his lieutenant (*kethüda*) to govern Egypt in 1670; this lieutenant came to Cairo with 2,000 new Janissaries and his own household, some members of which remained in Egypt after he left and influenced Egypt's political culture. With the central and provincial administration under his control, Köprülü Fazıl Ahmed was able to turn his attention to the battlefield, where he achieved notable successes against the Venetians, the Habsburgs and the Russians. Doubtless his most striking accomplishment was the conquest of Crete from Venice in 1669. The Ottoman attack on the island, including the siege of the Venetian capital, Candia, had commenced a quarter of a century earlier, then stagnated. Large contingents of troops from the Arab provinces, above all Egypt, had participated in the seemingly endless struggle to win the island. On receiving word of Köprülü Fazıl Ahmed Pasha's victory, Cairo and other provincial capitals were illuminated for seven nights.

With the Köprülüs, the seventeenth-century crisis recedes, not simply because of the family's administrative and military skills but also because Ottoman dynastic politics had stabilized during the long reign of Mehmed IV, while the Ottoman economy had begun to recover. This did not, however, mean an end to political upheaval, as two major military rebellions in the capital in 1703 and 1730 would demonstrate. Nor could the upturn in the empire's military fortunes be taken for granted. In July 1683, the grand vizier Merzifonlu Kara Mustafa Pasha, a son-in-law of Fazıl Ahmed, besieged the Habsburg capital of Vienna, encouraged by recent Ottoman victories in Hungary and Poland and urged on by a zealous spiritual advisor. The disastrous results are well-known: after coming perilously close to capitulating, the city was saved in September by Polish relief forces, before whom the Ottoman army fled in utter disarray. Late summer rains and mud turned the retreat into a rout, allowing the reinvigorated Habsburg armies to retake virtually all of Hungary. Hostilities dragged on fitfully until 1699, when the humiliating Treaty of Karlowitz obliged the Ottomans to recognize the Habsburgs as an equal power for the first time. Kara Mustafa Pasha himself had been deposed and executed at the end of 1683.

Despite Kara Mustafa's debacle, the Köprülü family continued to supply the Ottoman Empire with grand viziers well into the eighteenth century. The family name retained its cachet well into the twentieth century, when the Turkish historian and parliamentarian Mehmed

Fuad Köprülü (1890–1966) claimed descent from the fabled grand viziers.

Vizier and pasha households such as that of the Köprülüs did not, in any event, simply compete with provincial households in a centre–periphery struggle. The Köprülü household was not fundamentally different in character from that of Abaza Mehmed Pasha or any of the other provincial governors. Nor was it fundamentally different from the local notable households that began to dominate at the provincial level in the eighteenth century, as will be detailed in the following chapter. A degree of continuity can be demonstrated between the vizier and pasha households, on the one hand, and those of the local notables, on the other. The link consists in part in the clients injected into provincial political culture by provincial governors or by far-reaching grand viziers such as the Köprülüs. In addition, local notables, from *sanjak beyi*s to regimental officers to prominent Muslim scholar-officials, cultivated ties with governors and other members of the Ottoman administration, and used the administrators' households as models for households of their own. Keeping this continuity in mind, the following chapter addresses the changes in the eighteenth century which allowed the households of local notables to assume a leading role in the Arab provinces.

Notes

1. Jean Deny, 'Chansons des Janissaires turcs d'Alger', in *Mélanges René Basset*, 2 vols (Paris, 1925), II, p. 82; quoted in translation in André Raymond, 'Soldiers in Trade: The Case of Ottoman Cairo', *British Society for Middle Eastern Studies Bulletin* 18 (1991), p. 16.
2. Mustafa Ali, *The Matchless Tarji' Band entitled Summary of Circumstances involving the Pleasantness of Truthful Sermons*, trans. in Andreas Tietze, 'The Poet as Critic of Society: A Sixteenth-Century Ottoman Poem', *Turcica* 9 (1977), pp. 120–60.
3. Ahmed Chelebi ibn Abd al-Ghani, *Awḍaḥ al-ishārāt fī man tawalla Miṣr al-Qāhira min al-wuzarā' wa'l-bāshāt* (*The Clearest Signs: The Viziers and Pashas Who Governed Cairo*), ed. A.A. Abd al-Rahim (Cairo, 1978), p. 131 (my translation).
4. Mustafa ibn Ibrahim al-Maddah al-Qinali, *Majmū' laṭīf* (*Pleasant Compendium*), quoted in P.M. Holt, 'Al-Jabarti's Introduction to the History of Ottoman Egypt', *Bulletin of the School of Oriental and African Studies* 25 (1962), pp. 42–3.
5. Mehmed ibn Yusuf al-Hallaq, *Tārīḫ-i Miṣr-ı Ḳāhire* (*History of Cairo*), Istanbul University Library, T.Y. 628, ff. 169v, 173v (my translation).
6. Hajji Ali, *Aḫbār ül-yamānī* (*Yemeni Events*), Süleymaniye Library (Istanbul), MS Hamidiye 886, f. 219r (my translation).
7. Silahdar Fındıklılı Mehmed Agha, *Silahdar Tarihi* (*Silahdar's History*), 2 vols (Istanbul, 1928), I, p. 154 (my translation).

chapter five

PROVINCIAL NOTABLES IN THE EIGHTEENTH CENTURY

Ayan

The eighteenth century is sometimes called the age of *ayan*, which is an Arabic word often used for provincial political elites. Literally, the word is a seldom used plural for the Arabic word for 'eye'; metaphorically, it has the sense of prominent or visible persons. These were not the Ottoman governor and his administration but entrenched provincial administrators, such as *sanjak beyi*s and Janissary commanders, who by the eighteenth century had established power bases in the Arab provinces. They were able to do so because, by the eighteenth century, the Ottoman Empire had entered a new phase of decentralization. In the seventeenth century, provincial governors such as Abaza Mehmed Pasha, many recruited by and trained in Topkapı Palace, had emerged as alternative power centres to the imperial government in Istanbul. In the eighteenth century, however, the loci of power shifted to notables, or grandees, who forged their careers entirely in the provinces and who, unlike most vizier and pasha household heads, amassed economic and military resources completely independent of the imperial centre.

Another term for *ayan* is 'local notables', the phrase introduced by the late historian Albert Hourani in a seminal paper first published in 1966. Hourani, however, portrayed the *ayan* as one of three key groups of potential notables, along with the ulema and the commanders of local garrison troops. (In this book, to avoid confusion, *ayan* and 'local notables' will be used more or less interchangeably and will encompass all three groups.) He defined notables as those 'natural leaders' of Arab provincial society who could serve as intermediaries between the Ottoman administration and the populace at large. While acknowledging the interdependence of the *ayan* and the Ottoman provincial government, he tended to stress the *ayan*'s isolation from the central government, as if the government could not have played any role in their formation. As to the *ayan*'s entrenchment in the provinces, Hourani at least implicitly stressed their Arabization rather than a more complex process of localization, described in more detail below. This enables some readers of Hourani to portray Ottoman Arab society as essentially tripartite: the Ottoman administration comprised one group, consisting of the governor, appointed from Istanbul, and his entourage; any troops who might have accompanied him from Istanbul; and his bureaucracy, which might well include local personnel but which was essentially there to carry out his orders. To this group also belonged the chief judge of the province and other top religious officials appointed from Istanbul. This administration was essentially 'Turkish' and therefore alien, foreign, occupying and imperialist, with all the accompanying negative connotations. A far larger group consisted of the 'native' population, meaning the 'ordinary people', comprising artisans and merchants in the cities and peasants and tribespeople in the countryside. These were essentially 'Arabs', the natives who had populated Egypt, Syria or Iraq for centuries and seen foreign occupying regime after foreign occupying regime come and go. In a separate category stood the notables, who were either Arabic-speaking natives or Arabized residents of long standing but who acted as intermediaries between 'the people' and 'the Ottomans'. It was at least theoretically possible for a peasant or a townsman to ascend to notable status, but the 'Turkish' administration was fundamentally separate from the other two categories.

This scheme, however, is far too neat and, moreover, anachronistically assumes that the tensions among emerging national groups which characterize late Ottoman history were already present during the eighteenth century. In reality, the Ottoman administrative stratum did not remain completely separate from the 'natives'. Personnel dispatched to the provinces from Istanbul became localized to different degrees. An aide to the Ottoman governor, for example, might stay behind when the governor went back to Istanbul or was rotated to some other province. He might establish a household of his own, with local clients, right there in the province. He might learn the local language; indeed, this was more likely in the Arab provinces than in the Balkans, as Ottoman officials usually knew some Arabic to begin with since it was part of their religious educations.

Ottoman soldiers were even more likely to strike roots in the province. As noted in the previous chapter, the Ottoman armies were not professional armies in the modern sense. While they resided in barracks, they did not engage in regular training drills throughout the year. With the wave of inflation that began in the late sixteenth century, furthermore, they increasingly sought new sources of income to supplement their fixed stipends. Thus, most Janissaries in the Arab provincial capitals, as in Istanbul, engaged in trade of some description. A lower-ranking soldier might open a shop in the bazaar; he might even purchase a small house near the bazaar. Indeed, a neighbourhood of Turkish-speaking Janissary artisans grew up near the Khan al-Khalili bazaar in seventeenth-century Cairo. High-ranking Janissary officers were more likely to participate in long-distance trade or to farm the customs of port cities. Localization, then, was not necessarily equivalent to Arabization, although it could, and often did, include adoption of the language and many of the province's entrenched customs, particularly among members of the military-administrative class born and bred in the Arab provinces. In general, however, localization was a multifaceted, as well as multilingual and multicultural, process which did not follow a set trajectory.

For their part, 'civilian' notables native to an Arab province, such as ulema and local bureaucrats, frequently cultivated ties to the Ottoman governor or members of his entourage; some even enjoyed connections to the imperial government in Istanbul. What linked members of the government to *ayan* or potential *ayan* were patron–client ties, which likewise bound the *ayan* to certain groups and individuals among the general population. These ties shaped the framework within which provincial *ayan* functioned. More specifically, the *ayan* operated within networks of patron–client ties which coalesced in patron-led households. A member of the *ayan* almost invariably headed such a household. However, he might also have started his career in the household of one of an older generation of *ayan* or in the household of a member of the government.

The *ayan* household

We may, in fact, regard the *ayan* household as a descendant of the 'vizier and pasha' household of the seventeenth century with deeper roots, including an independent source of wealth, in the province and a larger provincial component to its membership. Like the vizier and pasha household, the *ayan* household was not, strictly speaking, a kin-based household, although members of the founder's family almost always belonged to it, but a collection of patron–client ties radiating out from the patron who founded the household. This patron was often a member of the provincial military/administrative elite, such as a Janissary officer or the governor of a district or subprovince, although he might also be a long-distance merchant or a high-ranking member of the ulema. He secured a source of wealth, typically some form of trade or the right to collect taxes or customs duties; collected clients, or followers, a number of whom might form his private army; and gathered them in a central location, which served as the household's headquarters. This was often a large house, resembling a mansion or even a fortress, but, particularly in the case of smaller households founded by military officers, it might also be a military barracks.

A key eighteenth-century development which enabled *ayan* households to accumulate amounts of capital far beyond the capabilities of the earlier vizier and pasha households was the life-tenure tax farm, or *malikane*. Conceived in 1695 as a means of reforming the imperial treasury, the *malikane* system allowed wealthy administrators to bid on packages of urban and rural taxes throughout the Ottoman provinces. The purchaser submitted a bid based on the revenue he expected to collect within a fiscal year; any amount that he collected in excess of this purchase price he kept as profit. Even major provincial governor-ships were for sale as conglomerations of key tax-collection rights. Initially, *malikane* holdings were dominated by the administrative elite of Istanbul, who sent their agents to collect taxes and deal with the day-to-day business of provincial governance. Soon, however, provincial grandees joined the bidding game. Although they were obliged to retain agents in Istanbul to improve their chances of winning tax farms, they were able to hold the farms they did win for life and even to treat them as heritable property. While they dramatically augmented the *ayan*'s wealth and influence, then, the *malikane*s also bound them to Istanbul and the imperial government. *Malikane*s were essential to the rise of *ayan* households in Syria and Iraq. In Egypt, although the term *malikane* appears not to have been in general use, the 'traditional' tax farm, known as *iltizam*, came to be treated in practice as property held for life.

In the following sections, we shall focus on five Arab provinces in which specific *ayan* households or groups of *ayan* played decisive roles during the eighteenth century. Egypt's Kazdağlı household was founded by an Anatolian Janissary officer in Cairo; in contrast, the Azms of Damascus were an old Arab provincial family who entered Ottoman service. In Aleppo, as in Cairo, localized Janissaries wielded preponderant influence in the early eighteenth century; in later years, however, they were challenged by a population of purported descendants of the Prophet Muhammad, led by the Tahazade family. Meanwhile, Mosul's Jalili family came from a background not unlike that of the Azms. Finally, the regime that dominated Baghdad throughout the eighteenth century originated in the Georgian mamluks of the Ottoman governors of that province.

The Kazdağlıs of Egypt

Mustafa al-Kazdağlı, the founder of the Kazdağlı household, apparently came to Egypt in the early decades of the seventeenth century from western Anatolia: specifically, the region of the Kazdağı, known in the West as Mount Ida, the mountain from which, in Greek mythology, the gods watched the Trojan War. He must have been either a Greek Orthodox Christian living along the coast of the Gulf of Edremit, then as now prime olive-growing territory, or one of the Shiite-leaning Turkish nomads who migrated into the region in the fifteenth century and encamped in the Kazdağı range. Many Anatolian soldiers came to Egypt during the seventeenth century, some of them trying to flee the economic and demographic crises of the time, others perhaps recruited for the naval effort against Crete. Mustafa first appears in Ottoman archival documents as a lower-ranking officer in Egypt's Janissary regiment during the 1640s. At some point, he joined the household of the commander (*agha*) of one of Egypt's cavalry regiments, a leading figure in the Faqari faction who may even have brought Mustafa to Egypt in the first place. (As noted in Chapter 4, the rivalry of the Faqari and Qasimi factions permeated Egyptian society during the seventeenth century.) By the 1670s, and perhaps much earlier, Mustafa had attained the rank of Janissary second-in-command (*kethüda* or *kâhya*). He attracted followers, many of them fellow Anatolians, from among the lower-ranking officers and enlisted men who served under him, and probably formed a rudimentary household of his own in the Janissary barracks in Cairo's citadel. At the same time, he would already have had a house or houses outside the citadel, perhaps in the Turkish-speaking neighbourhood near the Khan al-Khalili market. Before his death in 1704, moreover, he had begun to acquire mamluks from the Caucasus, whom he injected into the Janissary corps and promoted through the officer ranks. Under the mamluk who succeeded him as household head, the Kazdağlıs came to dominate the Janissary officer stratum, surviving challenges not only from other households led by Janissary commanders but from lower-ranking officers who resented the disproportionate wealth and influence of this top echelon.

At first, the Kazdağlıs were one of numerous households under the umbrella of the Faqari faction; as such, they supported the Faqaris in their conflicts with the enemy Qasimi faction and played a part in a Faqari rout of the Qasimis in 1730. In the wake of this resounding Faqari victory, however, the Kazdağlıs turned their attention to overcoming rival households within the Faqari faction. Ultimately, the household transcended the faction which had spawned it. By the 1740s, the culture of bilateral factionalism had grown obsolete in Egypt as the Kazdağlıs increasingly dominated the province.

Until the mid-eighteenth century, the leader of the Kazdağlı household always held the rank of Janissary *kethüda*. By the 1720s, however, the Kazdağlı headquarters was no longer the Janissary barracks, or even a small house near the Khan al-Khalili, but a huge mansion in what was at the time Cairo's premier elite neighbourhood. Meanwhile, the household's leaders were purchasing more and more mamluks from the Caucasus, and above all Georgia. For the *ayan* of the Arab provinces, as for the Jelali governors of the preceding century, the Caucasus was the logical source of elite slaves since they did not have access to *devshirme* recruits. By the eighteenth century, in any case, the *devshirme* had been abandoned, and mamluks, along with Albanian mercenaries, were playing an increasingly prominent role throughout the Ottoman Empire.

Coffee was the initial source of the Kazdağlı household's wealth. The plant, native to Ethiopia, had been introduced into Yemen in the fifteenth century while the beans had begun to be shipped through the Red Sea during the following century, largely in merchant vessels from the western coast of India. Jidda, the port serving Mecca, was a key port of call for these ships; consequently, the annual pilgrimage to Mecca became a prime opportunity for coffee-trading. From Egypt, Yemeni coffee was transshipped to Syria and Istanbul. In short order, European merchants began purchasing the beans in Egypt, then transporting them to their home countries. The coffee trade helped to compensate for the damage to the transit trade, via the Red Sea and the Mediterranean, in Indian and Indonesian spices which resulted from the Portuguese discovery at the end of the fifteenth century of the route to the Indian Ocean around the Cape of Good Hope.

Officers of Egypt's Janissary regiment were prime beneficiaries of the coffee trade, for they held the tax farms of the customs at the Red Sea port of Suez and at the Mediterranean ports of Alexandria, Rosetta and Damietta, and provided security for the massive pilgrimage caravan which departed Cairo for Mecca each year. While the Kazdağlıs faced competition from other Janissary households for control of Egypt's customs, they had succeeded by the mid-1720s in monopolizing the positions attached to the pilgrimage caravan. Meanwhile, they cultivated ties to merchants in Jidda, Mecca and Medina, as well as Cairo's increasingly influential overseas merchants, all the while maintaining links to key personnel in Istanbul. By 1748, they had all but displaced rival households, not only within the Janissary corps but throughout Egypt, and achieved a position of unchallenged political and economic authority.

Around 1730, however, the French began importing coffee into the Mediterranean from their Caribbean colonies. The cheaper French beans eroded sales of Yemeni coffee as Yemeni-French Caribbean blends became the beverages of choice for the middle classes. French merchants even began to sell their coffee in Egypt itself. These new circumstances posed an obvious threat to the source of the Kazdağlıs' wealth. Therefore, the household changed with the times. Leadership of the household by 1754 had shifted from Janissary officers to *sanjak beyi*s, including Egypt's chief financial officer, or *defterdar*, and the governors of Egypt's major subprovinces, who controlled the lucrative tax farms of much of the Egyptian countryside, including those of villages whose revenues were endowed to the Holy Cities of Mecca and Medina. These villages supplied the Holy Cities with grain, which was transported by the annual pilgrimage caravan. The two most influential offices held by *sanjak beyi*s were those of pilgrimage commander and a new position, *shaykh al-balad*, equivalent to governor of Cairo. By monopolizing these positions, the Kazdağlıs were able to extend their control over the pilgrimage, over Cairo and over Egypt's economy at large. Moreover, they retained their dominant position in the Janissary corps, although Janissary officers now held a subordinate position in the household to beys.

One of the first generation of Kazdağlı leaders to hold the rank of *sanjak beyi* was the famous Ali Bey al-Kabir, who in 1770 allegedly rebelled against the Ottoman sultan. A great deal has been written about Ali Bey, and just who he was and what he hoped to achieve have been debated, sometimes hotly. He was, in fact, the Georgian mamluk of the Janissary officer Ibrahim Kethüda al-Kazdağlı, the first head of the Kazdağlı household to promote his clients to bey. Named *shaykh al-balad* in 1760, Ali Bey began systematically to eliminate his rivals, who were for the most part other members of the greater Kazdağlı household, while filling key posts with his own protégés. In 1768 and 1769, he deposed two Ottoman governors in a row, after which he allowed his name to be recited during the Friday midday sermon immediately after that of the sultan and in lieu of that of the governor.

Some historians have insisted that Ali Bey intended to remove Egypt from Ottoman sovereignty and interpret his actions as a foretaste of Egyptian nationalism. Others have claimed that he sought to restore the Mamluk sultanate, although his knowledge of that long-defunct polity would probably have been based largely on popular tales of the early Mamluk sultans rather than on detailed knowledge of Mamluk administration. An alternative explanation is that Ali Bey sought, above all, the governorship of Egypt; hence his deposition of two governors and insertion of his own name, rather than that of the governor, in the Friday sermon. It seems possible, too, that his rebellion was, at least in part, motivated by his inability to win appointment as governor in an era when Georgian mamluks of provincial grandees had risen to the governorships in Damascus and Baghdad. In Cairo, by contrast, the governor remained a palace official dispatched from Istanbul.

In any case, Ali Bey was hardly the first Egyptian grandee to pursue an autonomous course; even his patron, Ibrahim Kethüda, had disobeyed sultanic orders. He differed from most of his predecessors, however, in extending his ambitions beyond Egypt's borders, allying with Shaykh Zahir al-Umar, the chief of a clan of Arab tax-farmers, the Zayadina, in northern Palestine. Since the early part of the century, Zahir al-Umar had been steadily expanding his territory; in the process, he had resurrected the old Crusader capital of Acre, turning it into a thriving port from which cotton and wheat were shipped to France. Both Zahir al-Umar and Ali Bey harboured grudges against the governor of Damascus, Osman Pasha al-Sadiq, an emancipated Georgian mamluk of the Azm family (on whom see below). While earlier governors, including several from among the Azms, had tolerated Zahir's expansionism, Osman Pasha attempted to thwart it. Ali Bey, for his part, had had a hostile encounter with Osman Pasha at Mecca, where each man was leading his province's pilgrim caravan, years before. He therefore joined forces with Zahir al-Umar to overthrow Osman Pasha and take control of Damascus.

Far more alarming to the imperial authorities, however, was the possibility of an alliance between Ali Bey and Catherine the Great's Russia, with which the Ottomans were then at war. A Russian fleet under Catherine's sometime lover Count Grigorii Orlov had destroyed the Ottoman navy at Cheshme, west of Izmir on the Aegean Sea, in July 1770. In the months preceding this victory, Orlov had cruised the eastern Mediterranean in the hope of inciting Ottoman provinces bordering the sea to rebel; in the case of Crete and the Morea, or southern mainland Greece, he succeeded, although the risings were swiftly quashed. Catherine herself was certainly aware of Ali Bey's venture, which also captured the imagination of her frequent correspondent, the French Enlightenment philosopher Voltaire. To a January 1771 letter in which Voltaire predicted that Catherine would divide the Ottoman Empire with the ambitious bey, the empress teasingly replied, 'If I go to Istanbul, I will ask [Ali Bey] to come there so that you can see him with your own eyes. And as I have no doubt that you will not favour me by accepting the post of patriarch, you will have the consolation of administering the sacrament of baptism to Ali Bey, by immersion or otherwise.'[1]

As enticing as such scenarios may have been to Catherine, there is no evidence of direct Russian aid to Ali Bey until it was, to be blunt, too late. The conquest of Damascus fell to Ali Bey's Georgian mamluk Mehmed Bey Abu al-Dhahab, who had earned his sobriquet, which translates to 'Father of Gold', when his patron promoted him to the rank of *sanjak beyi* in 1764 and he dispensed gold, rather than the customary silver, coins to the crowds during the ensuing celebration. In April 1771, Abu al-Dhahab led an army into Syria and occupied Damascus, but then seems to have had a change of heart. For reasons that are still unclear, he swore allegiance to the Ottoman sultan and turned back towards Egypt, where, in early 1772, he attacked his patron militarily. Only in June 1772, two months after Ali Bey had fled to Zahir al-Umar in Palestine, did the Russian navy bombard Beirut in support of the two grandees' expansionist designs. The following year, however, Ali Bey was tricked into returning to Egypt by Abu al-Dhahab, who again attacked him, this time mortally wounding him. As for Zahir al-Umar, he died in 1775 while fleeing Acre, which was under siege from the sea by an Ottoman naval force and from land by the army of the new governor of Damascus.

In broad terms, both Ali Bey and Zahir al-Umar bear a certain resemblance to the Jelali governors of the seventeenth century. (In fact, an aide to one of the governors whom Ali Bey deposed, in a history he composed years later, describes Ali Bey as an Abkhazian supremacist, perhaps harking back to the rebellious Abkhazian governors of the previous century, discussed in Chapter 4.) The difference is mainly one of scale: each eighteenth-century grandee commanded a much larger household, possessed of much greater and more sustainable material resources, than any of the Jelali governors had done; moreover, neither Ali Bey nor Zahir al-Umar had been trained in the imperial palace or relied on palace troops, even as the starting point for a household army. Their households were much closer to being on an equal footing with the imperial household, even if they did not seek to supplant the imperial household.

Despite Ali Bey's defeat, members of the greater Kazdağlı household were able to retain de facto control of Egypt until 1798, when the French under Napoleon Bonaparte invaded and put Ibrahim and Murad, the two beys then administering the province – both mamluks of Mehmed Bey Abu al-Dhahab – to flight. Even so, the household's power was not entirely broken until the massacre of most of its last surviving remnants by the autonomous governor Mehmed Ali Pasha in 1811.

The Azms of Damascus

By the time the Kazdağlıs were coming to prominence in Egypt, the Azm family had already begun to dominate Syria. Unlike the Kazdağlıs, the Azms did not originate with a Janissary or other military officer, or an administrator transplanted from Istanbul or elsewhere in Anatolia. Rather, they were a venerable Sunni Arab family with deep roots in Syria. Although the family is thought to have originated in the vicinity of the western city of Hama under the Mamluk sultanate, branches soon emerged in nearly all the major Syrian provincial capitals, including Damascus. Azms were apparently serving as administrators for the Mamluks in Damascus when Sultan Selim I conquered the city in 1516. One of the Azms entered Ottoman military service in the seventeenth century and was awarded a *timar* – that is, a grant of revenue from a plot of land from which he was expected to raise a troop of cavalry. Later generations rose through the provincial chain of military-administrative command until, by the eighteenth century, members of the Azm family were appointed governor of Damascus itself, as well as various surrounding provinces and districts, including Aleppo in northern Syria and Tripoli in northern Lebanon. Ostensibly, they governed at the pleasure of the Ottoman central authority; each term as governor in each locale had to be negotiated separately with Istanbul, and in theory the Azm governors, like other Ottoman provincial governors, could be transferred to any province in the empire. Nonetheless, from the 1720s until the early nineteenth century, the Azms retained a remarkable lock on the Syrian governorships, largely through the astute purchase, as *malikane*, of the rights to major sources of urban and rural revenue. Although one family member served as governor of Egypt from 1738–40, posting outside Syria was a distinct aberration. The main Azm sphere of operations was Damascus. There, they built several mansions, today usually referred to as palaces, as well as commercial and religious establishments, and gathered a variety of clients: Janissary commanders, merchants, ulema, and Bedouin and Turcoman tribal shaykhs. They did not rely on Damascus' Janissaries for military might, however, but amassed private armies, in parallel with the Jelali governors of the preceding century.

Like the Kazdağlıs, the Azms recognized the opportunities afforded by the annual pilgrimage to Mecca, which became their chief source of wealth and influence. Under the Ottomans, two major pilgrimage caravans were outfitted every year: one from Cairo, led by the bey who held the office of pilgrimage commander (after 1750 almost always a Kazdağlı); and one from Damascus, led, beginning in 1708, by the provincial governor. (In this fashion, Osman Pasha al-Sadiq, as governor of Damascus, and Ali Bey, as Egypt's pilgrimage commander, met in Mecca, as described above.) By monopolizing the governorship of Damascus, then, the Azms monopolized the pilgrimage command, which gave them access to an immense array of commerce and contacts with merchants, ulema and other military commanders. Since the pilgrimage took several months to complete, the governor of Damascus spent much of the year either on the road or preparing to depart. While away, he was obliged to leave his deputy in charge of day-to-day business in Damascus. This meant that the deputy had to be a reliable member of the governor's household, often a mamluk from the Caucasus. Occasionally, these deputies proved trustworthy enough to serve as governors in their own right, as in the case of Osman Pasha.

Azm control of Damascus was challenged only twice between 1720 and 1800, both times, intriguingly enough, at the instigation of the Chief Eunuch of the Ottoman imperial harem. As superintendent of the imperial pious endowments to the Holy Cities of Mecca and Medina (discussed below), the Chief Eunuch was vitally concerned with the conduct of the major pilgrimage caravans from Cairo and Damascus. Since the governor of Damascus, as of 1708, led the pilgrimage in person, his office was a source of particular interest to the Eunuch, who occasionally promoted his own clients for the post. In the late 1730s, the extraordinarily long-serving and influential Chief Eunuch el-Hajj Beshir Agha (term 1717–46) began to patronize an opponent of the Azms: the Damascene notable Fethi Efendi, grandson of a weaver from western Syria, who in 1736 succeeded his father as chief financial administrator, or *defterdar*, of the province of Damascus (for this reason, he is commonly known as Fethi the *defterdar*). When the governor Süleyman Pasha al-Azm died in 1743, Fethi, in his capacity as *defterdar*, zealously confiscated his estate, alienating the rest of the Azm family and their supporters. Süleyman was succeeded by his nephew Esad, whom Fethi attempted to undermine so as to win the governorship for himself. His efforts were cut short in 1746, however, by the superannuated Beshir Agha's death, after which Esad Pasha al-Azm exploited his own connections in Istanbul to secure Fethi's execution for corrupt practices.

Roughly a decade later, the Chief Harem Eunuch Abu al-Wuquf Ahmed Agha (term 1755–8) succeeded in having his protégé Hüseyin ibn al-Makki ('son of the Meccan', also rendered by the Persianate Mekkizade) appointed governor of Damascus, replacing Esad Pasha al-Azm. Ibn al-Makki, a native of Gaza, was not as solidly entrenched in the province as the Azms and consequently did not enjoy the ties to the Bedouin tribes along the pilgrimage route that the Azms had forged. By the time he set out on the pilgrimage in 1757, moreover, the region had suffered from two years of drought. Perhaps as a partial result, the pilgrimage caravan which he led was brutally attacked by a massive Bedouin force on its return to Damascus. As the Damascene chronicler Ahmad al-Budayri tells it, in rather tabloid-esque fashion, the Bedouin stripped men and women alike of their money and clothing, 'put their hands on the men's testicles and the women's pudenda', then abandoned them, naked, in the desert, so that many 'died of hunger, thirst, cold, and heat, even after drinking one another's urine'.[2] Some 20,000 pilgrims died. Ibn al-Makki himself escaped and made his way back to Damascus but was rusticated to Gaza the following year (in later years, he was appointed to less prestigious provincial governorships). His patron Abu al-Wuquf Ahmed Agha, meanwhile, was executed on the orders of the grand vizier, as was Esad Pasha al-Azm, whom the grand vizier suspected of inciting the Bedouin attack. The administration of Damascus reverted to the Azms in 1760, when Osman Pasha al-Sadiq, the Georgian former mamluk of Esad Pasha al-Azm, was appointed to the governorship.

Whereas the Kazdağlıs were displaced by the French invasion and the autonomous regime founded by Mehmed Ali Pasha, so that they did not really leave a mark on the modern history of Egypt, the Azms continued to be an influential Syrian family well into the twentieth century. From their ranks came several prominent Syrian nationalists who steered the nation's course following the break-up of the Ottoman Empire after World War I. One, Khalid al-Azm, was known as the Red Millionaire for his flirtation with socialism; he served in several Syrian cabinets until one of Syria's many post-World War II military coups led him to seek asylum in, rather ironically, the Turkish embassy in Damascus. On the other hand, the latter-day Azms did have a genuine Turkish connection, for one branch of the family had migrated to Anatolia after World War I and essentially become Turkish, even changing their name. Ultimately, the Syrian Azms ran foul of the Baathist regime of Hafez al-Asad (1930–2000), which, after coming to power in the early 1960s, confiscated the Azm palaces and turned them into museums. Until the late 1990s, several prominent Azms lived in exile outside Syria.

Janissaries vs. *ashraf* in Aleppo

As the Kazdağlıs' experience indicates, the story of *ayan* ascendancy in the eighteenth century was not entirely one of local families overcoming or outflanking provincial Janissary regiments. In Aleppo, as in Cairo, the Janissary corps remained a locus of provincial influence during the eighteenth century, although Aleppo's Janissaries were never displaced by another class of provincial officials but, on the contrary, had consolidated their hold on Aleppo's major sources of wealth and channels of political power by the end of the century. This is somewhat surprising given the fact that Aleppo, unlike Damascus, Cairo or Baghdad, was not garrisoned with Janissaries following its conquest by the

Ottomans. The city acquired a Janissary population towards the end of the sixteenth century, when, as noted in the preceding chapter, imperial Janissaries stationed in Damascus extended their sway over Aleppo. In 1602, however, the governor of Aleppo joined forces with the Kurdish chieftain Hüseyin Pasha Janbulad to defeat these Janissaries and subsequently organized a new Janissary corps composed entirely of local and regional elements. These 'localized' Janissaries were known in Ottoman Turkish as *yerliyye*s ('locals') to distinguish them from new Janissary contingents dispatched directly from Istanbul, who were called *kapı kulları*, literally 'servants of the gate', referring to the imposing gate separating the first court of Topkapı Palace from the second court (today the main entrance to the palace museum).

In Damascus itself, these two categories of Janissaries clashed periodically in violent confrontations. Meanwhile, opponents of the Azm governors occasionally attempted to join forces with the *yerliyye* troops, against whom the Azms employed not the *kapı kulları* but their own private troops. The *kapı kulları* were more of a nuisance than anything else, rebelling against their commanding officers and imposing their will on Damascus' artisans. In 1740, one of the rare non-Azm governors of Damascus joined with the city's ulema to request that Sultan Mahmud I take punitive action against the *kapı kulları*; as a result, those *kapı kulları* who were not expelled from the city or hunted down and killed gave up their military status and became ordinary tax-paying reaya.

Aleppo, in contrast, never had to accommodate fresh contingents of *kapı kulları* troops during the eighteenth century. In consequence, the city's Janissaries remained a relatively homogeneous body who served as citadel guards. (In Damascus, the *yerliyye* protected the pilgrimage route while the *kapı kulları* guarded the citadel.) As in Cairo, influential Janissary officers moved out of the barracks in the citadel and took up residence in fortress-like mansions in various urban locations. Like the Kazdağlıs in Cairo, they drew their wealth from monopolizing the farms of Aleppo's customs, a highly lucrative source of revenue given the city's status as a regional commercial hub. As early as the seventeenth century, moreover, they had begun to acquire the tax farms of villages in Aleppo's rural hinterland, combining urban and rural revenues without giving up Janissary status in the manner of the beys who dominated the Kazdağlı household after 1754.

During the latter decades of the eighteenth century, a faction of self-styled descendants of the Prophet Muhammad emerged to challenge the Janissaries in Aleppo. One scholar has described these *ashraf* (the plural of the Arabic *sharif*) as the closest thing Islamic society had to a nobility; their Prophetic lineage absolved them of tax responsibilities and commanded the esteem of their fellow Aleppines. Although *ashraf* were a social force in all major Ottoman provincial cities, only in Aleppo and the south-eastern Anatolian cities of Ayntab (today Gaziantep) and Marash (today Kahramanmaras) did they form powerful factions that contended for political and economic dominance. The lack of *kapı kulları* troops in these cities may have been a factor in the *ashraf*'s prominence, but regional mores may also have played a role.

By the eighteenth century, to be sure, not all those who claimed *ashraf* status in a given Arab or Anatolian provincial capital were genuine descendants of Muhammad. The head, or *naqib*, of the local *ashraf*, who was appointed by the imperial *naqib* in Istanbul, ostensibly scrutinized the genealogies of prospective *ashraf* and weeded out those he deemed spurious, but by the eighteenth century he was clearly allowing non-*ashraf* with falsified genealogies to purchase places on the *ashraf* lineage rolls, which were kept by Aleppo's chief judge. By this time, too, provincial *naqib*s were chosen from among the local population rather than from the *ashraf* of the imperial capital; this development may have facilitated the purchase of positions since local *ashraf* might have had prior connections to those seeking spots on the rolls. The process resembled nothing so much as the widespread purchase of places in the provincial Janissary regiments. In fact, the similarity is more than coincidental, for by the eighteenth century the *ashraf*, like many other social groupings, had become militarized to the extent that they were armed and could serve as an informal local militia. Like the Janissaries, they amassed clients and established influential households.

Leadership of Aleppo's *ashraf* rested with the Tahazades, an entrenched Hanafi ulema family who had dominated the influential post of *naqib* since the late seventeenth century. The Tahazades enjoyed ties to the imperial court in Istanbul and to military-administrative grandees in Aleppo; in addition to serving variously as *naqib* and judge, family members invested heavily in textile and food production while amassing urban commercial and rural real estate. A sign of the family's efflorescence was the modification of the family name sometime in the seventeenth century from Tahaoğlu to Tahazade: while both names mean 'son of Taha', referring to the family's eponymous founder, the Persian –*zade* suffix was considered to have more panache than the Turkish –*oğlu*. Ahmed Efendi Tahazade, who served as *naqib al-ashraf* during the late 1730s and early 1740s, was prosperous enough to found his own *madrasa*, or Islamic theological college, the Ahmadiyya, in 1752 in Aleppo's central commercial district. Intriguingly, the *madrasa*'s foundation deed stipulates that it should serve first and foremost the Kurds of the region of Mosul, a condition which could indicate a Kurdish strain within the Tahazade family itself or, on the other hand, personal affinity for Kurds on the part of Ahmed Efendi, who had noted the poverty of northern Iraq's Kurdish population during his tenure as *qadi* of Baghdad in 1750–1. The *madrasa*'s distinctive mission might also reflect a rivalry with the Jalilis of Mosul (on whom see below), who sought to promote the Shafii legal rite, to which most Kurds belonged, in the region.

Ahmed Efendi Tahazade's son Mehmed, popularly known by the Turkish honorific Chelebi Efendi, served as *naqib al-ashraf* for roughly twenty-five years all told (*c*.1747–67 and 1782–86), becoming 'master of Aleppo', in the words of a French consul,[3] and forging Aleppo's *ashraf* into a coherent political faction which fought the Janissaries in pitched battles. On his death in 1786, he was succeeded as faction leader, although not as *naqib*, by his former servant Ibrahim Qataraǧası, who had previously commanded Aleppo's pilgrimage caravan (*qatar*), which linked up with the mammoth Damascus caravan each year (hence his sobriquet, which signifies *agha*, or commander, of the *qatar*). When Bonaparte invaded Syria, Ibrahim led Aleppo's *ashraf* in the defence against the French; the city's Janissaries fought as a separate contingent. In 1802, following this successful effort, he was appointed governor of Aleppo; two years later, he assumed the governorship of Damascus, leaving his son in charge of Aleppo. The Qataraǧasıs now seemed on the verge of establishing an Azm-like dynasty which would dominate Syria, in the process marking a decisive victory for Aleppo's *ashraf* over the rival Janissaries.

Not long after Ibrahim's installation in Damascus, however, the Janissaries and *ashraf* of Aleppo, along with the city's Christian population, jointly rebelled against the depredations of his son and drove him from the city. He returned two months later as a figurehead. The following year, he combined with the *ashraf* to attack the Janissaries, only to have the Janissaries score a decisive triumph in a week of bloody city-wide fighting. Ibrahim Qataraǧası was reappointed to Aleppo in 1807 but removed by the young sultan Mahmud II the following year, leaving Aleppo's Janissaries triumphant. The Janissaries utterly dominated the city until 1813, when the governor Jelal al-Din Pasha, himself a member of an Anatolian *ayan* family, invited their commanders to a meeting, then massacred them in a move strikingly similar to the destruction by Mehmed Ali Pasha, the autonomous governor of Egypt, of the remaining grandees of the Kazdaǧlı household and its offshoots two years earlier.

Eighteenth-century Aleppo, then, combined powerful localized Janissaries, similar to those of Cairo and Damascus, with ascendant *ashraf*. *Ashraf* arguably made natural *ayan* during the eighteenth century, when local families of alleged Prophetic descendants began to monopolize the post of *naqib*, previously appointed from Istanbul. Yet while the *ashraf* and their *naqib* became quite wealthy and influential in other Arab capitals, notably Cairo and Damascus, Aleppo's powerful, militarized *ashraf* have no real parallel in any other major Arab provincial city. On the other hand, the striking similarity they bear to their counterparts in Ayntab and Marash leads one to suspect that northern Syria and south-eastern Anatolia during the Ottoman period should properly be analysed as a discrete region. What is striking about Aleppo's Janissaries, meanwhile, is that they persisted as a locus of influence, resisting the efforts of both rival *ayan* and governors to dislodge them until their fateful meeting with Jelal al-Din Pasha.

The Jalilis of Mosul

Patterns of *ayan* influence in Ottoman Iraq are distinctive because of the Iraqi provinces' status as border territories with hostile Iran. In close geographical proximity to the frontier between the Ottoman and Safavid domains, the northern city of Mosul was also an ethno-cultural frontier between the Kurds of northern Iraq and south-eastern Anatolia, and the Sunni Arab populations farther south. The city was also home to an ancient Christian population belonging to the Nestorian and Jacobite rites, while both Christians and Yazidi Kurds inhabited its rural hinterland (on these sects, see Chapter 1). Indeed, the Jalili family, which dominated the city for much of the eighteenth century, originated with a Christian merchant from the south-eastern Anatolian city of Diyarbakır who migrated to Mosul in the late seventeenth century. This merchant was known as Abd al-Jalil, Arabic for 'servant of the Exalted' – 'Exalted' being, naturally, an epithet of God – and his descendants took the adjectival form of 'Exalted' as their family name. His seven sons converted to Sunni Islam of the Shafii rite, and two of them contracted to supply grain to Baghdad; several later purchased offices in Mosul's Janissary regiment.

In 1726, Ismail ibn Abd al-Jalil purchased the farms of Mosul's urban taxes and, with them, the governorship of the province on the promise of provisioning the Ottoman armies along their route of march through south-eastern Anatolia and into Iraq. Provisioning was a constant preoccupation in this region and a burden on the populace; as a Mosul proverb puts it, 'The armies take those things that we cannot taste.'[4] Ismail took office just as a massive Ottoman army commanded by the governor of Baghdad was withdrawing into Iraq from western Iran after suffering defeat at the hands of the Afghan tribesmen who had displaced the Safavids in 1722. Following Ismail Pasha's tenure, five successive generations of Jalilis governed Mosul until 1834, when a cross-section of Mosul society, weary of the household's exactions, overthrew the last Jalili governor.

For much of this period, Mosul was a crucial link in the defence of the Ottoman Empire's eastern front against the various rulers of post-Safavid Iran. Afghan tribesmen who were nominal vassals of the Safavids had rebelled and overthrown the dynasty in 1722. Following some fourteen years of military and political turmoil, featuring Ottoman attempts to occupy former Safavid territory in western Iran and Azerbaijan, the pro-Safavid military commander Nadir Shah took Isfahan from the Afghans and claimed to rule Iran as regent for a young Safavid prince; he ultimately declared himself shah in 1739. In an attempt to reclaim all former Safavid territories, Nadir engaged the Ottomans in Azerbaijan and the Caucasus, and attacked Ottoman Iraq repeatedly. Overall, his armies posed a greater threat to Baghdad and Basra than they did to Mosul; nonetheless, he besieged the northern city in 1736, prompting Hüseyin Pasha al-Jalili, the son of Ismail Pasha, to lead a vigorous, and ultimately successful, defence. This victory proved a key source of legitimacy for the Jalilis over the next century.

Like the Azms, then, the Jalilis were an old, established, if somewhat less venerable, family who joined the Ottoman administration and eventually acquired prominent offices, although the Jalilis, unlike the Azms, never succeeded in spreading their authority far beyond their home district. While Hüseyin Pasha al-Jalili was briefly appointed governor of Basra in 1741 on condition he provide grain to Ottoman forces fighting Nadir Shah in southern Iraq, Jalili aspirations of extending their influence southward were for the most part thwarted by the mamluk governors of Baghdad (on whom more below). Even more than the Azms, furthermore, the Jalilis depended on the goodwill of the central government in Istanbul to govern. Despite the family's dominance in the region, no Jalili governor administered Mosul continuously for years on end; instead, each governor's tenure was routinely interrupted by the appointment of alternative candidates. For these reasons their impact on Mosul and vicinity, while considerable, was arguably less profound than that of the Azms on Syria.

Georgian mamluks in Baghdad

Far more so than Mosul's, Baghdad's history, as well as that of Basra to the south, was affected by the actions of the Arab tribes who operated freely in central and southern Iraq, south-western Iran and the northern Arabian peninsula, rarely observing provincial or even imperial borders.

Following the collapse of Basra's local Afrasiyab dynasty in the 1660s, the ancient Muntafiq tribe, which had migrated into southern Iraq from the eastern Arabian peninsula at the time of the original Muslim conquest, occupied the political vacuum in the region; they managed to unite the Arabs of the deserts south-east and south-west of Baghdad, most of whom were Sunni, with the predominantly Shiite Arabs of the marshes south of Basra. In 1694, the Muntafiq seized Basra itself from its Ottoman governor and were evicted only by the Safavid shah, who, not wishing to encumber himself with a continual Muntafiq challenge, returned the territory to the Ottomans. The Muntafiq were, in any event, not vanquished but continued to pose a threat to Ottoman authority in the region. The dynasty of Georgian governors who took over Baghdad in the eighteenth century cemented their reputation with their ability to check the Muntafiq and other tribes in southern Iraq, although, admittedly, this sometimes took the form of placating the tribes in question.

Like Mosul, however, Baghdad was a forward position against the Safavids and their successors as rulers of Iran. Thus, like the Jalilis, the governors of Baghdad were obliged time and time again to prove themselves capable of defending the Ottoman frontier against the Iranians.

The line of governors began with Hasan Pasha. The son of a Georgian official at the court of Sultan Murad IV (r. 1623–40), he held the governorships of Konya (central Anatolia), Aleppo, Urfa (south-eastern Anatolia) and Diyarbakır (north-east of Urfa) before being appointed to Baghdad in 1704 – an indication, incidentally, of just how closely linked Iraq, northern Syria and south-eastern Anatolia were through the Ottoman army's route to the eastern front. Over the next several years, he launched a series of attacks on the Muntafiq which severely diluted their strength in the vicinity of Basra. To secure his victories, he named his lieutenant, or *kethüda*, who also happened to be his son-in-law, governor of Basra on the approval of the Ottoman central authority. This set a precedent: when the son-in-law died in the early 1720s, Hasan Pasha appointed his natural son, Ahmed, who had also served as his father's *kethüda*, to Basra, which remained a dependency of Baghdad until the collapse of the Ottoman Empire after World War I.

During the 1720s, Hasan Pasha's duties shifted from confronting the Muntafiq and other tribes in southern Iraq to contending with the aftermath of the Safavids' collapse. He died in 1724 while on campaign in western Iran, which the Ottomans had hoped to take from the Afghans. His son Ahmed Pasha succeeded him as governor of Baghdad and as commander of one of two enormous Ottoman armies invading Iran, for which troops had been levied from Egypt and other provinces far away from the front. Fighting on the Iranian front dragged on almost continuously for twenty years, with Ahmed Pasha in the forefront. The expansionist Safavid revivalist Nadir Shah proved a more formidable threat than the Afghans. In 1733, he besieged Baghdad itself, which was rescued only by a relieving force from Anatolia led by a former grand vizier. Repeated attempts to negotiate a peace treaty were only sporadically successful, even after Nadir Shah proposed in 1739 that Twelver Shiism be recognized as a fifth Sunni legal rite. Only Nadir's assassination in June 1747 brought an end to the Iranian threat to Ottoman Iraq.

Ahmed Pasha himself died only two months later and, having left no sons, was eventually succeeded as governor of Baghdad by his Georgian mamluk Süleyman, though only after a two-year struggle between the latter and the troops of a new governor appointed from Istanbul. Süleyman had served as *kethüda* to Ahmed Pasha, who married him to his daughter; at the time of Ahmed's death, Süleyman was governing Basra. In this way, he duplicated the career path that Ahmed Pasha himself had followed in the service of his father Hasan Pasha. Moreover, Süleyman was one of a large number of Georgian mamluks whom Hasan and Ahmed Pashas had acquired over the forty-odd years during which they administered central and southern Iraq, taking advantage of the collapse of the Safavid hold over eastern Georgia with the end of the dynasty in 1722. In the same way that the Safavids had used Georgian mamluks (or *ghulam*s, as they were called in Safavid circles) to circumvent the Turcoman tribesmen who had brought them to power, so Hasan Pasha and his son used them as an alternative to the Ottoman garrison troops who had stymied so many provincial governors during the preceding century. Unlike the Kazdağlıs of Egypt, the governors of Baghdad did not employ the infrastructure of the regiments of garrison troops to build their household but sidestepped the regiments altogether, using their mamluks as an entirely separate military force. They also integrated these mamluks fully into their household, employing them as *kethüda*s and marrying them to their daughters.

In addition to military efficacy, the Georgian mamluk regime displayed impressive commercial savvy, forging an alliance with the British East India Company in the late eighteenth century, then thoroughly dominating transshipment of the Indian goods to Aleppo, whence they were distributed to other Ottoman provinces and to Europe. Baghdad's governors even prevented the merchants of Basra from shipping directly to Aleppo without stopping in Baghdad. They also cultivated ties with Mosul's merchants, ultimately undermining the Jalilis' economic hegemony in northern Iraq.

The mamluk regime continued until 1831, though not without conflicts among the households of different mamluk commanders, not unlike those that plagued the Kazdağlıs of Egypt towards the end of the eighteenth century. As under Hasan and Ahmed Pashas, the office of *kethüda* to the governor of Baghdad continued to be a critical stepping-stone to regional influence. Meanwhile, Basra continued to function as a virtual dependency of Baghdad, often administered by a mamluk of the Baghdad governor.

Georgian mamluks in *ayan* households

It will now be apparent that mamluks from Georgia played sometimes pivotal roles in most, if not all, of the *ayan* households examined here. This was hardly a coincidence. On the contrary, the pattern resulted from increasing importation of Caucasian mamluks throughout the Ottoman domains combined with the new geopolitical realities created by the collapse of the Safavid empire in 1722.

Mamluks from the Caucasus, above all Circassia – today a southerly region of Russia, north-west of the Republic of Georgia – as opposed to Turks from Central Asia, began to be employed by the Mamluk sultanate towards the end of the thirteenth century. From the end of the fourteenth century until the Ottoman conquest of the sultanate in 1516–17, most Mamluk sultans were themselves Circassian. Once they had conquered the Mamluk sultanate, the Ottomans began to purchase mamluks from the same regions; by the seventeenth century, in consequence, Circassians, Abkhazians and other Caucasian peoples came to be well represented within the imperial palace and in the administrative elites of the provinces. Since the *devshirme* had been abandoned by the middle of that century, mamluks from the Caucasus, as well as born Muslims from the Balkans and Anatolia, began to fill more and more military and administrative positions. Indeed, several of the Jelali governors discussed in Chapter 4 were Abkhazian. In seventeenth-century Egypt, as noted in Chapter 4, prominent *sanjak beyi*s tended to be emancipated Circassian mamluks, in many cases clients of an earlier generation of Circassian beys, while their private armies, like those of the Jelali governors, consisted of mercenaries of various regional provenances.

With the fall of the Safavids to Afghan invaders in 1722, however, a new source of mamluks opened for the Ottomans: namely, eastern Georgia, which the Safavids had held as a protectorate and from which they had purchased large numbers of Georgian boys for service in their armies and at their court. The Safavid Shah Abbas I had supposedly hoped to use these Georgian *ghulam*s to curtail the influence of the Turcoman tribesmen who had formed the backbone of the original Safavid armies, much as Sultan Osman II had sought to use mercenary troops to counter the influence of the Ottoman *kuls*. In the aftermath of the Safavid collapse, however, eastern Georgia became an open pool of man- and woman-power of which governors and grandees in the Ottoman Arab provinces appear to have taken full advantage.

As a result, the late eighteenth century was a period of something approaching Georgian administrative hegemony in the Arab provinces. We have already noted Osman Pasha al-Sadiq, the Georgian mamluk of Syria's Azm family who governed the province of Damascus from 1760–72, as well as the 'dynasty' of Georgian mamluks who governed Baghdad and Basra from 1747 through 1831. In Egypt, meanwhile, the leadership of the Kazdağlı household was almost exclusively Georgian by 1750. The rebellious Ali Bey al-Kabir was Georgian, as was his mamluk Mehmed Bey Abu al-Dhahab and Abu al-Dhahab's mamluks Ibrahim and Murad Beys, who were administering Egypt when Bonaparte invaded in 1798. When Bonaparte returned to France in 1799, leaving a subordinate general in charge of Egypt, he took a number of Georgian mamluks with him.

There is even evidence that Georgian mamluks in different provinces were aware of each other and felt a certain degree of ethnic solidarity. Hence, when the Georgian mamluk of a defeated Kazdağlı ally was forced to flee Cairo in 1755, he went to Baghdad, where he must have known a Georgian regime was already firmly entrenched and where he may even have had relatives.

Women in the household

Despite the heavily militarized character of many eighteenth-century provincial *ayan* households, they included a substantial female component which played a critical, albeit frequently understudied, role in shaping their character. The head of an elite household such as that of the Kazdağlıs, the Azms, the Jalilis, or the mamluks of Baghdad was surrounded not only by his aides, mercenaries and mamluks but also by a substantial number of women, including his wife or wives, concubines and daughters, who might even be joined by his mother. Although female members of the household were largely relegated to the harem – that is, the portion of the residence's private quarters reserved for women – this by no means implied that wives, concubines and daughters lacked political and economic influence. On the contrary, each wife or concubine might well head her own female household, parallel to that of her husband, within the harem or even in a separate house, which in Egypt, at least, was therefore termed a 'harem house'. So far from being the household head's sexual playpen, then, the harem more closely resembled a female dormitory.

It is worth noting that the harem as parallel female household is apparently a venerable institution dating back at least to the Achaemenid Empire, which ruled Iran and Iraq from roughly 550–330 BCE. Thus, when King Ahusuerus gives a banquet in the Biblical Book of Esther, which is set in a fictionalized Achaemenid court, Queen Vashti gives a parallel banquet in the women's quarters (Esther 1:9). The Ottoman imperial harem, a vast network of rooms and passageways that takes up much of the western side of Topkapı Palace in Istanbul, functioned in much the same way, and served as a prototype and model for the harems of provincial *ayan* households. In an *ayan* household, however, the household head's mother did not usually wield the formidable influence exercised by the sultan's mother from about 1600 onwards. Competition among the wives and concubines of an *ayan* household to produce a successor to the (male) household head was, moreover, muted; any struggle over household leadership following the head's death was far more likely to pit his son against one of his mamluks or other clients.

In other respects, the sexual politics of the *ayan* household was similar to that of the imperial household. A household head might well marry his daughter to his favourite mamluk or other subordinate by way of reinforcing ties of patronage within his household, or to a key ally by way of cementing ties between two households. As noted above, the daughter of Ahmed Pasha, who governed Baghdad from 1724–47, married her father's Georgian mamluk, who ultimately succeeded to the governorship. Likewise in Egypt, Kazdağlı daughters routinely married their fathers', or occasionally brothers', mamluks. In a famous example, Ali Bey al-Kabir, who later rebelled against the sultan, in 1766 married his sister to his mamluk Mehmed Bey Abu al-Dhahab in a lavish ceremony.

A female member of an *ayan* household was likely to have acquired considerable political savvy by the time she reached marriageable age and could use it to the advantage of her husband's household. For example, Adila, the daughter of Ahmed Pasha, played an influential role in Baghdad's politics during the tenure of her husband Süleyman Pasha. Once she had lived through numerous marriages to influential grandees, a woman's political acumen was incalculable. Ambitious clients of deceased household heads therefore occasionally found themselves marrying ageing widows possessed of vast political experience and considerable wealth. In Cairo and Baghdad, it became common for a household head's favourite client to marry his patron's widow as part of assuming leadership of the household. Sitt Nafisa, the widow of Ali Bey al-Kabir, skipped a 'generation' of clients when she married Murad

Bey, the mamluk of Mehmed Bey Abu al-Dhahab, in 1773; the couple then moved into Ali Bey's old house. By the time of Bonaparte's invasion of Egypt in 1798, she was such a formidable political operator that the French imprisoned her on suspicion of smuggling supplies to Murad, who had fled to Upper Egypt.

In addition to its political advantages, this sort of marriage was also a canny economic strategy. The daughter of a wealthy grandee would naturally enhance her husband's standing. But since, under Islamic law, a wife retained any property she brought to her marriage and could acquire more in her own right after marriage, she could also keep a portion of the household's wealth from being confiscated by the state should her husband be executed or die without heirs. Some *ayan* encouraged their wives to make investments – for example in ships, in merchandise to be traded, or in quarrying operations – for precisely this reason. Other female members of a household could fulfil this role, as well. In 1746, the sister of Fethi Efendi, the *defterdar* of the province of Damascus mentioned above, was entrusted with much of his wealth after his execution at the hands of the Azms. In Egypt, meanwhile, the sister of the influential Qasimi chieftain Ismail Bey ibn Ivaz controlled much of the wealth of her brother's household following his assassination in 1724; with this fortune and her political astuteness, she was courted assiduously by other Qasimi leaders and ultimately married a series of them. A grandee's wife could also endow her own pious foundations (Arabic singular *waqf*), which similarly could not be touched by the state. Sitt Nafisa, for a notable example, endowed a Quran school over a public drinking fountain, known in Arabic as a *sabil-kuttab*, just outside Cairo's Bab Zuwayla, the tenth-century gate marking the southern boundary of the original city founded by the Fatimids.

A wife could, moreover, protect the household's wealth if her husband went off to war or on a long commercial journey, or were forced to flee his city or town by local rivals or a hostile governor. In that case, the wife, along with her entourage, would remain behind in her husband's residence. While enemies would feel no compunction about attacking the house or even razing it to underline the household head's defeat, they would usually stop short of invading the harem, for to do so would be considered an unacceptable violation of the family's intimate space. As a result, the male household head might deposit money and valuables in the harem. If his wife had her own 'harem house', these riches would be that much more secure.

An *ayan* wife, as head of such a parallel female household, presided over a hierarchy of female slaves corresponding to her husband's hierarchy of mamluks or mercenaries. Female slaves were imported from the

Caucasus along with mamluks and often fulfilled this role. In fact, the wives and concubines of the Kazdağlıs, Azms and governors of Baghdad by at least the mid-eighteenth century were usually themselves freed Caucasian slaves. Not all such slaves were potential wives or concubines, however; some lived lives of celibacy in the harem, serving as aides and factotums to the lady of the house or performing far more menial chores, although there were far fewer such slaves in provincial *ayan* households than there were in the imperial harem.

On the other hand, *ayan* households in the Arab provinces took advantage of the slave trade through the Sudan to acquire eastern African slave women, some of whom might serve as concubines while others attended to mundane household chores. By 1800, the majority of African slaves entering the Ottoman domains came from what are now Sudan and Ethiopia, and a majority of these were women. While certain Kazdağlı grandees towards the end of the eighteenth century acquired small numbers of African mamluks, military use of male African slaves remained a rarity until the nineteenth century; far more were employed as household servants, or castrated and employed as eunuch harem guardians. Each year, a series of caravans transported these slaves to Egypt, whence substantial numbers were transshipped to Syria and Anatolia. The *ayan* of Baghdad and Basra acquired African slaves via Anatolia or Syria or, alternatively, via the route that took slaves across the Red Sea to Yemen, then through the Arabian peninsula.

African eunuchs and *ayan* households

As noted above, a portion of the African slaves incorporated into *ayan* households were eunuchs. In Egypt, however, eunuchs delivered to the province by the trans-Saharan slave caravans or by Red Sea ships were augmented by eunuchs exiled from the Ottoman imperial harem in Istanbul. These two groups of eunuchs, in point of fact, represented different stages of the eunuch career.

Because castration is against Islamic law, young male slaves from Ethiopia, Somalia, Sudan and Nubia were castrated in Coptic Christian villages in Upper Egypt, then transported to Cairo for sale in the slave markets. They were not infrequently purchased by the Ottoman governor or by Egypt's grandees, who were among the few elements of the population wealthy enough to afford costly East African eunuchs. Thus, a recently castrated eunuch often began his new life by joining an *ayan* household, such as that of the Kazdağlıs, or the governor's household. The governor of Egypt often presented African eunuchs to the sultan's palace as gifts – a key means of currying sultanic favour. Increasingly, as the eighteenth century progressed, Egypt's *ayan*, and the Kazdağlıs above all, also presented eunuchs to the palace. In this fashion, a young eunuch could serve as a link between Egypt and the imperial capital very early in his career.

Exiled Chief Harem Eunuchs in Egypt

Early in the seventeenth century, eunuchs of the imperial harem, the over-whelming majority of whom were African, began to be exiled to Egypt when they were removed from office, doubtless in part because of this pre-existing connection to the province. By the middle of the century, even the Chief Harem Eunuch, one of the most influential figures in the entire empire, was routinely exiled to Cairo upon his deposition. For Ottoman officials, this sort of exile did not normally mean ruination for life but represented either a career lull or a comfortable retirement. For Chief Harem Eunuchs, it meant the latter. An exiled Chief Eunuch received a stipend and, furthermore, would have planned ahead for his last years in Cairo, so that by the time he arrived in Egypt he would have a large, comfortable house waiting for him, along with a number of agents and followers. In Egypt, he could amass property, endow pious foundations, and even purchase his own elite slaves from the Caucasus, creating the curious phenomenon of a castrated African ex-slave who owned uncastrated Caucasian slaves. He might also purchase his own eunuchs or cultivate ties of patronage with lower-ranking harem eunuchs already in Egypt.

In other words, exiled Chief Harem Eunuchs built up their own house-holds in Egypt. Indeed, a neighbourhood west of Cairo's citadel had become a virtual eunuch enclave by the end of the seventeenth century, thanks to a concentration of mansions there owned by exiled Chief Eunuchs and their clients. Arabic chronicles of Ottoman Egypt feature an influential late seventeenth-century grandee known as Mustafa Bey Kızlar (literally, 'the girls') because he was the mamluk of the exiled Chief Harem Eunuch (Kızlar Ağası, or 'agha of the girls', in Turkish) Yusuf Agha, who held office from 1671 to 1687. As a rule, though, households founded by Chief Eunuchs did not become particularly influential in Egypt. Even Mustafa Bey Kızlar, when he died, left a single impoverished mamluk living in Yusuf Agha's old house. In contrast, however, the founder of the Jalfi household, which functioned for many years as a sort of subordinate partner to the Kazdağlıs, is said by provincial chroniclers to have been a mamluk of el-Hajj Beshir Agha, the most powerful Chief Harem Eunuch in Ottoman history. Beshir Agha was Chief Eunuch for nearly thirty years, from 1717–46, and was one of the rare holders of

Figure 5.1 African eunuchs surrounding Sultan Ahmed III, from the 1720 *Book of Festivals* illustrated by the court painter Levni. Ahmed III is seated at the centre. To his immediate right is the grand vizier. Behind the grand vizier and to his left is the Chief Harem Eunuch, el-Hajj Beshir Agha; behind to his right is the Chief White Eunuch.
Source: Topkapı Palace Library Museum, MS A. 3593, folio 20b

that post to die in office. A few years before being named Chief Eunuch, however, he had spent a year or so in exile in Cairo, just around the time when the Jalfi household first appears in the historical record.

Quite apart from their personal mamluks and households, Chief Eunuchs wielded most influence, both in Egypt and in other Ottoman provinces, through their supervision of a set of pious endowments (Arabic singular *waqf*, Turkish singular *vakıf*) founded in the sixteenth and seventeenth centuries by members of the imperial family to benefit the poor of, and Muslim pilgrims to, the Holy Cities of Mecca and Medina. By the terms of these endowments, the tax revenues generated by specified lands and urban properties in numerous provinces of the Ottoman Empire were earmarked for the operation and maintenance of wells and caravanserais along the pilgrimage route, as well as soup kitchens and hospitals in the Holy Cities themselves. Egyptian villages endowed to the foundations provided grain for the Holy Cities, whose climate was too arid and barren to support cereal cultivation. Tax collection on all these lands and properties was farmed out to provincial notables in a process not unlike the purchase of *malikane*s. The tax farms of properties endowed to Mecca and Medina were highly prized, and it appears that the Chief Harem Eunuch was able to ensure that they were assigned to his clients in the provinces. In Egypt, members of the Kazdağlı household and their partners from the Jalfi household had monopolized the tax farms of the endowed grain villages by the 1750s.

Indeed, the Chief Harem Eunuch kept a permanent agent (*wakil* in Arabic, *vekil* in Turkish) in Cairo to see that grains and revenues earmarked for the Holy Cities were duly collected and sent on their way thither. This agent was usually a member of Egypt's military-administrative elite, often a high-ranking regimental officer or a *sanjak beyi*, although not ordinarily a member of one of Egypt's leading households. There is, in fact, some evidence that Mustafa Bey Kızlar, the mamluk of the exiled Chief Eunuch Yusuf Agha, served as agent to el-Hajj Beshir Agha when the latter was acting Chief Eunuch. This 'agent of the harem', as he was known, was thus himself one of Egypt's *ayan* and a full participant in that province's household politics.

Tomb Eunuchs in Medina

African harem eunuchs not only supervised the Holy Cities endowments but established a sizeable physical presence in the Holy Cities themselves. In Mecca, a corps of about eighty, mostly palace eunuchs, some of whom had previously been exiled to Egypt, stood guard at the Great Mosque, site of the Kaba. In Medina, some 120 guarded the entrance to the Prophet Muhammad's tomb; they were, in fact, the only people allowed to enter the tomb chamber. The custom of the eunuch guard began under the Ayyubids in the late twelfth century and was reinforced by the Mamluk sultans, who sought to buttress Sunni Islam in a region which at the time was heavily populated by Zaydi and Ismaili Shiites. Shiites resented the Sunni imams who led prayers in Medina's Mosque of the Prophet. Occasionally, furthermore, they sought to defile the graves of Abu Bakr and Umar, which lie within the Prophet's tomb compound; while Sunnis recognize these two figures as Muhammad's immediate successors as leaders of the Muslim community, or caliphs, Shiites regard them as usurpers of Ali's right to the caliphate. The eunuchs acted as a check on disruptive Shiite behaviour. Under the Ottomans, they kept a watchful eye on Twelver Shiite pilgrims from Iran, as well as Zaydis from Yemen, while enforcing decorous behaviour among tomb visitors as a whole.

In a parallel to the exiled harem eunuchs in Cairo, the 'Tomb Eunuchs' of Medina joined the ranks of Medina's notables, residing in their own quarter adjacent to the tomb. At the entrance to this quarter stood the house of the Chief Tomb Eunuch, known in Arabic as Shaykh al-Haram. This official appointed his subordinate Tomb Eunuchs and acted as a sort of local coordinator for the delivery of grain and revenues to Medina's poor. He must certainly have consulted fairly closely with the Chief Harem Eunuch in Topkapı Palace. Beginning with Yusuf Agha in the 1690s, furthermore, the Chief Tomb Eunuch was often a former Chief Harem Eunuch who had earlier been exiled to Cairo. Thus, the harem eunuch career bound Istanbul, Cairo and Medina in a 'eunuch network' which ensured the proper functioning of the Holy Cities foundations while serving as a multidirectional channel of influence.

Eunuchs and provincial intellectual life

The provincial religious influence of Chief Harem Eunuchs, acting and exiled alike, went well beyond guardianship of the Prophet's tomb and the Great Mosque of Mecca. Eunuchs also affected religious and intellectual life in the Arab provinces at large through their personal charitable endowments. Numerous Chief Eunuchs founded *madrasas*, or Islamic theological colleges; Sufi lodges; and libraries in various provinces. The great el-Hajj Beshir Agha established a library of theological works in Medina, where he served as chief of the Tomb Eunuchs before his appointment as Chief Harem Eunuch in 1717.

A similar purpose was served by the Chief Eunuchs' endowment of books from the extensive libraries that many of them accumulated over their long careers. The core of such a library was the palace school curriculum, which included a thorough grounding in Islamic law according to the Hanafi rite. El-Hajj Beshir Agha endowed a portion of his library to the residential college of the Turks at Cairo's al-Azhar university, thus assuring that this Hanafi student population was supplied with manuscripts of seminal Hanafi legal texts. He established a similar endowment at the mosque of Abu Hanifa, namesake of the Hanafi rite, in Baghdad, which throughout the 1730s and 1740s was under continual threat from the Shiite Safavid revivalist Nadir Shah. (Today, this mosque is most famous as the site of the last public appearance of Saddam Husayn before his capture in late 2003.) Chief Harem Eunuchs exiled to Egypt, meanwhile, carried their libraries with them and must, like el-Hajj Beshir Agha, have made books available to members of the ulema.

This is not to imply, of course, that non-eunuch *ayan* did *not* contribute to provincial religious and intellectual life; they did, as will become clearer in the following chapter. However, the eunuchs' endowments were distinguished by their unusually systematic character, whereby a lengthy series of eunuchs established substantial endowments in numerous provinces, and the clearly pro-Hanafi purpose many of them served.

Ayan architecture

In the sixteenth and seventeenth centuries, many, though by no means all, publicly visible architectural monuments in the Arab provinces were commissioned by governors sent out from Istanbul. In a few instances, the sultan himself commissioned high-profile monuments, as in the case of Damascus' Tekke, or Takiya, Mosque, founded by Süleyman I in 1554 though not completed until after his death. (Süleyman also rebuilt the walls of Jerusalem and restored the Dome of the Rock, replacing the derelict exterior mosaics from the era of the structure's founding under the Umayyads with tiles from the famous kilns of Iznik in western Anatolia.) During the eighteenth century, however, the *ayan* of the Arab provinces increasingly took the initiative in commissioning publicly visible architectural monuments, from mosques and *madrasas* to caravanserais and fountains. Architecturally, many of these monuments combined stylistic elements typical of the imperial capital with ones drawn from pre-Ottoman provincial building styles and occasionally even from the latest European styles, all the while making allowances for the availability or unavailability of certain building materials, the proclivities of local architects and craftsmen, and the realities of climate.

The Azm style in Damascus

In some cases, an *ayan* household would cultivate an architectural style which served as a veritable signature of its sponsorship. In Damascus, the Azms commissioned a number of mansions, mosques and *madrasas*, as well as an enormous caravanserai, the Asad (Esad) Pasha Khan, named after Esad Pasha al-Azm, governor of Damascus from 1743–57, constructed of alternating stripes of white limestone and black basalt. Occasionally, as in Esad Pasha al-Azm's residential palace in Damascus, stripes of red granite entered the mix for a trichromatic effect. Although this bichromatic and multi-chromatic construction had been used in earlier Damascene monuments and in structures in other provinces, and continued to be used in non-Azm structures, it quickly became an Azm trademark.

The Abdurrahman Kethüda style in Cairo

At around this same time in Cairo, Abdurrahman Kethüda al-Kazdağlı, a Janissary commander who led the Kazdağlı household in the late 1750s before being displaced by Ali Bey, pioneered a unique architectural style that makes his mosque, fountain, and additions to al-Azhar university instantly recognizable. Characteristic of this style are recessed arches and a combination of classical Ottoman decorative elements with others derived perhaps from the architecture of North Africa or of the western Arabian peninsula, where Abdurrahman Kethüda spent several years during the late 1740s.

Ottoman 'retro' style

In other cases, provincial notables deliberately adhered to classical Ottoman styles in order to make specific political points. In 1774, Mehmed Bey Abu al-Dhahab, the emancipated mamluk of Ali Bey, built a mosque just outside the main gate of al-Azhar. The mosque's dome and minarets resemble those of sixteenth- and seventeenth-century mosques in Istanbul itself. When we recall that Abu al-Dhahab had thwarted his patron's rebellion by retreating from Damascus, the mosque's design seems calculated to underline its sponsor's loyalty to the sultan.

Much the same could be said of the mosque of Ahmed Pasha al-Jazzar in the northern Palestinian seaport and sometime Crusader capital of Acre. A Bosnian mercenary, al-Jazzar arrived in Egypt from Istanbul in 1756 in the entourage of the new governor. When the governor was reassigned, al-Jazzar attached himself to the household of the future rebel Ali Bey,

Figure 5.2 The house of Esad Pasha al-Azm in Hama, Syria (*c*.1740),
showing both the Azm 'trademark' black-and-white striped masonry and the
characteristic features of the courtyard house, discussed in Chapter 7.
Source: Author's photo

which at the time consisted overwhelmingly of Georgian mamluks.
(He thus provides an example of an appointee from the imperial capital
participating fully in the household culture of a province.) It was Ali
Bey who promoted him to the rank of *sanjak beyi*. He acquired the
sobriquet al-Jazzar, Arabic for 'the butcher', for the ruthlessness with
which he subdued a Bedouin rebellion in the Nile Delta. Although he
appears to have served as a close aide to Ali Bey, he ultimately incurred
his wrath when he warned a sometime ally of Ali Bey's plan to assassin-
ate him. Al-Jazzar fled to Syria, where he built up his own household.
His troops helped to defeat Ali Bey's ally Zahir al-Umar, after which al-
Jazzar was named governor of the province of Sidon, which, as noted
in Chapter 4, had been created in 1614. From 1775 until his death in
1804, he ruled not from the city of Sidon in southern Lebanon but from
Acre, which Zahir al-Umar had transformed into a flourishing centre
of commerce with Europe. Among his most notable achievements was

preventing Bonaparte from capturing Acre in 1799; the town's successful resistance forced the French evacuation of Syria.

Although al-Jazzar was a despotic governor who sought to bring both Lebanon and Damascus under his sway, his mosque in Acre, built in 1781, is a relatively unassuming, quintessentially Ottoman affair such as a government minister, or vizier, might have built in Istanbul. The design appears to have been deliberately chosen to invoke al-Jazzar's status as the sultan's servant, perhaps in implicit contrast to Zahir al-Umar.

The *sabil-kuttab* in Cairo

A smaller form of architectural monument began to pop up all over Cairo in the eighteenth century: the *sabil-kuttab* or, in Turkish form, *sebil-mekteb*, a Quran school (*kuttab* or *mekteb*) over a public drinking fountain (*sabil* or *sebil*). This may seem an unlikely juxtaposition architecturally, yet in religious terms the structure combined two pious acts: providing basic Islamic education, often for orphaned and/or impoverished boys, and supplying clean drinking water to the thirsty, as the Quran repeatedly urges believers to do. While the boys memorized the Quran and learned basic Muslim doctrine upstairs, a functionary inside the *sabil* drew water from a cistern beneath the fountain's floor and passed it in metal cups to thirsty passers-by. Both the Quranic instruction and the water were provided free of charge; the founder of the *sabil-kuttab* established a *waqf*, or pious endowment, to cover all costs.

Although unattached Quran schools and fountains can be found throughout the Muslim world, the *sabil-kuttab* combination appears to be restricted to Egypt, where the form dates back to the late Mamluk sultanate. By the eighteenth century, the *sabil-kuttab* had become the most common religious foundation in Cairo. Most were built by local notables. Abdurrahman Kethüda al-Kazdağlı founded one, featuring the recessed arches characteristic of his monuments, at Bayn al-Qasrayn, the busy commercial thoroughfare which runs through the heart of the original Fatimid city. As noted above, Sitt Nafisa, wife of Ali Bey and, later, of Murad Bey, commissioned one just outside Bab Zuwayla, the southern gate of the original Fatimid city. Among the more active founders of *sabil-kuttab*s were exiled harem eunuchs. In 1715, the future Chief Harem Eunuch el-Hajj Beshir Agha commissioned a *sabil-kuttab* during a brief period of exile in Cairo; he placed it in the north-western neighbourhood that was just becoming the hub of elite residence. Some forty years later, his successor as Chief Eunuch, Moralı Beshir Agha, commissioned another just across the road. Both these structures are in close proximity to the *madrasa* of Sultan Mahmud I (r. 1730–54), built in

Figure 5.3 Abdurrahmah Kethüda al Kazdağlı's *sabil-kuttab* at Bayn al-Qasrayn, Cairo (1744).
Source: André Raymond, *Le Caire des Janissaires: l'apogée de la ville ottomane sous 'Abd al-Rahmân Katkhudâ*. Paris: CNRS Editions, 1995, p. 33.

1750 under Moralı Beshir's supervision as the first sultanic *madrasa* the Ottomans had ever constructed in Egypt. The *madrasa* boasts its own *sabil-kuttab*, which closely resembles that of Moralı Beshir Agha in the bowed façade of the *sabil* and the polygonal shape of the *kuttab*.

It may not be a coincidence that *sabil-kuttab*s were commissioned by Hanafi rulers and grandees in a land where followers of the Shafii and Maliki legal rites far outnumbered those of the Hanafi rite. Most founders of *sabil-kuttab*s specified in their endowments that the *kuttab* would provide instruction according to the Hanafi rite. Since, furthermore, many *sabil-kuttab*s provided Quranic education to orphans, they could help to ensure Hanafism's continued viability in Egypt. Meanwhile, the drinking fountain, where scores of people might stop daily, guaranteed wide public exposure for the foundation's mission. Overall, the *sabil-kuttab* gave the Hanafi rite much-needed public visibility in a region where it was decidedly in the minority. It made a fitting endowment for Chief Harem Eunuchs, who identified strongly with Ottoman Hanafism.

Collectively, these monuments founded by the *ayan* of the Arab provinces sent an array of political, economic and religious messages. Through the founder's choice of style and ornament, a building could mark a notable household as a power in its own right and/or as the loyal servant of the Ottoman sultan. Its size and ostentation, or the extent of its charitable or intellectual effect, could attest to the founder's wealth and influence. A space in which Islam could be practised testified to the founder's piety while a structure that reinforced the Hanafi legal rite bespoke the founder's commitment to the brand of Islam promoted by the Ottoman central authority. What seems clear, in any case, is that these monuments represent a form of *ayan* assertion peculiar to the eighteenth century, when provincial *ayan* had acquired the means and the local or regional clout necessary to make such architectural statements. Still, this sort of assertion did not automatically connote a desire for autonomy from Istanbul.

Conclusion

Whether they began as members of prominent Arab families, as localized Janissaries, as Caucasian mamluks, or as transplanted officials from the imperial palace, the *ayan* of the Arab provinces nurtured households, modelled ultimately on the sultan's household, which in large measure determined the political culture and economic trajectories of the provinces in which they flourished. Although these *ayan* households can be seen as an outgrowth of the seventeenth-century vizier and pasha households, they controlled far larger accumulations of human, fiscal and, in most cases, territorial resources and were far more entrenched in the provinces where they operated. In dealing with the Ottoman central authority, therefore, the *ayan* came much closer to being on an equal footing.

Scholars and observers alike have therefore asked why the *ayan* of the Arab provinces did not rebel en masse against the Ottoman sultan and declare themselves rulers of independent states. Such a question, however, is coloured by modern-day nationalist assumptions, chief among which is the assumption that these *ayan* must have felt oppressed by, rather than empowered by, Ottoman rule. Yet in most cases, grandees such as the Azms or the governors of Baghdad seem to have regarded their regional autonomy as a complement to the overall sovereignty of the sultan. Even the provocative acts of Ali Bey al-Kabir in Egypt and

Shaykh Zahir al-Umar in Palestine were circumscribed by regional rivalries. Moreover, loyalty to the Ottoman sultan was a source of social cohesion that would have been difficult to recreate in an *ayan*-ruled independent statelet with a population of wildly diverse ethnicities, confessions and degrees of material wealth. It also provided a degree of security vis-à-vis the growing encroachments of France, Britain and Russia.

Above all, we should remember that the relationship between the Ottoman central authority and any given province during the eighteenth century was not a question of two rival power centres; rather, it resembled a dialogue or negotiation, with much give and take of personnel and resources. The fact that the provincial *ayan* households had become self-sustaining loci of power arguably made the relationship less potentially antagonistic than that between the central authority and the Jelali governors of the preceding century, who were essentially attacking a palace system that would not accommodate them rather than creating their own parallel system. For, whereas the Jelali governors and their equivalents struggled to persuade the Ottoman central authority to recognize their legitimacy, the eighteenth-century *ayan* had the means to establish their own legitimacy, whereupon the central government was obliged to recognize a *fait accompli*. At the same time, the *ayan* households in any given province forged relationships with *ayan* in other provinces or, on the other hand, pursued rivalries and even vendettas with these *ayan*. They also cultivated their own relationships with the European powers, often in blatant disregard for the wishes of the imperial government. This increasing autonomy of activity, even without rebellion, prepared the ground for the Porte's efforts to recentralize control in the nineteenth century.

Notes

1. W.F. Reddaway, ed., *Documents of Catherine the Great: The Correspondence with Voltaire and the Instruction of 1767 in the English Text of 1768*, reissue (New York, 1971), p. 96 (my translation).
2. Ahmad al-Budayri al-Hallaq, *Ḥawādith Dimashq al-yawmiyya* (*Daily Events of Damascus*), condensed by Muhammad Saʿid al-Qasimi, ed. Ahmad Izzat Abd al-Karim (Damascus, 1959), p. 208 (my translation).
3. Quoted in Abraham Marcus, *The Middle East on the Eve of Modernity: Aleppo in the Eighteenth Century* (New York, 1989), p. 84.
4. Quoted in Dina Rizk Khoury, *State and Provincial Society in the Ottoman Empire: Mosul, 1540–1834* (Cambridge, 1997), p. 45.

chapter six

RELIGIOUS AND INTELLECTUAL LIFE

Islam was, obviously, an integral part of Ottoman identity. Islamic law underpinned the Ottoman judicial system, even if it were supplemented by sultanic *kanun*, and, as noted in Chapter 3, the Ottoman state actively promoted Sunni Islam of the Hanafi legal rite. Many of the *ayan* introduced in the preceding chapter reinforced their legitimacy by founding religious and charitable institutions; some of them even intermarried with families of Muslim scholar-officials. At the same time, descendants of the Prophet Muhammad, whether real or manufactured, enjoyed esteem by virtue of their presumed lineage.

By the sixteenth century, a highly articulated system of religious education and a corresponding hierarchy of religious officials had taken shape in the imperial capital and the provinces alike. Not all religious figures belonged to this hierarchy, however. Muslim mystics, or Sufis, traditionally received a quite different form of religious instruction and stood outside the official religious establishment, although by the eighteenth century a complete rapprochement had been achieved between 'mainstream' forms of mysticism and religious orthodoxy, so that even high-ranking religious officials, in the Arab provinces as elsewhere, were often practising Sufis as well.

Muslim scholar-officials, known collectively as ulema, were key contributors to intellectual activity in the Ottoman Arab provinces, producing not only religious treatises and commentaries but also historical chronicles, biographical dictionaries, poetry, works on grammar and the like. They did not hold a monopoly on such activity, but were joined by government bureaucrats of various sorts, as well as Sufis and others who held no formal position in the religious hierarchy. What united all these writers, however, was some form of religious education, which before the late eighteenth century was the foundation of all education, though it might occur in different settings and be supplemented by training of a more practical sort. In the society of the premodern Ottoman Arab

lands, in short, no rigid boundary existed between religious life and intellectual life in general, or between religious functionaries and intellectuals as social groups.

This is not to say, of course, that all religious functionaries were
intellectuals. Many lower-ranking professionals, such as Quran-school
teachers and the various scribes and other aides who kept the mach-
inery of the Muslim religious courts, indispensable for a vast array of
transactions, operating on a daily basis, left no written legacy and probably did not participate in the intellectual discussions common among
the higher echelons of ulema and other scholars. Some were probably
not highly literate in the first place. And while many high-ranking ulema
might belong to Sufi orders, there were many other Sufis who laboured
at humbler occupations, such as those of ordinary craftsmen, and produced no written works.

The purpose of the present chapter, then, is to introduce the principal religious institutions and personnel of the Ottoman Arab provinces, and to show how they functioned within provincial society and how
they contributed to the intellectual life of the provinces. We must bear
in mind throughout, however, that these institutions and categories were
never mutually exclusive, nor did membership of one or another of them
prevent a scholar-official or a Sufi from interacting with or belonging to
other social groups.

The ulema

In very general terms, a given Muslim society recognizes a large body
of 'learned people', that is, men, and occasionally women, learned in
Islamic traditions, theology and law. These people, comparable in
certain ways to rabbis in Judaism, are known collectively as ulema; this
is the Arabic plural of *alim*, which means simply one possessing knowledge (Arabic, *ilm*). Theoretically, ulema can include everyone from
the world's greatest experts in Islamic law to a humble Quran-school
teacher. Usually, however, the label 'ulema' refers to Islam's intellectual
elite, the professorial and juridical class, somewhat like the English
'intelligentsia' but with an unmistakeable theological component. As
bearers of the literate tradition of Islamic culture, the ulema acquired
considerable moral authority, though occasionally they were targeted for
arrogance and profligacy. On the other hand, they did not constitute a
clergy, for they did not mediate sacraments, nor did they stand apart
from ordinary people through a process of initiation.

The ulema first came to be recognized in the early centuries of Islam
as an identifiable category of people who were thoroughly familiar with

the text of the Quran and with the reports of the sayings of the Prophet Muhammad, known collectively as *hadith* (Arabic for 'speech'), or the broader corpus of sayings and deeds of the Prophet and his companions, including the early caliphs, or successors to Muhammad as leaders of the Muslim community, known as *sunna* ('custom'). They made legal decisions based on these sources, as well as on community consensus, logical analogy and independent rational enquiry, and, through their varying emphases on these different sources of legal authority, contributed to the formation of the Sunni legal schools, or rites, mentioned in Chapter 3. Likewise, they laid the ground for Islamic theology, which covers not only mundane matters of ritual practice but also fundamental metaphysical questions, such as the nature of God and his relationship to his creation.

We may divide the Ottoman ulema into three broad categories: those who handled legal decisions (*qadi*s and *mufti*s), those who oversaw religious-cum-legal education (*madrasa* professors), and those who preached in the mosques. To be sure, these categories were not employed by the Ottoman government itself, although they correspond very roughly to distinct roles within the ulema profession. In any case, they were by no means mutually exclusive.

Qadis

To oversee the administration of *sharia* in each province, the Ottoman central government appointed a chief judge, or *qadi* (*kadı* in Turkish). Sultan Mehmed II, the conqueror of Constantinople, had instituted two supreme judges overseeing all the other judges in the empire: one for Rumelia, that is, the empire's European provinces, and another for Anatolia. Each of these officials held the title *qadi askar* (*kazasker* in Turkish), literally, 'judge of the military'. The *qadi askar* of Rumelia was considered somewhat superior in rank to that of Anatolia and often ascended to the post of Shaykh al-Islam, or chief *mufti* of Istanbul, the highest religious official in the Ottoman Empire. Following his victory at Chaldiran and subsequent conquest of south-eastern Anatolia and northern Iraq, Selim I established a third *qadi askar*, based in the south-eastern Anatolian city of Diyarbakır, for the 'Arab and Persian' lands. He abolished this new judgeship, however, after his conquest of Syria and Egypt. (Nonetheless, the chief judge of Egypt was accorded the title *qadi askar* as an honorific; he was also called *qadi al-quda*, or 'judge of judges'.) Thus, oversight of the Arab provinces' legal administration quickly came to rest with the *qadi askar* of Anatolia, who appointed a chief judge to each provincial capital. During the reign of Süleyman I, however, the extraordinarily influential Shaykh al-Islam Ebussuud Efendi (term

1545–74) assumed a leading role in choosing the provincial chief judges, setting a lasting precedent. Following his tenure, the *qadi askar* of Anatolia selected only lower-ranking provincial judges, usually on the recommendation of the chief judges of the provinces concerned.

By the terms of the Ottoman judicial hierarchy, each province consisted of a number of judicial districts (Arabic singular *qada*, related to *qadi*), and each district in turn consisted of numerous subdistricts (Arabic singular *nahiya*). Ordinarily, the capital and its immediate hinterland constituted one *qada* under the authority of the province's chief judge, but this *qada* was subdivided into numerous *nahiyas*. The chief judge served for one year, occasionally longer; district judges, who administered lesser *qadas* within a province, were appointed by the Anatolia *qadi askar* for similarly brief terms. Thus, they had little opportunity to strike roots in the province in the manner of the *ayan*. On leaving his post in one Arab capital, a chief judge might well be appointed to the same post in another Arab province or perhaps in Anatolia or Rumelia. An informal pecking order obtained among the Arab provincial chief judgeships, with Mecca, Medina, Cairo, Damascus, Aleppo and Jerusalem carrying the greatest prestige. The chief judgeship of one of these cities could serve as a stepping-stone to the post of *qadi askar* of Anatolia or Rumelia.

As Hanafism was the official legal rite of the Ottoman Empire, provincial chief judges and district judges were without exception Hanafi. Nonetheless, the Shafii, Maliki and Hanbali rites were well established in the Arab provinces, and deputy judges belonging to these rites presided over Muslim law courts at the subdistrict, or *nahiya*, level in locales where their fellow adherents lived in significant numbers. These non-Hanafi deputy judges did not exist solely for the benefit of followers of their own rites, however, for litigants often 'played the courts', bringing cases before courts of whatever rite they calculated would render the most favourable decision. Deputy judges went by the Arabic title *na'ib* (literally, 'representative'). Whereas Hanafi *na'ib*s were often students or even relatives of the chief judge, whom they accompanied to the province and with whom they departed, their non-Hanafi counterparts often belonged to prominent local families and usually served for life.

The judge ruled on cases subject to the *sharia*, or Islamic law as derived from the Quran, the *hadith*, and the legal decisions of the first few generations of ulema. Such cases included marriage, divorce, custody of children, property transfers, and business partnerships and disputes arising therefrom – in short, all personal status cases with the exception of inheritance, which, although subject to the *sharia*, was adjudicated in the provincial capitals by special inheritance courts set up under the provincial *kanunname*s. He also ruled on *sharia* criminal cases and enforced the *kanun*, or sultanic law, which covered matters not addressed by the *sharia*, as well as local customary law.

In short, the chief judge exercised an authority separate from that of the provincial governor, and he did not ordinarily serve at the governor's pleasure. When the provincial governor perceived a clear and present threat to public security and order, however, he had the authority to sentence trouble-makers without the judge's intervention. Meanwhile, commanders of the corps of Ottoman soldiery adjudicated disputes within their respective regiments, rather in the manner of a military tribunal.

Whereas judges under the Mamluk sultanate and other pre-Ottoman regimes apparently kept records of their cases among their personal papers, which they presumably stored in their homes, an Ottoman court was required to maintain a register, known in Turkish as a *defter*, of cases in the court building itself. The judge and his assistants recorded court cases in summary form, so that a case encompassing sporadic hearings over several days, weeks or even months might be reduced to a single register entry of only a few lines, such as this one from the court register of the Palestinian town of Nablus in 1656:

> Muhammad, of the village of Isdud in the district of Gaza, sues master barber Yusuf ibn Abdallah. In his complaint, the plaintiff claimed that the master Yusuf has employed his son, Hasan, without due authorization from the child's father. He demands that the master return the son to his parents' custody. Master barber Yusuf, questioned on the matter, said that the boy joined his employ of his own free will and wishes to stay with his master and learn the trade. The boy was therefore summoned and questioned, and he, too, replied that he wishes to stay with his master in order to learn the barber's profession.
>
> In view of these declarations the *qadi* informed the plaintiff that he is not to get custody of his son unless the son himself so wishes, since the boy is now a mature companion. He warned the plaintiff against trying to harm the defendant or harass him.[1]

Despite this terseness, the registers of Ottoman *qadi* courts constitute one of the few records of Muslim court practice from the premodern period to have survived to the present day; as such, they are a vital source for Ottoman social and economic history. In the Arab provinces, these registers were kept in Arabic, in Anatolia and the European provinces in Ottoman Turkish. Since most judges assigned to the Arab provinces were Turcophone, they relied on court translators to communicate with litigants. Most judges, regardless of provenance, acquired a knowledge of legal Arabic in the course of their religious educations, but for a native Turkish speaker, or at least someone who had spoken Turkish since his youth, running a court in Arabic several days a week was another matter.

Another Ottoman innovation in the Arab lands was the designation of specific buildings as courthouses, at least for the chief provincial judges. Under pre-Ottoman regimes, courts had convened in mosques, and this practice continued among lower-ranking judges and *na'ib*s. In the case of the chief judge, the 'courthouse' often doubled as his residence, putting the judge's house in the same league as the palatial residences of local notables. In Cairo, the chief judge, who was, naturally, a Hanafi, lived and held court in a fifteenth-century Mamluk palace located in the city centre and known as the Bab al-Ali (literally, 'highest gate'), duplicating the name of the grand vizier's council room in Topkapı Palace; he was joined here by four *na'ib*s representing the four Sunni legal rites. Roughly fifteen more subdistrict, or *nahiya*, courts, run by *na'ib*s, met in mosques spread throughout the city. For example, a key Hanafi court, which during the seventeenth century was frequented by many of the city's notables, met in a mosque situated outside Bab Zuwayla, the southern gate of the original Fatimid city of Cairo; this was a mosque in which prayers were conducted according to the Hanafi rite. Damascus' chief judge presided in a building, no longer extant, thought to be near the tailors' bazaar in the heart of the old city, near the covered markets built by two Azm governors and a stone's throw from the Umayyad Mosque. *Na'ib*s ran four additional subdistrict courts. Similar arrangements prevailed in Aleppo.

There was no jury in these courts; rather, the judge decided cases on the spot. Oral testimony was the most important form of evidence, particularly in cases involving conflicting accounts of an incident, such as the case of the barber's apprentice cited above. Physical evidence was far less important. In this attitude towards evidence, Muslim legal procedure shows its partial descent from Roman practice, in which rhetoric was so critical to swaying an audience. Although the 'ideal witness' was a free Muslim male, women and non-Muslims could also give testimony. However, a woman's testimony counted for only half that of a man while a non-Muslim could not testify against a Muslim unless there were extenuating circumstances – for example, if a non-Muslim were the sole witness to the death of a Muslim whose estate was being divided. These limitations, however, did not stop women and non-Muslims from making fairly frequent use of the Muslim courts. Non-Muslims even resorted to Muslim courts in cases not involving Muslims when they thought that Muslim law promised a more beneficial outcome than the laws of their own communities. Slaves, meanwhile, had little role in court cases since their testimony was not normally admitted. According to the *sharia*, slaves could be witnesses only in cases involving certain monetary transactions and, if of good character, in those involving religious matters.

As the barber's case attests, witnesses were of critical importance since they vouched orally for the character of the plaintiff or defendant, or for the status of a business partnership, a marriage or a piece of property. The importance of witnesses gave rise to a category of 'permanent' witnesses (Arabic plural *shuhud al-hal*). These were not like today's expert witnesses but were rather an informal body of 'court watchers' who scrutinized cases to make sure that they followed correct legal procedures and, where necessary, adduced relevant precedents to the case at hand. They were not appointed officials who served fixed terms but simply community members from various classes and walks of life who habitually made themselves available at court or, on the other hand, who happened to have business at court on a particular day and were pressed into service on the spot. A good proportion could be labelled upstanding members of the community, and some clearly belonged to the local *ayan*. In addition to knowing proper court procedure, they were intimately familiar with the community, including the status and reputations of many of its members. Thus, a key part of their value lay in their ability to provide oral testimony in contentious cases or to witness and sign documents such as property transfers, partnership agreements, and deeds establishing pious endowments.

Muftis

While the *qadi* dealt with the day-to-day application of the *sharia*, the *mufti* was the official who made rulings about what was acceptable according to Islamic law; we might say that while the *qadi* wielded executive power, much as a mayor or prime minister, the *mufti* wielded interpretive power, much as the High Court – or as a rabbi. In practice, the *mufti* responded to specific questions regarding proper Islamic conduct; many of these were submitted by judges or litigants involved in specific court cases. His ruling, known in Arabic as a *fatwa* (*fetva* in Turkish), was thus analogous to the Jewish responsum. *Fatwa*s can run the gamut from the late Ayatollah Khomeini's 1989 opinion sanctioning the killing of the British author Salman Rushdie to everyday questions concerning, for example, the proper manner in which to wash before prayer. Notwithstanding the esteem in which his opinions were held, the *mufti* did not have veto power over the *qadi*; rather, his *fatwa*s were non-binding advisory positions which a judge could accept or reject, as he saw fit, in deciding a given case. Yet because *mufti*s were renowned for their learning and their probity – and sometimes for their political connections as well – someone pleading a case before a judge would find himself in a strong position if he could produce a *fatwa* in his favour.

Beginning with the great Ebusuud Efendi under Süleyman I, the chief *mufti* of Istanbul, or Shaykh al-Islam, appointed the chief *mufti*s of the European provinces and Anatolia, all of whom were Hanafi, in keeping with the legal rite of the overwhelming majority of the population. Where the Arab lands were concerned, however, he ordinarily recognized a chief *mufti* for each legal rite represented in a particular province. Furthermore, because a *mufti* was a giver of legal opinions, rather than an enforcer, many provincial *mufti*s had no official appointments but were simply acknowledged by their communities as sources of juridical authority. This meant that the number of religious scholars acting as *mufti*s in the Arab lands could vary rather considerably from one province to another and over time. There need not be a *mufti* in every major provincial city, in the way that there had to be a *qadi*, since the *mufti*'s rulings did not have a direct impact on day-to-day affairs as the *qadi*'s judgements did. By the seventeenth century, *mufti*s of all rites came from leading local ulema. In some cases, prominent local families dominated the post. In Damascus, the Muradis, a family of purported descendants of the Prophet, monopolized the office of Hanafi *mufti* during the second half of the eighteenth century; in seventeenth- and eighteenth-century Mosul, the post was held by members of the Umari, Fakhri and Yasin families, who also supplied Mosul with *na'ib*s. And while this pattern of family dominance did not obtain in Egypt, the Hanafi, Maliki and Shafii *mufti*s unquestionably numbered among Cairo's local notables.

Madrasas

*Qadi*s and *mufti*s, as well as theologians and legal theorists (who were often current or former *qadi*s or *mufti*s), normally received their education in a Muslim theological college, or *madrasa* (*medrese* in Turkish). The *madrasa* seems to have emerged in the tenth or eleventh century in Iran and Central Asia as a central location where ulema and the students from many far-flung places who sought their knowledge could come together and even live. The Great Seljuks, who ruled Iran and Iraq from the mid-eleventh century until the Mongol invasions of the thirteenth century, heavily patronized the *madrasa* as a means of shoring up normative Sunni Islam against the ideological threat posed by Ismaili Shiites at the time (although recent research points to the concurrent existence of Ismaili *madrasa*s). By the Ottoman period, *madrasa*s were well established as the site of Islamic higher education, not only among the Ottomans themselves but among their Twelver Shiite rivals, the Safavids.

Ordinarily, a *madrasa* was founded by means of a pious endowment, known in Arabic as a *waqf* and in Turkish as a *vakıf.* In the imperial capital, the founder was often the sultan, another member of the Ottoman royal family, or a powerful vizier. Although sultanic *madrasas* do exist in the Arab provinces, far more typical were those founded by provincial governors or, particularly in the eighteenth century, local notables. The prospective founder went to a *qadi* court to draft a deed endowing the revenues from a group of shops or, on the other hand, from specified lands, to the *madrasa*'s maintenance and upkeep (the same process was used to endow other charitable foundations, such as mosques, soup kitchens, Quran schools and Sufi lodges). As endowed monies, these revenues were permanently exempt from government taxation. The deed specified a superintendent of the *waqf* to oversee collection and distribution of these revenues; the commander of the local Janissary regiment was a popular choice for foundations established by provincial governors during the sixteenth and seventeenth centuries. Also spelled out in the deed were all expenses associated with the *madrasa*, from teachers' salaries and students' bread rations to prayer rugs and oil for lamps. In consequence, these deeds (Arabic singular *waqfiyya*) can serve as rich sources for social and economic history while providing clues to the material culture of the time.

In such a *madrasa*, a student studied a particular text with a particular professor, who usually went by the title shaykh, a broad and flexible term connoting leadership in a variety of contexts. For example, a student who belonged to the Hanafi legal rite might study one of the classical works of Hanafi law, composed in medieval Central Asia, with a Hanafi shaykh. This meant that he would memorize the text or take down the shaykh's commentary on the text verbatim, then memorize the commentary. Once he had completed this task to the shaykh's satisfaction, the shaykh wrote out an *ijaza*, that is, a certificate testifying that the student had mastered this text and could now teach it. Thus, a *madrasa* education consisted not so much in passing prescribed courses as in collecting *ijaza*s for prescribed texts. Possession of such *ijaza*s was also a way to establish and maintain connections with teachers and to introduce oneself to new teachers.

In the central lands of the Ottoman Empire, the entire legal administration was staffed by a hierarchy of *madrasa*s determined by the annual salaries the teachers earned: hence, twenty-, thirty- forty-, fifty-, sixty- and hundred-*akche madrasa*s. The last three categories included the most prestigious *madrasa*s, founded by the towering sultans of the fifteenth and sixteenth centuries in Istanbul, Edirne and Bursa; graduates of these institutions would be candidates for the top religious posts in the empire, including the chief judgeships of the Arab provinces. *Madrasa*s in the Arab provinces, however, did not belong to this hierarchy, a fact which some historians have taken to signify that these provincial *madrasa*s were not really part of the Ottoman system and that, consequently, the ulema of the Arab provinces were not truly Ottoman ulema. Yet the fact that they did not participate in the central *madrasa* hierarchy did not necessarily mean that they were not Ottoman ulema, any more than the fact that a modern-day academic is not employed by Oxford or Cambridge means that he or she cannot be one of the top experts in his or her field. There were other, less formal, ways of participating in Ottoman intellectual life, as will be pointed out below.

The great *madrasa*s in the Arab provinces tended to be attached to the ancient mosques which had historically been the centres of Islamic learning in the major provincial cities. Thus, in Damascus, the Umayyad Mosque, and in Cairo, al-Azhar were the sites of prestigious *madrasa*s during the Ottoman era. Most of these *madrasa*s accommodated ulema and students of all four Sunni legal rites. Iraq and Yemen were somewhat special cases. Southern Iraq was home to the great Twelver Shiite centres of education, located in the cities where Ali and Husayn, the Prophet Muhammad's cousin and grandson, were martyred: respectively, Najaf and Karbala. Even under Ottoman rule, these continued to be important sites of Shiite education. Yemen was home to a confessional mosaic in which the northern highlands were dominated by Zaydi Shiites, the central highlands by Ismaili Shiites, and the coastal region by Sunnis of the Shafii legal rite. The hub of Sunni intellectual life under Ottoman rule was the city of Zabid in the south-western coastal region. A number of prominent ulema, both Shafii and Hanafi, came out of Zabid, including Shaykh Murtada al-Zabidi (1732/3–91), a Hanafi from north-western India who sojourned in Zabid for three years before settling in Cairo in 1753; he is famous as the author of a massive commentary on a treatise by the great eleventh-century theologian al-Ghazali, as well as one of the greatest dictionaries in the Arabic language.

Al-Azhar *madrasa* in Cairo was and is one of the world's oldest centres of Islamic learning. It was founded in 969 CE by the Fatimids, the Ismaili Shiite dynasty who founded Cairo in the same year. Until recently, historians believed that al-Azhar was originally the seat of the secretive Ismaili proselytizing mission, which directed the operations of missionaries deep in enemy Seljuk territory; now, however, they doubt that it was anything other than an important Ismaili mosque. Under the Ayyubid dynasty founded by Saladin, which displaced the Fatimids in 1171, it became a Sunni *madrasa*. Even by the time Selim I conquered Egypt, however, al-Azhar was not unquestionably the most

Figure 6.1 Al-Azhar *madrasa* in Cairo. Note the Ottoman minarets in the front. The dome of the Mosque of Mehmed Bey Abu al-Dhahab (1774) is visible at centre rear.
Source: © Gary Otte/Aga Khan Trust for Culture.

important *madrasa* in Egypt or even in Cairo; other establishments, such as the Husayniyya shrine, where the head of Ali's martyred son Husayn is said to be entombed, rivalled it in authority. But by the late seventeenth century, al-Azhar had emerged as Egypt's premier institution of Islamic learning. It was a diverse institution, accommodating all four Sunni legal rites and housing students from all over the Muslim world. By the eighteenth century, Egypt's Hanafi, Shafii and Maliki *mufti*s were all chosen from among al-Azhar's shaykhs. Towards the end of the seventeenth century, furthermore, a new office emerged: that of rector of the *madrasa*, or Shaykh al-Azhar. Historians are still not sure exactly how and why this post materialized, but by the mid-eighteenth century the Shaykh al-Azhar had become Egypt's most important religious authority, which he remains to this day. Of the first several Shaykhs al-Azhar, a number were Maliki, reflecting the intellectual vigour of that legal rite in Egypt at the time, as well as its predominance in Upper Egypt, from which numerous students and ulema migrated to Cairo to study at al-Azhar. In the 1770s, however, Shafiis, who are dominant in Cairo and Lower Egypt, established a monopoly of the post that has lasted until the present day.

Ulema who held such prestigious posts would have had links to ulema in Istanbul, as well as to the sultan and important viziers. Shaykh Hasan al-Jabarti (1699–1774), the father of the chronicler Abd al-Rahman al-Jabarti, was a prominent Hanafi shaykh at al-Azhar, head of the residential college for students from Jabart, now known as Djibouti, the bit of the Horn of Africa directly across the Red Sea from Yemen. He was a multilingual and multi-talented scholar who had impressive connections to the Kazdağlı grandees, to several governors of Egypt, and to several sultans and grand viziers. By his son's account, Sultan Mustafa III (r. 1757–74) used to send him books of Islamic theology and law.

Al-Azhar's students, unlike those at most *madrasa*s, were organized in residential colleges known in Arabic as *riwaq*s. Most *riwaq*s were based on region of origin, rather like Collèges in the pre-1789 French university system. Thus, there was a *riwaq* of students from Upper Egypt, one for students from the Blue Nile, one for students from the province of Damascus, one for Turks, and so on, as well as a special *riwaq* for blind students and a few based on legal rite. In the late eighteenth century, notables of the Kazdağlı household added *riwaq*s for students from India and Indonesia, demonstrating how famous al-Azhar had become, as well as how far the local notables' commercial connections extended.

Mosque preachers

Despite the eminence of the shaykhs who taught in the great *madrasa*s, the most publicly visible representatives of the ulema were arguably the preachers at the Friday mosques. Interestingly, mosque preachers in the Ottoman Empire did not necessarily come from the same backgrounds as judges or *madrasa* professors, although at the highest levels they sometimes did: in the seventeenth century, for example, the preachers of Istanbul's largest and most prestigious mosques, such as Aya Sofya and the Süleymaniye, tended to come from the central hierarchy of *madrasa*s. But this was not necessarily the case, and certainly not in the Arab provinces. Mosque preachers in smaller cities and towns might be the sons of local judges or, for that matter, the sons of previous mosque preachers. Aspiring mosque preachers in the Anatolian provinces were also far more likely than ulema trained in the elite *madrasa*s of Istanbul, Edirne and Bursa to seek training in the Arab provinces. There was, in short, broader geographical circulation at the mosque preacher level – another source of integration between the central lands and the Arab provinces.

A mosque preacher was responsible for delivering the sermon, known in Arabic as the *khutba*, which followed public midday prayers each Friday (for this reason, he was often known as a *khatib*). This sermon usually included the expected pious exhortations; however, it was (and is) also an opportunity for political statements reflecting the agenda of either the ruler or of the preacher himself and the social tendencies he represented. The *khutba* thus gave the mosque preacher a good measure of social influence, and the larger and more heavily attended the mosque was, the more dramatic this influence became.

As to the sermons themselves, styles of delivery varied widely from one Arab province to another. A scholar from seventeenth-century Medina, after hearing a sermon by a Damascene preacher, delivered this verdict: 'In Damascus and Rum [the Ottoman central lands] and adjacent lands, they chant the sermon well and are known for it. But they do not know the meaning of linguistic purity and eloquence.'[2] Clearly, this denizen of the city where the Quran was compiled considered himself an authority on correct Arabic pronunciation and usage. His observation is a reminder of the variety of local cultures and styles in the Arab lands, to say nothing of the Ottoman Empire as a whole.

Sufism

Mysticism in Islam often goes under the name Sufism. This name supposedly derives from the Arabic word for wool, *suf*, because the early Muslim mystics were ascetics who wore rough woollen cloaks. (An alternative theory proposes that the word derives from Arabic *saf*, or 'pure'.) Sufism does not prescribe a particular doctrine, nor is it a separate sect of Islam comparable to Sunnism or Shiism. Rather, it is a mystical tendency within Islam which over the centuries has manifested itself in a number of forms and which can be compatible or incompatible with various forms of Islamic orthodoxy. In these characteristics, it resembles mystical strains in most other major religions.

A mystical tendency is evident almost from the very beginning of Islamic history; the earliest mystics were ascetics who strove individually to obtain a more direct experience of God than they felt could be had simply by following the *sharia*. Often, this meant giving up worldly goods and concentrating their entire attention on God in the hope of ultimately achieving an ecstatic mystical union with him. The most active of these early mystics were concentrated in Iraq and Iran. They might attract small groups of followers who met informally at their houses. Many explored their spirituality in poetry which their followers would memorize and repeat. In the twelfth century, the Andalusian mystic Muhyi al-Din ibn Arabi (1165–1240) took this individual spiritual quest to what some would consider its limit when he articulated the doctrine of 'unity of being', which conceives of all of creation as part of God. Although he was accused of pantheism by some ulema, most Sufis ultimately adopted his principle.

In the same way that the *madrasa* coalesced and became institutionalized in the tenth and eleventh centuries CE, so Sufi brotherhoods, or orders, began to coalesce in the twelfth and thirteenth centuries. Such an order is known in Arabic as a *tariqa*, which literally means a road or path: specifically, the path to union with God. The *tariqa* gave institutional form to the already established practice whereby individual mystical adepts attracted disciples to themselves. Within each order, the core of the mystical experience remained the relationship between the individual and his Sufi guide, who served as intermediary between him and God. In this relationship, the disciple was known in Arabic as the *murid*, literally, the seeker – in this case, the seeker after mystical union with God. The *murid*'s spiritual instructor was known as the *murshid*, literally, 'he who guides'. The guide could also be called by the omnibus title shaykh, which is the term one encounters most frequently in the Arab provinces. (The Persian word *darvish*, commonly anglicized to 'dervish', meanwhile, originally denoted a wandering ascetic who begged for alms.)

The function of the Sufi order, then, was to collect sizeable numbers of *murids* under the guidance of a particular shaykh. Especially talented disciples of a shaykh might be sent out to found, then to direct, branches of the order in different locales. It was by this means that the orders spread. In this fashion, numerous initiates of a single shaykh could become shaykhs of widespread branches of the same order.

At the same time, the order formalized the process whereby a shaykh passed the mystical tradition which he had nurtured down to his successors. As Sufi orders spread, the concept emerged of a mystical chain of transmission from shaykh to shaykh; this chain is known simply by the Arabic word for 'chain', *silsila*. A shaykh drew his mystical legitimacy from his *silsila*. Eventually, the tradition evolved of tracing the *silsila* back not only to the founder of the order but all the way back to the companions of the Prophet, in particular Ali. The Sufis tended to have a certain fondness for Ali, who Shiites in particular believe received esoteric knowledge from the Prophet. This, however, did not necessarily make the Sufis Shiite, although certain orders, such as the one from which the Safavid dynasty emerged, nurtured pronounced Shiite tendencies. Nor did it render them incapable of living in a Sunni society.

The Sufi orders thus moulded the individual mystical quest into the group spiritual quest. A group spiritual exercise developed called the *dhikr* (*zikir* in Turkish), which literally means 'remembrance', in this case remembrance of God. *Dhikr* had begun among the early Sufis as set recitations, often performed privately, designed to concentrate the attention on God and remind the individual of his presence. During the Middle Ages, however, the *dhikr* became an often elaborate ritual which served as the signature of the individual Sufi order. The *dhikr* usually consisted of a series of utterances, notably of the ninety-nine names of God (e.g. *al-rahman*, 'the most merciful', *al-hakim*, 'the all-knowing'), or simply of the Arabic word *huwa* ('he'), often shortened to *hu*. These utterances were often accompanied or followed by ritual movements, known as the *sama* (*sema* in Turkish), or 'listening'. Some of these rituals could last for hours; when coffee from Yemen began to circulate through the Ottoman lands in the sixteenth century, much of its initial popularity was among Sufis struggling to remain alert during their *dhikr*s and *sama*s. The *sama* could have cosmic significance, as in the case of the Mevlevi order, whose ritual casts the shaykh as symbolic axis of the universe, his disciples circling around him like planets or cosmic spheres (a practice that earned them the sobriquet 'whirling dervishes' in the West).

In the early centuries of Islam, Sufis had simply gathered in the house of a spiritual master for prayer and devotions. With the advent of the orders, however, bigger spaces became necessary, as well as permanent spaces specifically for the *sama*. Thus began the tradition of the Sufi lodge, known variously as *khanqah* (Persian), *tekke* (Turkish) and *zawiya* (Arabic). Generally, one of these lodges consisted of a hall in which the *sama* was performed, attached to a small mosque, school and often cells for individual devotions and even ascetic isolation. Some rulers even endowed Sufi lodges, using the mechanism of the *waqf* to fund them. If a Sufi shaykh had amassed sufficient wealth and prestige, he might even endow his own lodge. Quite often, the shaykh would be buried in a tomb attached to his lodge, which then became a centre of pilgrimage not only for his disciples but for masses of Muslims at large. The veneration of the tombs of such Sufi 'saints' is perhaps the most visible legacy of Sufism in the Muslim world. Tombs exist throughout the region which are still the objects of pilgrimage. The tomb of the Mevlevi order's namesake, the thirteenth-century mystic Mevlana Jelal al-Din Rumi, in the central Anatolian city of Konya is a notable example. This pervasive 'saint-worship', as it is characterized by its detractors, was and is one of the pet peeves of some puritanical Muslims.

The rise of Sufi orders did not mean that all Muslim mystics were now affiliated with one *tariqa* or another. Lone wandering ascetics could still be found throughout the Muslim world until well into the twentieth century (one very occasionally encounters them even today); antinomian mystics who could not easily find a niche in normative Muslim society found this lifestyle particularly appealing. In addition, an informal, non-*tariqa* mysticism persists to this day among Iranian Shiites; the late Ayatollah Khomeini is said to have been an adherent. Sufi orders, however, made it possible for ordinary folk to participate regularly in mysticism while continuing to pursue their mundane, day-to-day activities in the wider society. Because of their broad appeal and adaptability to existing social conditions, the Sufi orders spread rapidly and quickly became entrenched.

A number of Sufi orders which originated in Iraq achieved widespread popularity in the Ottoman Arab provinces. Among these were two, the Qadiris and Rifais, which trace their spiritual lineages to, respectively, a Hanbali preacher and a reclusive ascetic in twelfth-century Iraq; during the fourteenth and fifteenth centuries, both orders spread into Syria and, in the case of the Rifais, Egypt. The Rifais are well-known for putting themselves through extreme physical ordeals, such as walking on hot coals and piercing their cheeks with swords, to prove their unwavering faith in God. Meanwhile, the less flamboyant Shadhili order, whose namesake lived in North Africa and Egypt, took root in these regions, giving rise to numerous sub-orders.

Special mention should be made of the Naqshbandis, an order which during the fifteenth century spread from Central Asia into the Caucasus and Anatolia. Reaching India at the height of the Mughal Empire in the late sixteenth century, it was transformed early in the following century by an orthodox Sunni reformist wave, as will be explained in Chapter 10. From India, this reformed Naqshbandi *tariqa* made its way to Yemen and the western Arabian peninsula along pilgrimage and trade routes. An Egyptian Sufi initiated into the order in Yemen brought it back to his homeland in the early eighteenth century. The order came to Syria with one Murad ibn Ali (1640–1720), a scholar from Tamerlane's old capital of Samarkand in today's Uzbekistan who joined the order in India, then ultimately settled in Damascus in the late seventeenth century, founding his own local sub-branch. Patronized by Sultan Mehmed IV (r. 1648–87), Murad also introduced the reformed Naqshbandi order into the imperial capital. Following his death, the Muradi family which he founded dominated the post of Hanafi *mufti* of Damascus, thus giving the Naqshbandi order a noteworthy degree of public prominence.

Khalwatis/Halvetis

An extraordinarily wide-ranging and influential order in the Arab lands was that of the Khalwatis (Halvetis in Turkish). The order's name comes from its members' practice of occasionally retiring to cells (Arabic singular *khalwa*) for periods of isolated prayer and meditation. A forty-day stint in a *khalwa* was required for initiation into the order, and Khalwati lodges commonly featured multiple cells both for this purpose and for voluntary seclusion.

Like the Naqshbandis, the Khalwatis were founded in Central Asia during the Middle Ages. Khalwati shaykhs had settled in Egypt and founded branches of the order, along with prominent lodges, in the last years of the Mamluk sultanate. In Anatolia and the Balkans during the sixteenth and seventeenth centuries, the order gave rise to several different branches. This pattern of branch formation was, in fact, characteristic of the Khalwatis and a key reason for their rapid proliferation: shaykhs founded branches which operated in decentralized fashion, without firm allegiance to a central lodge or shaykh. Another reason for the order's success was that it, like the Mevlevi, Shadhili and Naqshbandi orders, meshed well with mainstream Sunni Islam. It was quite possible to be a shopkeeper and also to belong to the Khalwati order; a shopkeeper might go to the lodge once a week for *dhikr* and *sama* (as people still do today) and perhaps participate in a special celebration on the birthday of the founder of the branch to which he belonged. He might also visit the founder's tomb.

In the same fashion, it was possible to be an important mosque preacher or professor of Islamic law at a *madrasa* and at the same time to be a Khalwati. By the seventeenth century in Istanbul, this was not simply possible; it was the norm. The preachers at the largest and most influential mosques, such as Aya Sofya and the Süleymaniye, were Khalwatis. Several sultans and grand viziers had ties to the order.

During the seventeenth century, this symbiosis between Sufism and Sunni orthodoxy was challenged by a puritanical tendency which has come to be known collectively as the Kadızadeli movement, after its first prominent exponent, the Anatolian mosque preacher Kadızade ('son of the judge') Mehmed Efendi (1582–1635). Drawing its adherents from the class of provincial mosque preachers who resented Khalwati domination of the premier religious posts in the Ottoman central lands, the Kadızadelis espoused a version of Hanafi orthodoxy devoid of all practices that they regarded as innovations to the Prophet Muhammad's custom, chief among them Sufism. By mid-century, its leaders were able to rally urban mobs to burn Sufi lodges. Ascending to the post of sultan's spiritual advisor, the late seventeenth-century Kadızadeli leader Vani Mehmed Efendi in 1683 encouraged the grand vizier Merzifonlu Kara Mustafa Pasha to attack Habsburg Vienna, whose fall he believed would have messianic implications for the Muslim community. When the siege of Vienna degenerated into a disastrous rout for the Ottomans, the grand vizier was executed while Vani was banished in disgrace. This effectively ended the Kadızadelis' political influence. Although the movement had only indirect repercussions in the Arab provinces, it is important to note that it represented the only major threat during the Ottoman period to Sufism's integration with Hanafi orthodoxy. In the course of the following century, the Khalwati order, having weathered this challenge, would attract large numbers of followers among the ulema of the Arab provinces, Egypt in particular.

The ulema in social protest

Quite apart from their religious duties and mystical affiliations, the ulema of Arab provincial cities played a pivotal role in social protest. The conventional wisdom holds that the ulema were mediators between 'the people' and the *ayan* who, by the eighteenth century, dominated the Arab provinces. In actual fact, the network of patronage and influence binding provincial society was more complex, so that the chief ulema of the most noteworthy mosque or *madrasa* in a given provincial capital formed just one link in a chain of influence stretching from the marketplace to the leading grandees.

Nonetheless, in an incident of social protest, a prominent member of the ulema could be the most visible and audible participant. Ordinarily, this sort of protest was quite limited in its aims, seeking redress for a specific instance of injustice rather than attempting to overturn the prevailing social order. In Cairo in 1786, for example, a mamluk of one of the Kazdağlı beys galloped into a poor neighbourhood in the north of the city and ransacked the home of the shaykh of a sub-branch of the Khalwati order. The shaykh's followers, most of them butchers, closed their shops and marched to al-Azhar, where they approached Shaykh Ahmad al-Dardir, Maliki *mufti* and head of the *riwaq* of the Upper Egyptians, who they knew had strong ties to the leading Kazdağlı beys. 'I am with you!' al-Dardir declared, and swore to lead the mob in plundering the homes of the beys if the shaykh's belongings were not returned. This prompted the *shaykh al-balad*, or 'mayor' of Cairo, Ibrahim Bey, to send his lieutenant, along with the commander of the Janissaries, who patrolled Cairo's markets, to negotiate with al-Dardir. On their suggestion, and presumably with the help of the butchers, al-Dardir drew up a list of the stolen possessions, which he presented to Ibrahim Bey. The latter was, however, unable to punish the perpetrator, who was in fact not his own mamluk but the mamluk of his comrade-in-arms Murad Bey.[3]

In this episode, Shaykh al-Dardir did indeed act as a mediator, but only one in a fairly complex network of mediation that also included the butchers of the impoverished neighbourhood, the Janissary commander and Ibrahim Bey. Although al-Dardir, as a symbol of religious authority, would certainly have got Ibrahim Bey's attention, it was arguably the disruption to Cairo's commercial life caused by the market shutdown that forced the bey's hand. Essential to resolution of the crisis, furthermore, was the Janissary commander, who was intimately familiar with the city's markets and neighbourhoods.

In any event, al-Dardir's role was typical of that played by high-ranking members of the ulema in such social disturbances: spokesman for and spearhead of a limited movement to restore social order. There was nothing anti-establishment about such activity; on the contrary, the fact that the high ulema were very much part of the establishment made them effective in relaying public dissatisfaction to the administrative elite. Moreover, they did not instigate these protests but allowed themselves to be co-opted into them. On the other hand, we do have examples of prominent ulema taking the initiative to effect changes within the administrative establishment. Thus, in Damascus in 1746, the Muradi family procured the overthrow of Fethi the *defterdar*, mentioned in Chapter 5, who dared to challenge Azm hegemony, by launching a petition drive that won the signatures of forty-six ulema and fifty-four localized Janissaries and *timar*-holders. Fethi was ultimately executed.

The ulema as intellectuals

Thus far, we have been considering the ulema as a social group. However, they also produced many of the writings in the religious sciences which circulated in the Ottoman Arab provinces. Their written output extended to works that could not really be called religious, such as histories, biographical compendia, poetry, grammars and dictionaries, although these sorts of compositions were also penned by intellectuals who were not members of the ulema.

Where the religious sciences were concerned – that is, Islamic law and theology, Quranic exegesis, and study of the sayings of the Prophet – the accepted wisdom maintains that little of great originality or intellectual value appeared during the period of Ottoman rule in the Arab lands, citing the disproportionately large number of commentaries on 'classical' works produced in the Middle Ages, as opposed to treatises on wholly new topics. This sort of appraisal, however, overlooks the signal importance of commentaries and supercommentaries in Islamic intellectual tradition and in religious writing more generally. As in the case of Christian and Jewish theology, some landmarks of Islamic theological and juridical writing originated as commentaries on earlier works. To give one example from the Ottoman Arab provinces, Abd al-Rauf al-Munawi (1545–1621), considered one of Ottoman Egypt's greatest religious scholars, compiled a widely used explication of the shorter *hadith* collection of his illustrious predecessor Jelal al-Din al-Suyuti (1455–1505). Similarly, the Egyptian historian al-Jabarti's teacher and sometime collaborator, the Indian scholar Murtada al-Zabidi, authored a commentary on the great eleventh-century theologian al-Ghazali's *Revitalization of the Religious Sciences*. Even al-Zabidi's monumental Arabic dictionary, entitled *Taj al-arus* (*The Bride's Crown*), originated in a commentary on a much shorter fourteenth-century dictionary.

In addition, the range of scholars, mystics, government officials and soldiers coming to the Arab provinces from Istanbul, going from one province to another, and going from the Arab provinces to Istanbul dramatically increased the circulation of hand-written and lithographed manuscripts of religious works, as well as all other kinds of literature. Ottoman officials posted to the Arab provinces brought their personal libraries with them; in the case of former harem eunuchs exiled to Egypt, these libraries became permanent additions to the province and had a direct impact on theological and legal instruction. Because books could be endowed as pious foundations, furthermore, the libraries of Ottoman officials, as well as provincial grandees, could benefit ulema and their students anywhere in the empire, as in the case of the books endowed by the Chief Harem Eunuch el-Hajj Beshir Agha, noted in the preceding chapter. Provincial notables, such as Mehmed Bey Abu al-Dhahab of Egypt and Syria's Azm governors, likewise endowed libraries to the *madrasa*s they commissioned.

Chronicles and regional cross-fertilization

Despite what appears to have been a flourishing book culture, much has been written about the stagnation of Arab intellectual life during the Ottoman period. This characterization has a nationalist cast, for it implies that the production of Arabophone ulema and other intellectuals in the Arab provinces was inherently separate from that of their counterparts, Arabophone or otherwise, in other parts of the Ottoman Empire. A consideration of a single category of intellectual output, historical chronicles, which were often composed by ulema, demonstrates the shortcomings of such an assumption. With the conquest of the Mamluk sultanate, to be sure, the centre for the production of lavishly illustrated annalistic histories for presentation to the sultan shifted to Istanbul;

nonetheless, writers, whether ulema or otherwise, in the Arab provinces continued the chronicling traditions of the pre-Ottoman era while modifying them and taking them in new directions.

As might be expected, the period of conquest and incorporation during the sixteenth century constrained intellectual production to a great degree. Yet the conquest could also inspire literary creativity, as witness the spate of *Selimname*s, panegyric accounts of Sultan Selim I's life and military exploits, giving prominence, naturally, to his conquest of Syria and Egypt. Specimens of this genre were produced both in the imperial capital and in Cairo. Although most were composed in Ottoman Turkish, a number were written in Arabic, including the seminal account of Ahmad ibn Zunbul (d. 1553), a Cairene chronicler about whom little is known beyond the fact that he witnessed the Ottoman conquest of his city. Ibn Zunbul's short, highly mythologized account of 'Selim's struggle with the Circassians' contains more than simply praise of the Ottoman sultan, however, for the author is sympathetic towards the defeated Mamluks and portrays the last sultan, Tumanbay, as something of a martyr. In fact, Ibn Zunbul's work did much to establish the paradigmatic pro-Mamluk account of the conquest, whereby the Ottomans violated the laws of chivalry by employing cannon and guns. In this context, Selim emerges, perhaps rather ironically under the circumstances, as the hero who welcomes defeated but repentant Mamluks into the Ottoman administration, thus saving Circassian chivalry. The chronicle is written in a simple, colloquial Arabic and contains lengthy stretches of imagined dialogue, suggesting that it was sometimes recited, and perhaps even performed, aloud. It was translated into Turkish by various slightly later authors who used it as the basis for their own works. The *Selimname* genre, in other words, provides an example of cross-fertilization between central and provincial literary compositions, and between works in Turkish and in Arabic.

A similar process appears to have occurred in succeeding generations. Provincial chroniclers writing in Arabic adopted the central Ottoman system of organizing political annals according to the tenures of rulers: in their case, Ottoman governors, although the sultans' reigns are also tracked in such chronicles. However, they retained the medieval practice, visible as early as the history of the Abbasid-era chronicler al-Tabari (*c*.838–923 CE), of listing the deaths of notable political and religious figures at the end of each Muslim year. Locally produced chronicles of the Arab provinces increased in the seventeenth century, with the likes of Muhammad ibn Abi al-Surur (*c*.1596–1676) in Egypt and Muhammad Amin al-Muhibbi (1651–99) in Damascus. In Yemen, an ancient Zaydi chronicling tradition competed with a more 'conventional' tradition maintained by Shafii and Hanafi ulema and other intellectuals in the coastal regions. While the Zaydi tradition continued virtually unbroken through the Ottoman period and beyond, the Sunni tradition would seem to have come to a temporary halt with the prolific Zabidi chronicler Abd al-Rahman ibn al-Dayba (d. c.1537) before resuming in the early seventeenth century with the likes of Abd al-Qadir al-Aydarus (1570–1627), a descendant of the Prophet from the southern Hadramawt region, and Shams al-Din Muhammad al-Mawza'i (flourished 1618–22), a resident of the south-western city of Taizz, inland from Mocha. Al-Aydarus composed a history of his own time, al-Mawza'i a description of the Ottoman conquest of Yemen in 1538.

These chronicles were by no means divorced from events in other provinces or in Istanbul, although the degrees to which they engaged with this broader Ottoman context varied. The Meccan judge Qutb al-Din Muhammad al-Nahrawali's (1511–82) sprawling chronicle of Yemen, the Holy Cities and the Red Sea region is virtually unique in its trans-provincial purview; in an example of bilingual cross-fertilization similar to that provided by the circulation of Ibn Zunbul's chronicle, it was translated into Ottoman Turkish and continued by an Anatolian military commander posted to Yemen during the last vain Ottoman attempt to hold the province in the early 1600s. Meanwhile, beginning in the late sixteenth century, a small group of provincial administrators started to produce chronicles of their respective provinces, written in Ottoman Turkish with fairly heavy admixtures of Arabic but also incorporating imperial decrees and similar documents from Istanbul.

At the same time, ulema and other literati in the Ottoman capital were producing biographical dictionaries, usually of members of a certain profession, such as ulema and poets. These were undoubtedly influenced by the great Mamluk-era prototypes, as were the provincial chronicles that summarized the lives of recently deceased prominent personages at the end of each year. The genres of annalistic chronicle and biographical dictionary fused and culminated in Abd al-Rahman al-Jabarti's chronicle of Egypt, which covers the period from the Muslim year 1100 (1688) to 1236 (1821), roughly four years before the author's death. Contrary to long-held opinion, however, al-Jabarti did not single-handedly resurrect the Mamluk historiographical tradition. His narrative owes far more than he himself admits to earlier eighteenth-century annals while his biographies-cum-obituaries take their place beside a spate of eighteenth-century biographical dictionaries composed in the provincial and imperial capitals. In fact, the historian had begun collecting biographies in support of a vast interprovincial biographical project conceived by Khalil al-Muradi, the chief *mufti* of Damascus, in collaboration with Murtada al-Zabidi. By some twist of fate, both his collaborators died in the plague year of 1791, leaving al-Jabarti with al-Zabidi's unfinished collection of biographies until he saw the opportunity to incorporate them into his history decades later. Al-Muradi, before his death, had compiled the material he had collected into a biographical dictionary of ulema and notables, primarily of Syria, during the twelfth Muslim century, roughly equivalent to the eighteenth century CE.

Demographic flux and literary culture

In general, the circulation of ulema, bureaucrats, Sufis, soldiers and merchants through the Ottoman Arab domains yielded compositions which reflected the cultural and linguistic encounters and exchanges among the various regions of the Ottoman realm. The sixteenth-century bureaucrat and 'decline writer' Mustafa Ali's 1599 *Description of Cairo* falls into this category, even though, like most of his works, it is driven by an agenda related to his professional rivalries in Istanbul. Dictionaries might also fit this category; some notable ones were, not coincidentally, written by scholars with roots in distant places, as in the case of a dictionary of colloquial Egyptian Arabic by Yusuf al-Maghribi (d. 1610), whose sobriquet indicates North African descent, or even the Indian expatriate al-Zabidi's great *Taj al-arus*. The seventeenth-century Syrian historian al-Muhibbi, meanwhile, composed a dictionary of non-Arabic words that had entered spoken Arabic, indicating an awareness of the linguistic impact of the Ottoman era's demographic fluidity. The seventeenth-century Ottoman courtier Evliya Chelebi's (*c*.1611–82) *Book of Travels* deserves special mention in this connection since it was composed during the final decade or so of the author's life, which he spent in Cairo. This work shows an often astonishing sensitivity to the cultural differences of the myriad peoples populating the Ottoman domains, and even contains examples of their languages and popular legends. Why the author chose to settle in Cairo, however, is far from clear, as is the place he occupied in Cairene society. Indeed, his sojourn in the city, including the circumstances in which he compiled his travel account and its early audiences, is a subject ripe for study.

Conclusion

In summary, religious and intellectual life in the Ottoman Arab provinces encompassed a vast array of offices, movements and tendencies, and absorbed people from a wide variety of classes, regions, occupations and educational levels. The effect of religious figures, to say nothing of the broader category of intellectuals, on society was likewise wildly varied, ranging from the barely perceptible transmission of ideas among the intellectual elite to legal rulings affecting a broad cross-section of society to public activism that could close down a major urban bazaar. Almost every member of Ottoman provincial society participated in a religious institution or group in some fashion at some point in his or her life, and usually with some degree of regularity. Thus, a consideration of religious institutions and their exponents is a fitting preliminary to a broader examination of social groups in the Ottoman Arab provinces, which will occupy the next three chapters.

Notes

1. Quoted in Dror Ze'evi, *An Ottoman Century: The District of Jerusalem in the 1600s* (Albany, NY, 1996), p. 155.
2. Ibrahim al-Khiyari, quoted in Karl K. Barbir, *Ottoman Rule in Damascus, 1723–1783* (Princeton, NJ, 1980), p. 77.
3. Abd al-Rahman al-Jabarti, *Abd al-Rahman al-Jabarti's History of Egypt*, eds Thomas Philipp and Moshe Perlmann, 4 vols in 2 (Stuttgart, 1994), II, p. 174 (trans. Gerard Salinger).

chapter seven

URBAN LIFE AND TRADE

Arab provincial cities

Four or five decades ago, 'The Islamic City' was a convenient and widely used label that owed its origin to the fact that scholars of the Middle East noticed certain structures and functions common to cities that had historically belonged to Islamic polities. As more recent scholarship has pointed out, however, it is erroneous to believe that Islam itself can explain the appearance and workings of these cities. The forms and functions of these cities were heavily influenced by the circumstances of their founding, their locations, climatic factors and, of course, the precedents set by the cities of earlier polities.

Location

Many of the great Arab cities, such as Cairo, Damascus, Aleppo, Baghdad and Mosul, are situated inland. Even Basra in southern Iraq is located slightly inland, on the edge of what was until the early 1990s a system of marshes (currently taking the first steps towards regeneration). Such a location has historically given these cities a natural defence against enemy attack: they are not vulnerable from the sea, and their hinterlands make them relatively invulnerable by land. These cities, by and large, do not follow the rationale behind numerous Greco-Roman cities and certain European capitals, which were commercial entrepôts located on the seacoast. This is certainly not to say that Islamic governments cared nothing for trade, for all of the cities listed above were situated to take advantage of overland and, in the case of Cairo and the Iraqi cities, riverain commercial routes. Still, where the question of location was concerned, commerce was not always the first priority.

Layout

The military impetus behind certain of these cities carried over to their layouts. Many cities were centred on a military fortress, or citadel, where the city's main body of troops was garrisoned and where the city's military governor held council. The citadel became a widespread phenomenon after the eleventh century CE, when Abbasid central control had given way to rival autonomous principalities, when nomadic Bedouin and Turcoman tribesmen threatened much settled life, and when Crusaders made their first appearance on the scene. Thus, Salah al-Din (Saladin), the Kurdish general who displaced the Fatimids, built Cairo's imposing citadel in the late twelfth century. His brother likewise rebuilt the citadel of Damascus, originally constructed by the Seljuks, while his son added substantially to Aleppo's citadel, founded under a tenth-century Arab Shiite dynasty.

Strong walls were also critical to a city's defence. Space nearest to the walls or just outside was reserved for a city's dirtiest and most malodourous industries, above all tanning and dyeing. The area outside the walls was also a popular site for livestock markets; sheep markets exist outside the old city walls of Jerusalem and Sanaa to this very day, while in Cairo one may be found at the entrance to the southern quarter of Fustat, in Ottoman times a separate town.

It would be natural to assume that the citadel or the ruler's palace would stand at the centre of a city. This was less and less frequently the case by the Middle Ages, however, as the great Arab cities expanded beyond the cores established by the original Muslim conquerors or founders. A city's layout likewise varied according to the city's political and economic status – the imperial capital, a provincial capital, a regional market town – and how the city evolved from one dynasty to another, as well as the vagaries of local topography. In 762 CE, for example, when Baghdad was founded as the new capital of the Abbasid caliphate, the caliph's palace was erected at the centre of the original round city. By the time the Mongols invaded in 1258, many other palaces had been built outside the round city and along the western bank of the Tigris River while the original caliphal palace and other early structures had fallen into decay or disappeared entirely. After the Mongol invasion, Baghdad was never again an imperial capital; under the Ottomans, the city lacked major military structures, despite its strategic location near the Iranian front. In Cairo, meanwhile, Saladin built the citadel south-east of the old Fatimid city, perhaps to distance himself from the seat of Fatimid power but also, no doubt, so as to take advantage of the elevation offered by the Muqattam Hills. In both Aleppo and Damascus, by contrast, the medieval citadel stood in the city centre, in the case of Aleppo on an ancient mound around which the city had taken shape.

Mosques

Even more critical to urban infrastructure were mosques and markets, which were often located in close proximity to one another. The scholarship of half a century ago attributed this feature to what it regarded as Islam's inherently urban and commercial character: the Prophet Muhammad, after all, lived in an urban commercial hub and was himself a caravan trader. While cities have certainly played a key role in Islam's development, a less essentialist explanation would suggest that a mosque provides the sort of central gathering place that also supports a market. Certainly, the phenomenon of a place of worship next to or near a market is common to a wide range of societies adhering to various religions. In the major Arab cities, a central mosque and marketplace often served (and still serve) as a hub of urban life. In late Mamluk and Ottoman Cairo, al-Azhar mosque-*madrasa* and the adjacent market known as Khan al-Khalili, commissioned by the Mamluk emir Cherkes ('Circassian') Khalil in 1382, provided such a hub. In Damascus, the ancient Umayyad Mosque stood near a number of Ottoman-era markets, including two built by the Azms. It was much the same in Aleppo, Baghdad, Basra and Mosul.

The manner in which these mosques were funded contributed to the mosque–market nexus. During the Middle Ages and under the Ottomans also, the most common means of funding the construction and maintenance of mosques, as well as *madrasa*s, soup kitchens, hospitals and other public and charitable works, was the pious endowment known in Arabic as *waqf*. If an Ottoman governor or a provincial grandee wished to build a mosque, he had to provide for the mosque's maintenance, as well as all the costs the mosque's operation would incur: the salaries of the imam who led daily prayers and the *khatib* who preached the Friday sermon, the muezzin who called the faithful to prayer, the workers who swept the floors, and so on. In much the same process as that described in Chapter 6 for a *madrasa*, he would therefore go to a *qadi*'s court to draw up a deed stipulating that the rents from specified shops or lands would go towards the upkeep of this mosque. This process tended to result in a sort of complex consisting of the mosque or other charitable institution and the market whose rents were endowed to it. The creation of *waqf*s endowed to large, centrally located mosques was, in fact, one key way in which cities developed and grew during the Ottoman period.

Markets

The mention of markets in Arab cities often conjures up images of crowded, colourful bazaars. Open-air bazaars are often called *suq* in Arabic, a term that can also apply to a street along which practitioners of a particular craft happen to concentrate. Most major Arab cities have or had a *Suq al-Nahhasin*, or 'street of the coppersmiths', since copper pots and utensils were indispensable for cooking and washing, as well as for more arcane tasks such as mixing medicines.

In contrast, the name *khan* (or *han*, to use the Turkish rendition) applies to elaborate, roofed structures which, as early as the eighth century, began to be designed specifically for long-distance merchants. These were typically two-storey buildings which, on the ground floor, provided storage facilities for merchandise and stables or hitching posts for pack animals; upstairs were rooms where the merchants could stay. This, in fact, is precisely what Cairo's Khan al-Khalili market is. Most western readers probably know these structures best by the name 'caravanserai' because they served as halting places for caravans, often in-between major towns. The Seljuks commissioned caravanserais on lonely stretches of road throughout Iran and central Anatolia. During the Ottoman era, however, *khan*s were commonly found in major cities, where they became centres for the purchase and sale of particular items of long-distance trade, notably textiles and coffee. In Istanbul and other cities in Anatolia, in fact, such a covered market was often called a *bedestan*, a contraction of the Persian *bezzaz-istan*, literally, 'place of the cloth'. Typical of this sort of urban caravanserai in the Arab provincial capitals are the large *khan*s endowed by the Azms in Damascus, notably the Asad (Esad) Pasha Khan, founded in 1752, whose black-and-white striped masonry, the Azm 'trade-mark' (see Chapter 5), makes it a particularly striking specimen.

In Egypt, the commodity-specific urban caravanserai was known as a *wakala* (or *wikala* in Egyptian pronunciation), the Arabic word for 'agency', as in commercial agency. As early as the Fatimid era, *wakala*s became widespread in Cairo and Alexandria, as well as in subprovincial trading towns. The fact that these structures were also called, in the singular, *qaysariyya* (from *qaysar*, the Arabicization of 'Caesar') indicates that they may even have existed when Egypt was part of the Roman Empire.

Merchants often used the *wakala* as a virtual office; they could receive mail there, sell their goods out of storage facilities on the ground floor, even negotiate deals. *Wakala*s could be part of the property endowed to the *waqf* of a mosque; the merchants' shops provided the revenues for the mosque's upkeep. At the same time, less well-to-do merchants and even the artisanal class might live in what amounted to tenements

Figure 7.1 The Asad (Esad) Pasha Khan in Damascus (1752). The *khan* was restored in the 1980s and today is an exhibition space. Here, a photography exhibit is on display.
Source: Author's photo

above or near the *wakala*. Such a 'tenement' was known as a *rab'*, from the Arabic verb for 'to stay or live', and derived from urban housing in the Mediterranean provinces of the Roman Empire. It was a sort of apartment house of two or three storeys where multiple families lived, sharing stairs, a well and a latrine. A *rab'* could either stand alone or occupy the top two or three floors of a *wakala*. Merchants and artisans whose shops were located in the *wakala* in question found it convenient to resort to this type of housing. During the Ottoman period, a number of governors of Egypt endowed *wakala*s, as did exiled harem eunuchs. Endowment deeds often earmarked these *wakala*s for specific commodities, such as flax, silk or coffee.

Streets, neighbourhoods and houses

One of the first things to strike the western traveller about the older quarters of Arab cities is the tangled street network, apart from a few major axes. Instead of the broad streets laid out according to a grid that characterize some western European and North American cities – and which, not coincidentally, characterized Roman cities – one finds a rabbit warren of exceedingly narrow streets that seem to follow the lie of the land. More than one scholar of the Middle East has regarded the twisted street network as a metaphor for the 'Oriental mind': characterized by an intricate and tortuous thought process, not lucid and rational like the western mind. There are, however, rational explanations for this street network, notably the ever-present need for security, the very principle on which many Islamic cities were founded. The stranger, the thief or the brigand would be discouraged by these tortuous streets from entering an unfamiliar quarter. Moreover, such narrow, winding streets did not seem so very illogical in a society which, by and large, had given up wheeled vehicles. Richard Bulliet, in his engaging study *The Camel and the Wheel*, demonstrates that the camel, used as a pack animal, largely replaced the wheel as a means of transport in the Middle East outside Anatolia and North Africa, beginning with the decline of the Roman Empire and continuing until the reintroduction of the wheel with the European intrusions of the nineteenth century.[1]

The obsession with security also lay behind the layout of residential quarters, which were known in Arabic as *harat* (singular *hara*) or *mahallat* (singular *mahalla*). A typical quarter consisted of a network of narrow streets, often no more than alleyways, lined with houses and often converging on a cul-de-sac. Often the quarter was gated off at night to ensure that only those who lived there could get in. Who lived in a given quarter was not dictated by any higher authority. Often merchants dominated the neighbourhood adjacent to the market or *wakala* where their shops were located. Sometimes a quarter was dominated by members of a certain ethnicity or religion. In certain instances, Christians or Jews tended to cluster together in the vicinity either of the markets they frequented or of a church or synagogue. Muslim court records and *waqf* documents, however, reveal that Muslims not infrequently lived next to Christians and Jews, and that the rich frequently lived next to the poor or less well-off.

Leadership of the quarter often rested with a quarter shaykh, ordinarily a long-term male resident who was relatively secure financially, well-known to his neighbours, and of good character. This sort of grass-roots leadership was critical to the functioning of Arab provincial cities, indeed of Ottoman cities generally, since there was no municipal government in the modern sense. To be sure, municipalities had existed in Egypt and Syria under the Roman Empire, but they had disintegrated during the Byzantine period, while in Iraq they may never have been established before the nineteenth century. In the absence of a mayor, judges and deputy judges played a major role in overseeing the daily functioning of civic institutions. In addition, most larger cities had a chief of police, known as *wali* or *subashi*, a military office often filled by localized Janissaries; this official was responsible for maintaining public order. The quarter shaykh was informally recognized by the residents of his neighbourhood as the party who represented them to these authorities.

In the quarters, residential houses clustered tightly together, following the dictates of a need for security and a relative lack, in most regions, of building materials such as wood. Generally, two houses shared a common wall. Yet despite this extreme proximity – or perhaps because of it – privacy was highly valued. Ordinarily, what faced the person who approached a house from the street was nothing but a blank wall of whitewashed stone or brick. The visitor turned a corner and found himself facing an entryway. Inside might be a courtyard.

In fact, the so-called courtyard house has become a virtual stereotype, much like the 'Islamic city'. In this type of house, rooms are arranged around a central courtyard open to the air. Reception rooms and private chambers, including the harem where the women stayed, were located on the house's upper floor while the ground floor was reserved for storerooms and kitchens. This, then, was the typical Islamic house, yet, as André Raymond has pointed out, such houses are more properly referred to as Mediterranean houses, for Roman villas followed this general pattern, which was retained in Christian Spain. Moreover, non-Mediterranean Islamic regions displayed considerable variation in house type. In Yemen, for a notable example, the typical house was a very distinctive sort of high-rise apartment of mud brick. In Anatolia and northern Syria, where the relatively cold climate made a courtyard inadvisable, an entirely enclosed house was often built, the bottom floor of insulating stone, the upper floor of wood or wood interspersed with masonry. Quite apart from the dictates of climate, the one-family courtyard house was a cultural ideal that much of society simply could not afford. Often, a large extended family would be obliged to cram into a single courtyard house, or several unrelated families would have to share a courtyard, where there might be a common well and latrine. In such cases, a harem, a separate suite of rooms serving as quarters and social space for the women, was unfeasible.

Urban change in the Ottoman era

Arab cities changed under Ottoman rule. Most obviously, they grew, both in terms of population and in terms of built space. André

Raymond was one of the first scholars to point this out, in the process exploding the tenacious myth that, under Ottoman rule, urban life stagnated and population declined. Physical remains point to increasing construction during the Ottoman period outside the old medieval walls of Cairo, Damascus, Aleppo, Mosul, Baghdad, Basra, Tunis and Algiers. Meanwhile, chronicles and Muslim court records document the relocation of aesthetically distasteful industries, above all tanneries, as population spread beyond the old walls. By the same token, mosques and cemeteries sprang up where none had existed before, and public baths increased in number, indicating larger concentrations of people in a broader expanse of territory. Court records, in addition, note property purchases and disputes in new neighbourhoods, or certain populations – elites, non-Muslims, merchants – living in neighbourhoods where they were formerly unrepresented, indicating demographic shifts. Drawing on Raymond's findings, we may estimate that Arab cities grew by an average of about fifty per cent between the early sixteenth century and the mid-eighteenth century. Thus, Cairo grew from a population of well under 200,000 souls at the time of the Ottoman conquest to a peak of over 300,000 by the end of the seventeenth century, before a series of climatic crises, plagues and food shortages, combined with elite infighting, in the late eighteenth century caused the population to drop.

Another persistent myth or, more properly, interpretation of urban realities in the Ottoman Arab provinces is that the Ottomans left no appreciable architectural imprint on the provincial capitals; rather, their chief aim was to preserve the pre-Ottoman, and above all Mamluk, heritage. Certainly, the Ottomans pursued a somewhat different agenda in the Arab provinces from that which prevailed in the Ottoman Balkans. The Arab provincial capitals, after all, had been the premier cities of great Muslim empires – in some cases, as in that of Cairo, the imperial capitals. Ottoman constructions in such cities show a clear desire to pay due respect to the structures of preceding Sunni Muslim regimes and even to improve upon them by, for example, attaching new *waqf*s to existing Mamluk *waqf*s. By the same token, Ottoman governors and provincial grandees repaired, renovated and, in some cases, expanded pre-Ottoman structures and added large numbers of distinctive, pencil-like Ottoman minarets to existing mosques. Thus, the Umayyad Mosque in Damascus boasts one distinctly Ottoman minaret, artfully perched atop a thirteenth-century base, while al-Azhar in Cairo features an unmistakably Ottoman-style addition to the main gate, courtesy of the eighteenth-century grandee Abdurrahman Kethüda al-Kazdağlı. Mosques, *madrasa*s and other buildings commissioned by Ottoman governors and provincial grandees might combine pre-Ottoman local styles with classic Ottoman elements or might stress one style over the other, as observed in Chapter 5.

Nevertheless, the Ottoman approach to pre-existing symbolic architecture in the Arab provinces shared certain features with the approach pursued in the Balkans and Anatolia. In Anatolia, to be sure, the Ottomans did not allow the palaces of the pre-existing Turkish emirates to survive. But in Constantinople and the Balkans, there was a clear pattern of preserving Byzantine (and, in southern Greece and Cyprus, Venetian and Lusignan) structures, churches above all, and Ottomanizing them through redecorating and adding structures. Naturally, turning a Byzantine church into a mosque has a very different kind of public resonance from adding Ottoman touches to a Mamluk *madrasa*. Architecturally, however, the effect is similar: to mark the urban landscape as Ottoman.

At the same time, the conquest of territories that were home to sites sacred to Muslims gave the Ottomans opportunities to display their piety architecturally through renovations and additions to existing Islamic structures. Under Süleyman I, as noted in Chapter 5, the exterior of Jerusalem's Dome of the Rock, built under the Umayyads in the late seventh century CE, was transformed with the application of distinctively Ottoman tiles from the famous western Anatolian tile centre of Iznik (the Byzantine Nicaea). In Baghdad, Süleyman replaced the dome over the tomb of Abu Hanifa (699–767), the inspiration for the Hanafi legal rite to which the Ottomans adhered, after the structure had been demolished by the Safavid empire-builder Shah Ismail. He also oversaw the restoration of the Prophet Muhammad's mosque and tomb complex in Medina, adding an Ottoman-style minaret and a new niche (*mihrab*) indicating the direction of Mecca while replacing the green dome over the Prophet's tomb, originally added by the Mamluk sultan Qaytbay (r. 1468–96). In Mecca, the master architect Sinan renovated the prayer hall of the Great Mosque in 1571 at the behest of Süleyman's son Selim II (r. 1566–74). Sixty years later, after floods ravaged Mecca, Sultan Murad IV (r. 1623–40) had the Great Mosque and the Kaba substantially rebuilt in a massive project overseen by the Egyptian pilgrimage commander. Murad's reconquest of Baghdad from the Safavids in 1638 inspired another major refurbishment of Abu Hanifa's tomb, which had been destroyed during Shah Abbas' occupation of the city. These renovation projects allowed the Ottoman dynasty to emphasize their custodianship of sites associated with the Prophet, as well as the Sunni Hanafi religious identity of the ruling house, while at the same time marking these sites as Ottoman through the judicious use of minarets and tile decor.

This policy of renovation-cum-Ottomanization extended even to the Ottoman treatment of Iraq's Shiite shrines. The two shrines most sacred to Shiites, the mausoleum of Ali ibn Abi Talib in Najaf and that of his son Husayn in Karbala, date from the late tenth century, when the Shiite Buyid emirs, who had invaded Iraq from northern Iran a few decades earlier, administered the region, ostensibly in the name of the Abbasid caliph. Succeeding dynasties restored the structures and made improvements to their surroundings. The shrines were especially important to the Safavids, who vigorously promoted Twelver Shiism in their territories. After conquering southern Iraq from the Akkoyunlu Turcomans, Shah Ismail made a pilgrimage to both sites and renovated Husayn's tomb. During the period between 1623 and 1638, when he had managed to retake Baghdad and southern Iraq from the Ottomans, Shah Abbas I covered the exterior of the dome over Husayn's mausoleum with blue tiles from Kashgar in western China (the domes of the two mausolea were not covered with gold until the mid- to late eighteenth century, after the Safavid collapse). Given the shrines' close association with Shiism, and more particularly with the Safavid enemy, we might expect the Ottomans to have treated them harshly once Najaf and Karbala fell under or returned to their jurisdiction. Yet the Ottomans, as Sunnis, revered Ali and Husayn, even if they did not regard them as rightful successors to Muhammad as leaders of the Muslim community. They would therefore never have razed or damaged the shrines. On the contrary, Süleyman I visited both mausolea following his conquest of central and southern Iraq from the Safavids in 1534, restoring the irrigation canal and gardens near Husayn's tomb. Murad III (r. 1574–95) further restored Husayn's tomb and added a minaret to the adjacent mosque. The only 'retributive' action of which the Ottomans could be accused against either of the shrines occurred in 1638, when Murad IV, having just regained central and southern Iraq from the Safavids, had the elaborately tiled dome covering Husayn's tomb whitewashed. Even this, however, was at most an anti-Safavid move rather than an act of disrespect towards Husayn. Indeed, Murad and those around him, steeped in the conservative religiosity of the seventeenth-century Ottoman Empire, may have felt that an austere white dome accorded better with the reverence due a member of the Prophet Muhammad's family.

Government regulation of markets

In the marketplace, as elsewhere, the Ottoman administration in the Arab provinces attempted to maintain some form of order and control. In the absence of municipalities, market regulation had to be carried out through the local or neighbourhood Muslim law court, through the soldiery stationed in any given town, and through the very merchants and craftsmen who sold their wares in the market.

The *muhtasib*

A town's markets were overseen by a market regulator known as the *muhtasib*, an Arabic word derived from the verb for 'to calculate'. His duty was known as *ihtisab*, which today means 'computation' or 'calculation', or *hisba*, which today signifies an arithmetical problem. Yet he was far more than an accountant or records-keeper. His chief task was to ensure that buying, selling and general behaviour in the marketplace accorded with the *sharia*. In order to accomplish this goal, he made a daily tour of inspection through the market, accompanied by an armed escort. The Quran, like the Hebrew Bible, repeatedly inveighs against selling at false weight: selling the equivalent of a half-kilogram of dates, for example, at the price of a full kilogram by falsifying the small, solid metal weights that merchants weighed against goods in a double-panned scale. The *muhtasib* took this injunction seriously, frequently carrying out spot checks of the metal weights. Likewise, the Quran forbids usury, and the *muhtasib* was on the lookout for anyone taking interest, although there were legal subterfuges, such as fictive sales, by which merchants could circumvent this prohibition. Offenders were often subject to summary justice meted out by the *muhtasib* himself, and their punishments could be dire. The Egyptian chronicler al-Jabarti reports merchants being beaten to death or nailed to the doors of their shops by their earlobes for charging exorbitant prices. They might also be bastinadoed, that is, beaten on the soles of their feet with a cane or short whip. In such cases, the *muhtasib* resorted to public humiliation so as to set an example for other merchants. Ultimately, however, the *muhtasib* was responsible to the *qadi*; he might therefore bring offenders before the *qadi* for punishment or ask the *qadi* to approve of such summary punishments as nailing by the ears.

In any case, the *muhtasib*'s jurisdiction was far from arbitrary. The standards and prohibitions he was to enforce were laid out in a book commonly known today as an *ihtisab* manual. In addition to rigorous and detailed standards of quality control for goods bought and sold in the market, and rules of proper business practice, such a manual included guidelines on public morality, often interspersed among the more mundane regulations. Thus, an *ihtisab* manual from medieval Seville reads, 'If someone assays gold or silver coins for a person, and later it emerges that there is base metal in them, the assayer must make good, for he deceived and betrayed the owner of the coins, who placed his trust in him . . . ,' and immediately afterwards, 'Women should not sit by the river bank in the summer if men appear there.'[2] This might seem a strange juxtaposition until one considers that the marketplace is, above all, a public arena. In this setting, both cheating a customer and prostitution constitute public immorality and thus a violation of the *sharia*. Preventing both was part of the *muhtasib*'s general duty of ensuring that all activity in the public market fell within the bounds of Islamic law.

During the Ottoman period, the duties of *muhtasib* were sometimes assumed by another official, typically a local grandee. In Cairo, the commander (*agha*) of the local Janissary regiment had taken over the *muhtasib*'s functions by the late seventeenth century. In Aleppo, the *muhtasib*'s authority appears to have been displaced by that of the craft guild leadership in combination with the chief judge. These shifts occurred as local *ayan* became the most influential public forces in the Arab provincial cities.

Price and import controls

A *hadith*, or saying attributed to the Prophet Muhammad, states that 'it is God who fixes prices'. Although this would seem to imply that human beings should not undertake to regulate prices themselves, the advice was not always heeded by the Ottoman central authority. The central government not infrequently resorted to a package of price controls known collectively by the Persian word *narh*. Lists of set prices for essential commodities such as olive oil, grain, cheese, sugar, flax and silk fibres, and animal skins were registered in Muslim law courts throughout the empire so that local *qadis* could impose them. Merchants who sold their goods at prices higher than those specified by the *narh* risked the full wrath of the *muhtasib* or his equivalent.

Some medieval Islamic polities, most notably the later Mamluk sultanate, had attempted to impose government monopolies on certain commodities, which they then forced merchant and craftsman conglomerates to purchase in a process known as the *tarh*. The Ottoman government did not resort to such a policy, but provincial authorities occasionally did, often to rid themselves of staples such as grain and livestock which they had hoarded in an effort to drive up prices. Egypt's beys were notorious for this sort of behaviour towards the end of the eighteenth century, and several governors of Aleppo alternately forced their leftovers on the city's butchers and millers and obliged them to supply the governor's household at below-market prices.

Where foreign trade was concerned, the Ottomans generally welcomed imports as increasing the volume of goods available to the empire's subjects. Yet even in the absence of formal import quotas, non-Ottoman merchants were obliged to pay customs duties in order to bring their merchandise into Ottoman territory while non-Muslim foreign merchants were charged a higher rate than their Muslim counterparts. Indeed, the Capitulations, largely commercial agreements that the Ottomans signed with various European states, beginning with Genoa in the fourteenth century but most famously with France in the sixteenth century, were designed in the first instance to relieve European merchants of the burden of excessive customs dues.

On the other hand, the Ottoman central authority did curb exports of certain goods from the empire. It was particularly eager to eliminate exports of critical commodities such as grain and animal skins to enemy powers such as the Habsburgs in time of war. Nonetheless, sultanic orders to the provinces demanding that such exports cease indicate that local notables often ignored these bans. During wartime, as well, the central authority sought to keep gold and silver specie, necessary for paying standing infantry troops and mercenaries, within the empire and out of its enemies' hands. This would appear to have been a difficult proposition if the Ottomans were paying cash for foreign goods, as they often did, while limiting exports. Until the eighteenth century, nevertheless, exports of non-essential goods, such as coffee, to Europe yielded a net inflow of bullion into the empire.

The overall rationale behind all these controls was to keep goods within the empire so that all provinces of the empire would be well provisioned and all merchants would produce and sell optimal volumes of goods. This strategy arguably reduced competition for basic resources among different strata of society and thus helped to maintain social order. At the same time, it provided Ottoman society some measure of preparedness during wartime. In effect, this economic philosophy, sometimes termed provisionism or even consumerism, ostensibly sacrificed a degree of free-market competition in pursuit of widespread economic security. Lately, however, the notion that the Ottoman authorities even pursued such a policy has come under criticism as historians gain an ever greater appreciation of the profit-consciousness and commercial savvy of the Ottoman state. It was not at all the case, in any event, that market forces did not operate in the Ottoman economy or that competition had no effect on the marketplace.

Guilds

Merchants and craftsmen themselves coalesced in loose organizations which arguably added another degree of regulation to the marketplace. The question of craft organizations, or guilds, is, however, a particularly vexed one in Islamic history. Some historians have insisted that craft guilds simply did not exist before the Ottoman period. If, by 'craft guild', we mean a guild in the medieval European sense – that is, a corporation that organized all practitioners of a given trade in a strict hierarchy of apprentice–journeyman–master while electing officers and setting prices and quality standards – then, clearly, there is no evidence of guilds before or even during the Ottoman period. Under the Ottomans, the government, whose dictates were enforced by the *qadi* and the *muhtasib*, regulated the market. Such craft organizations as existed were loose associations that the government regulated via foremen or representatives appointed to head the craft.

Notwithstanding, there is no denying that merchants and artisans in Ottoman cities did tend to form professional associations of one kind or another, even if they did not approach the regimentation of their European counterparts. As early as the Abbasid period, groups of young artisans in Muslim cities formed brotherhoods that followed certain codes of initiation and fellowship, rather like Masonic lodges or even orders of chivalry. This sort of code was known by the Arabic word *futuwwa*, which translates roughly to 'young manhood'. Members of the brotherhoods could be distinguished by the colours and styles of their clothing, by the banners and other heraldic emblems they might display, and even by the way in which they wore their hair. *Futuwwa* gave artisans a sense of identity, community and tradition; in effect, it functioned as a sort of working-class Sufism. Members of a certain trade in a particular town might undergo an elaborate ritual, curiously similar to Masonic initiation, in which they were invested with the apron of their trade or, alternatively, with knee-length trousers specifically associated with *futuwwa*, and received the trade's characteristic tools. Elaborate *futuwwa* manuals were compiled, giving each craft a patron saint, normally from among the companions of the Prophet Muhammad but occasionally from pre-Islamic history also. Still, the *futuwwa* organization was not a corporative body as the European guild was; in other words, it did not incorporate its members into a discrete, autonomous economic body with its own internal government and standards. Instead, the *futuwwa* organization imparted a sort of artisanal consciousness to the trade. It defined the identity of the practitioners of a certain craft, setting them off from other artisans and from the government. On the other hand, it did not regulate prices or monitor the quantity or quality of a certain good.

The late historian Gabriel Baer has argued that the Ottoman state itself imposed craft guilds on the artisans of the various provinces: that is, the governor of a province or the judge of a city or district would approve a master craftsman, who in the Arab provinces went by the omnibus title shaykh, who would be that craft's intermediary with the government and would thus help the government to control the craft. In this sense, the guild shaykh performed a role similar to that of the neighbourhood shaykh discussed above. The Ottoman government wished to ensure that raw materials were evenly distributed among the practitioners of a particular craft, that prices and quality were uniform, and that there was an equal distribution of goods empire-wide. This attitude was long held to be characteristic of so-called provisionism: the emphasis was not on selling as much as possible and making the largest possible profit but on ensuring that the entire empire was supplied with necessary provisions and, at the local level, that a steady flow of raw materials and finished products was maintained so that markets flourished in a general way.

The guilds pictured in the well-known collections of Ottoman miniatures showing the extravagant public celebrations surrounding the circumcisions of Ottoman princes in 1582 and 1720 are presumably these state-sponsored Ottoman guilds. Yet even these guilds retained their own lore and traditions, much like the *futuwwa* brotherhoods of young artisans that characterized medieval Islamic cities. When the traveller Evliya Chelebi describes the guilds of Istanbul and Cairo, he depicts them as they appear in processions, and in processions they were less like state-sponsored economic entities and more like *futuwwa* brotherhoods, with patron saints and rituals. Moreover, such processions included groups that one would not normally consider craft guilds, such as thieves and prostitutes on the one hand, and archers on the other. Perhaps such groups did not really exist outside processions but rather had a certain transient processional identity that was not the same as the identity of the guilds taxed by the government and regulated by the *muhtasib*. The guilds, in short, were not simply economic entities but social institutions; their identities and their places in the societies of the Ottoman Arab provinces were multifaceted.

If all guild members cooperated to ensure a reliable supply of raw materials and finished goods, then we might expect each craft to be concentrated in a certain neighbourhood, or even street, of a given city so as to ensure easier regulation, or as a result of professional solidarity and simple habit. This was, in fact, the case in many Arab cities and Ottoman cities in general. As indicated above, most major Arab cities had streets or covered markets inhabited solely by copper-makers, leather-workers or tailors. This was not always and everywhere the rule, however. In some cities, certain crafts would congregate in particular neighbourhoods or streets; others would not. Craftsmen who produced

Figure 7.2 Guilds processing, from the 1720 *Book of Festivals* illustrated by the court painter Levni. Pictured are the gold and silver thread-makers, blacksmiths, shipbuilders, silk-weavers and saddlers. The dark, outsized figure at centre is a puppet belonging to the saddler's guild. Note the two Janissaries, in high white headdresses, at centre rear, and next to them a party of French and Russian emissaries.
Source: Topkapı Palace Library Museum, MS A. 3593, folio 140a

luxury goods destined for the long-distance trade, such as jewellers, silk-workers and goldsmiths, might be concentrated in a central covered bazaar while humbler crafts would be dispersed throughout the city according to where they were needed. Indeed, although the term *bedestan*, or 'place of cloth', as noted above, came to apply to covered markets in general, such markets were built in the first place to house the merchants who participated in the lucrative long-distance textile trade.

Long-distance trade

Not all commerce in the Ottoman Arab provinces was confined to the shops in the *suq*s or to the craft guilds. As the presence of *wakala*s and *bedestan*s attests, Ottoman Arab society also included a stratum of long-distance merchants. These merchants, who are usually called *tujjar* (singular *tajir*) in Arabic, dealt in the luxury goods, notably textiles, coffee and spices, which were exported to Europe or imported from Yemen, India and the Far East, as well as more mundane products shipped from one Ottoman province to another. They did not belong to the usual run of craft guilds but might form a loose, informal consortium, although their organization varied a great deal from city to city. At the head of such an organization was an informal representative of the long-distance merchants to the authorities; he was often known by the Persian title *shahbandar*, literally, 'king of the port'. In some large cities, this post was in practice hereditary within a single wealthy family.

Seaborne trade

By and large, shipping goods by sea was faster, cheaper and safer than transporting them overland. That said, however, conditions along the two chief oceanic trade routes, through the Mediterranean Sea and through the Indian Ocean, differed considerably. Mediterranean shipping generally involved shorter distances and was more predictable than shipping in the Indian Ocean. Most ships carrying goods to or from the Ottoman Empire's Mediterranean ports were European vessels contracted to Ottoman merchants, most of whom were Turcophone or Arabophone Muslims. Ottoman war galleys – long, wooden craft manned by oarsmen – were far less suitable for commerce, although during the sixteenth and seventeenth centuries dual-purpose galleys were built in Istanbul and in the port of Damietta on the eastern branch of the Nile, while a species of 'clumsy, maladroit Alexandrine vessels'[3] lumbered across the Mediterranean to supply Istanbul with Egyptian crops, notably rice for the imperial court. In the course of the seventeenth century, however, European ships largely displaced these indigenous varieties, not least because continuous naval warfare rendered Ottoman galleys unavailable for trade.

Despite the involvement of European ships and their crews, much of the Ottoman Empire's Mediterranean trade was internal and, in fact, contributed to a commercial symbiosis among the Ottoman cities and provinces of the Mediterranean basin. As one recent study of the subject puts it,

> Rice cultivated in Egypt is consumed in the sultan's palace and in North Africa, Macedonian tobacco is smoked in Egypt and Anatolia, wood from southeastern Anatolia is used in Egypt, fezzes from Tunis are imported throughout the Levant, Syrian silk is woven in Anatolia, and the surviving African slaves, arriving in Libyan Tripoli, are sold in the market of Izmir.[4]

This commerce tended to follow highly specialized trajectories. Whereas most ships from Alexandria sailed to Izmir, for example, Damietta trafficked with the ports of Greater Syria: Tripoli, Beirut and Sidon, which supplied Damascus, and Latakia and Alexandretta (Iskenderun), which supplied Aleppo.

As for international trade through the Mediterranean, textiles played a huge role, as they had in the Middle Ages. During the Ottoman period, however, the balance of the textile trade shifted somewhat. Under the Fatimids and Mamluks and their neighbours, Muslim and European merchant ships had transported flax from Egypt to Tunisia, linen cloth from Egypt and Tunisia to the Byzantine Empire, and silk cloth from Spain and Italy to Egypt and North Africa. Under the Ottomans, European ships transported more and more finished cloth from France, Holland and, above all, England to the Ottoman capital and the provinces. By the seventeenth century, the palace pages were wearing garments of English wool. The ships returned to Europe carrying chiefly Ottoman and transshipped Asian luxury goods, such as silk (both raw and finished), coffee, spices and porcelain. Boatloads of European specie, payment for these goods, also travelled between Europe and the Ottoman provinces, fuelling the wave of inflation that hit the Ottoman Empire towards the end of the sixteenth century, then supplying the coinage the Ottomans needed to offset their own debased currency. On the other hand, the Ottomans themselves shipped specie to Iran, Yemen and above all India to pay for imported coffee, textiles and spices.

European merchant ships also introduced New World crops to the Ottomans. While tobacco, discussed in tandem with coffee below, had a widespread, highly visible and occasionally controversial impact on Ottoman society, new food crops left a subtler, if no less lasting, imprint. Many, but by no means all, of these crops travelled from the Americas to western Europe, then across the Mediterranean to Ottoman territory. Tomatoes, which would become an indispensable ingredient of Ottoman and post-Ottoman Middle Eastern and Mediterranean cuisine, probably reached the Ottoman domains from Italy, while haricot, or navy, beans most likely entered through Spain. Sweet potatoes and chili peppers, on the other hand, were shipped by the Portuguese to India in the early seventeenth century and may have arrived in Ottoman territory from there. Intriguingly, the most transformative New World food crop, American corn, or maize, came to the Ottoman Arab lands directly from the New World, perhaps in Spanish ships captured by Ottoman pirates or with Muslim (or Jewish) refugees from southern Spain following the Christian reconquest in 1492. Maize may have taken root in Egypt even before the Ottoman conquest; this would explain why the Ottomans called it *mısır*, the Arabo-Turkish word for 'Egypt', which is still used in modern Turkish. Hardier than wheat or barley and with a higher calorie yield per acre, maize quickly became a vital supplement to these Old World crops, particularly in time of drought or scarcity. By the seventeenth century, a parody of rural society in Egypt, to be discussed in the next chapter, describes maize bread as a staple food of peasants. Recounting a period of severe shortages and inflation in 1804–05, the Egyptian historian al-Jabarti remarks, 'Had God in his mercy toward his creatures not provided maize, the granaries and warehouses would have been empty, and the docks would have been as devoid of grain this year as they had been in the previous one.'[5] From Ottoman territory, maize was shipped to western Europe, where it was known as 'Turkish wheat' or 'Saracen millet'.

As commerce with the European powers, above all Britain and France, accelerated in the seventeenth and eighteenth centuries, the port cities of the Ottoman Mediterranean increased in size and economic importance. Cities such as Izmir, Alexandria, Tripoli and Sidon in Lebanon, and Acre in Palestine attracted colonies of European merchants, some of whom stayed for years. To communicate with indigenous merchants and with each other, they cultivated a *lingua franca*, which one eighteenth-century French merchant described as 'a mélange of Provençal, of vulgar Greek, and especially of corrupt Italian'[6] – a patois which has left its mark, however faint, on the modern-day Arabic dialects of the region and on modern Turkish. Their presence facilitated the introduction not only of European woollen cloth but also of European luxury goods, which imperial officials and provincial grandees alike began importing in record quantities early in the eighteenth century. Combined with intra-imperial shipping, then, this external commerce linked all the ports of the Mediterranean, and by extension the inland cities dependent on them, in an intricate commercial network.

Piracy and the weather were the two chief dangers to Mediterranean shipping. Ships left port in two major seasons – autumn and spring – to avoid winter storms. Still, shipwrecks and leakage were not uncommon. Meanwhile, European pirates lurked in the eastern Mediterranean, hoping to catch Ottoman ships unawares. The Knights of St John, who had relocated to Malta in 1533 after being expelled from Rhodes in 1522 by Süleyman I, remained a persistent threat until late in the seventeenth century. One reason the Ottomans conquered Cyprus in 1570 and Crete in 1669 (after a twenty-five-year siege of Candia), in fact, was that they suspected the Venetian rulers of these islands of allowing the Knights to use their territories as bases of operations against the Ottomans in the eastern Mediterranean. It was a Maltese attack on an Ottoman ship carrying a deposed Chief Harem Eunuch to exile in Egypt in 1644 that supposedly triggered the assault on Crete.

The longer, more unpredictable Indian Ocean route was dominated by merchants from India and the Arab principalities bordering the Arabian Sea who relied on a relatively small but hardy ship known as a dhow, more particularly a special type of deep-sea dhow that is no longer built. Constructed in large part along the western coast of India, these dhows were durable vessels with hulls made of teak, which was native to South Asia, and triangular, or lateen, sails, that made them especially manoeuvrable. Even armies depended on these Indian dhows. When the Ottomans were expelled from Yemen in the 1630s by the Zaydi Shiite imam, the last remaining Ottoman military commander, an Albanian bey from Egypt, evacuated the remnant of his troops from Mocha on an Indian merchant vessel. Some forty-three years later, when the Zaydi imam attempted to expel the Jews from his domain, they decamped to the town of Mawza in the coastal plain just inland from Mocha, where they waited in vain for an Indian ship to pick them up and transport them to a 'safe haven' (after a year, the imam allowed them to return).

To merchants and adventurers alike, the Indian Ocean route was legendary as the source of exotic spices. Black pepper and ginger were cultivated in India itself, cinnamon in Ceylon (Sri Lanka); meanwhile, India was the transit point for spices native to what is now Indonesia, above all cloves and nutmeg. Yet India also had a long history of producing high-quality cotton textiles, which were in great demand in the Ottoman Arab provinces. Slaves from eastern Africa were also transported in Indian dhows across the Red Sea to Yemen and through the Indian Ocean to Oman, the Persian Gulf and India itself, where they were employed at the Mughal court, often as eunuchs.

Indian Ocean ships sailed at the pleasure of the monsoon winds. Between October and April, winds blowing from the north-east carried vessels southwards, down the coast of East Africa, on the one hand, or towards China, on the other. In summer, when the winds blew from the south-west, ships sailed northwards back to India or to the Persian Gulf and the Red Sea. Thus, Indian ships would have arrived in Ottoman territory during the summer months. Any shift in the winds or unpredictable storms could easily wreck a ship or drive it seriously off course. As in the Mediterranean, a ship might also become becalmed. Hence it was not unusual for an Indian Ocean merchant to be absent from home for many months, and sometimes even years. Not surprisingly, colonies of Indian merchants could be found in all the ports along the route.

Commerce in the Indian Ocean connected a wide array of Muslim polities, from East Africa to Yemen, Oman, the kingdoms of the Persian Gulf, Iraq, Iran and India itself – and this is not even taking into consideration the kingdoms east of India that participated in the trade. Understandably, these polities all wished to profit from this trade; hence, they jockeyed for dominance at various points. A powerful motivation for the Ottomans to retake Iraq from the Safavids in 1638 was to reap the benefits of the sea trade through Basra. In the Arabian peninsula and around the Persian Gulf, competition erupted among the smaller kingdoms and tribes that dominated the coastline. During the eighteenth century, the rulers of Oman founded a veritable naval empire which, by the end of the century, dominated the route between East Africa and India, along which their fleet carried coffee. Neither Sunni like the Ottomans nor Shiite like the Safavids and later Iranian dynasties, the Omanis followed one strain of Kharijism, the sect that stemmed from the soldiers in Ali ibn Abi Talib's army who mutinied when he accepted arbitration during his battle with the Umayyads, who disputed his claim to the caliphate. In 661 CE, Ali was stabbed to death by a Kharijite in the Iraqi city of Najaf, where he is buried.

Ever since the Portuguese discovery of the Cape Route in 1498, of course, European merchant vessels had shipped Indian and Indonesian spices directly to Europe, although this was often less cost-effective than acquiring them second-hand in Ottoman entrepôts such as Aleppo. In the eighteenth century, however, French and British ships began to import Indian spices, above all pepper, to Ottoman Mediterranean ports such as Alexandria. Yet even after this European intervention, Indian dhows continued to carry cotton cloth, indigo (used in dyeing), incense, perfumes and gums to ports on the Persian Gulf and the Arabian Sea. They likewise transported the all-important coffee beans from the Yemeni port of Mocha to Jidda, the Red Sea port serving Mecca.

Curiously, though, the dhows almost never ventured into the northern half of the Red Sea. Instead, coffee was delivered from Jidda to Suez in ships even larger and clumsier than the 'maladroit Alexandrine vessels' of the Mediterranean; constructed at Suez, these behemoths were of such questionable seaworthiness that they were obliged to sail close to the shoreline, despite the hazards posed by rocks and coral reefs, and only during daylight hours. (Small wonder that coffee was also carried along the overland pilgrimage route.) Towards the end of the eighteenth century, they began to give way to Indian vessels piloted by Egyptian crews. Clearly, the dhow remained indispensable to Red Sea and Indian Ocean commerce.

Overland trade

Merchants from the Arab provinces who carried goods overland had access to two ancient major routes and a number of minor ones. One key route followed the old Silk Road from Aleppo eastwards through northern Iraq and Iran to Central Asia and, ultimately, China. Subsidiary routes branched south-westwards towards the Arabian peninsula and Egypt, and south-eastwards to the port of Basra. In Africa, meanwhile, a trans-Saharan route ran from the southern part of what is now the country of Sudan northwards through Egypt. Smaller routes fed into this route from the west, linking the Sudanese trade to markets as far away as Morocco and Mali.

Aleppo was an old-fashioned caravan city whose covered markets brimmed with the trade goods that entered the city from the east and south-east. Horses, weapons, animal skins and such luxury items as Chinese porcelain followed the ancient Silk Road while Indian spices were transshipped through Iraq, camels from the Arabian desert were driven from Basra, and Yemeni coffee arrived with pilgrims returning from the Holy Cities. Nonetheless, textiles, and above all silk, formed the bulk of Aleppo's trade from the East. Raw silk from China and Safavid Iran reached Aleppo for transshipment to weaveries in Istanbul, Bursa, Cairo and various cities in Europe. The countryside around Aleppo likewise produced raw silk, and the city had its own population of silk-weavers, who sold their product locally and regionally. The prospect of rich profits from the textile trade through Aleppo was a major incentive for the duke of Tuscany to ally with the Lebanese Druze leader Fakhr al-Din Ma'n II in the early seventeenth century, as described in Chapter 4. In return, European merchants brought silver specie, weapons and, above all, finished woollen cloth to trade in the East. In the early eighteenth century, British merchants in Aleppo bartered wool for locally grown raw silk, leading one British factor to insist, 'If we can have no silk we can sell no cloth. . . .'[7]

If piracy were a threat to merchants shipping by sea, robbery was an even greater danger to overland caravan trade. The annual pilgrimage caravans from Cairo and Damascus were attractive targets for Bedouin bands precisely because they included vast numbers of merchants who used the pilgrimage as an opportunity to sell their wares and purchase others. Damascus' caravan became especially vulnerable towards the end of the seventeenth century because of a massive movement of tribal populations within the province. In particular, as will be noted in Chapter 8, the large Anaza confederation was moving northwards into Syria from the Arabian peninsula, perhaps in response to population shifts within the Arabian peninsula which would culminate in the explosive Wahhabi movement in the latter part of the eighteenth century. The Ottoman central administration responded by attempting to incorporate the leaders of the Anaza and neighbouring tribes into the Ottoman bureaucracy as salaried caravan escorts. This policy had the unintended consequence of providing the tribal chieftains with cash with which they could then purchase firearms from provincial notables such as Zahir al-Umar, enabling them to launch far deadlier raids in the latter half of the eighteenth century. Even outside the pilgrimage season, however, Bedouin or Turcoman bands, as well as bands of non-tribal brigands, might attack smaller commercial caravans; vigilance and appeasement were therefore constant necessities.

Apart from physical attacks on caravans, the economic policies of Safavid Iran arguably posed the biggest threat to Ottoman overland commerce. In the last decade of his reign, Shah Abbas I (r. 1588–1629) imposed a monopoly on silk, meaning that the shah now licensed all production and trade of silk within the Safavid domains. He negotiated directly with European merchants for their trade, with the result that the British and Dutch East India Companies began to load Iranian silk directly on to their ships in the Persian Gulf. This tactic was designed to allow the shah to profit from the demand for Iranian silk by taxing the European merchants who exported it. The effect of the shah's monopoly on Aleppo was, not surprisingly, negative, as for ten years virtually no Iranian silk entered the city. Nonetheless, the city suffered much more severely when the Safavid dynasty collapsed in the early eighteenth century, as turmoil within Iran and border warfare with the Ottomans disrupted the Iranian transit trade for decades.

Even within the Ottoman Empire, Aleppo by the mid-seventeenth century was losing importance as a trade entrepôt to the booming southern Anatolian port city of Izmir (Smyrna), which had begun to encroach on Aleppo's trade with Europe. In the following century, its value to British textile merchants eroded as cheaper, high-quality Bengali and Chinese silk shipped directly to Europe by the East India Company began to compete with raw silk produced in or shipped through Aleppo. By the end of the century, Aleppo had become something of a commercial backwater so far as the long-distance caravan trade was concerned. It was still, however, a very important centre for regional trade in goods such as soap, coffee, rice, dried fruits and silk cloth.

Far to the south-west, African luxury goods were transported along the desert route which traversed the vast Sahara. Notable among these were ivory and ostrich feathers, which were needed for the plumes in the headdresses of pashas, Janissary officers and the sultan himself. By far the most lucrative item of this trade, however, was slaves. Each year, two major slave caravans assembled in the city of Sennar in what is now south-eastern Sudan and in the now notorious western Sudanese district of Darfur for the trek northwards across the desert to Egypt. Sennar actually dispatched several relatively small caravans in the course of a year; these merged into one large caravan, carrying several hundred slaves, at Egypt's southern border before following the Nile down to Cairo. The Darfur caravan, by contrast, was a single massive operation which brought several thousand slaves to Cairo each year.

Robbery was a hazard on this route, as on the pilgrimage routes and the Silk Road. The Bedouin, Berber and Nubian tribes of the Sahara, like their counterparts along the other routes, were tempted by the lucrative cargoes, both human and material, that the caravans carried; they might also be even more hard-pressed than the tribes of the Syrian and Arabian deserts by periodic livestock shortfalls and shortages of the crops and material goods they normally acquired from villages and towns. Meanwhile, the challenges the slaves faced from the harsh desert climate were compounded by the actions of avaricious slave-traders, who often withheld food and shelter from their charges so as to expend as few of their own resources as possible during the journey. In consequence, a high percentage of slaves died en route, without ever reaching the market in Cairo.

As for political challenges along the trans-Saharan trade route, the Portuguese, who had established fortified bases all along the African coast by the time of the Ottoman conquest of Egypt, posed a potential, if relatively remote, threat throughout the sixteenth century. Otherwise, Saharan territory featured nothing comparable to the Ottoman conflict with the Safavids, but petty rulers along the route were a potential source of obstruction. Securing the trade route was a secondary objective of Süleyman I's conquest of 'Habesh' during the 1550s, carried out by the former Mamluk emir Özdemir Pasha, as noted in Chapter 2. Through-out the Ottoman period, the governor of Egypt was intensely interested in protecting the route through Sudan. In the 1820s, the autonomous governor Mehmed Ali Pasha went so far as to conquer Sudan outright (founding the present-day capital, Khartoum, in the process) in order to use it as his personal source of slaves.

The Red Sea coffee trade and its cultural effects

A uniquely Ottoman component of long-distance trade was the trans-port of coffee from Yemen through the Red Sea to the port of Jidda, then to Egypt, whence it was transshipped to Syria, Anatolia and Europe. Inasmuch as the Ottomans were administering Yemen when the craze for Yemeni coffee began and took a leading role in its shipment even after their expulsion from Yemen in 1636, coffee can be regarded as an Ottoman gift to the world.

How coffee was discovered is the stuff of legend; one origin tradition claims that an Ethiopian goatherd noticed his flock growing unusually frisky after eating the berries of a certain tree. The coffee tree grew wild in Ethiopia, from where it seems to have been introduced to Yemen some-time in the fifteenth century. It is interesting to note, in any case, that well into the twentieth century many Yemenis spurned brewed coffee in favour of a sweetened infusion, known as *qishr*, made from the husks of the coffee bean. Coffee itself seems first to have caught on among the Sufi brotherhoods, who used it to stay awake and perhaps to achieve a certain 'buzz' during lengthy mystical rituals. Yemeni tradition asso-ciates the popularization of the drink in Yemen with the career of the rather mysterious Sufi shaykh Ali ibn Umar (d. 1418), known as al-Shadhili from his adherence to the Shadhili Sufi order, who lived at the Ethiopian court before founding his own Sufi lodge in Mocha. He allegedly praised coffee for its power to ward off sleep and improve mystical concentration. The communal function of coffee-drinking was as important as its stimulant effect. In some Sufi lodges, passing the porcelain coffee cup became an unofficial part of mystical ritual and a symbol of brotherhood.

From Yemen, the new drink crossed the Red Sea to Egypt, whence it made its way to Syria and North Africa, the Ottoman heartland in Anatolia, and the Balkans. At first, Muslim religious authorities were unsure what to make of this strange brew, which, as it happened, had appeared on the scene at about the same time that an equally mysterious stimu-lant, tobacco, arrived in the Ottoman lands from the Americas. Some ulema actually wrote anti-coffee tracts. In the long run, the nay-sayers had little effect as coffee spread from the mystical orders to virtually the entire spectrum of Ottoman society. The responsa of Cairo's chief rabbi in the mid-sixteenth century show that the beverage was already in widespread use as a remedy for stomach disorders. By the 1740s, the British physician Alexander Russell could report that in Aleppo, 'few of the lower people drink less than three or four cups of coffee in the twenty-four hours; their superiors drink more; and persons who frequent the great, drink perhaps twenty cups daily'.[8]

European ships carried coffee beans from Egypt to France and to Italy, where they entered the Habsburg Empire through the Adriatic port of Trieste. By the end of the seventeenth century, the middle and upper classes of western Europe were in thrall to the beverage. The seventeenth-century English traveller Sir Henry Blount makes extravagant claims for coffee's medicinal properties, asserting that the people of the eastern Mediterranean, 'using Cophie morning and evening, have no Consumptions, . . . no Lethargies in aged people, or Rickets in Children; and but few qualmes in women with child'.[9]

What this meant, of course, was that, some two hundred years after the Portuguese discovery of the Cape Route around Africa to India, Europe was once again dependent on the Ottoman Empire to satisfy its insatiable demand for a luxury good. The old spice route through the Red Sea and the Mediterranean, which had been challenged by the Cape Route, was now the scene of quite a lucrative business. In the course of the seventeenth and early eighteenth centuries, in fact, the Ottoman Empire recouped the revenues it had lost from the temporary diversion of the spice trade as a result of the discovery of the route around Africa.

Egypt was the linchpin of the Ottoman coffee trade. Coffee was shipped from the port of Aden in southern Yemen, and later from Mocha on Yemen's Red Sea coast, to the Arabian port of Jidda, then across the Red Sea to Suez, from where it went overland to Cairo. Provincial merchants transshipped coffee to other Egyptian towns and into the countryside, as well as down the Nile to Alexandria to await shipment across the Mediterranean. European, and above all French, merchants came to Cairo and Alexandria to load coffee on to their ships, which sailed back across the Mediterranean full of beans. Cairo thus became a coffee hub. At least one Ottoman governor and one exiled harem eunuch founded *wakalas*, or 'urban caravanserais', specifically for coffee merchants and their product.

The coffee trade had an enormous impact on Egyptian society during the seventeenth and eighteenth centuries. The regimental, and above all Janissary, officers who controlled Egypt's Mediterranean and Red Sea ports made fortunes in this trade. During the seventeenth century,

Janissary officers monopolized the tax farms of the customs of Alexandria, Damietta and Rosetta on the Mediterranean Sea, and were thus able to cut lucrative deals with European merchants hoping to ship coffee out of these ports without paying ruinous customs duties. They also bought shares in the ships, both Indian and Suez-built, which transported the coffee through the Red Sea. By the end of the seventeenth century, Janissary officers were able to amass huge households of the sort described in Chapter 5 based on their coffee wealth; the Kazdağlı household, which would come to dominate Egypt completely during the following century, was the largest and most successful of these households. Moreover, coffee merchants who did not belong to the military were able to build their own households and forge links with the Janissary households through business partnerships and marriage alliances. Cairo's most prominent coffee merchants during the eighteenth century were the Sharaybi family, well attested in provincial chronicles, whose fortunes were inextricably intertwined with those of the Kazdağlıs. Ottoman governors of Egypt, as well as the central Ottoman government in Istanbul, found that they had no hope of controlling the province unless they cooperated with – or appeased – these households.

It is worth emphasizing that Egypt's coffee fortunes peaked *after* the Ottoman expulsion from Yemen at the hands of the Zaydi imams of the Qasimi dynasty during the 1630s. The Qasimi imams unquestionably took advantage of the demand for coffee. During their reign, the coffee-growing region expanded far south of its core in Yemen's central highlands; meanwhile, the imam received a quarter of the retail price of all coffee sold. And yet Yemen's core growing region lay in territory inhabited mainly by Ismaili, as opposed to Zaydi, Shiite tribes whose loyalty to the Zaydi imam was tenuous at best. (The Ismaili communities had their own missionaries, whose authority they generally heeded.) At the same time, Yemen lacked a ship-building industry that could supply the means to ship the coffee beans out of Mocha. Yemeni coffee-growers and even the Zaydi imam himself thus depended on the Indian merchant ships, often partially owned, as they well knew, by Janissary officers from Egypt, to conduct the trade from which they profited. By means that are still unclear, these grandees must have made deals with both Zaydi and Ismaili tribes in order to transport the coffee beans to the Red Sea coast, where the merchant vessels waited.

The coffee fortunes of Egypt's grandees began to erode in the eighteenth century, when French merchants began importing coffee from their colonies in the Caribbean into the Mediterranean, and ultimately into Egypt itself. Though of lower quality than Yemeni coffee, the Caribbean beans were cheaper. French Caribbean coffee did not drive

Yemeni coffee out of the market completely; instead, affordable blends of Yemeni and Caribbean beans became the preferred libations for Ottoman subjects of middling means. As a result, however, market prices for Yemeni coffee dropped dramatically beginning in the 1730s. Rather than face ruination, Egypt's great households, the Kazdağlıs above all, shifted the basis of their wealth from the coffee trade to the control of rural tax farms, as documented in Chapter 5.

Coffee culture

The method of preparing 'Turkish coffee' has changed relatively little since the days when laden merchant vessels plied the routes connecting Mocha, Jidda and Suez. Coffee beans are pounded into a powder which is finer than the ground roast to which many European coffee-drinkers are accustomed. One places this powder in a brass coffeepot or a small cooking pot with a long handle, adds water and perhaps the aromatic Indian spice cardamom, and heats the brew over a flame. Each Arab province came to have its distinctive brass coffeepot: the Yemeni pots are large, with pronounced spouts, the Syrian pots less exaggerated; the Palestinian pots are often topped with rooster figurines. The brew is poured into small, handleless cups and drunk with a measured amount of sugar – at least today; European observers reported that coffee-drinkers in Aleppo shunned sugar until well into the eighteenth century.

As it spread from the Sufi orders into Ottoman society at large, coffee-drinking remained a communal activity. In the seventeenth and eighteenth centuries, as today, Turkish coffee was seldom used as a means of waking up in the morning. Instead, coffee was usually drunk after an afternoon or evening meal, or at communal gatherings, whether in a private home or in a coffeehouse, a new kind of establishment where men gathered to imbibe the brew, smoke water pipes, and listen to story-tellers and gossip. Coffee could also mark important events and achievements. In the Damurdashi chronicles, which cover events in eighteenth-century Egypt, the province's grandees often drink coffee after reaching a milestone political agreement.

By the seventeenth century, the coffeehouse had become an institution in many Ottoman cities. Sultan Murad IV (r. 1623–40) went so far as to close down all of Istanbul's coffeehouses because he suspected that the sorts of people who gathered there, notably un- or underemployed elements such as demobilized Janissaries, would foment social unrest and even political subversion. Ulimately, this sort of tactic failed, as did the preaching of anti-coffee puritans among the ulema. As a case in point, the Chief Harem Eunuch Abbas Agha, exiled to Egypt just when these puritanical types were riding high in the 1670s, founded a massive coffee establishment in a Nile Delta town, whereby coffee spread through Egypt's subprovinces. Even well after Yemeni coffee prices had declined, this feature of the coffee culture remained entrenched in the region. Late in the eighteenth century, the German surveyor Carsten Niebuhr, travelling through Yemen with a Danish scientific expedition, reports the existence of what he calls coffee huts – i.e., little shacks where the beverage was brewed and sold – even in quite remote areas.

An association between coffee and tobacco was not slow to appear, even though tobacco was a New World crop while coffee was a decidedly Old World one. Tobacco was introduced into Europe and the Ottoman lands from the British colonies in North America not long after coffee made its appearance. It, too, was regarded with some suspicion by the ulema but proved immensely popular among the general population, above all the Ottoman soldiery. The early seventeenth-century Egyptian chronicler al-Ishaqi quotes Galen and Maimonides in building a medical case for smoking tobacco. It could be smoked in a water pipe in a coffeehouse but more conveniently in a simple clay pipe. By the middle of that century, chroniclers tell of Janissaries who kept their tobacco pipes in their sleeves, and even of condemned Janissaries who smoked on the way to their own executions. In Istanbul's naval museum are artefacts recovered from an Ottoman vessel sunk by the Russian navy at the Anatolian port of Cheshme, near Izmir, in 1770. The number of clay pipes found amid the wreckage is so enormous that one can imagine that the ship might well have burned accidentally had it not been attacked by the Russians.

Storytelling and popular culture

It was, in many respects, the coffeehouse that brought coffee and tobacco together, since both stimulants lent themselves to lengthy communal gatherings. The coffeehouse was, moreover, the ideal place for communal storytelling, which cannot be neglected as a feature of Ottoman coffee culture. Public storytelling was, to be sure, a tradition that dated back many centuries before the appearance of coffee. The Middle East has a rich oral narrative tradition dating from well before the advent of Islam. Professional or semi-professional storytellers held forth at coffeehouses on certain evenings, often dramatizing their renditions with drums, fiddles or painted backdrops. Although most stories originated in legends that were passed down orally, many had been written down by at least the eighteenth century, and there is even evidence that some storytellers read their tales, or at least memorized them from written manuscripts before performances. In the Ottoman period, epic adventure stories featuring larger-than-life heroes were the most popular fare: for example, the stories of Alexander the Great, who had been transformed into a Persian hero-king in medieval Iranian literature. Tales of the Prophet Muhammad and his companions, as well as various Sufi 'saints', likewise had widespread appeal. In the Arab provinces, the epic of the eleventh-century migration from the Arabian peninsula to North Africa of the Banu Hilal Bedouin was frequently recited and wildly popular, as were tales of Baybars (r. 1260–77), the founder of the Mamluk sultanate. The demographic shifts which followed the Ottoman conquest of the Arab lands and attended the seventeenth-century crisis undoubtedly resulted in additions to the body of popular tales current in the societies of the Arab provinces. True, Niebuhr reports that pre-Ottoman lore dominated the tales most popular in Yemen during his stay there, citing the Baybars stories and those of the mythical African culture hero Antar. However, he also mentions the tales of Rüstem from the Iranian national epic known as the *Shahname*, which had been translated into Turkish under the late Mamluk sultan Qansuh al-Ghuri (r. 1501–16); its popularity in Yemen perhaps implies a species of bilingual exchange between Egypt and Yemen during the Ottoman era.

Recitations-cum-performances of these tales took place not only in public venues such as coffeehouses but also in private homes and, in that context, no doubt in harems. 'In the winter evenings,' notes the physician Alexander Russell, who resided in Aleppo during the 1740s, '. . . the ladies often pass the time in attending to Arabian tales, which are recited, but more commonly read, by a person who has a clear distinct voice.'[10] The frequency in some of these epics of heroines of super-human strength who do battle and even wrestle with male enemies may conceivably reflect the importance of the harem or other kinds of female gathering-places, such as public baths, as sites for storytelling of this sort. In an era when women and men from a vast array of provenances were arriving in the Arab provinces, storytelling, in private venues as in public coffeehouses, served as a means of acculturation.

Conclusion

The commerce in coffee, in short, gave rise to a whole cultural complex, ranging from elite provincial households to popular gathering places and forms of entertainment. It is perhaps the most dramatic example of the manner in which trade shaped Ottoman social life. More generally, the opportunities and demands of commerce shaped the topography, institutions and popular culture of Ottoman Arab provincial cities more forcefully than any other single factor. During the Ottoman era, in fact, commerce and natural growth transformed the layout and functions of Arab cities which had originally been conceived as or which, during the Middle Ages, had become military bastions. At the same time, commercial pursuits frequently overlapped with, intertwined with and clashed with public religious life and religious dictates. Meanwhile, irrepressible commercial energies ran up against the need for government regulation of the marketplace. All these interactions contributed to the dynamic of urban life in the Ottoman Empire's Arab provinces.

Notes

1. Richard W. Bulliet, *The Camel and the Wheel* (Cambridge, MA, 1975).
2. Bernard Lewis, ed. and trans., *Islam from the Prophet Muhammad to the Capture of Constantinople*, II: *Religion and Society* (New York, 1974), pp. 160–1.
3. Daniel Panzac, *La caravane maritime: marins européens et marchands ottomans en Méditerranée (1680–1830)* (Paris, 2004), p. 210 (my translation).
4. Ibid., p. 207 (my translation).
5. Al-Jabarti, *Al-Jabarti's History of Egypt*, III, p. 492 (trans. Moshe Perlmann).
6. Quoted in Panzac, *La caravane maritime*, p. 162 (my translation).
7. Quoted in Ralph Davis, *Aleppo and Devonshire Square: English Traders in the Levant in the Eighteenth Century* (London, 1967), p. 32.
8. Alexander Russell, *The Natural History of Aleppo*, 2 vols (London, 1794), I, pp. 119–20.
9. Quoted in Ralph S. Hattox, *Coffee and Coffeehouses: The Origins of a Social Beverage in the Medieval Near East* (Seattle and London, 1985), p. 69.
10. Russell, *The Natural History of Aleppo*, I, p. 251.

chapter eight

RURAL LIFE

As difficult as it is to piece together a complete picture of life and customs in the cities of the Ottoman Arab provinces, reconstructing life in the countryside is a far greater challenge. While historians are able to determine with a fair degree of accuracy the administrative and legal structures within which the rural population operated, the daily routines of country-dwellers and the internal hierarchies that prevailed among them remain, to a large degree, elusive. This circumstance is all the more frustrating given that the vast majority of the Ottoman sultan's subjects lived outside the cities and large towns, making their living from cultivating crops or raising livestock. Nevertheless, tax registers, pious endowment deeds, certain eccentric narrative sources, and above all the records of cases that came before the Muslim law courts allow us at least a glimpse of how most of the sultan's subjects lived.

Land tenure

The official Ottoman administrative structures governing the apportionment, use and taxation of land are well-known. In all Islamic empires, going back to the original empire founded by the Prophet Muhammad and the early caliphs, all conquered land belonged to the state rather than to any family or individual who cultivated it. This principle may in turn have derived from Sasanian and late Byzantine prototypes. State-owned land, that is, the vast majority of land in the Ottoman Empire, was known in Ottoman Turkish by the adjective *miri*, from *mir*, a contraction of the Arabic word for 'prince' – i.e., the prince's land. Those who cultivated the land or grazed livestock on it enjoyed only the right to the land's usufruct, as noted in Chapter 3.

*Timar*s

State ownership of land allowed for the systematic organization of the expanding Ottoman territories, beginning in the fourteenth century, under the *timar* system. A *timar*, as explained in Chapter 3, was a grant of land which a member of the imperial or provincial cavalry received in exchange for military service. He used the land and the tax revenues it produced to equip a certain number of horsemen for the sultan's army. However, he did not own this land but merely exploited its productivity; the central government could reassign his *timar* if he abandoned the land, failed to perform his military duty, or died. Land revenues came from taxation of the peasantry who lived on and worked the land assigned as *timar*; in the Balkans and much of Anatolia, these were overwhelmingly Greek Orthodox Christians. These peasants, however, were not serfs of the timariot but free farmers who could dispose of their crops as they wished and who technically had the right to leave the land if they so desired, although they could incur fines and loss of usufruct rights if they left the land uncultivated for long periods. In fact, cultivable land in all Ottoman provinces in which *timar*s were the norm was divided into single-household freehold farms, each of which was known in Ottoman Turkish as a *chiftlik*, from the Turkish word for 'pair', *chift*, alluding to the amount of land that could be ploughed by a pair of oxen. For this reason, the great historian Halil Inalcik maintains that this '*chifthane* system', referring to the household (*hane* in Persian) that formed around a *chiftlik*, constituted the foundation of the Ottoman agricultural economy. Nonetheless, the presence of cavalrymen and their officers in the countryside created what amounted to a class of landed gentry.

While an ordinary member of the cavalry held title to a single *timar*, perhaps comprising little more than a village and the lands farmed by its inhabitants, an officer received a larger conglomeration of *timar*s known as a *zeamet*, from the Arabic word for 'responsibility' or 'surety'. These powerful officers were far less likely than ordinary timariots to live on their land; instead, they often employed agents to oversee their holdings and collect taxes on their behalf. Meanwhile, a government minister (vizier) or the governor of a province in which *timar*s predominated received an even larger grant of landed revenue known as a *hass* (literally, 'special' or 'private').

Tax-farming (*iltizam*)

After conquering the Arab lands, as noted in Chapter 3, the Ottomans extended the *timar* system to Syria and northern Iraq but not to Egypt, southern Iraq, Yemen or North Africa. In Egypt, the Ottoman administration, after confiscating the defeated Mamluks' landholdings, experimented with a system of inspectors (Ottoman Turkish singular *emin*) appointed from Istanbul; these, however, lasted only through the early seventeenth century, after which tax-farming became the norm. By the end of the seventeenth century, in fact, tax-farming had spread through the Ottoman provinces, Arab and non-Arab alike, in many cases displacing the venerable *timar* system.

A government that practises tax-farming 'farms' the right to collect taxes on a given enterprise or property by selling this privilege, often to the highest bidder at auction. In the Ottoman case, the buyer paid a purchase price equivalent to the estimated revenue the land or property would produce within a fiscal year. In practice, naturally, this meant that only the wealthiest grandees could become tax-farmers; in many cases, a single wealthy individual or family held multiple tax farms within a given province. Any surplus revenue was for the tax-farmer to keep as a profit. Clearly, this system absolved the Ottoman government of responsibility in the case of unanticipated revenue shortfalls caused by crop failures and the like. On the other hand, at least according to conventional arguments, it gave the tax-farmer little incentive to maintain the lands whose taxes he farmed, notably by keeping irrigation works in good repair – unless, of course, lack of maintenance would reduce the revenues he collected.

It now appears that tax farms were much more widespread far earlier than historians had long thought. Even during the sixteenth century, control of port customs and similar, largely urban, operations was purchased by wealthy notables, above all Janissary officers – although, in the case of Egypt's port customs, wealthy members of the province's Jewish community played prominent roles. Moreover, land tenure institutions closely resembling the Ottoman tax farm had existed in various Islamic empires as far back as the Abbasid era.

Malikane

Initially, the Ottoman provincial administration auctioned tax farms for a year at a time. In 1695, however, ostensibly in an attempt at fiscal reform, Sultan Mustafa II, as noted in Chapter 5, introduced the life-tenure tax farm, known as *malikane*. In many cases, this new measure more or less codified existing practices since many tax farmers retained control of their holdings year after year and were even 'succeeded' in their posts by their children. Notwithstanding, the institution of *malikane* contributed to the ascendancy of provincial notables since it gave them an unassailable revenue source while at the same time reinforcing their ties to the imperial capital, where the tax farms were auctioned.

Sultanic properties and *waqf*

Not all land in the Ottoman Empire was *miri*, or state, land; hence not every piece of land was divided into *timar*s or tax farms. Some land, known in Ottoman Turkish as *havass-i hümayun*, 'imperial private properties', was earmarked for the imperial family's use. Regardless, revenue collection rights to these lands were not infrequently sold as tax farms to wealthy bidders, who delivered the income not to the sultan but to the imperial treasury. In all Islamic empires since at least the time of the Abbasids, furthermore, large amounts of land were endowed to pious foundations (Arabic singular *waqf*) so that the revenues they yielded would contribute to the upkeep of a mosque, *madrasa* or other religious or charitable institution. *Waqf* land was not taxed and, indeed, a wealthy personage might use a personal private endowment to keep a piece of land in the family while avoiding land taxes. In that case, he would draft a pious endowment deed naming himself superintendent of the foundation and stipulating that his descendants would succeed him in this position. (Women could, and did, endow *waqf*s of their own, as well.)

Mülk

Finally, state-owned, or *miri*, land could occasionally be reallocated as private property (*mülk*) as a reward for meritorious military service or some other favour to the state. Members of ruling families or households whom the Ottomans had conquered but retained as administrators might also be allowed to keep their private landholdings, while anyone who reclaimed wasteland was legally entitled to hold it as *mülk*. In addition, orchards and gardens – agricultural properties not classified as farms – fell under the category of *mülk*. Only privately owned land could be endowed to a pious foundation. If an endower wished to attach state-owned land to his foundation, he first had to follow a legal procedure to transform the land from *miri* into *mülk*.

Village life

If the superstructure of the Ottoman land regime is relatively easy to ascertain, the culture of the peasants whom it affected is far more difficult of access. Nonetheless, three principal types of archival document

– the official land tax register, the pious endowment deed and the Muslim law court register – provide a window onto the circumstances of villagers and even, occasionally, onto their personal predicaments.

During the reign of Sultan Süleyman I, as the central Ottoman government was assimilating the recently conquered Arab provinces, provincial administrators in each province conducted a cadastral survey: that is, a village-by-village survey of all revenue sources and taxable units. The resulting registers list every village in every province and, within each village, all households. In this context, a household is a family, headed by an adult male (or occasionally an adult female) inhabiting a single dwelling. Unattached bachelors are also recorded. Known as a *tapu tahrir defteri* (literally, 'register of title deed certificates'), such a register reveals village resources; population, including non-Muslims; and, to some extent, social structure. If the household heads' ethnicities are recorded, such a document can also shed light on village demographics, perhaps indicating patterns of migration and settlement. Registers of villages in the hinterland of Damascus during the sixteenth century, for example, show growing numbers of Turcoman tribespeople and unmarried young men, both indications of demographic flux in the decades following the Ottoman conquest.

Technically, a new *tapu* register was to be prepared for each province at the accession of each new sultan. Towards the end of the sixteenth century, as economic and demographic crisis gripped the empire, systematic registration was abandoned, although registers for individual provinces and districts were prepared sporadically through the seventeenth and eighteenth centuries. Less detailed registers of tax-farm holdings are also available for these later periods. Land held as a tax farm is frequently termed *muqataa*, literally, 'that which is separated out'; therefore, such a register is known as a *muqataa defteri*. These registers list villages, along with the tax farmers who collect their revenues, and various village resources, such as the number of oars a village can contribute to the imperial galleys (via a special tax).

Pious endowment deeds (Arabic singular, *waqfiyya*) are revealing in a different way from land tax registers. When a government official or provincial grandee went to a *qadi*'s court to draw up an endowment deed, the court clerks identified each property – from a grove of fruit trees to a residential complex – which he endowed by describing the properties that bordered it. Thus, the deed can constitute a snapshot of holdings in a given village or district at a given time. The individual property-holders mentioned give us an idea of village demographics and the status of women and non-Muslims, who often held property. In addition to who held what, we get a sense of the key crops cultivated and the sorts of commodities, such as soap and olive oil, produced in these villages. In the early eighteenth century, the Chief Harem Eunuch el-Hajj Beshir Agha (term 1717–46), for a notable example, endowed a wide range of properties in two villages near Aleppo. His lengthy endowment deed, of which these villages form only a small part, lists scores of orchards and mulberry trees, plus an astonishing number of olive trees.

Valuable as they otherwise are, land tax registers and pious endowment deeds do not record the voices of the peasants who lived in these villages. Virtually the only sources in which these are present are the registers of Muslim law courts. Ordinarily, a peasant had recourse to the court located in the sizeable town nearest his village. Since peasants might have to walk for days to reach the court, they appeared before the judge only in the most pressing cases: major property theft or land disputes, quarrels over inheritance, accusations of marital infidelity, and the like. While the judge and his scribes normally summarized cases, leaving out details of testimony, conversations and outbursts that could supply extraordinarily rich insights into peasant self-presentation, what they did record nonetheless serves as an unmatched source for village social dynamics, town–village relations and, perhaps most intriguingly, the confrontation between peasants and Ottoman officials. The court registers of sixteenth-century Jerusalem present the spectacle of an Ottoman surveyor, charged with compiling a *tapu* register, complaining to the judge that the peasants of a village to the south refused to give him accurate information about their vineyards, jeering, 'Write down what you want!'[1] Elsewhere, villagers violently attacked timariots and police chiefs who came to collect taxes and debts. Leslie Peirce's close examination of a Muslim court register covering the year 1540–41 from the south-eastern Anatolian city of Ayntab, a former Mamluk city in close proximity to Aleppo, reveals that a village south-east of the city, known for its moral rigour, served as a haven for a child bride who had allegedly been raped by her father-in-law.[2]

Social historians have been able to deduce from a combination of these sources, as well as more conventional narrative sources, that a 'typical' village in rural Egypt featured a number of shaykhs, each of whom headed a large household, consisting chiefly of his family. By the eighteenth century, these shaykhs recognized a sort of *primus inter pares* known as the *shaykh al-balad*, who acted as 'mayor' of the village. (The office of *shaykh al-balad* of Cairo, discussed in Chapter 5, which was normally filled by a *sanjak beyi*, appears to have derived from its rural counterpart.) In the province of Damascus, the equivalent official held the title *ra'is al-fallahin*, or 'head of the peasants', in the sixteenth century and almost certainly before, as well; like the *shaykh al-balad*, he represented a collectivity of village household heads, although in a given village several men might hold the title *ra'is* at the same time. During the seventeenth and eighteenth centuries, the title appears to have changed to *shaykh al-qarya* ('leader of the village'). This loose hierarchy of a head-man representing various household and family heads prevailed in other Arab provinces also, although nomenclature differed from one province to another. Although he might have the approval of other village shaykhs, the headman, rather like the head of a craft guild, was officially appointed by the provincial or subprovincial governor and served as a conduit for government authority in the village. Not surprisingly, the headman was usually one of the wealthiest villagers: someone who could guarantee the village's taxes to the tax farmer (or *timar*-holder in Syria and northern Iraq) while also ensuring that the village's land was cultivated without disruptions by peasant unrest. He had the authority to arrest peasants whom he deemed trouble-makers. An ability to negotiate with tribes in the surrounding countryside would also have been an asset in most cases. Often, the office was passed from father to son and remained in the same family for generations.

An unusual source for the living conditions and customs of Egypt's peasantry – and perhaps by extension for the peasantry of the Arab provinces as a whole – is a prose work entitled *Hazz al-quhuf fi sharh qasid Abi Shaduf*, which a recent translator has rendered as *Brains Confounded by the Ode of Abu Shaduf Expounded*, ostensibly compiled in the late seventeenth century by one Yusuf ibn Muhammad al-Shirbini. This extraordinary work, distributed as a lithograph as early as 1800, then printed in the late nineteenth century, was most famously exploited by the historian Gabriel Baer in the 1970s. In an introductory section, al-Shirbini describes Egypt's peasantry and Egyptian village life in disparaging terms; his commentary is followed by what purports to be the poetic *oeuvre* of a humble village ploughman ('Abu Shaduf') whom he has 'discovered'. In an article analysing the work, Baer argues that al-Shirbini was not himself an outraged urban sophisticate but probably a member of the rural ulema who had migrated to Cairo and was now attempting to demonstrate to his big-city colleagues that he had abandoned the retrograde culture of the countryside. In Baer's opinion, al-Shirbini invents Abu Shaduf as a caricature of the dirty, ignorant, lazy and untrustworthy country bumpkin; his putative poem demonstrates all the unsavoury qualities al-Shirbini has enumerated in his 'commentary': 'they are always in tatters and rags'; 'they express happiness with shouting, screaming and shrieking'; when they eat, they shovel huge amounts of food into their mouths all at once; and so on.[3] At the same time, however, the poem provides an invaluable glimpse of peasant speech, attitudes and customs.

Additional detail on country life comes from an even more obscure source, namely, a collection of documents from the Jewish community of Fustat, now a southerly neighbourhood of Cairo. Known as the Cairo Geniza, the Hebrew word for 'archive', this collection consists of documents and manuscripts of every conceivable kind, deposited in a specially built structure inside Fustat's Ibn Ezra Synagogue so as to avoid destroying any paper inscribed with the name of God. Although the Geniza documents date from the ninth to the nineteenth centuries CE, scholarly interest has centred on those produced in the Middle Ages, when luminaries such as the great Jewish philosopher Maimonides (1135–1204) frequented the synagogue. (By the Ottoman period, Fustat was an impoverished district, as it remains today.)

Nonetheless, at Gabriel Baer's urging, the eminent Geniza scholar S.D. Goitein published a humble seventeenth-century Geniza document which provides something of a window onto the growing tension between Cairo and its rural hinterland during this period. Written in colloquial Arabic but, like most Geniza documents, in Hebrew letters, the document presents 'The Story of the Cairene and the Country-Dweller'. In strikingly similar fashion to Aesop's well-known fable of the city mouse and the country mouse, the story's two characters extol the virtues of city life – more specifically life in Cairo – *versus* country life. Although the document is fragmentary, so that we cannot tell whether the urbanite or the peasant is victorious, the story depicts the rural lifestyle, as well as the culture clash between rural and urban.

To judge from 'The Story of the Cairene and the Country-Dweller', the feature that most differentiated city from countryside was the abundance and variety of goods and services available in an urban milieu, particularly in a major metropolis and commercial hub such as Cairo. Whereas the Cairene can choose from a wide array of exotic foodstuffs and textiles, his rural counterpart lives on what he can grow or raise on his plot of land. His clothing and surroundings are likewise far humbler than those of the urbanite. 'In the [countryside]', declares the Cairene, 'even the fortunate walks barefoot.'[4] Otherwise, the dialogue makes much of the cleanliness of urban life relative to the peasant's unavoidable proximity to soil and animals – a point also emphasized in al-Shirbini's work. As in *Hazz al-quhuf*, the peasant fears the exactions of the military-administrative elite, based in the cities. Naturally, these contrasts would register most forcefully with someone who has experienced both environments – say, a rural migrant. In this respect, both *Hazz al-quhuf* and the Geniza fragment reflect the uneasy encounter between urban and rural populations, as well as between administrators and peasants, that characterized much of the seventeenth century.

Cash crops

The Geniza dialogue gives the impression that peasants lived by subsistence farming; the country-dweller rhapsodizes about 'seeds and wheat and eggs and soft butter'.[5] Yet cash crops were by no means unknown in the Ottoman provinces before the nineteenth century. Chapter 5 described how Zahir al-Umar, overlord of northern Palestine for much of the eighteenth century, gave the region over to cotton and wheat cultivation for the French market, perhaps providing a model for Mehmed Ali Pasha, the autonomous governor of Egypt in the nineteenth century, who mobilized that province's peasants to supply cotton to the mills of Lancashire. Even villages that did not produce cash crops for international markets belonged to localized networks of town and village markets which often determined what crops and livestock they would raise. Al-Shirbini, to say nothing of the Geniza story, may conceivably exaggerate the economic and cultural isolation of the typical villager.

Before the nineteenth century, the only other major cash crop besides cotton and wheat grown in the Arab provinces for export outside the Ottoman domains was coffee, which, of course, was cultivated in the highlands of Yemen. Here, however, the Ottomans encountered a pre-existing, largely locally controlled pattern of cultivation. How Ottoman officials intervened in Yemen's coffee cultivation, transportation and marketing during their century of rule there is still, unfortunately, little understood. The trade in coffee, on the other hand, affected both urban and rural life in Yemen and other Arab provinces, as sale of the beans and the beverage penetrated even the smallest provincial towns and their rural hinterlands. During the 1670s in the Nile Delta town of Minyat Zifta, which 500 years earlier had been a centre for the regional redistribution of raw silk imported from the Mediterranean, the exiled Chief Harem Eunuch Abbas Agha, as noted in Chapter 7, endowed an immense coffee complex where, apparently, beans were ground and roasted, and the beverage was prepared and consumed. It seems likely that coffee beans, like raw silk half a millennium before, were traded through the surrounding countryside also.

Although silk appears no longer to have been traded in the Egyptian countryside during the Ottoman period, it was produced in those regions of the Arab provinces where the climate was suitable for cultivating mulberry trees – primarily Syria and Lebanon. In the course of the seventeenth and eighteenth centuries, in fact, Ottoman governors of Aleppo and Damascus, to say nothing of Chief Eunuchs and other imperial personnel, greatly expanded the acreage devoted to mulberry trees, which, like olive trees, were quick and dependable generators of revenue. Villagers in Syria and Lebanon nurtured cocoons and spun silk thread, while silk cloth was woven in Aleppo and Damascus and sold in the bazaars of those cities. As noted in the preceding chapter, Aleppo remained an important regional centre of silk production and redistribution even after its role in the transshipment of raw silk from Iran had eroded in the eighteenth century.

Olive trees, veritable signposts of settled agriculture in the Mediterranean region since the dawn of civilization, can grow in a wider range of climates than mulberry trees. In the Ottoman provinces, olive cultivation stretched from the Greek mainland through western and southern Anatolia to Greater Syria and the North African coastal plain. In Palestine, the large-scale production and sale of olive oil and of soap made from olive oil and potash provided a stable source of wealth for several influential families based in the countryside around Nablus during the eighteenth and nineteenth centuries.

Changes

This generalized description of peasant life should not, however, be taken to mean that conditions in the countryside remained unchanged through the ages. On the contrary, the countryside was in flux during the seventeenth century, above all, as a result of the society-wide economic and demographic crisis described in Chapter 4. True, armed brigandage was less of a problem in the Arab lands than it was in Anatolia since considerably fewer mercenaries – mainly tribesmen – were hired from the Arab territories. Still, farmers and herders suffered no less than their Anatolian counterparts from the wave of inflation and concomitant currency debasement. Meanwhile, their lives were disrupted by the machinations of the Arab provincial versions of the Jelali governors covered in Chapter 4.

Inflation, as well as political and economic uncertainty, put pressure on the region's tribes, increasing competition and, therefore, conflict among them and encouraging tribal attacks on settled populations, to say nothing of the pilgrimage caravan. Peasant response to the growing turmoil was inevitably to flee to large towns and cities when possible. As a result, the major Arab capitals – Cairo, Damascus, Aleppo, Mosul, Baghdad, Basra – while perhaps not overrun with desperate peasants, found themselves with much enlarged populations of recent rural migrants.

Gabriel Baer has pointed out that the guild structure that obtained in most provincial cities tended to discourage peasants from migrating since the guild hierarchy severely restricted the entry of 'outsiders' into any given craft. Although more recent scholarship has questioned the uniformity and rigidity of guild superstructure in provincial cities, some country folk may well have opted for larger villages, small towns or, as Baer puts it, 'the hills' when disaster threatened, rather than relocating to the disorienting milieu of a major metropolis.

One of the groups who unquestionably moved regularly from countryside to city were the ulema, or Muslim scholar-officials. After all, it was usually necessary for an aspiring village judge or theologian to relocate at least temporarily to a city where reputable *madrasa*s and eminent scholars could be found in order to pursue his religious education. The scholar wandering in search of knowledge is as enduring a type in Islamic as in western European or Chinese civilization, going back to the early centuries of Islam. Over the course of the seventeenth century, the major cities of the Ottoman Arab provinces received large numbers of students from their rural hinterlands. This was particularly true of Cairo and Damascus, which were home to some of Islam's greatest *madrasa*s, but also of Mecca and Medina, traditional gathering places for Muslim scholars. Upper Egyptian students adhering to the Maliki legal rite flooded Cairo's venerable al-Azhar *madrasa*; ultimately, a separate residential college, or *riwaq*, was added to accommodate them. This influx of ulema of rural origin supposedly inspired al-Shirbini to pen his *Hazz al-quhuf*; he may himself have been, as Baer argues, a rural scholar working 'under cover'. Some of these intellectual refugees from the countryside became eminent legists and theologians in their own right, contributing to a critical mass of Maliki luminaries in Cairo during the second half of the seventeenth century and the first half of the eighteenth. When the office of Shaykh al-Azhar, equivalent to rector of the institution, was created in the late seventeenth century, several of its early occupants were Maliki. Damascus, meanwhile, attracted students from not only the Syrian but also the Anatolian countryside; one of the leaders of the puritanical Kadızadeli movement, which swept Istanbul towards the middle of the seventeenth century, had received the major part of his education in Damascus. Meanwhile, one of the most influential mystics of the premodern era, Abd al-Ghani al-Nabulsi (1641–1731), migrated from the Palestinian market town of Nablus to Damascus; there, he founded a *madrasa* where he and his descendants held sway and where they are entombed.

As the Ottoman economy recovered during the eighteenth century, the wave of rural-to-urban migration slowed, and earlier generations of migrants assimilated. In the countryside, some peasant families of relative means were able to acquire tax farms, although this was in no sense the norm. A few enterprising peasant families even managed to purchase the life-tenure tax farms (singular *malikane*) which so profoundly shaped provincial land tenure during the eighteenth century. In this fashion, families of peasant origin were transformed into provincial notables. Among Egypt's eighteenth-century grandee households was one known as the Fallah, literally, 'peasant', whose founder was 'a peasant orphan lad from a village in Manufiyya Province . . . [who] worked as a servant for one of the village shaykh's sons'.[6] When the shaykh was unable to repay a debt to the grandee who held the tax farm of his village, he gave him his son's servant, whom the grandee raised as a member of his household. Arguably more typical were the Palestinian villagers who grew rich from the sale of olive oil, above all the Abd al-Hadis, a clan from the village of Arraba who used their olive oil profits to penetrate Nablus' soap-making industry, for which olive oil was the prime ingredient.

Subsistence crises

Towards the end of the eighteenth century, however, a series of sharp economic downturns and meteorological irregularities combined to throw the rural population of the Ottoman Arab provinces back into crisis. This was particularly the case in Egypt, where, in the 1780s and again in the 1790s, a series of low Nile floods led to crop failures and famine, which left the population especially susceptible to repeated outbreaks of epidemic disease. These already miserable conditions were exacerbated by the behaviour of the province's two governing beys, Ibrahim and Murad, who invariably hoarded already scarce grain in order to drive up prices. The predictable result was renewed peasant flight from the land and a corresponding decline in tax revenues. Ironically, when the French invaded in 1798, they found Egypt's peasantry in the worst straits they had seen in nearly a century – yet still the attraction of the province as the 'breadbasket' of countless empires drove the Napoleonic expedition on.

Tribes

No discussion of rural life would be complete without due attention to the various tribes that inhabited the Arab countryside. These ranged from settled agriculturalist Bedouin in the Nile Delta to semi-nomadic Turcomans in northern Lebanon to wealthy Kurdish princes in northern Iraq and south-eastern Anatolia.

When the Ottomans conquered the Arab lands, they were obliged to make administrative arrangements with various tribal groups, many of whom had performed military and administrative duties for the Mamluks (in Egypt, Syria and the western Arabian peninsula) and for the Akkoyunlu and the Safavids (in Iraq). In the Nile Delta, the Ottomans entrusted a large, diffuse group of Bedouin known as the Banu Baqara (literally, 'sons of the cow') with tax collection in numerous villages in several key subprovinces. While the Banu Baqara had been allies of the late Mamluk sultans, under whom they had attained a position of unassailable authority in the Delta, they ultimately betrayed the last Mamluk sultan, Tumanbay, and turned him over to the forces of Selim I. The situation in Greater Syria was more volatile because of the region's mountainous topography and ethno-religious variety. In the hinterland of Damascus, for example, which included Lebanon's Bekaa Valley, the Ottomans initially relied on the Hanash family of Sunni Arab tribal shaykhs, who had carried out the policies of the Mamluk sultans in the region since the late fourteenth century. By 1570, however, the Hanash, whose loyalty to the Ottoman sultan was at best unpredictable, had been displaced in the region by the Furaykhs, a small Bedouin family from the Bekaa who, however, ultimately fell victim to attacks by larger, more established regional families, including the Ma'n, a Druze clan that controlled much of Lebanon during the seventeenth century, as noted in Chapter 4.

In Greater Syria, the Ottomans confronted not only Muslim sectarianism – of particular concern during the first half of the sixteenth century, when the struggle with the Safavids of Iran was acute – but also the ancient rivalry between 'northern' and 'southern', or Qaysi and Yemeni, Arabs, briefly described in Chapter 4. Originating in the cultural cleavages separating the tribes of pre-Islamic Yemen from those farther north in the Arabian peninsula, this division spread throughout the Middle East with the Muslim conquests, quickly losing its original geographical connotations. Qays-Yemen conflict permeated Palestine, Lebanon and parts of Syria into the twentieth century. Rather ironically in view of their mutual antagonisms, the three Syrian families mentioned above were Qaysis; however, the Ottomans seemingly had no systematic preference for one faction over the other and, in fact, promoted the Yemeni Alam al-Din family against the Ma'ns following Fakhr al-Din's defeat.

Because the Iraqi provinces comprised the frontier with the enemy Safavid empire, the Ottomans treated the tribal populations operating there with extreme caution following the conquest of the region by Selim I and Süleyman I. In fact, the rebellion during the 1540s of the Arab chieftain who controlled Basra and environs, and who had submitted to Süleyman in 1538, triggered the region's formal incorporation as an Ottoman province. Large swathes of northern Iraq, as well as north-eastern Syria and south-eastern Anatolia, in contrast, were the preserve of powerful Kurdish emirs whom the Ottomans invested as leaders of tribal confederations and who remained semi-autonomous in return for paying tribute to the imperial treasury and lending military support to the Ottoman armies. The seventeenth-century Jelali governor Ali Pasha Janbulad, whose rebellion is covered in Chapter 4, was the nephew of the Kurdish emir of Kilis in south-eastern Anatolia. Even after the demise of the Janbulads, Kurdish chieftains remained prominent in the region.

This is not to say that the Ottomans took no action to manipulate the tribal populations of the Arab lands apart from playing one group off against another. The Ottoman central authority created many of the Kurdish emirates described above by imposing the *timar* system on pre-existing independent Kurdish statelets; in a departure from established usage, however, *timar*s and *zeamet*s remained within a restricted group of ruling Kurdish families through hereditary succession. The families who controlled these emirates thus came to depend on the Ottoman state for their status and authority. During the sixteenth century, in addition, the Ottomans introduced substantial numbers of Turcoman tribes-people into northern Iraq and Syria for reasons that remain largely unclear. With the rise of the Safavids, who were themselves Turcomans, such tribes were on the move in the region in any case, and channelling Sunni Turcomans into relatively remote, mountainous parts of the Ottoman Arab provinces arguably created a buffer against Safavid influence. More generally, the addition of these Turcomans to the ethnic mix in Syria and Iraq diluted the impact of other tribal populations, such as those mentioned above. These were not, however, the first Turcomans to enter the region. The Turcoman Akkoyunlu and Safavids had, of course, ruled Iraq before the Ottoman conquest. But even in Syria and Lebanon, smaller Turcoman tribal groups had been present since at least the late four-teenth century, presumably part of the larger movement of Turcoman tribes which followed the Mongol invasions and of which the Ottomans themselves had been a part.

In Yemen, of course, the Ottoman governors confronted the challenge of various Arab Zaydi tribes who were never content to live under Sunni Ottoman rule. Nonetheless, the Ottomans managed rather cannily to play rival Zaydi tribes off against each other. Following the defeat of the militant imam al-Mutahhar ibn Sharaf al-Din in the 1560s, for the most notable example, the Ottomans took his sons onto their payroll and even paid one of them to spy for them. These Mutahharids were presumably of some use to the Ottomans a few decades later against the imams of the Qasimi dynasty, whom al-Mutahhar's line cordially detested. Notwithstanding, as pointed out in Chapter 4, the Qasimis ultimately forced the Ottomans from Yemen entirely. Ottoman governors were arguably more successful in co-opting certain of Yemen's equally divided Ismaili tribes, chiefly by granting them tax farms in exchange for loyalty, as they did an Ismaili missionary of the venerable Hamdani clan.

Changes

Tribal configurations in the Arab provinces changed considerably during the Ottoman era as a result of both the all-encompassing crisis of the seventeenth century and regional transformations during the following century. In seventeenth-century Egypt, the demographic dislocations which had produced factionalism in Cairo and other urban centres had more subtle repercussions in the countryside, where tribal factionalism had already existed for some centuries. Egypt's Banu Baqara tribe, mentioned above in connection with the Ottoman conquest, belonged to a large bloc of related, or at least allied, tribes known collectively as the Banu Haram which had inhabited the Nile Delta since at least the late Mamluk period. The Haram had seemingly always entertained a conflict with another huge tribal bloc whose identity varied over the centuries. By the seventeenth century, their rivals were the Banu Saʻd. The two blocs' names seem to have an almost ritualistic significance: *haram* signifies 'forbidden' or 'taboo' in Arabic, while *saʻd* means 'felicity'. These labels may point to the ritually positive and negative roles the two blocs played in popular tales seeking to explain their origins.

These two blocs fought for control of tax farms in key subprovinces of both Lower and Upper Egypt, so that Saʻd–Haram violence threatened to engulf the Egyptian countryside. Al-Shirbini, in his *Hazz al-quhuf*, uses 'Saʻd–Haram' as a byword for rural upheaval, treating the pair as if they were inseparable one from another. This tribal rivalry was directly related to the emergence of the Faqari and Qasimi factions during the same century, for the grandees of the Faqari faction were allied with the Saʻd, those of the Qasimi faction with the Haram. Indeed, the Saʻd–Haram rivalry can be regarded to some degree as the rural analogue to the Faqari–Qasimi struggle.

In the course of the following century, the pace of change among tribal groups in the Ottoman Arab provinces intensified. Tribal migrations in southern Syria, the Arabian peninsula and western Iraq led to a reconfiguration of political and economic influence among the region's Bedouin. Members of the ancient, enormous Anaza (or Anayza) confederation began moving from central Arabia into the Euphrates valley in Syria and Iraq in the late seventeenth century. These transhumants ranged in the course of a year over a territory stretching from north-western Syria to western Arabia. In western Syria, they displaced the Mawali confederation, a population of sheep-, horse- and camel-herders who had controlled the region since the thirteenth century and received official sanction from the Ottoman authorities in the late sixteenth century. Inevitably, the Anaza encountered the pilgrimage caravan from Damascus; by 1700, they were regularly supplying mounts and provisions to the pilgrims while protecting the caravan from attacks by other Bedouin tribes in return for a payment from the central Ottoman treasury. If they failed to receive this payment, they might not only withdraw their protection but even join in the plundering of the caravan, as in the infamous attack of 1757, discussed in Chapter 5.

To the south-west, meanwhile, an enormous Berber confederation known as the Hawwara had achieved near-total control over Upper Egypt by the 1730s. Originating in Algeria under the Roman Empire, the Hawwara had very gradually migrated eastwards across North Africa, reaching Egypt in the thirteenth century. Although the confederation was divided into several subunits, all recognized an overall shaykh who had his seat in Farshut in the Upper Egyptian superprovince of Jirja. In the 1750s, Shaykh Humam ruled Upper Egypt as a veritable fiefdom. He was finally broken, however, by the rebellious grandee Ali Bey after sheltering the bey's enemies from what remained of the Qasimi faction.

In the late eighteenth century, the aggressive expansionism of the Banu Saud, allied with the puritanical Wahhabi movement, in the eastern Arabian peninsula drove hostile tribes into Iraq. Although one subgroup of the Anaza espoused the Wahhabi cause, the remainder of the confederation shifted their base from central Arabia to central and southern Iraq in an attempt to escape Wahhabi demands for revenue. In southern Iraq, the Anaza challenged, although they could not undermine, the hegemony of the Muntafiq confederation, whose expansion was described in Chapter 5. After reaching a modus vivendi with the Georgian mamluk governors of Baghdad, the Anaza became one of the region's largest and most influential tribal populations. Another large, influential Bedouin confederation of central Arabia, the Shammar, were the lineage group of the Banu Rashid, enemies of the Saudis in the late nineteenth and early twentieth centuries. Initially, however, the Shammar supported the Saudis but fell out with them and gradually migrated into northern Iraq, where by the early nineteenth century they exercised undisputed hegemony.

For the Ottomans, of course, the rise of the Wahhabis in the interior of the Arabian peninsula and their alliance with the Banu Saud, to be treated in Chapter 10, constituted the most fateful transformation to occur among the tribes of their Arab territories. This combination would fuel an explosive rebellion against Ottoman rule in the peninsula which would ultimately succeed in the early twentieth century.

Tribal life

About the daily lives of these different tribal groups we know little apart from what we can extrapolate from their modern-day descendants and the occasional detail provided by travel accounts such as that of the seventeenth-century Ottoman courtier Evliya Chelebi. While a number of the tribes of southern Syria, Iraq and the Arabian peninsula, including the Anaza, were entirely nomadic, those of northern Syria, Lebanon, Egypt and Yemen were more likely to be semi-nomadic. In the Nile Delta, many tribes were settled agriculturalists. The women of the Banu Haram tribes in the Nile Delta apparently embroidered textiles.

Tribes were instrumental in supplying livestock for the Ottoman armies and administrators. Numerous Arab, Kurdish and Turcoman tribes in Syria and Lebanon provided donkeys and sheep for the army, imperial court and provincial administrators. The Anaza confederation not only protected the Damascene pilgrimage caravan but also supplied it with camels, horses and donkeys. Camels were so critical to overland trade in the Arab provinces, to say nothing of military administration and expeditions, that a caravan consisting of nothing but camels raised by the Anaza and other tribes trundled from Basra to Aleppo once a year. In Upper Egypt, the Hawwara had raised horses for the sultans and emirs of Egypt during the Mamluk period; there is no reason to doubt that they continued to provide this service for Ottoman administrators also. Tribes inhabiting Iraq and the Arabian interior had for centuries supplied fine Arabian horses to India; by the eighteenth century, Ottoman governors in Iraq, including the Georgian mamluks of Baghdad, had come to rely on these mounts, some of which came from the Anaza and Shammar once they had established themselves in the region. Horse merchants drove the herds from the tribal lands to Basra for shipment to India or farther into the Iraqi interior, and sometimes as far as Aleppo and Diyarbakır for further redistribution. Given the importance of horses in premodern societies, it is hardly surprising that the trade in Arabian horses through Iraq and the Arabian peninsula, as well as through the Persian Gulf, was vast, complex and highly lucrative. 'In five or six months, about 3,000 horses were received from the ports of the Persian Gulf,' a former British consul-general in Bombay estimated in 1894. '. . . Every day witnessed the sale of horses, and when the season closed, the unsold residue was inconsiderable. . . .'[7] Some tribes even used horses as a means of paying taxes, tribute and war reparations; they were also highly prized as gifts.

A new and distinctive element in the overland caravan trade was the population known as Uqayl or Agayl, who were at least nominally connected to the ancient central Arabian Uqayl tribe, ancestors of the Muntafiq Bedouin of southern Iraq. 'Uqayl' appears to have been a blanket term for a conglomerate of members of various Bedouin tribes, particularly those of central Arabia, and certain other elements, allied for commercial purposes. They cultivated ties with the merchants of Baghdad and Damascus, for whom they served as agents, as well as guides for the caravans linking the two cities; in fact, several hundred of them took up residence in Baghdad. Furthermore, they transported camels from central Arabia to these two entrepôts, returning with trade goods for the tribes of the region. By the end of the eighteenth century, Uqaylis utterly dominated overland trade among Syria, Iraq and the Arabian peninsula. In addition, the Ottoman governors of Baghdad and Damascus came to rely on them as protectors of the pilgrimage caravan, particularly in the face of the Wahhabis.

Conclusion

By 1800, the rural population of the Ottoman provinces was being wrenched out of a long period of relative economic and social stability. In addition to an empire-wide economic crisis, various localized subsistence crises and major tribal realignments, the provincial peasantry was beginning to feel the effects of western European, and above all French and British, intervention in the Ottoman economy. To be sure, the notion that the Ottoman Empire had by 1800 already been incorporated into the so-called European world economy has recently been challenged. Agricultural production continued to be overwhelmingly for intra-provincial, or at least intra-imperial, consumption until at least the mid-nineteenth century. But combined with these other pressures, that of the expanding European market seemed to exacerbate the sense of crisis.

In addition, tribal realignments of the period foreshadowed profound political changes in the region. Most significant in this regard, naturally, was the emergence of the Wahhabi movement in the depths of the Arabian peninsula, its alliance with the Banu Saud, and the combined forces' astonishing military and ideological success.

Such, then, is the picture we are able to assemble of conditions in the countryside of the Ottoman Arab provinces. Regrettably, rural populations, although they far outnumbered city-dwellers throughout the Ottoman Empire during the entire period covered by this study, are almost inevitably marginalized in the historiography of the empire and its various provinces because of the lack of sources revealing the conditions under which they lived relative to those available for urbanites, as well as the tendency for city-dwellers to serve as the standard by which a society is evaluated. In recent years, happily, this underrepresentation of the rural populace, both peasant and tribesperson, has begun to be redressed. Much the same can be said for marginal groups among both the urban and rural populations, who form the subject of the following chapter.

Notes

1. Quoted in Amy Singer, *Palestinian Peasants and Ottoman Officials: Rural Administration around Sixteenth-Century Jerusalem* (Cambridge, 1994), p. 91.
2. Leslie Peirce, *Morality Tales: Law and Gender in the Ottoman Court of Aintab* (Berkeley, CA, 2003), pp. 136–9.
3. Quoted and paraphrased in Gabriel Baer, 'Shirbini's *Hazz al-quhūf* and Its Significance', in Baer, *Fellah and Townsman in the Middle East: Studies in Social History* (London and Totowa, NJ, 1982), pp. 11, 12, 35.
4. S.D. Goitein, 'Townsman and Fellah: A Geniza Text from the Seventeenth Century', *Asian and African Studies* (Haifa) 8 (1972), p. 259.
5. Ibid.
6. Al-Jabarti, *Al-Jabarti's History of Egypt*, I, p. 311 (trans. Daniel Crecelius and Boutros Abd al-Malik).
7. Quoted in Hala Fattah, *The Politics of Regional Trade in Iraq, Arabia, and the Gulf, 1745–1900* (Albany, NY, 1997), p. 170.

chapter nine

MARGINAL GROUPS AND MINORITY POPULATIONS

The populations of rural and urban spheres alike were far from homogeneous. In addition to Arabophone Sunnis, large numbers of non-Muslims and significant groups of non-Sunni Muslims and non-Arabs of various confessions inhabited the Ottoman Empire's Arab provinces. Nor were all these populations free. Slaves, not only influential elite slaves but also more humble domestic servants and agricultural workers, played critical roles in provincial economic, social and political life. Furthermore, at least half, and sometimes a higher percentage, of all these populations were women, while a not insignificant proportion were impoverished and/or disabled. This chapter, therefore, explores the status and roles of these different groups, keeping in mind the difficulty of generalizing about such diverse populations.

Each of these groups, with the exception of women, was a decided minority in the societies of the Arab provinces. We can also assert that all of them, women included, were marginal populations inasmuch as they did not enjoy the officially sanctioned social legitimacy and public centrality of free, mentally and physically sound Sunni Muslim males, along with the legal rights that status conferred. On the other hand, 'marginal' in this context does not necessarily connote oppression or even subordination. Although members of some of these groups were certainly disadvantaged and even wretched, others, notably prominent non-Muslim merchants, occupied privileged positions of influence; their minority status arguably helped them to attain such heights. Their cases represent a phenomenon that we may call 'marginality at the centre', for, although they belonged to communities that were officially denied the full rights of the Ottoman sultan's free male Sunni subjects, they operated close to the very power centre that defined and upheld these rights.

Religious minorities

The Pact of Umar

Muslims had first had to contend with large numbers of non-Muslim monotheists living under their rule during the reign of the second caliph, or successor to the Prophet Muhammad as leader of the Muslim community, Umar ibn al-Khattab (r. 634–44). Under Umar, Arab tribal armies penetrated deep into Byzantine territory and brought the Sasanian Empire to an end. Before the nineteenth century, the template for treatment of non-Muslims under Muslim rule was a document known as the Pact of Umar, supposedly the peace treaty between Umar and the residents of Byzantine Jerusalem, whose population at the time was overwhelmingly Orthodox Christian. Many scholars, however, are convinced that at least parts of the Pact date from as much as a century later, for certain clauses display thorough familiarity with Muslim norms, which a newly conquered population could not have had.

As central as the Pact of Umar was in determining the place of non-Muslims in the premodern Ottoman world, two of the most fundamental features of non-Muslims' status were not specified in the document. First of all, non-Muslims who were subject to the Pact must be monotheists with a revealed scripture, who came to be known as People of the Book. Polytheists, notably animists of the sort who dominated Mecca throughout most of the Prophet Muhammad's lifetime, were not allowed to keep their religion and live peacefully under Muslim rule. They must convert, leave the community or face military attack. In the territories the Ottomans came to rule, People of the Book comprised for the most part Christians and Jews.

Although they were officially tolerated, People of the Book who did not convert to Islam had to pay a special poll, or head, tax that Muslims did not have to pay. This was the *jizya* (*cizye* in Turkish), a tax which, like the stipulation of monotheism, is not mentioned in the Pact of Umar, although it was often justified by the Quranic verse exhorting Muslims to 'fight against those to whom the Scriptures were given, who do not believe in God and the Last Day, who do not prohibit what God and his apostle have forbidden, . . . until they pay the tribute (*jizya*) out of hand and are humbled' (9:29). Under the Umayyads and later dynasties, including the Ottomans, the *jizya* was graduated so that the wealthiest, middling and poorest members of the non-Muslim population paid three different rates corresponding to their economic status. Unlike most taxes, notably land taxes, the *jizya* was an individual tax, calculated according to the estimated numbers of the adult male non-Muslim population. This did not mean, however, that each male non-Muslim paid his tax individually to a government official. Ordinarily, the leader of each major non-Muslim community in a given locale would collect the *jizya* household by household and deliver it to representatives of the government. As early as the sixteenth century, the Ottoman central authority began to auction off *jizya* collection rights in various provinces as tax farms; like most tax farms, they were usually held by military and administrative grandees, who often sent their agents to collect the tax.

As to what *is* included in the Pact of Umar, the document, in the form of a letter to Umar from the leader of the Christian community, opens, 'When you advanced against us, we asked you for a guarantee of protection for our persons, our offspring, our property, and the people of our sect.' The Arabic word for 'protection' is *dhimma*, for which reason non-Muslim subjects of a Muslim ruler came to be known as *dhimmi*s (*zimmi* in the Turkish singular), or 'protected ones'. The remainder of the document consists of a series of restrictions that the Christians volunteer to observe in their public behaviour in exchange for being allowed to keep their religion and community structure and to live peacefully under Muslim rule. The restrictions most commonly remarked upon are: 'We shall not build . . . any new monasteries, churches, hermitages, or monks' cells. We shall not restore . . . any of them that have fallen into ruin . . . ,' and, above all, 'We shall not attempt to resemble the Muslims in any way with regard to their dress.'[1] In the days of the original Islamic conquests, such clothing restrictions were probably designed to prevent non-Muslims from attempting to join the Arab military elite by adopting its costume. In premodern Islamic societies, furthermore, different confessional and ethnic communities dressed differently as a matter of course. In this context, the sumptuary laws may be regarded as something other than an unprecedented, draconian imposition. Likewise, the restriction on building non-Muslim houses of worship may originally have been designed to reinforce the presence of a tiny Muslim ruling elite amid an overwhelmingly non-Muslim population. Thus, while they unquestionably promoted inequality between Muslims and non-Muslims, the stipulations of the Pact of Umar must be viewed within the context in which they probably originated.

In any case, the Pact of Umar's restrictions were not rigidly enforced by every Muslim regime throughout the ages until the westernizing reforms of the nineteenth century. Most modern-day scholars interpret the sporadic appearance under a variety of premodern Muslim regimes of orders and decrees reimposing the Pact as evidence that its strictures were being ignored. The Ottomans are generally regarded as one of the most lax regimes in enforcing the Pact, although, as we shall see, society-wide crises not infrequently led to more rigorous application of its stipulations.

Communal administration and leadership

Before the conquest of Egypt, Syria and the western Arabian peninsula in 1516–17, the Ottoman Empire was a Balkan and Anatolian empire a majority of whose population was Orthodox Christian. The early Ottomans even accepted unconverted Orthodox Christians into their ranks and gave them *timar*s, or grants of land revenue in return for military service. After Mehmed II conquered Constantinople in 1453, however, administration of Christian and Jewish communities was standardized. According to the conventional wisdom, Mehmed II established an empire-wide community, or *millet*, for each major non-Muslim community under his rule, with community leaders whose authority extended empire-wide. *Millet* is simply a Turkicized pronunciation of the Arabic word for 'nation', but before the nineteenth century, as the historian Benjamin Braude has pointed out, it was ordinarily used to designate either the Muslim community as a whole or a foreign Christian community, such as the Genoese merchants who inhabited the neighbourhood of Galata on the northern shore of Istanbul's Golden Horn.

Braude argues persuasively that the conventional view stems from foundation myths constructed centuries later by the Jewish and Christian communities themselves.[2] In fact, Mehmed II recognized those individual Christian and Jewish religious leaders whom he found in Constantinople, although not necessarily without hesitation and false starts. Every new religious leader had to be reapproved, and the status of the different communities' leadership varied markedly. Whereas the Greek Orthodox patriarch's authority extended, at least theoretically, throughout the empire, the Jewish chief rabbi's jurisdiction before the nineteenth century was apparently limited to Istanbul. As for the Armenians, Mehmed II was able to establish only a sort of symbolic patriarchate in Istanbul because the seat of the ancient Armenian Orthodox Church was located at the time in the territory of the Akkoyunlu, or White Sheep Turcomans, who were hostile to the Ottomans. As a result, the Armenian patriarchate of Istanbul had very little authority, even within the city itself. In short, the *millet* system in the sense of uniform empire-wide non-Muslim community administration was not put in place until the nineteenth century.

With the conquest of the Arab lands, similarly ad hoc policies were applied to the non-Muslim communities there, who included, in addition to Jews and Orthodox Christians, Coptic Christians and Christians of the smaller eastern rites, enumerated in Chapter 1, as well as minuscule numbers of adherents of non-Jewish and -Christian monotheisms. Unlike previous regimes, the Ottoman central authority was most concerned with the lay leadership of these communities, as opposed to rabbis, bishops and even patriarchs, for the lay leaders ensured that the communities paid their taxes to the imperial treasury. In each Arab provincial capital, the Ottomans recognized a secular community representative who usually received the omnibus title shaykh; in Anatolia and the European provinces, he went by the equally flexible title *kâhya*, a contracted rendition of *kethüda*. This personage was normally a well-to-do merchant or money-lender who could stand surety for the community's collective *jizya* if necessary, as well as taxes not specific to non-Muslims; he was appointed by the Muslim chief judge on the recommendation of prominent members of the non-Muslim community in question. In seventeenth-century Cairo, for example, the head of the Jewish community was the Ottoman governor's banker, who went by yet another fluid title, *chelebi*, which can perhaps be likened to 'esquire'. The Ottoman authorities had abolished the religious office of Head of the Jews, which dated to Fatimid times, shortly after the conquest. In general, we may regard this community representative as a sort of secular deputy to the community's religious leader. Notwithstanding, such representatives arguably impinged in certain respects on the authority of the non-Muslim religious leadership in the Arab provinces. For administrative and economic purposes, they, not the chief rabbis and bishops, occupied the most critical positions.

The major non-Muslim communities over whom the Ottomans came to rule in the Arab lands were described in Chapter 1. Here, we shall explore how the conditions of certain communities changed during the Ottoman period as a result of the policies of the Ottoman government and those of other states, as well as shifts in demographic and commercial patterns.

Jews

Towards the end of the fifteenth century, the composition of the Ottoman Empire's Jewish population changed drastically as a result of developments in distant Spain and Portugal. In 1492, Spain's Roman Catholic monarchs, Ferdinand and Isabella, conquered the kingdom of Granada at Spain's south-eastern tip, bringing an end to nearly eight centuries of various forms of Muslim dominion in various parts of Spain. Ferdinand and Isabella regarded their military victory as part of a broader Catholic crusading mission. Their patronage of the Genoese merchant-explorer Christopher Columbus – who, of course, set off on the first of his famous voyages that same year – contributed in some respects to this mission, for they wished him to discover a route to India which would not pass through the territory of any Muslim regime. In the summer of 1492, the king and queen formally expelled Spain's sizeable Jewish population, which, along with the remaining Muslims, prevented Spain from becoming a purely Catholic realm. Some Jews outwardly converted to Catholicism in order to remain but were frequently harassed by the Inquisition, who suspected them of harbouring their former faith. Most Muslims who chose to remain in Spain converted to Christianity, frequently under duress, but, like the Jews, often attempted to observe their original faith clandestinely. These Moriscos, as they were known, were ultimately expelled from Spain in 1609. In Portugal, meanwhile, the king, not wanting to lose the economic productivity of his Jewish subjects, simply issued a decree in 1497 unilaterally declaring them Christian. Not surprisingly, many Portuguese Jews fled the kingdom as a result.

Sultan Bayezid II (r. 1481–1512), the son of Mehmed II, issued a decree ordering his provincial governors not to hinder the immigration of these Iberian Jews. Over the next several decades, in consequence, a demographic transformation occurred whereby the Ottoman Empire's Jewish population became majority Spanish and Portuguese, or Sephardic, an adjective derived from Sepharad, the traditional Hebrew name for Spain. This happened not only in the Balkans and Anatolia but in the Arab lands as well, where the Jewish population had historically consisted of Arabic-speaking Jews known as Mustarabs. By the time Selim I conquered Syria and Egypt in 1516–17, the change was already well under way. The Mustarabs were soon eclipsed by the well-educated, commercially active Sephardim, although ultimately Arabic would reassert itself as the daily language of most Jewish communities in the Ottoman Arab provinces.

Under Süleyman I, a small but visible elite of Sephardic Jews attained positions of great influence around the sultan. Particularly striking is the story of Doña Gracia Nasi (ca. 1510–69) and her nephew Don Joseph Nasi (ca. 1520–79), as they are most commonly known. They belonged to a large family of Portuguese Jews, the Mendes family, who had outwardly converted to Christianity. Even in this situation, the Mendeses founded and participated in a family import–export business which traded heavily throughout Europe and the Mediterranean, largely in pepper transshipped from India, cloth and grain. Under pressure from the Inquisition, Doña Gracia and her nephew ultimately emigrated to Ottoman territory, where Don Joseph became a sort of Rothschild to the Ottoman court, lending the palace huge sums of money and arguably exercising more influence with the sultan and his family than any other Jewish or Christian subject in Ottoman history. Both he and his aunt reconverted to Judaism and even launched a project to reinforce the Jewish presence in Palestine by restoring the ancient city of Tiberias, just west of the Sea of Galilee. In 1558, Sultan Süleyman leased Tiberias to Doña Gracia, who commissioned a *yeshiva*, or Jewish theological school, there while her nephew oversaw the rebuilding of the city's walls. (In the late 1730s, these walls would be reinforced and extended by the Arab grandee Zahir al-Umar, discussed in Chapter 5.) They then appealed to the Jews of Italy to settle in the town, although the settlement programme was hindered by the outbreak of war between the Ottoman Empire and Venice in 1570, hostilities that would result in the Ottoman conquest of Cyprus that same year and the destruction of the Ottoman fleet at Lepanto the following year.

During these same years, north-east of Tiberias, a group of Sephardic rabbis were creating what one twentieth-century scholar has called 'the strangest, strictest, maddest, most amazing community in Jewish history',[3] in the process making the greatest contribution to Jewish mysticism since the body of mystical oral tradition known as the Kabbalah was compiled in thirteenth-century Spain. These mystical luminaries lived in the city of Safed in what is now northern Israel. In the sixteenth century, Safed grew larger than Jerusalem, and its Jewish community outstripped that of Jerusalem in regional influence (Ottoman Jerusalem was a provincial town a majority of whose population was Muslim and Arab Christian). Safed became a thriving regional commercial centre, thanks in large part to the textile, and above all wool, industry, in which Jews participated heavily, particularly in dyeing. Some of the great mystics were also wealthy textile merchants. Perhaps the most famous of these scholar-mystics was Rabbi Isaac Luria (1534–72), who developed a distinctive messianic interpretation of the Kabbalah which is still known as Lurianic Kabbalah. The longer-lived Rabbi Joseph Karo (1488–1575) wrote a practical guide to Jewish law known as the *Shulhan Arukh* (literally, *The Set Table*) which is still used today; when not pondering Jewish law, he had visions of angels which informed his influential mystical writings.

The general condition and treatment of Jews and Christians in the Ottoman Empire took a turn for the worse at the end of the sixteenth century. As noted in Chapter 4, this was a period of social and economic crisis for the empire, combining the dislocations of the Long War (1593–1606) against the Habsburgs with massive inflation exacerbated by the influx of silver from Spain's colonies in Mexico and Peru. Generally speaking, economic crisis tends to have negative effects on minority populations. While there was no wave of bloody persecution, authorities tended to take a somewhat harsher line with Jews and Christians alike, although circumstances varied widely from place to place. In Istanbul, a large Jewish neighbourhood down the hill from Topkapı Palace, at the edge of the Golden Horn, was cleared for the completion of the New Mosque (Yeni Jami), commissioned by the mother of Murad III.

Sabbatai Sevi

In the late seventeenth century, Jewish communities throughout the Ottoman Empire and beyond were rocked by the affair of Sabbatai Sevi. The son of a merchant in the booming Anatolian port of Izmir, Sabbatai Sevi declared himself the long-awaited Jewish messiah in 1665 and began spreading the news of the imminent messianic age to Jewish communities in the eastern Mediterranean. His disciple Nathan of Gaza

Figure 9.1 Sabbatai Sevi.
Source: Thomas Coenen, *Ydele Verwachtinge der Joden getoont in den Persoon van Sabethai Zevi*. Amsterdam: Joannes van den Bergh, 1669.

was instrumental in whipping up enthusiasm, composing letters of glad tidings which circulated throughout the empire. Meanwhile, the movement was bankrolled by the head of Egypt's Jewish community, who was also the personal banker to the Ottoman governor. The messianic tidings followed the trade routes through the Aegean, the Mediterranean and the Red Sea, ultimately spreading to Yemen, North Africa, the Balkans, Italy and even as far afield as Holland and England. Jews throughout this vast region began to sell their property and prepare to be miraculously transported to Jerusalem.

Understandably alarmed, the Ottoman authorities imprisoned Sabbatai Sevi in the spring of 1666 on the grounds that, by purporting to be the Jewish messiah, he threatened the sultan's rule while fomenting social unrest. Originally held in Istanbul, he was moved after a few months to Gallipoli, then to Edirne, where Sultan Mehmed IV (r. 1648–87) was in residence and where Sabbatai Sevi faced a council of high officials. He was apparently given the choice of conversion to Islam or death and ultimately converted after intense discussions with the sultan's personal spiritual advisor, Vani Mehmed Efendi, who led the puritanical, ostensibly anti-mystical Sunni Muslim tendency commonly known as the Kadızadeli movement, discussed in Chapter 6, which had gained unprecedented influence in the central Ottoman lands. 'And now let me alone,' Sabbatai Sevi wrote to his brother nine days after his conversion, 'for God has made me a Turk.'[4] Now called Aziz Mehmed Efendi, he became Vani's personal assistant.

Sabbatai Sevi's conversion left Ottoman Jewish communities in shock. A number of Sabbatai Sevi's disciples followed him into Islam, laying the foundations for what is commonly known as the Dönme sect, a tiny, nominally Muslim faith whose three branches observe their own highly mystical, post-messianic versions of Jewish rites, which often feature violations of normative Jewish law and which in some cases are influenced by Islamic practice. Other disciples retained their Judaism while continuing to believe in Sabbatai Sevi's mission. The banker to the governor of Egypt was mysteriously murdered in 1670 while Nathan of Gaza, after undertaking a proselytizing mission through Anatolia, the Balkans and Italy, died in Macedonia in 1680. In 1679, the Zaydi Shiite imam of Yemen attempted to expel Yemen's Jews, who had been swept up in a messianic fervour coloured by, even if not directly inspired by, Sabbatai Sevi's mission. They were corralled in the city of Mawza, just inland from Mocha, where, because Yemen had no ship-building industry of its own, they were obliged to wait for an Indian ship to carry them into exile. None ever arrived, however, and in the meantime, large numbers of Jews died of starvation and disease brought on by overcrowded living quarters and the torrid climate of the coastal plain. After a year, the imam, realizing what a blow he had dealt Yemen's economy, allowed the survivors to return to their native towns.

Back in Ottoman territory, the remaining Jewish leadership tried strenuously to control the damage wrought by Sabbatai Sevi's movement while rejecting the movement itself. Internal sources, both those emanating from the Jewish community and those produced by the Ottoman government, are curiously reticent on the subject of Sabbatai Sevi's career and its effects. But there is little doubt that it represented a serious blow to Ottoman Jewry at a time when treatment of minorities generally was growing more stringent.

Syrian Catholics

With the penetration of the European commercial powers into the Ottoman Empire, however, new economic opportunities opened for Jews and Christians. During the seventeenth century, British, French and Italian merchants importing goods, above all cloth, into the Ottoman provinces began to employ Jews and Christians as commercial intermediaries so as to facilitate their trade, particularly in smaller towns and in the countryside. After all, many upper-class Jews and Christians spoke both Arabic and European languages, either as a result of speaking Spanish or Italian at home, in the case of Sephardic Jews, or as a result of being educated in European universities. Beginning in the eighteenth century, the consuls of the European powers in question applied to the Ottoman central authority for *berat*s, or certificates, of honorary European citizenship, which these agents then purchased so that they would be immune from Ottoman law in their commercial transactions. In consequence, the agents were often popularly known in Ottoman Turkish as *beratlı*s.

The French in particular took advantage of these circumstances to spread Roman Catholicism, not among Ottoman Muslims but chiefly among Orthodox Christians working as agents for them in Syria. Large numbers of these Syrian Christians reconciled with the Vatican and became what are commonly known as Syrian Catholics; they resemble Greek Orthodox Christians in many of their rituals but recognize the Pope, rather than the Greek Orthodox Patriarch in Istanbul, as their spiritual leader. With French backing, they became a commercial force in the late eighteenth-century Mediterranean.

A virtual colony of Syrian Catholics formed even in Egypt, where they were instrumental in commerce between their native Syria and the Mediterranean ports of Alexandria, Damietta and Rosetta. The famous Kazdağlı household leader Ali Bey, whose 1770 rebellion against the

Ottoman sultan was discussed in Chapter 5, in an attempt to establish his own commercial hegemony in the eastern Mediterranean, initially patronized Jewish customs directors who operated under the protection of Venice. In 1768–9, however, he transferred his patronage to Syrian Catholics under French protection; he went so far as to beat the Jewish customs directors of Alexandria and the Nile port of Bulaq to death and seize their wealth. This move had less to do with the bey's religious sympathies than it did with commercial opportunities; the French simply had more to offer him in the 1760s, when France was arguably the dominant power in the eastern Mediterranean.

Jews and Christians in financial service

One of the more pervasive truisms of scholarship on the Ottoman Empire is that Ottoman Muslims tended to disdain trade and other financial activities, thus leaving these fields almost entirely in the hands of *dhimmi*s. While this generalization is demonstrably inaccurate, it is nonetheless true that in many Ottoman cities Jews and Christians of certain denominations concentrated in the commercial and financial sectors. Although the vast majority of the empire's Greek Orthodox and Armenian Orthodox Christian populations were peasant agriculturalists, members of these communities were also prominent merchants in the major Arab provincial cities. Armenians also tended to be overrepresented in the profession of *sarraf*, or money-lender, a profession also frequently practised by Jewish merchants, at least in part because Jewish law does not prohibit interest on loans to non-Jews.

Non-Muslims were also overrepresented in financial posts in the provincial governments. In a few cases, this resulted from historical precedent. Egypt's financial administration, as a notable example, had been run by Coptic Christians before the initial Muslim conquest of the country in the seventh century; following the conquest, the Copts continued in their positions, even employing the Coptic language for record-keeping until late in the seventh century. They were still prominent in such positions throughout the Ottoman period. Even the rebellious Ali Bey employed a prominent Coptic merchant, Muallim Rizq, as manager of his financial affairs – and as his personal astrologer; Rizq, according to the historian al-Jabarti, 'attained in Ali Bey's days a position no other Copt . . . had ever achieved'.[5] Jews also served as financial officials, in large part because of their relative lack of grass roots community ties that might dilute their loyalty to the rulers who employed them. Abraham Castro, the Sephardic Jew who ran Egypt's mint in the years following the Ottoman conquest and who reported to the imperial capital on the rebellion of the governor Ahmed Pasha al-Kha'in, is a case in point. Shortly after Ali Bey's rebellion, meanwhile, Ahmed Pasha al-Jazzar, the autonomous governor of northern Palestine and southern Lebanon, appointed Haim Farhi, a member of a prominent Jewish banking family with a tradition of government service, as his financial officer. In a fit of rage one day, the pasha ordered Farhi's right eye gouged out and his nose cut off for some infraction, yet later restored him to his post. (He is depicted waiting on al-Jazzar in this unfortunate condition in a drawing by the British naval surgeon F.B. Spilsbury.)[6] Non-Muslims, like anyone else who held a position of trust close to a powerful authority figure, suffered the insecurity of their offices.

Twelver Shiites

Although Shiites are not, of course, non-Muslims, the Ottomans' continuing warfare against the Safavids and their successors in Iran made the status of Twelver Shiites living under Ottoman rule uniquely problematic. Since the rise of the Safavid empire at the beginning of the sixteenth century, in fact, the Ottomans had regarded themselves as the guardians of Sunni Islam. Sultan Selim I, the conqueror of Egypt and Syria, not only waged war against the Safavids but launched a veritable inquisition against Safavid-leaning inhabitants of eastern Anatolia. More generally, the Ottomans steadfastly refused to recognize Twelver Shiites as a distinct religious community, separate from Sunni Muslims. Ottoman provincial authorities even occasionally co-opted provincial Sunni ulema to write propaganda works against Shiites, inveighing against intermarriage between Sunnis and Shiites in particular.

Nonetheless, there remained sizeable Shiite populations under Ottoman rule, above all in Iraq, conquered from the Safavids by Süleyman I in 1534, retaken by Shah Abbas in 1623, then reconquered by Sultan Murad IV in 1638. Ottoman Iraq's Shiite population lived as a virtually autonomous religious community under the direction of the Shiite ulema in the shrine cities of Najaf and Karbala. Twelver Shiite ulema differ from their Sunni counterparts in their emphasis on independent reasoning (*ijtihad*) in reaching legal decisions. Their independently arrived-at legal judgements are regarded as binding; they do not depend so heavily on precedent and consensus as Sunni ulema. Moreover, the leading Shiite ulema are the closest authority the community has to the occulted Twelfth Imam, who disappeared in the ninth century and who, Twelver Shiites believe, will return as a messianic figure at the end of time. Shiite ulema are able to collect a tithe from community members for a fund to be used by the Imam on his return. Because of their seminal legal and spiritual roles, they receive extraordinary loyalty from their constituents and are able to project an unusual degree of authority.

Ottoman provincial officials treated the leading ulema of the shrine cities with wary respect while preserving the lavish tomb complexes their predecessors had built to house the remains of Ali in Najaf and Husayn in Karbala, as noted in Chapter 7. Occasionally, however, provincial authorities restricted popular Shiite festivals, above all the public commemorations of the martyrdom of Husayn, which could become wildly emotional and hence struck the authorities as potential vehicles for expression of discontent with Sunni rule. The Jalili family, who, as discussed in Chapter 5, dominated Mosul in the eighteenth century, banned these rituals outright.

Other Twelver Shiite populations could be found in Lebanon, Palestine and Syria. In southern Lebanon and northern Palestine, the Shiites known as Matawila were largely peasants who participated in the factional infighting among Lebanon's notables. In seventeenth-century Aleppo, however, a prominent family of descendants of the Prophet, the Zuhris or Zuhrizades, were Shiite; as descendants of the Prophet, they may have been involved in early confrontations with Aleppo's Janissaries.

Non-elite slavery

Despite their disproportionate influence on the administration, political culture and intellectual life of the Ottoman Arab provinces and of the Ottoman Empire in general, elite slaves of the sort discussed in Chapter 5 were a small minority among slaves in Ottoman service. The vast majority of slaves were decidedly non-elite. Most were female, came from eastern Africa and worked as domestics of one kind or another. In these respects, as in others, Ottoman slavery differed from that with which most readers will be familiar, namely, that of the Americas, where a majority of slaves were males from western Africa who worked in agriculture. The Ottomans occasionally employed eastern African slaves in agriculture, but not on anything like the scale of earlier empires. In the ninth century CE, African slaves had toiled for the Abbasids in appallingly brutal conditions on rice plantations and in salt pans in the marshes of southern Iraq. Under the Mamluk sultanate, African slaves had worked on sugar plantations in Upper Egypt. The Ottomans, in contrast, do not appear to have engaged in plantation agriculture to any significant degree; in comparison with the *chifthane* system, described in the preceding chapter, it was not cost-effective.

Female domestic slaves performed the tasks one would expect household slaves to have performed: caring for children, cooking, cleaning, sewing. It was not uncommon for a female slave to have children by her male owner; in that case, the children were legally free Muslims while their mother became free on her master's death. This mitigating circumstance has contributed to the reputation of slavery under Islamic regimes as a 'kinder, gentler' form of slavery than the trans-Atlantic variety, but, in fact, the potential for a male (or female) owner to abuse his female slaves was vast. Although the experiences of individual household servants are well-nigh impossible to recover, the historian Ehud Toledano found an account in the police records of nineteenth-century Cairo of a Circassian slave girl called Shemsigül ('Sunny Rose' or 'Sunflower') whose case combines elements of elite harem slavery and domestic slavery. Delivered to the harem of no less a personage than the son of Mehmed Ali Pasha, the autonomous governor of Egypt, Shemsigül was unceremoniously expelled when she was found to have been impregnated by the slave dealer who had brought her there. As she later told the police, 'He forced me to have sexual relations with him; he continued to sleep with me until he sold me.'[7] Returned to the slave dealer's house, she was savagely beaten by his wife, who later spirited away the newborn baby. She then passed from slave dealer to slave dealer until one of these men discovered that she was the mother of her original purchaser's child and turned her over to the police. If a prospective elite slave suffered such physical and psychological abuse, it must have been all the more common among the average run of domestic slaves. Yet before the nineteenth century, when the punctilious record-keeping of the modernizing Ottoman state resulted in standardized police blotters and similar documents, there is very little trace in the historical record of what Toledano calls 'the other face of harem bondage', let alone the circumstances and experiences of ordinary female domestics. For the most part, historians can only extrapolate from extremely terse passing mentions of these slaves in historical chronicles and nineteenth-century memoirs.

Slave trade routes

Domestic slaves from the Caucasus followed the same route as mamluks and elite female slaves from that region: they were transported along the southern Black Sea coast to Istanbul, or occasionally to a Black Sea port east of the imperial capital, such as Sinop, where they were either sold in the markets or transshipped to the Arab provinces. In many cases, a trader would purchase a group of slaves in Istanbul, then sell them in Cairo or Damascus. As for the African trade, as noted in connection with long-distance commerce, two major slave caravans left Sudan for Egypt each year: one – actually a conglomeration of several which converged at the Egyptian border – from the eastern city of Sennar, another from the western district of Darfur. The several hundred slaves carried by the Sennar caravan each year were overwhelmingly female; the Darfur caravan shipped several thousand, with a larger proportion of males. Slaves who reached Cairo alive were then sold in the city's vast slave market. The trip from Sudan was treacherous and gruelling. Traders often beat the slaves, underfed them and forced them to sleep outside with inadequate protection from heat or cold. Raids on the caravans by brigands and hostile tribesmen were likewise not uncommon. A widely cited truism has it that, in the 'Islamic slave trade', the trade itself – that is, transport and sale – was brutal, but conditions once the slave was in service were mild compared with slavery in the Americas. But as we have seen, this was not necessarily the case. In many cases, slavery was simply brutal from beginning to end.

Women

Shemsigül's wretched condition might strike some readers as consistent with the condition of women in predominantly Muslim societies as portrayed by European and North American mass media. Closer examination, however, reveals that the status of women in premodern Islamic societies, and certainly in Ottoman society, was in many respects not radically different from that of their counterparts in other premodern societies of Europe and Asia. Generally, in approaching this issue, we must acknowledge that the tenets of Islam were not, in and of themselves, solely responsible for every feature of women's condition in Muslim societies; rather, women's experiences were shaped by a complex combination of factors, including the political, economic and natural environments in which they lived and the precedents set by previous societies, whether predominantly Muslim or otherwise. Above all, we must bear in mind that women's position in Muslim societies changed over time and that within a given society women's status varied a great deal depending on their socio-economic conditions and ages.

The pre-Islamic societies of the Middle East – Byzantine, Sasanian, those of the Arabian peninsula – were all highly patriarchal. In the western Arabian peninsula, where Islam emerged, the new social order it engendered arguably improved the lot of women in many respects. The Quran inveighs against female infanticide, which was widespread in the region during the Prophet Muhammad's lifetime, and indeed the Prophet himself raised four daughters. In addition, the new emphasis on belonging to the Muslim community, as opposed to tribal affiliation, improved the social standing of members of smaller, humbler tribes, as well as those unattached to any tribe at all; this change benefitted men and women alike.

Veiling and seclusion

Veiling and seclusion, which seem to figure prominently in western stereotypes of women in Islamic society, were initially prerogatives of the urban elite. During the premodern era, it was the face covering that distinguished Muslim women of the urban elite from most, though by no means all, of their European counterparts since until relatively recently most women and men in most societies wore some form of head covering. The face veil was not initially regarded as a means of guarding a woman's modesty. The Quran does not specifically mention it; all it says about feminine modesty, in fact, is, 'Tell the believing women to lower their eyes, guard their private parts, and not display their charms except what is apparent outwardly, and cover their bosoms with their veils and not to show their finery' (24:31). The wives of the Prophet Muhammad, however, did wear face veils as a sign of their exalted position within the early Muslim community. It was considered disrespectful for an unrelated male to see the uncovered faces of such distinguished personages. As Islam spread into areas where a sophisticated urban culture existed, as in the Byzantine and Sasanian empires, the face veil was adopted as a custom first of all of elite urban women whose husbands were wealthy enough to keep them veiled and secluded as a sign that they did not have to perform menial chores such as milking goats or tending crops. Since the urban elite ordinarily set the cultural ideal for society at large, the veil and seclusion came to seem desirable to people of all socio-economic strata.

The harem

Even more misunderstood than the veil in European perceptions of Islamic societies is the harem. The word comes from the Arabic for 'forbidden' in the sense of off-limits or sacred. Thus, the Holy Cities of Mecca and Medina are often referred to as the two *harams* (*haramayn* in Arabic). In Asian societies dating back to the earliest human civilizations, the ruler and his family inhabited an inner sanctum deep inside the palace. This exclusive space comprised the harem for both male and female members of the ruling family. In the palaces of most Muslim dynasties, there were, in fact, two harems – one for men, one for women – although only the women's space is popularly known as a harem today. Power was measured not by public visibility, as it is in most societies today, but by seclusion. Only someone as powerful as the ruler (or his wives) could achieve total seclusion. Meanwhile, the closer one could get to the ruler's inner sanctum, the more powerful one was. Thus, the eunuchs who guarded the (male or female) harem came to be some of the most influential figures at court while the ruler's wives and concubines, who controlled their own harem, could exercise formidable degrees of power.

The harem of Topkapı Palace was not, as many western travellers imagined, a den of iniquity where the ruler came to slake his depraved desires; on the contrary, it was more like a girls' dormitory: a highly structured female hierarchy, usually presided over by the sultan's mother. The women who inhabited this harem were not simply glorified prostitutes but stateswomen and their administrators. In addition to the wives and concubines, there was a full female staff (some of them the slaves of the sultan's wives and mother) who were responsible for everything from laundering clothing to cooking to teaching to managing the harem budget. This was, in short, a female household parallel to the male palace household, and with many of the same concerns. In the provinces, the households of provincial governors and grandees featured the same parallel female structures, modelled on the imperial harem albeit on a considerably smaller scale.

Marriage

Even below the elite level, Muslim women enjoyed certain legal rights which enabled them to exercise a degree of autonomy within a highly patriarchal society. Although most marriages were arranged, for example, and the bride rarely even saw her prospective husband before their wedding, she retained her own property after marriage. Her husband assumed the responsibility of supporting her even apart from any money and property she might possess. Ordinarily, the groom's family paid a dowry (Arabic, *mahr*) to the bride, who frequently received half at the time of marriage and the remaining half in the case of a divorce or the husband's death. With this money, the bride assembled a trousseau (*jihaz* in Arabic, *ceyiz* in Turkish) of household items, textiles for the most part, to put to use in her new home. After marriage, bride and groom moved to the groom's family's house, where, as in the harem of Topkapı Palace, the groom's mother exercised a formidable degree of authority and might treat her new daughter-in-law as a veritable slave. Domestic housing patterns varied widely, however, with economic status and locale. Whereas a wealthy family inhabiting a courtyard house could easily accommodate the new member and, later, her children, a family living in a cramped urban tenement, such as the *rab*'s of Cairo, might be obliged to build a makeshift extra room out of scraps of construction materials. In crowded urban quarters, moreover, the extended family ideal was often simply untenable; newly married couples often had to find their own accommodations.

Islamic law also allowed for the annulment of a dysfunctional marriage – one that was never consummated or one in which the husband failed to provide for his wife's material needs – thus enabling a woman to escape an intolerable situation. The husband's legal obligation to support his wife materially impinged on his legal right to take up to four wives, much remarked upon by western observers. Because a man who married more than one woman was obliged to support his wives equally, polygamy was rare in most Islamic societies; even the very wealthy seldom had more than two wives. Admittedly, it was far easier for a husband to obtain a divorce. He need only repeat the phrase 'You are divorced' three times; no justification was necessary, nor were witnesses unless the man were Shiite, in which case two witnesses were required. The wife, on the other hand, had to be able to produce two witnesses who could testify in a Muslim court to her mistreatment or to her husband's prolonged absence. In some cases, a wife might persuade her husband to agree to divorce by forfeiting the remainder of her dowry. In addition, certain Sunni legal rites more readily granted divorce than others in certain instances. If a husband had been absent for a number of years during which he failed to provide for his wife's support, a Hanafi judge would annul the marriage only if the wife received reliable word that her husband had died, divorced her or apostatized from Islam. Judges of the other three Sunni rites did not require such evidence. Thus, a woman of the Hanafi rite seeking divorce from a long-absent husband might deliberately appeal to a Shafii, Maliki or Hanbali judge. If a man divorced his wife before he had paid her dowry in full, moreover, she was entitled to the remainder at the time of divorce. Occasionally, Christian and Jewish women brought their divorce petitions before Muslim courts, thus attesting that Islamic law provided relatively favourable terms in such circumstances and gave women a degree of agency they did not necessarily enjoy in other legal frameworks.

Inheritance

Key to the question of women's property are inheritance laws. Islamic law guarantees women a share in family inheritances; in this respect, it represents a vast improvement over the conditions of pre-Islamic Arabia, where a woman had few if any inheritance rights and might herself, in certain circumstances, be bequeathed as part of the family estate. The Quran stipulates that 'the share of the male is equivalent to that of two females' (4:11), although this is almost universally taken to apply only to children inheriting from a parent. Otherwise, the Quran (4:11–12) is fairly explicit regarding the division of inheritance within a family. If deceased parents leave behind only female children, the latter will collectively inherit two-thirds of their estate; a single female child will inherit one-half (Muslim governments assumed that the remaining half fell to the state). Parents of a deceased child with children or siblings of his own are each entitled to one-sixth of his estate; if the child leaves no offspring or siblings, each parent can expect one-third. A husband is entitled to one-fourth of his deceased wife's estate if the couple has children and half if they do not. In keeping with the 2:1 ratio, a widow receives one-eighth of her late husband's estate if there are children, one-fourth if not. Finally, if the deceased leaves behind neither parents nor children but only siblings, each sibling, regardless of gender, inherits one-sixth of the estate; if there are more than two siblings, they share one-third. Some Muslim legal scholars maintained that even these injunctions applied only to cases in which the deceased had not left a will; a will overrode these provisions and could impose any division of property the deceased had chosen. Meanwhile, virtually all Muslim jurists regarded as valid a saying of the Prophet Muhammad to the effect that a person can bequeath one-third of his or her property in any manner he or she chooses. While the four Sunni legal rites maintained that the 'one-third' exception did not extend to natural heirs, Twelver Shiite jurists held that it did.

Women in the Ottoman Arab provinces operated within the boundaries of these entitlements and constraints. Since the Ottoman central authority did not recognize Shiism as a separate sect or legal rite, a woman in the Arab provinces could not exploit the 'one-third' rule to inherit a one-third share from her father or, on the other hand, to bequeath a third of her own wealth to a blood relation. However, she could take advantage of it to provide for a slave or, if she herself were a slave, to inherit from her owner. Meanwhile, property could be bequeathed and inherited in shares of the owner's choosing through the institution of *waqf*; in that case, the endowment deed might simply name a female family member as superintendent of the foundation so that all rents and other revenues endowed to the foundation were remitted to her.

Christian and Jewish women frequently brought inheritance disputes to Muslim law courts because Islamic inheritance law usually allowed them a larger share of a deceased parent's or husband's property than the laws of their own communities. According to Jewish law, a daughter could not inherit from her father if she had any surviving brothers, although her father could set aside a portion of his money as a fund for her maintenance, nor could a widow inherit from her husband, although she normally received the remainder of her wedding portion, similar to the Muslim dowry, on his death. If a Jewish wife predeceased her husband, he received her entire estate. Most of the Christian communities followed similar guidelines. The major exception to this bias in favour of males in Jewish and Christian inheritance law occurred in the case of a Jewish man who left a single daughter. By Jewish law, she was entitled to her father's entire estate while, according to Muslim law, she could inherit only half. In Fatimid Egypt, the government frequently intervened illegally to divide Jewish and Christian estates according to Muslim legal prescriptions, and the Ottoman provincial administration in the Arab provinces probably did the same on occasion. In sum, while women as a rule did not inherit as large a share of property as men, Islamic law guaranteed them some portion of their parents' and spouses' estates. Among the poor, these estates might amount to little more than a collection of textiles and cooking utensils of various sorts; nonetheless, these were often crucial to the maintenance of a woman's home and expensive to replace. The same was true, naturally, of livestock in rural or semi-rural settings.

Occupations

Documents from the medieval and Ottoman periods reveal that women were active in spheres traditionally dominated by men even below the level of the palace or the grandee household. Women could participate very actively in trade, both local and international, without actually taking to the sea in ships, opening a shop in the bazaar or travelling around the countryside with a load of merchandise. To do so, they employed agents (Arabic singular *wakil*, Turkish *vekil*) to handle their commerce on their behalf. Rather than acting as a business partner, the agent handled his client's business interests in her stead, as a public proxy. Commercial agency allowed a woman to participate in even very sophisticated transactions, including the most costly sorts of long-distance trade. Court records from the Jewish community of Cairo in the Middle Ages and Muslim court records from the Ottoman era include many contracts of agency in which women empower men to act as their commercial agents. Although a woman was likely to choose her husband or brother as agent, it was not uncommon for a woman's agent to be a man unrelated to her, implying that the woman's circle of contacts was a bit wider than the harem.

Figure 9.2 Women in rural Egypt, from the *Description de l' Égypte*. The woman in the foreground is preparing pieces of sod to be used as fuel.
Source: *Description de l'Égypte, ou, Recueil des observations et des recherches qui ont été faites en Égypte pendant l'expédition de l'Armée française.* Paris: Impr. C.L.F. Panckoucke, 1821–9, *État Moderne, Arts et métiers*, vol. II, plate XXVIII

Trade by means of an agent was largely restricted to women of some financial means. Records of women of humble substance are lamentably scarce. Nonetheless, we are able to deduce that in villages and small towns women often cultivated kitchen gardens and cared for domestic livestock while their husbands pursued a living as small-time travelling merchants. In the countryside, they performed these tasks while male family members ploughed the fields, then took an active part in planting and harvesting crops. Because of their critical role in the agricultural economy, in fact, women contributed significantly to the Ottoman Empire's tax base.

At the same time, women in villages and towns often worked in the textile industry, particularly as spinners of thread and weavers of cloth, tasks for which their relatively small fingers were better suited than those of men. (For the same reason, children were also employed as weavers.) A twelfth-century Arab Muslim geographer describes Egyptian villages in which the chief economic activity was the weaving of linen by Coptic women; at the end of the eighteenth century, the scholars of Bonaparte's expedition report similar conditions, although the market for linen had declined somewhat since the Middle Ages. Likewise in the Ottoman period, many of the silk spinners of Lebanon and Syria would have been women and children. In these mountainous regions, the climate was cool enough to grow mulberry trees, and the Ottoman provincial administration actively encouraged mulberry cultivation so as to boost production of silk for domestic consumption and export; thus, female spinners would have found even greater demand for their skills. As cotton textiles increased in popularity as a result of growing imports of Indian cotton cloth, peasant women in southern Syria and northern Iraq contributed to a limited 'import substitution' by cultivating the cotton crop, spinning thread and weaving cloth. The role of women in the Palestinian chieftain Zahir al-Umar's experiment in exporting cotton to France is probably incalculable.

Society-wide economic crises could throw women of the lower economic strata into marginal occupations, such as rag-dealing and prostitution. The same was true of warfare, particularly in provinces such as Mosul and Baghdad that were situated close to a hostile frontier. Although such wrenching transformations struck the lower classes regardless of gender, women, whose livelihoods might be precarious in the best of circumstances, were often disproportionately affected. For the period before the nineteenth century, unfortunately, there are woefully few records of these dislocations in the lives of lower-class women. We are therefore often forced to extrapolate from nineteenth-century conditions, unsatisfying though this may be.

The poor and disabled

Most marginalized of all, both in times of social dislocation and otherwise, were the desperately poor, including those unable to function in accordance with society's norms either physically or mentally. Physical and mental disabilities were undoubtedly widespread in Ottoman provincial society, yet available primary sources make little mention of them, perhaps because the disabled were for the most part sequestered, either at home or in institutions, and/or did not live particularly long or full lives.

The singular exception to this circumstance was the situation of the blind. Blindness was not uncommon in Ottoman Arab society, particularly among the lower socio-economic strata. Well into the twentieth century, blindness caused by trachoma and other bacterially transmitted ocular diseases occurred with great frequency among the poor in Egypt and other Arab countries. Lack of sight, however, did not prevent a male child from acquiring an education, particularly in a culture in which oral transmission and memorization occupied places of such high esteem. Hence a rural family might send a blind child who was of little use in agricultural pursuits to the nearest city or large town to receive an Islamic education. Cairo's great al-Azhar *madrasa* still boasts a special residential college for blind students, who in the late eighteenth century were notorious for their militancy. In his obituary of Sulayman al-Jawsaqi, who headed this college towards the end of the eighteenth century, the historian al-Jabarti describes the shaykh 'sending the gangs of the blind' to tax farmers who owed him grain and money, 'and then there remained no way to escape paying'.[8] In 1798, Shaykh al-Jawsaqi was one of the instigators of the first revolt against the French occupation, for which he was executed.

For those with other physical and mental disabilities, life was usually more constrained. Some provision did exist for treating the afflicted. During the Middle Ages, wealthy notables and members of the Mamluk, Seljuk, Timurid and early Ottoman royal families endowed numerous insane asylums, as well as medical hospitals, in the Arab lands, Anatolia, Iran and Central Asia. Justifiably famous is the enlightened asylum of the fourteenth-century Mamluk emir Argun al-Kamili in Aleppo, which soothed its patients with light, music and running water; a similar facility forms part of the religious complex of Sultan Bayezid II (r. 1481–1512) in Edirne. During the later Ottoman period, however, the number of such facilities appears to have decreased.

As for the desperately poor, neither the central Ottoman government nor the provincial or local authorities provided systematic attention to their needs. On the other hand, notables and members of the imperial family endowed soup kitchens in major provincial cities which fed and sometimes sheltered the indigent. In Jerusalem, for example, the soup kitchen founded by Süleyman I's wife Hürrem in 1555 served two meals a day to scores of people. Sultans and imperial women alike paid particular attention to the poor of the Holy Cities; the mammoth pious foundations of the Holy Cities provided them with grain while several smaller endowments established soup kitchens and wells. In nineteenth-century Cairo, meanwhile, the soup kitchen at Mahall al-Khayriyyat served 1,000 meals a day while the hospital of the Mamluk sultan Qalawun, erected in 1284, served as a shelter for homeless beggars. In addition, most Sufi lodges provided basic food and lodging to all who sought their shelter.

Beyond this, responsibility for the maintenance of the poor rested with the religious communities to which they belonged. Soup kitchens were a major form of Muslim charity, although most of the larger ones, including Hürrem's complex in Jerusalem, served the poor indiscriminately, with no regard for their religious affiliation. Apart from such establishments, charity was voluntary and ordinarily took the form of alms. The Jewish and the various Christian communities, however, established more rigorous mechanisms for poor relief. In predominantly Jewish or Christian neighbourhoods, rabbis and priests commonly collected a regular sum of money from residents for a community charitable fund, which purchased bread and other foodstuffs for the needy. In this way, the indigent were kept from starving while their more fortunate coreligionists performed a good deed which all three monotheisms believed would ultimately be rewarded in heaven. Major religious holidays, notably the Muslim month of Ramadan and the feast of the sacrifice ('Id al-Adha in Arabic, Kurban Bayramı in Turkish) during the pilgrimage season, the Jewish holidays of Yom Kippur and Passover, and Christmas and Easter, provided special opportunities for charity and distribution of food to the poor. Generally speaking, communal charitable institutions provided a safety net of last resort for the poor when family members could or would not contribute to their support, although homeless beggars nonetheless appeared on the streets of the major Arab cities.

The dislocations of wartime and social unrest, of course, put extraordinary pressure on these community resources. Before the nineteenth century, the Ottoman Arab lands, in contrast to Hungary and the Balkans, were spared major invasions and reconquests by European powers, with the waves of refugees desperately seeking food and shelter which these events inevitably produced. Nonetheless, the soldiery revolts, rebellions of provincial governors, and Bedouin attacks described in previous chapters, to say nothing of Safavid and post-Safavid incursions into Iraq, must have created sizeable numbers of displaced persons stripped of their belongings, albeit in relatively circumscribed regions.

Conclusion

These diverse minority and/or marginal groups, underrepresented in both primary sources and secondary historical studies, comprised an important part of Ottoman Arab society. Women made vital contributions to the economies of the Arab provinces while shaping social life in critical ways. Because mothers were the major influence in the early lives of men and women alike, women also played a vital role in transmitting social and religious mores, practical knowledge and regional lore. Slaves and members of minority religious communities likewise made essential contributions to the provincial economies, while the elite among these groups proved indispensable to the functioning of central and provincial governmental institutions.

The condition of a society's most vulnerable, finally, provides telling clues to the overall well-being of that society. It is thus all the more frustrating that so few traces remain of the experience of the destitute and disabled of the Ottoman Arab provinces. Such evidence as we have suggests that they were fed and maintained, if not rehabilitated, by their communities. This in turn contributes to the impression that the social infrastructure of the Arab provinces was fundamentally sound, particularly in the absence of wrenching political and social dislocations. Towards the end of the eighteenth century, however, provincial society began to experience just this sort of dislocation, as the following chapter will explain.

Notes

1. Quoted in Norman A. Stillman, *The Jews of Arab Lands: A History and Source Book* (Philadelphia, 1979), p. 157.
2. Benjamin Braude, 'Foundation Myths of the *Millet* System', in Braude and Bernard Lewis, eds, *Christians and Jews in the Ottoman Empire: The Functioning of a Plural Society*, 2 vols (New York and London, 1982), I, pp. 69–83.
3. Cecil Roth, *The Duke of Naxos of the House of Nasi* (Philadelphia, 1948), p. 102.
4. Quoted in Gershom Scholem, *Sabbatai Sevi, the Mystical Messiah*, trans. R.J. Zwi Werblowsky (Princeton, NJ, 1973), p. 686.
5. Al-Jabarti, *Al-Jabarti's History of Egypt*, I, p. 638 (trans. Charles Wendell and Michael Fishbein).
6. F.B. Spilsbury, *Picturesque Scenery in the Holy Land and Syria Delineated during the Campaigns of 1799 and 1800* (London, 1823); reproduced in Stillman, *The Jews of Arab Lands*, following p. 316.
7. Quoted in Ehud R. Toledano, *Slavery and Abolition in the Ottoman Middle East* (Seattle, 1998), p. 61.
8. Al-Jabarti, *Al-Jabarti's History of Egypt*, III, pp. 96–7 (trans. Thomas Philipp).

chapter ten

IDEOLOGICAL AND POLITICAL CHANGES IN THE LATE EIGHTEENTH CENTURY

B y the middle of the eighteenth century, the Ottoman economy and, with it, Ottoman society had regained a degree of stability not seen in some 150 years. The great social upheavals of the seventeenth century had come to an end as the Ottoman economy stabilized. Although debasement of the Ottoman silver *akche* continued to be a problem and the use of foreign currency became endemic, the galloping inflation that had characterized the era of the Jelali rebellions no longer plagued Ottoman society. And while increasing quantities of European goods entered Ottoman lands and French ships carried an ever larger proportion of Ottoman trade, the commercial sector nonetheless prospered; meanwhile, agricultural yields and, in consequence, land tax revenues had rebounded from the crisis.

At the same time, key sectors of Ottoman society that had been in ferment during the preceding century regularized, leading to a far greater degree of social stability. On the one hand, the spread of the life-tenure tax farm, or *malikane*, at the beginning of the eighteenth century helped to cement the influence of provincial *ayan*. On the other, the cessation of significant military activity on all but the Iranian front during the century's middle decades naturally reduced the number of hired mercenaries among the soldiery, thus eliminating a major source of political and social discontent. For their part, members of the permanent regiments of soldiery in the imperial capital and the provinces alike concentrated on commercial ventures and revenue collection.

Meanwhile, the ulema, having survived the demographic flux of the seventeenth century and the excesses of the puritanical Kadızadeli movement, retrenched. By 1750, a few wealthy ulema families dominated most of the top positions in the mosque and *madrasa* hierarchy of the central Ottoman lands. In the Arab provinces, the ulema families who had migrated from the countryside during the preceding century became entrenched and began to intermarry with local notables belonging to the military and administrative cadres. Within this context, two new tendencies appeared among the ulema of the Arab provinces. Mainstream Sufism absorbed what appeared to be a new strain of *sharia*-minded orthodoxy and achieved widespread popularity among leading provincial ulema. At the same time, in what may at first seem a paradoxical development, a rigorously pietistic and vehemently anti-Sufi movement, that of the Wahhabis, which combined Kadızadeli-esque puritanism with virulent anti-Ottomanism, took permanent root in the Arabian peninsula.

'Neo-Sufism'

What some scholars have labelled 'orthodox neo-Sufism' originated in the sixteenth century in northern India, which had fallen under the rule of the Mughals, a Turkic dynasty claiming descent from both Genghis Khan and Tamerlane which had swept into the Indian subcontinent from Central Asia in the early years of the century. They established their capital first at Agra, then at Delhi, and cultivated a highly sophisticated Persianate court culture. Ruling India presented something of a challenge because of the subcontinent's enormous Hindu population. The forms of Islam that had taken root in India under earlier Muslim dynasties had been unable to escape the influence of such an ancient and pervasive belief system as Hinduism, above all in the realm of mysticism. Likewise, the early Mughal rulers accommodated Hinduism. The emperor Akbar (r. 1556–1605) went so far as to grant Hindus equal rights with Muslims. Ultimately, Akbar established his own religion: a heavily mystical blend of Islam and Hinduism that accorded him the supreme right of independent legal reasoning, or *ijtihad*, and thus gave him a legal authority transcending that of the ulema.

Akbar's syncretism, to say nothing of his encroachment on the ulema's prerogatives, provoked a strong reaction among India's Muslim scholars, who demanded a return to the *sunna*, or custom, of the Prophet. What was unusual, however, was that the voices calling most loudly for a return to tradition belonged to the shaykhs of the Naqshbandi Sufi order, which had originated in Central Asia during the period following the Mongol invasions of the thirteenth century. The distinctive feature of the Naqshbandi order is its concept of 'solitude in society', that is, inner mystical devotion to God expressed in outward social and political activity. This concept found expression in the order's *dhikr*, which among many branches was silent and was, moreover, not performed at a set time and in a set place. Many Naqshbandis believed that the worshipper's attention was most effectively fixed on God in silence; freed from the physical space of the Sufi lodge and the time constraints of the organized *dhikr*, meanwhile, the believer could profess God's unity constantly while fully engaged in society. From Central Asia, the order spread into the Anatolian part of the Ottoman Empire in the fifteenth century, then through Iran to northern India, where it took root in the late sixteenth century. The Mughals themselves patronized the Naqshbandi order, to which most emperors belonged.

Notwithstanding, the emperor Akbar's eccentric new creed goaded India's Naqshbandi shaykhs into using their order as a vehicle for reform. One shaykh in particular, Ahmad Sirhindi (1564–1624), reacting against Hindu accretions in Indian Islam, undertook to reform Sufism so as to bring it strictly into line with Sunni orthodoxy. Sirhindi wished to purge Sufism of Ibn Arabi's influence, above all the concept of 'unity of being', whereby God was present in all of creation. As misunderstood by the common believer, Sirhindi maintained, this concept too readily accommodated pantheism and even polytheism, thus obscuring the distinction between Islam and Hinduism. (Here, Sirhindi's opinion mirrors that of medieval anti-Sufi critics of Ibn Arabi.) Sirhindi sought to reinforce the difference between the two faiths by reconciling Sufism with the *sharia*. Rejecting Ibn Arabi entirely, he turned to the example of the great medieval Baghdadi theologian al-Ghazali (1058–1111), who had combined profound mystical devotion with unwavering adherence to Islamic law. By the terms of al-Ghazali's example, the *sharia* was the true path to God; mystical seeking complemented and reinforced strict observance of the law but could never be a substitute for it. Clearly, such an attitude conformed to the general Naqshbandi principle of solitude in society.

Sirhindi's efforts triggered a general reform of Islamic practice under the later Mughal emperors. As noted in Chapter 6, the Indian Ocean trade and the annual pilgrimage to Mecca allowed this strain of Naqshbandi reformism to spread quickly from India to the Arab provinces of the Ottoman Empire. In the mosques and *madrasa*s of Mecca and Medina, scholars and merchants from India, Egypt, Syria, Yemen, eastern Africa and beyond debated the compatibility of Sufism and *sharia* and, in some cases, were indoctrinated into the Naqshbandi and other Sufi orders. By the late eighteenth century, reformist Naqshbandis numbered among the leading ulema of Damascus and Cairo, as well as Delhi. The founder of the Muradi family, who, as described in Chapter 6, dominated the office of *mufti* in eighteenth-century Damascus, established the order in that city, where his descendants perpetuated its influence.

Unlike the Naqshbandis, the Khalwati order never renounced the teachings of Ibn Arabi. During the eighteenth century, nonetheless, the Khalwati order spread along some of the same routes as the reformed

Naqshbandi order and even to some of the same groups of ulema. Seemingly instrumental in this expansion was the Damascene scholar Mustafa al-Bakri (1688–1749), member of a prominent family of descendants of the Prophet Muhammad, who belonged to a branch of the Khalwatiyya known as the Karabashiyya ('Black-Headed') established in Anatolia in the seventeenth century. Al-Bakri spent a year in Istanbul early in his career and later in life travelled extensively in the Arab lands, making four extensive visits to Cairo alone. Modern-day scholars have questioned the conventional narrative whereby Mustafa al-Bakri introduced a reformist strain into the Khalwati order similar to that which had galvanized the Naqshbandi order. Rather, his contribution may have consisted in introducing to the Arab lands, and particularly Egypt, the traditions of a prominent Anatolian branch of the Khalwati order. (As explained in Chapter 6, each branch of the Khalwati order was autonomous, so that rituals and traditions could differ markedly from one branch to another.)

This was unquestionably the role played by the Egyptian scholar Muhammad al-Hifni (1688–1767), whom al-Bakri initiated into the Karabashiyya branch of the Khalwati order. Al-Hifni was one of the most influential Egyptian ulema of the eighteenth century. 'His guiding influence reached throughout the country,' al-Jabarti recounts in his obituary of the shaykh. 'In many of the villages of Egypt he had a deputy, a lieutenant, and disciples invoking the name of God.'[1] He served as rector of al-Azhar for some twenty years during the middle decades of the eighteenth century, training scores of scholars in theology and law, and inducting an equal number into the Khalwati order.

As a result of al-Bakri's and al-Hifni's combined influence, the Khalwati order's membership in Egypt increased dramatically in the course of the century, to the extent that most of al-Azhar's shaykhs belonged to the order and even held leading positions within it. Critical to the order's success in Egypt was its appeal to adherents of different Sunni legal rites. Whereas the order had originated in an almost entirely Hanafi environment, its Egyptian members by the mid-eighteenth century also included large numbers of Shafiis and Malikis. Al-Hifni, as a prominent example, belonged to the Shafii rite while the historian al-Jabarti, also a Khalwati initiate, was a Hanafi. The late eighteenth-century Maliki *mufti* Ahmad al-Dardir (1715–86), whom we met leading a protest in Chapter 6, was initiated into both the Khalwati and Naqshbandi orders, and ultimately founded his own order, the Dardiriyya, which claimed to reconcile the practices of the two orders; construction of the order's lodge was funded by the sultan of Morocco, who revered al-Dardir as a great Maliki scholar. Maliki ulema from North Africa, many of whom studied at al-Azhar, likewise joined the Khalwati order and extended its influence to their homelands, where it ultimately gave rise to several influential orders in North and West Africa. Just as Cairo's Khalwati shaykhs had played a pivotal role in mobilizing popular protests, so these African Khalwati offshoots galvanized popular opinion against European imperialist encroachment during the nineteenth century.

By the late eighteenth century, then, from all appearances, Sufism, or at least certain Sufi orders, had triumphed over the Kadızadeli brand of puritanism and had even displaced it as a marker of Sunni orthodoxy in Ottoman society. Nonetheless, it would be simplistic to regard these two religious tendencies as diametrically opposed in perpetuity, with no common spiritual or intellectual ground. Despite their obvious differences, the two tendencies did share key features, above all the goal of emulating the Prophet Muhammad. While the Kadızadelis sometimes interpreted this goal quite literally, to the extent of trying to replicate conditions in seventh-century Medina, adherents of the Khalwati, Naqshbandi and other mainstream Sufi orders emphasized what they regarded as the Prophet's spiritual example. Yet this devotion to the Prophet could spring from common intellectual roots. The sixteenth-century Anatolian judge Birgevi Mehmed Efendi (*c*.1520–73), author of a basic treatise on proper Muslim practice which became a doctrinal touchstone for the Kadızadelis, was at the same time an exponent of a spiritual path that he called the 'way of Muhammad' (*tariqat-i Muhammadi*), which had great resonance for Kadızadelis and Sufis alike. New research indicates that Birgevi, though appropriated after his death by the Kadızadelis, was himself a mystic. More generally, the post-Sirhindi Naqshbandis' rejection of Ibn Arabi's doctrines and abandonment of ecstatic Sufi rituals would have been compatible with Kadızadeli principles. In Mecca and Medina, where the pilgrimage brought together Muslim scholars of every conceivable religious stripe, both Sufis and virulently anti-Sufi fellow Muslims studied with some of the same jurists and traditionists, occasionally drawing radically different conclusions from their teachings.

Wahhabism

Rather ironically, the founder of the Wahhabi movement, which at the end of the eighteenth century would pose a serious threat to Ottoman authority in the Arabian peninsula, studied in Mecca and Medina with members of the ulema who had previously taught Naqshbandi and Khalwati shaykhs. Muhammad ibn Abd al-Wahhab (1703–92) belonged to a family of *qadi*s in one of the towns of the peninsula's interior. Like the Kadızadelis, Ibn Abd al-Wahhab interpreted the injunction to emulate the Prophet Muhammad literally and thus vehemently opposed any innovation to what he perceived as the usages of the Prophet's time. He likewise anathematized all forms of Sufism, as well as Shiism.

Unlike the Kadızadelis, who adhered to the official Ottoman Hanafi legal rite, Ibn Abd al-Wahhab belonged to the Hanbali rite, at the time the smallest of the four surviving Sunni legal rites and the most literal in its interpretation of the Quran and the sayings of the Prophet. Nor did Ibn Abd al-Wahhab resettle in Istanbul or even in one of the urban centres of the Arab provinces, despite his studies in the Holy Cities and in Basra. Instead, he remained in the remote vastness of inner Arabia, which for all practical purposes lay outside Ottoman control, for, while the Ottomans administered the Holy Cities in the western region of the peninsula known as the Hijaz, they exercised little authority over the Bedouin tribesmen of the interior. In 1745, he acquired a base of support for his puritanical agenda by allying himself with the powerful Bedouin chieftain Muhammad ibn Saud. Ibn Saud's Bedouin fighters in turn spread this forceful new ideology throughout the Arabian peninsula, founding austere Wahhabi communities as they went.

Wahhabism promoted a return, in an almost literal sense, to the Islam of the original Muslim community of Medina, based on the *sharia* as it had evolved in Islam's first three generations. It stressed belief in a God who was absolutely transcendent, bearing no resemblance to his creation, although not a deity who had been reduced to an abstract principle by metaphysical exercises. According to Wahhabi doctrine, God could not be reached through mystical rituals or through the intercession of Sufi shaykhs. In their desert communities, not surprisingly, the Wahhabis prohibited anything remotely resembling an innovation to the Prophet's custom or remotely connected with Sufism, including coffee, tobacco and visits to the tombs of Sufi leaders. In the course of rooting out innovations, they actually brought orthodox Islam to certain parts of the Arabian interior for the first time. Certain populations in the peninsula's more remote wastes had never been thoroughly Islamized but still practised such ancient animist customs as making sacrifices at sacred groves of trees. The Wahhabis rooted out these customs and made the Arabian peninsula solidly Muslim.

Yet the success of the Wahhabi-Saudi military-religious alliance by no means translated into an extension of Ottoman authority in the Arabian peninsula. Perhaps the most striking difference between the Wahhabis and the Kadızadelis of the previous century was the fervent Wahhabi opposition to Ottoman rule. Muhammad ibn Abd al-Wahhab and his followers did not consider the Ottoman sultan a proper Muslim; above all, they rejected his claim to the title Custodian of the Holy Cities. Having secured a grip on the Arabian interior, therefore, the Wahhabis and their Saudi allies attempted to wrest Mecca and Medina from Ottoman control at the beginning of the nineteenth century. After years of raids in the area, the Saudi forces finally occupied Mecca in 1803 and Medina in 1805, taking advantage of the turmoil surrounding the waning years of Sultan Selim III's reign. In Mecca, the Wahhabis, to quote al-Jabarti, 'destroyed the dome over the well of Zamzam, the domes surrounding the Kaba, and all buildings higher than the Kaba; in Medina, they ordered 'the destruction of all dome-tombs, except that of the Prophet'.[2] Following Selim's deposition, to be described below, his young successor, Mahmud II (r. 1808–39), appealed to the autonomous governor of Egypt, Mehmed Ali Pasha, to retrieve the Holy Cities, which he succeeded in doing in 1811. Nonetheless, these initial Wahhabi-Saudi successes were a foretaste of what was to come in the early twentieth century, when a resurrected Wahhabi-Saudi alliance would take control of the Holy Cities for good.

The crisis of Selim III's reign (1789–1807)

The Wahhabi threat and the regional hegemony of Mehmed Ali Pasha were hallmarks of the troubled reign of Sultan Selim III, which in a sense embodied the crisis of the late eighteenth century. Unprecedented European encroachment on Ottoman territory prompted the sultan to undertake westernizing military reforms, which in turn alienated vested interest groups among the Ottoman military and administrative cadres. Meanwhile, provincial notables took advantage of the empire's dire military straits to press their claims for regional autonomy, as in the case of Mehmed Ali, or even to rebel outright, as in the case of Muhammad ibn Abd al-Wahhab and Muhammad ibn Saud. At the same time, economic crisis gripped the Ottoman territories after decades of relative prosperity. Enormous military expenditures only exacerbated the effects of yawning trade deficits and subsistence crises in key provinces, including Egypt and Syria.

Selim came to the throne during a period of renewed warfare between the Ottoman Empire and its traditional European enemies, Russia and the Habsburg Empire. Russia, under Catherine the Great (r. 1762–96), was in expansionist mode. In the course of the disastrous 1768–74 Russo–Turkish war, the Russians had destroyed the Ottoman fleet at Cheshme in south-western Anatolia (July 1770) and occupied the Crimean peninsula; Russian ships even appeared in the Bosphorus and threatened Istanbul itself. To end these hostilities, the Ottomans were obliged to sign the humiliating treaty of Küchük Kaynarja, which recognized Russia's territorial gains and allowed the Russian fleet free passage from the Black Sea to the Mediterranean through the straits comprising the Bosphorus, the Sea of Marmara and the Dardanelles. Where the Crimea was concerned, the treaty confirmed Russian political control but recognized the Ottoman sultan as caliph, in the sense of spiritual leader, of the peninsula's population of Muslim Tatars, descendants of the Mongols who had settled in the peninsula following the Mongol invasions of the thirteenth century. This was, in point of fact, the first time the sultan was acknowledged as caliph in a legally binding international agreement, although it had for at least a century been more or less tacitly understood that, for Sunni Muslims, the Ottoman sultan was caliph, that is, successor to the Prophet Muhammad as leader of the Muslim community.

Not content with occupying Ottoman territory outright, the Russians sought, in addition, to undermine the enemy empire from within by courting Ottoman provincial grandees. During the war, as noted in Chapter 5, the Russian admiral Count Orlov had fomented rebellion among the landholders of southern Greece and supported the regional ambitions of Ali Bey and Zahir al-Umar. A decade later, Ibrahim and Murad Beys, the Georgian freedmen of Ali Bey's client-turned-enemy Mehmed Bey Abu al-Dhahab, blatantly entertained Russian and Georgian envoys in Cairo, and even pursued an alliance with Russia through the mediation of the king of Georgia.

Selim III came to the throne in April 1789, in the midst of a war with the Habsburgs which ended in 1790 after a string of defeats. It was promptly followed by another demoralizing conflict with Russia, which came to a close only with the humiliating Treaty of Jassy in 1792. This seemingly endless series of battlefield defeats and territorial concessions led Selim to the inevitable conclusion that something was fundamentally wrong with the Ottoman armed forces, or at least that the Habsburg and Russian forces had fundamental advantages over their Ottoman counterparts.

In fact, Austria and Russia now had professional standing armies, while the Ottomans still relied on mercenaries and tribal levies who were called up as needed for battle. The imperial navy, meanwhile, consisted of little more than ordinary foot soldiers placed aboard ships. The once formidable Janissaries had by this time virtually ceased to exist as a fighting force; those still on the regiment's payroll were chiefly merchants who never saw battle. Selim therefore set out to establish a standing army. Like Osman II nearly two centuries before, he meant to supplement, not supplant, the traditional military forces. His new army, like the new administrative complex to which it gave rise, was called Nizam-i Jedid, or 'New Order'. Its troops were recruited largely from the Anatolian peasantry and urban working classes. Since a standing army had to have permanent quarters, they were housed in a huge new barracks built for them on the Asian shore of the Sea of Marmara; the building, still standing, is now a museum.

The Nizam-i Jedid troops comprised a European-style standing army with a revamped hierarchy and European-style military drill and discipline. They wore tight-fitting uniforms, just as European armies of the period did; these were supposed to make them more mobile in battle. Selim's government engaged French military officers to aid in the new army's organization and training, even though, in the wake of the French Revolution, the palace was suspicious of the anti-monarchical revolutionary government. Selim's father, Mustafa III (r. 1757–74), had already opened a naval engineering school, which his successor, Abdülhamid I (r. 1774–89), expanded. Selim's reformist chief admiral, or Kapudan Pasha, now built modern new warships. To pay for all this military renovation, Selim established a separate treasury which generated revenue by confiscating old *timar*s and neglected tax farms. To this treasury were attached specially appointed officials who inspected each corps of the traditional military: what little remained of the timariot cavalry; the Janissaries; and the various specialized corps of cannoneers, artillery and so on. Those found to be derelict in their military or fiscal duties were summarily removed from the payrolls while the tax farms or *timar*s to which they held title were confiscated.

Selim III further introduced a new system of rule by consultation: not only consultation with the grand vizier and the imperial *divan*, or governing council, but also consultation with notables, both provincial notables and leading religious figures, such as judges and *mufti*s. This was arguably the first tentative step towards a legislative assembly, which, however, would not even be attempted for nearly another century. In 1789, the sultan issued a call for reform proposals and later convened a consultative council to discuss these reforms. Despite the seeming novelty of Selim's approach, it harks back to an earlier tradition within the Ottoman state of internal reform through rooting out corruption, going back at least to Ahmed III (r. 1703–30). Ahmed III had even briefly set up a council of notables. Selim's chief reformers, furthermore, fit the pattern established earlier in the eighteenth century: they were Selim's palace companions, some of whom were appointed to positions of great influence. Among the most important were Selim's spiritual advisor, whom he appointed chief financial minister; the grand admiral, noted above; Selim's mother's most trusted aide, who was close to the commander of the imperial Janissaries and therefore functioned as the sultan's liaison with the regiment; and a series of reformist *reisülkuttab*s, or chief scribes. The Ottoman *reisülkuttab* had since at least the Treaty of Karlowitz in 1699 taken a leading role in diplomatic negotiations; by 1789, he functioned as a veritable foreign minister. More generally, the scribal class represented by the *reisülkuttab* submitted the largest number of reform proposals in response to Selim's call. Generally speaking, these new reformers came from the same professional cadres as the old decline writers. Their proposals likewise followed the classic decline literature strategy of appealing to the sultan to undertake internal reforms: pruning government payrolls, making promotions solely according to merit, and providing more effective administrative oversight. We might say that these late eighteenth-century scribes were the last of the decline writers, or that their reform proposals were the logical conclusion of the decline-writing tradition.

One reform that was not strictly military in nature but which nonetheless had far-reaching effects was the establishment of permanent Ottoman embassies in Europe. Previously, there had been no permanent Ottoman diplomatic presence in Europe but only irregular special envoys. In 1792, however, Selim sent the first permanent Ottoman ambassador to London. An ambassador to the Habsburg capital of Vienna followed in 1795, then one to Paris in 1796. Most of these ambassadors held the rank of *efendi*; that is to say, they were bureaucrats or occasionally members of the ulema rather than military officers or viziers. This development represented, in certain respects, the triumph of the office of *reisülkuttab*. In his dispatches, the first ambassador to France, a descendant of the Prophet from what is now mainland Greece, describes, among other things, a performance of the Oriental fantasy *Zaïre* by 'the famous, accursed Voltaire, may he burn in hell'.[3]

Selim's ambitious reforms ultimately failed because they hurt entrenched interest groups on whom the sultan remained dependent. He relied heavily on the *ayan* of the provinces, above all the Anatolian and Balkan provinces, to supply him with troops for his new army. Confronted with his efforts to force them to reform their operations and remit their tax revenues, to say nothing of his attempts to replace them with other provincial administrators, they were disinclined to support him, much less to send him the troops he needed. In addition, some conservative *ayan* with ties to foreign powers, especially Russia, tried to undermine Selim's reform efforts, not necessarily because they opposed them in principle but because they were alarmed at the heavy French influence among the reforming administrators. The cosy relationship between the Russians and Ibrahim and Murad Beys in Egypt benefitted from this atmosphere of provincial suspicion of the court's designs. As the eighteenth century drew to a close, in fact, the Ottoman Empire's administration was divided into two opposing camps: Conservatives, supported by the Russians, and Reformers, supported by the French.

The French invasion of Egypt

In July 1798, however, the French invaded Egypt, turning everything upside-down. After the French Revolution of 1789, France had gone through a series of regimes: a popularly elected National Convention established the republic in 1792 but was overthrown by peasant revolts, leading to the formation of the Committee of Public Safety and the 1793–4 Terror, which was brought to an end by the Thermidor Reaction and the declaration of the Directory. It was the Directory, now a de facto dictatorship, that ordered General Napoleon Bonaparte to invade Egypt.

Bonaparte's attack caught the Ottomans entirely unawares, despite their permanent ambassador in Paris. The chronicler al-Jabarti recounts how in June 1798 the people of Alexandria watched a British naval force sail into the harbour. When asked what they were doing there, the British warned that a French fleet was in the vicinity and offered their protection. Alexandria's governor, however, retorted, 'This is the sultan's land. Neither the French nor anyone else has access to it. So leave us alone!'[4] Once the French were established in Egypt, Bonaparte went on to Palestine, where, however, he was unable to defeat Ahmed Pasha al-Jazzar, the autonomous Bosnian governor of the province of Sidon, and was forced to withdraw. In any event, sentiment in France was turning against him; he returned in 1799 to overthrow the Directory and take over the government. Meanwhile, his generals remained in Egypt. Only in 1801 was a combined British-Ottoman force finally able to expel them.

The French posed as friends of the Egyptian 'people' who had come to liberate them from the tyrannical rule of the military grandees, whom they called simply Mamelouks (Mamluks) because most of them were, in fact, emancipated Georgian mamluks of the Kazdağlı household. Bonaparte emphasized his respect for Islam and appealed to Egypt's ulema to take the lead in a new French-sponsored government as representatives of the common people. The French more or less attempted to overlay traditional Ottoman governmental institutions with their own brand of republicanism. They established a governing council, which they called by the Ottoman name *divan*, with General Kléber as head and several members of the Egyptian ulema, including the historian al-Jabarti and several of his close friends and associates, as members. Meanwhile, the large team of scientists whom Bonaparte had brought

Figure 10.1 Murad Bey, from the *Description de l'Égypte*.
Source: *Description de l'Égypte, ou, Recueil des observations et des recherches qui ont été faites en Égypte pendant l'expédition de l'Armée française.* Paris: Impr. C.L.F. Panckoucke, 1821–9, *État Moderne, Costumes et portraits*, vol. II, plate G

with him surveyed Egypt's climate, plants, animals, human population and institutions, and, most famously, launched a massive archaeo-logical programme which more or less originated the field of Egypto-logy. The French Scientific Expedition, as it was called, published its collective findings in the massive, multi-volume *Description de l'Égypte*, a masterpiece of Enlightenment scholarship and still a useful historical source.

Al-Jabarti

Abd al-Rahman al-Jabarti (1754–1825) was the son of a great scholar and teacher at al-Azhar. His father Hasan, who died in 1774, had had to perform the sorts of duties that fell to 'professional ulema' in the eighteenth century: not just training students but mediating among rival grandees and heading delegations to Istanbul to negotiate particular matters between Egypt's grandees and the Ottoman court. His son, in contrast, lived on his late father's wealth, although he was trained at al-Azhar and was himself considered a member of the ulema. He began to write relatively late in his career, prompted in the first instance by the French invasion. In 1798, he composed a brief work known as the *History of the French Occupation of Egypt*; covering only the first six months of the French sojourn, it depicts Bonaparte's soldiers as uncouth, almost barbaric creatures while portraying the general himself as having no clue as to the true nature of Islam and little grasp of the Arabic language. Notwithstanding, the gist of the work is that the ulema can benefit from the scientific and technical expertise of the occupiers so long as they do not collaborate with them. After the Ottomans had expelled the French, with British help, in 1801, he crafted a revised history ignoring French technical achievements while lavishly praising the Ottoman sultan as the true defender of the *sharia*. Al-Jabarti was inspired to write a lengthy chronicle of Ottoman Egypt, beginning in the Muslim year 1100 (1688–9 CE) – a sort of 'prequel' to his earlier works – only several years later, in about 1805; this work takes the form of an annalistic narrative of key events, combined with extensive sections of what today we would call obituaries of prominent ulema and grandees.

By this time, Egypt had fallen under the rule of Mehmed Ali Pasha, who had come to Egypt with an Albanian contingent of the Ottoman army which had helped to expel the French. During the years of chaos that followed, he gradually established himself in authority; in 1805, Sultan Selim III recognized him as governor of Egypt. His governorship would ultimately be extended for forty-three years, until his death in 1848. Following his death, the dynasty that he founded ruled Egypt until the revolution of 1952.

Writing in 1805, al-Jabarti presents Mehmed Ali Pasha's regime as a new beginning for Egypt and the pasha himself as an ideal Muslim ruler who respects the *sharia* and heeds the advice of the ulema. By 1816, however, the ageing historian was bitterly disillusioned; his final revision of his chronicle, which he extended to 1821, makes little secret of his loathing for the pasha's increasingly autocratic rule and his disappointment in the heedless self-interest of Egypt's leading ulema. During Mehmed Ali's lifetime, al-Jabarti's history was banned in Egypt.

Epilogue

Selim III was deposed after a group of mercenary infantry opposed to the Nizam-i Jedid led a revolt in Istanbul. They were supported by Conservatives in the government, led by the Shaykh al-Islam, or chief *mufti*, who issued a *fatwa*, or legal opinion, supporting the rebels. Most of Selim's advisors were killed. Just as in 1623, when a provincial governor marched on Istanbul to avenge Osman II's overthrow, so the governor of a Balkan province marched to restore Selim in 1808. Selim's immediate successor, his cousin Mustafa IV, however, had him executed before the governor could enter the grounds of Topkapı Palace.

Meanwhile, in Egypt, Mehmed Ali Pasha implemented a series of drastic top-down military and economic reforms. Old vested interests that stood in the way were summarily eliminated. In the most notorious example of this systematic obliteration of obstacles, Mehmed Ali in 1811 summoned the surviving Mamluk commanders to Cairo's citadel to participate in a military procession preparatory to an expedition to Syria, only to order his new-model troops to open fire on them as they were descending from the fortress. Al-Jabarti's description of the massacre is chilling: 'The soldiers went berserk butchering the amirs and looting their clothing. . . . They cut down both those who had accompanied them and the citizens who were dressed in their clothing to embellish the procession.'[5] All Mamluks in the countryside were hunted down and killed, as well. Those few who escaped slaughter fled the province.

Sultan Mahmud II, who took the throne in 1808, would ultimately use Mehmed Ali's programme as a model for his own top-down reforms. Inspired by Mehmed Ali's wholesale annihilation of the Mamluks, which left the pasha free to implement his wide-ranging military and administrative reforms, Mahmud abolished the Janissary regiment altogether in 1826, thus eliminating the major source of opposition to his own westernizing reforms. His reforms were extended by his immediate successors, who inaugurated the era of westernizing political and administrative reforms known as the Tanzimat. These culminated, in the late nineteenth century, in a brief experiment in constitutional monarchy and representative parliamentary government that would be revived in the empire's final years.

Notes

1. Al-Jabarti, *Al-Jabarti's History of Egypt*, I, p. 500 (trans. Charles Wendell and Michael Fishbein).
2. Ibid., III, pp. 386, 529–30 (trans. Moshe Perlmann).
3. Stéphane Yerasimos, ed. and trans., *Deux Ottomans à Paris sous le Directoire et l'Empire: relations d'ambassade* (Paris, 1998), p. 95 (my translation).
4. Al-Jabarti, *Al-Jabarti's History of Egypt*, III, p. 2 (trans. Thomas Philipp).
5. Ibid., IV, p. 184 (trans. C. Peycheff and Thomas Philipp).

TRANSFORMATIONS UNDER OTTOMAN RULE

The effects of Ottoman rule

If we view Ottoman rule in the Arab lands before 1800 as a dynamic process that changed over time, we come to an assessment of developments in these territories quite different from that of the conventional historiography, whether Arab nationalist or Ottomanist-declinist. That is to say, we avoid the tendency to regard the Ottoman era as either an undifferentiated period of 'Turkish occupation' or as a century of robust, centralized sultanic rule followed by a two-century downward spiral. From this revisionist standpoint, there is no question of judging incorporation into the Ottoman Empire 'good' or 'bad' so far as the Arab provinces were concerned; such evaluations have little meaning when three hundred years in a variety of societies and among a wide array of social groups spread over a vast geographical space are at issue. Moreover, such a value judgment presumes to label this lengthy period in comparison with an arbitrarily chosen 'high point' of Arab or Islamic civilization, perhaps under the Mamluk sultanate, perhaps under the Abbasids or the Fatimids. In that respect, it reflects a 'declinist' approach to the entire sweep of Arabo-Islamic history which runs parallel to the declinist school within Ottoman historiography.

A review of the effects on the Arab lands of incorporation into the Ottoman Empire, free of declinist judgements, demonstrates how greatly changed the Arab territories were in 1800 from what they had been in 1516. Many of these changes resulted from the new imperial context within which the Arab provinces now operated, which allowed for new connections with distant lands that had likewise fallen into the Ottoman orbit. At the same time, the Arab provinces were affected by empire-wide trends which emerged in response to new internal and external challenges over the years.

Rural and urban life

Ottoman rule changed the face of both city and countryside in the Ottoman Arab provinces. In the decades following the conquest of the Arab lands, the Ottomans brought much new land under cultivation; while rural unrest in the seventeenth century temporarily threatened this trend, a far greater challenge was the tribal movements of the late seventeenth and eighteenth centuries, which turned large swathes of cropland into pasture for livestock. The *timar* system brought a new population of military administrators into the provincial countryside in Syria and northern Iraq while providing a mechanism to bind members of influential indigenous families, such as the Azms, to the Ottoman central authority, which assigned and redistributed the *timar*s. Much the same purpose was served by the life-tenure tax farms known as *malikane*s beginning in the late seventeenth century. At the same time, *malikane*s provided a secure financial foundation for the wealthy provincial notables who purchased these revenue-collection rights, thus paving the way for the near-hegemony in the eighteenth century of provincial *ayan* households such as the Azms of Syria, the Kazdağlıs of Egypt and the Jalilis of northern Iraq. During the late nineteenth and early twentieth centuries, certain of these notables, the Azms being the most prominent example, would join their provinces' nascent nationalist movements, using their familiarity with Ottoman government institutions to shape parallel institutions in the emerging Arab nation-states, much as Indian nationalists drew on their experience with the British Raj to mould their own independent society.

Towards the middle of the nineteenth century, both the Ottoman central government and the autonomous regime of Mehmed Ali Pasha's descendants in Egypt enacted far-reaching land reform laws. In Egypt, Mehmed Ali himself abolished tax-farming and confiscated some lands endowed to pious foundations, which he redistributed among the peasantry; the net effect of these measures was, however, to make the tiny echelon of already wealthy peasant families even wealthier. The land laws of 1847, 1855 and finally 1858 largely codified what Mehmed Ali had already achieved while preparing the ground for private landownership in the 1870s. A major land law passed in 1858 by the Ottoman central government and applied in all remaining Ottoman provinces was concerned primarily with establishing legal title to landholdings, a move that benefited both large and small landholders and, as in Egypt, contributed to the emergence of private ownership of land.

As for the peasantry, who were the most profoundly affected by these changes, as well as by the earlier introduction of *timar*s, tax farms and *malikane*, they are frequently depicted in secondary historical studies as an undifferentiated and unchanging mass who stoically watched the comings and goings of countless 'foreign' dynasties and administrators as they had since time immemorial. As Chapter 8 has attempted to demonstrate, this is an utterly inaccurate portrayal. No less than the urban population, the majority agricultural population was characterized by socio-economic and ethno-regional divisions. Certain of the more influential rural families acquired tax farms which they treated as heritable property and thus a form of sustainable wealth. A few, such as Egypt's Fallahs, formed their own elite households, complete with slaves and private armies. At the other end of the scale, impoverished peasants occasionally resisted the efforts of government authorities to register them for taxation purposes and to collect these taxes. In addition, many tribes were at least partially settled agriculturalists; while their chequered relations with government administrators are fairly well-known, the complex relationships that must have existed between them and non-tribal peasants remain largely unexplored.

To assume that the bulk of the peasantry lived an isolated existence, unaffected by far-away wars, international trade and the like is equally fallacious. Apart from the upheavals emanating from the Jelali rebellions in the late sixteenth and early seventeenth centuries, the peasants belonged to networks of regional markets that were highly sensitized to changes in provincial and international demand for particular crops and other commodities. By the end of the sixteenth century, furthermore, many peasant villages had adopted a cash economy and thus suffered directly from waves of inflation and currency debasement.

As for the cities of the Arab provinces, their populations unquestionably increased throughout most of the period under consideration here, largely through immigration from the countryside and other provinces, as well as a massive influx of government functionaries and military personnel, some of whom never left. The physical space occupied by these growing urban conglomerations likewise expanded, creating a need for new urban infrastructure: roads, wells, public baths, markets, occasionally new walls. In combination with local notables, Ottoman administrators marked the Arab capitals by establishing new neighbourhoods or expanding existing ones; providing this basic infrastructure; and building and restoring mosques, *madrasa*s and Sufi lodges. On the other hand, the Ottoman provincial administrations did not, for the most part, build new military fortifications in the major provincial capitals, though of course they used and extended the existing medieval citadels and built numerous forts in less densely populated rural areas. New architectural styles developed during the Ottoman period, drawn from the 'classical' Ottoman style (itself heavily influenced by the architecture of the Byzantines and the Seljuks of Rum) in Bursa, Edirne and Istanbul; the styles of the pre-Ottoman regimes in the Arab provinces; and other regional influences. Ottoman governors and local notables and the architects they hired emphasized different elements in shaping these styles. The Ottomans also left their stamp on these cities symbolically by building hundreds of the distinctive pencil-thin Ottoman minarets. These served as markers of Ottoman identity regardless of the architectural provenance of the mosques they adorned, just as the Ottoman standard, the *tugh*, a staff surmounted by a golden ball from which horsetails were suspended, signalled the Ottoman presence on the battlefield when it flew over the Ottoman troops.

Trade

Under the Ottoman aegis, trade between the Arab lands, on the one hand, and Anatolia and the Balkans, on the other, became commonplace; not only goods but occasionally merchants relocated from these regions to the Arab provinces and vice versa. Likewise, commercial connections between and among the different Arab provinces themselves became regularized as a result of these regions' inclusion in the same polity. In effect, the Ottoman conquests of the fourteenth, fifteenth and sixteenth centuries created a vast free-trade zone, despite the craft brotherhoods' restrictions on competition in some cities and government regulation of the quality and prices of staple commodities. This common commercial zone greatly facilitated not only the circulation of long-established crops and goods, such as wheat, wood, animal skins, textiles and Indian spices, but also the spread of new discoveries, notably Yemeni coffee, North American tobacco, and maize and other food crops from Spanish America. Although Ottoman merchants cultivated trading links to India, Central Asia, sub-Saharan Africa and western Europe, the vast majority of Ottoman trade between the sixteenth and nineteenth centuries was internal, as André Raymond has shown.

Language

Even more than merchants, government officials and military personnel circulated widely among the Ottoman provinces, Arab and non-Arab alike. Throughout the 300-year period covered by this book, governors, soldiers and financial officers of an unprecedented variety of ethnic and geographical origins entered the Arab provinces: Greeks, Hungarians, Serbs, Albanians and Bosnians recruited through the *devshirme*; Circassian, Abkhazian and Georgian mamluks; bureaucrats and soldiers from all parts of Anatolia. Many of these new arrivals stayed for a number of years or even settled permanently in the Arab provinces. Their presence affected local culture in a variety of ways. They made the provinces linguistically more diverse, adding the brand of Ottoman Turkish they spoke as a lingua franca to the dialects of Arabic, Kurdish, Persian, Armenian, Coptic, Circassian and Kipchak Turkish already spoken to varying degrees in the major urban centres.

The conventional dichotomous portrayal of Turkish as the language of the 'elite' and Arabic as the language of 'the people' obscures the linguistic diversity of the Ottoman Arab provinces, as well as the diffusion of dialects of non-Arabic languages among certain segments of the population. A form of simplified Ottoman Turkish was the common language of rank-and-file Ottoman soldiers, regardless of provenance, who not infrequently joined the middle- and working-class populations of artisans and small merchants in provincial cities, and presumably made contributions to the colloquial Arabic of the urban majority. More generally, the influence of Turkish on the colloquial languages of modern-day Arab nation-states, to say nothing of their Balkan counterparts, is readily evident to this day. On the other hand, Ottoman Turkish, already replete with Arabic loan-words before the conquest of the Arab lands, acquired many more in the centuries following their incorporation into the empire. Meanwhile, Georgian and Circassian mamluks, although they learned Ottoman Turkish for their military and administrative functions and at least enough Arabic to pray, still spoke their native languages among themselves to some degree. Not long before Bonaparte invaded Egypt, the *shaykh al-balad* of Cairo, Ibrahim Bey, corresponded with the king of Georgia in his native tongue.

The harem must have preserved some of these Caucasian languages, as well as Balkan languages, since harem women, sheltered as they were from the daily rough and tumble of the governing council, on the one hand, and the marketplace, on the other, presumably had greater opportunity to speak these languages in private. Even during the twentieth century, surviving members of the Ottoman royal family were thought to speak Turkish with Armenian or Circassian accents owing to their early upbringing in the harem, many of whose inmates were originally slaves from these and adjacent regions. We can only imagine the effects of such an upbringing on the speech and accents of the children of governors, other provincial administrators and provincial grandees.

Religious and intellectual life

Naturally, language was only one of the effects of the demographic shifts that accompanied Ottoman rule. Incorporation into the Ottoman

Empire profoundly changed the religious and intellectual life of the Arab provinces, not least by opening a much wider geographical space in which aspiring scholars could seek instruction and employment. Although Muslim scholars had crossed imperial boundaries in their quest for knowledge before the Ottoman conquest of the Arab lands and continued to do so during the Ottoman period, they could circulate with relative ease among Ottoman provincial centres of learning, and between these and the imperial capital. Ottoman promotion of the official Hanafi legal rite resulted in the posting of numerous Hanafi officials to provincial capitals, in some of which, notably Cairo and the Yemeni city of Zabid, Hanafis formed a minority to adherents of other legal rites. Hanafi law courts, Quran schools and *madrasa*s multiplied in the Arab lands in consequence, although in some cases they built on a pre-existing foundation of Hanafi institutions patronized by the Mamluks and the Akkoyunlu Turcomans.

Under the Ottoman aegis, meanwhile, Sufi orders spread through the Arab lands as never before. Particularly widespread in the Arab provinces were the Khalwati and Naqshbandi orders. The Khalwatis, as described in Chapter 6, had spread to Egypt from eastern Anatolia even before the Ottoman conquest and became popular among the Ottoman soldiery stationed in the province during the sixteenth century before becoming virtually universal among Egypt's higher ulema in the eighteenth. Arguably, incorporation into a vast common polity contributed to a heightened religious exchange of the sort that allowed the future Shaykh al-Azhar Muhammad al-Hifni, in the early eighteenth century, to be initiated into a Khalwati branch rooted in Anatolia. The spread of the Naqshbandi order to Syria and Egypt, on the other hand, owed much to commercial and intellectual exchanges between the Ottoman and Mughal empires, a topic that is still lamentably understudied. In any event, the annual pilgrimage to Mecca played a major part in bringing adherents of both these orders together with fellow members and potential recruits.

Non-Muslim communities

Like their Muslim populations, the Arab provinces' non-Muslim populations changed dramatically during the Ottoman period. Even before the Ottoman conquests, the Arab lands had absorbed large numbers of Jewish refugees from Spain and Portugal, an influx that transformed the composition of Jewish communities from Aleppo to Algiers and laid the ground for some of the greatest intellectual achievements in Jewish history. The émigrés and their descendants would be disproportionately represented among financial officials in the Arab provinces well into the eighteenth century. By then, however, their privileged position was being challenged by a wave of Syrian Christian merchants who had recognized the Vatican and received honorary European citizenship as a result of the commercial incursions of the European powers, above all France, in the region. These developments arguably had farther-reaching consequences for the Arab provinces, and for the Ottoman Empire as a whole, than the mission of the Jewish messianic claimant Sabbatai Sevi during the seventeenth century, as cataclysmic as his movement and ultimate apostasy seemed at the time. For while the aftermath of Sabbatai Sevi's mission would leave the Jewish communities of the Arab lands in temporary disarray and would add a small population of Dönmes to the confessional patchwork, European commercial encroachment would set the stage for the political and economic crises that characterized the end of the period covered by this book.

The Ottoman Arab provinces after 1800

Of course, 1800 did not mark the end of Ottoman rule in the Arab lands. Most of these territories remained part of the empire until after World War I. Even Egypt was technically an Ottoman province until 1914, when the war, in which Great Britain and the Ottoman Empire took opposite sides, forced the British to declare a protectorate over the province. British troops had initially occupied Egypt in 1882 following a nationalist army officers' rebellion which threatened British access to the recently completed Suez Canal and thus the all-important route to India. The North African provinces had been removed from Ottoman control somewhat earlier: the French occupied Algeria in 1830 and Tunisia in 1881. In 1912, Italy, like Germany trying to catch up to France and Britain in the game of African colony acquisition, took over Libya.

Nonetheless, the end of the eighteenth century is conventionally regarded as a milestone in Ottoman and more general Middle Eastern history because it marked the beginning of aggressive European polit-ical, military and economic intervention in the region; modern scholars not infrequently refer to this intervention rather portentously as The Impact. Bonaparte's occupation of Egypt was for many years considered the dividing line between 'tradition' and 'modernity' not only in Egypt itself but in the Middle East as a whole. This attitude resulted in large part from historians' habit of taking the French at their own word, in much the same way that they once took the decline writers at their word. Bonaparte's proclamations, as well as the writings of other promin-ent figures in the French delegation, portray the French as embarking on a 'civilizing mission' (*mission civilisatrice*) to bring the fruits of Enlightenment philosophy and science to the 'benighted' Egyptians. Certainly the French expedition laid the ground for modern Egyptology, even if the French made no attempt to train indigenous archaeologists, in contrast to British expeditions in the later nineteenth century. More recent analyses have tried to provide a context for the invasion by pointing out that France in 1798 was in the tenth year of revolutionary ferment and that the government of the Directory, while growing increasingly dictatorial, confronted a public desperate for affordable grain. In some respects, France's economy at the end of the eighteenth century was in straits similar to those of the Arab provinces, which during those years had suffered repeated market and subsistence crises. By bringing an end to the Georgian mamluk regime of the late Kazdağlı household, of course, the French served as catalysts for the rise of Mehmed Ali Pasha's dynasty, surely the greatest change Egypt experienced in the course of the nineteenth century. Elsewhere in the Arab lands, however, the French invasion had relatively little direct effect, apart from reinforcing Ahmed Pasha al-Jazzar's hold on northern Palestine and southern Lebanon.

Far more influential in bringing 'modernity' to the Arab provinces were the defensive westernization programmes attempted by Selim III and later undertaken by Mehmed Ali Pasha and Sultan Mahmud II (r. 1808–39). These measures responded to increasing European encroachment, both military and economic, on the Ottoman domains; inevitably, however, implementing them entailed inviting large numbers of European advisors into Ottoman territory so that their expertise would be readily available when new military strategies or financial institutions were introduced. To be sure, the Ottomans had a venerable history of importing European technical experts for military purposes, going back at least to the cannon-founders from the Italian city-states who were instrumental in Mehmed II's siege of Constantinople. This new importation of European expertise was, however, considerably larger in scale and formed part of a comprehensive effort to reshape the Ottoman armed forces on the European model. French military experts had begun introducing technical and tactical innovations to the Ottoman army and navy as early as the 1730s. When Selim III created the Nizam-i Jedid army, he imported French officers to teach the new troops military and naval sciences, as well as parade drill and military discipline; French instruction continued despite the Revolution and even after the French occupation of Egypt. Although Sultan Mahmud II, taking his cue from Mehmed Ali Pasha's 1811 destruction of Egypt's Mamluk elite, abolished the Janissaries in 1826 and resurrected the Nizam-i Jedid forces, the British army and navy repeatedly rescued the Ottoman military from disaster in the course of the nineteenth century.

Towards the middle of the nineteenth century, the much farther-reaching reforms of the Tanzimat era entailed far closer collaboration with the European powers, above all Britain and France. The British signed a commercial convention with the Ottomans in 1838 which codified free trade by foreigners within the Ottoman domains, and put pressure on the imperial government to abolish the trade in African slaves. At the same time, both the British and the French took advantage of the Capitulations to increase their exports of raw materials from, and imports of manufactured goods into, Ottoman territory without paying customs duties or taxes. British and French banks lent the Ottoman government large sums of money, in the first instance to finance the Ottoman military effort in the Crimean War of 1853–6, but later for such basic purposes as paying the army, in addition to financing public works programmes and more lavish 'vanity projects'. By 1875, the Ottoman Empire was entirely dependent on the British and French economically; unable to repay its debts, the central government defaulted on its loans, and an Anglo-French team took over the Ottoman economy. Thus, by the late nineteenth century, the European powers had truly peripheralized the Ottoman Empire, both economically and politically.

Certainly, continuity can be demonstrated between these nineteenth-century developments and those of the previous century. The Ottoman reform tradition, linked in its curious way to the 'decline-writing' tradition, can be traced at least to the reign of Ahmed III and possibly to that of Osman II. Sustained commercial, diplomatic and cultural contact with western Europe was well under way by the mid-1700s. Still, the eighteenth century was far more than a prelude to the peripheralization and dependence of the late nineteenth. Nor was it a foregone conclusion that the circumstances of the late eighteenth century would lead inexorably to those of the late nineteenth, even though the Ottoman economy was unquestionably in crisis during the 1790s, while the French occupation of Egypt created a military and political crisis on top of the continuing battlefield losses to Russia and the Habsburgs. In certain respects, the crisis of the late eighteenth century bears comparison to that of the late sixteenth century. Defensive westernization was part of the Ottoman attempt to adapt to this new crisis. Arguably, this attempt was not as successful as the empire's adaptation to the earlier crisis. Certainly it was of a fundamentally different character, predicated on acceptance of a greater European role in Ottoman government and society. As in the sixteenth century, however, and despite the empire's far more straitened circumstances, it was not a foregone conclusion that Ottoman fortunes were somehow preordained to spiral downwards. Rather, the course the Ottoman military, government and economy took resulted from rational choices by various elements within the Ottoman state and society in response to internal and external pressures.

At the same time, the Ottomans were inevitably affected by changes in the European countries over which they had little or no control. Bonaparte's invasion of Egypt and succeeding European interventions in Asia and Africa arguably marked a shift in the imperial strategies of the European powers: from the 'informal imperialism' of overseas trade to the formal imperialism of conquest and occupation, on the one hand, and direct, frequently overbearing economic and political inter-ference, on the other. Rivalry between France and Britain, and between both these powers and Russia, during the late eighteenth and nineteenth centuries intensified the intrusions of all three powers in the affairs of the Ottoman Empire and its Asian neighbours. Notwithstanding, Ottoman statesmen were occasionally able to take advantage of the rivalry among European powers, capitalizing, as a notable example, on Germany's industrialization and imperial ambitions in the wake of German unification in 1871 to encourage German investment and to court German technical expertise at the expense of the British between 1888 and 1914.

In short, the European Impact on Ottoman society need not be regarded as the unilateral introduction of western-style modernity to a passive, tradition-bound empire that had reached the nadir of a centuries-long decline. Instead, this encounter can be recast as a dynamic, if ultimately unequal, process of exchange which followed an already lengthy period of less intense contact.

The Ottomans and the world

Just as the Ottoman presence profoundly changed the Arab lands in the course of the three centuries examined in this book, so the world around the Ottomans changed during the same period. The drastic changes in western European government and society during this period are by far the most marked, and most accounts of the Ottoman Empire's non-military foreign relations focus almost exclusively on western Europe, particularly France, Britain and the Italian city-states. Where the Arab provinces are concerned, this western European focus can seem obses-sive, obscuring as it sometimes does the provinces' relations even with the rest of the Ottoman Empire. Examination of the Ottoman Arab provinces' connections to and similarities with regions outside western

Europe can, however, be enlightening, not least because it can provide a counterpoise to the relentlessly negative comparisons with western Europe that have dogged appraisals of the Ottoman Empire after 1600.

India

India under the Mughal Empire, which emerged in 1526, was a key trading partner of the Ottoman Arab provinces, as pointed out in Chapter 7. The commercial orientation of Basra and the port cities of Yemen, particularly Aden on the Arabian Sea, was primarily towards India, while Indian ships dominated trade in the Red Sea, forming a vital component of the regional coffee trade. Meanwhile, Indian merchandise loomed large in the overland transit trade through Aleppo.

In comparison with commercial ties, religious and intellectual links between the Mughal and Ottoman domains were more complex and ambivalent. As fellow Sunni, Hanafi regimes, the two empires ostensibly had many interests in common. Although both viewed the Shiite Safavid empire with suspicion, however, the Mughals seldom engaged the Safavids militarily but, at least during the sixteenth century, regarded them as potential allies against the Uzbeks and Afghans, who, though Sunni, were the early Mughals' chief enemies. The second Mughal emperor, Humayun (r. 1530–40, 1555–6), took refuge with the Safavids when he was driven from India by the Afghans; he regained the throne with Safavid aid. On the other hand, the Mughal emperor's attitude towards the Ottoman sultan was apparently somewhat ambivalent. There is certainly no indication that the Mughals recognized the Ottoman ruler as the leader of the world's Sunni Muslims. Rather, the Mughal emperor himself was a potential rival for this status. Khalil al-Muradi, *mufti* of Damascus during the late eighteenth century, as well as head of the city's population of descendants of the Prophet Muhammad, once referred to the Mughal emperor Awrangzeb (r. 1658–1707) as 'commander of the faithful', a title reserved for the caliph. In addition, the reformed version of the Naqshbandi Sufi order, which al-Muradi's ancestor had introduced to Damascus and which found a solid following in the Arab lands, had originated in India; apart from the emperor Akbar, whose religious syncretism had triggered the reformist trend, the Mughal emperors vigorously supported the Naqshbandis. Even Akbar, during the early decades of his lengthy reign, patronized shaykhs of the order. Large numbers of Mughal subjects, not surprisingly, made the pilgrimage to Mecca each year, and many Indian scholars took advantage of the opportunity to study with prominent scholars in Mecca and Medina, as well as Cairo, which was relatively close by. Egyptian historian Abd al-Rahman al-Jabarti's sometime collaborator Murtada al-Zabidi migrated from India to the city of Zabid in southern Yemen before settling in Cairo. The Kazdağlı grandee Abdurrahman Kethüda built a special residential college for Indian students at al-Azhar; this construction almost certainly reflected his own commercial links to the subcontinent, as well as his desire to accommodate foreign scholars.

So far as its internal administration was concerned, the Mughal Empire was curiously similar to its Ottoman counterpart. Decentralizing forces were even stronger in the Mughal provinces than they were in the Ottoman domains. In absorbing northern Indian territories which had belonged to earlier Sunni Muslim regimes, the Mughals faced many of the same challenges the Ottomans faced in incorporating former Mamluk, Akkoyunlu and Safavid lands, but with the additional challenge of an enormous Hindu population with a venerable military tradition of its own. Like the Ottomans, the Mughals awarded land revenue-collection rights in return for military service; those who held these grants, which resembled *timar*s, were known as *mansabdar*s, from the Arabic *mansab*, 'position', and the Persianate suffix indicating 'one who has'. Whereas Ottoman timariots were, by the mid-sixteenth century, entirely Muslim, some fifteen per cent of Mughal *mansabdar*s during the same period were unconverted Hindus belonging to a warrior caste known as Rajputs, who became an ever more potent force in the Mughal armies and in Mughal provincial administration. By the mid-eighteenth century, they were running the region of Rajputana (modern Rajasthan), west of Delhi, as a virtually autonomous kingdom. More serious was the revolt of the Marathas, a Hindu population based in the central Indian region known as the Deccan, whose leader Shivaji carved out an independent state in the Maratha homeland late in the seventeenth century. His successors expanded north-west, as well as south- and eastwards, and ultimately placed the Mughals under protectorate until a cataclysmic defeat by Afghan forces in 1761.

Even before the era of Maratha hegemony, much of the Mughal Empire's agricultural land was controlled by *zamindar*s, holders of revenue-collection rights whose functions were comparable to those of tax-farmers, although the term encompassed not only those who had purchased these collection rights but also hereditary chieftains similar to the Kurdish emirs of south-eastern Anatolia. During the seventeenth century, the Mughal central authority attempted to exert a degree of control over the *zamindar*s by enrolling them as *mansabdar*s so that their revenue-collection rights were subject to the state's approval. This policy, however, resulted in a codependence between the Mughal state and the *zamindar*s similar to that between the Ottoman state and the *ayan* during the eighteenth century. In the late seventeenth century, a time of agrarian crisis when the number of *zamindar*s far exceeded that of *mansab*s, rebellions by ambitious *zamindar*s became distressingly frequent. Like Ottoman provincial *ayan*, the *zamindar*s maintained private armies and sometimes large private estates. They were as well placed as the *ayan* to establish independent relations among themselves and with foreign powers, notably the European powers.

Africa

More than the slave trade linked the Arab provinces to Africa. With the North African provinces of the Ottoman Empire, as well as with Morocco, Egypt above all had a thriving commercial, religious and military relationship. In addition to the large numbers of North African pilgrims who joined the Egyptian pilgrimage caravan every year, many ulema and Sufis from Tunisia, Algeria and Morocco migrated to Egypt, adding to the strength of the Maliki legal rite there. The Maliki *mufti* Shaykh Ahmad al-Dardir was a favourite of the Moroccan sultan, who gave him a large sum of money which he used to build a Sufi lodge for adherents of his own order, described in Chapter 10. Partially through the mediation of Azhari shaykhs such as al-Dardir, the ever-adaptable Khalwati Sufi order spread across North Africa, where in several key cases it served as the basis for new Sufi orders which in turn extended into the burgeoning West African commercial kingdoms.

On the military front, large numbers of soldiers known simply as Maghariba ('North Africans') served as auxiliary forces in Syria and, under Ali Bey al-Kabir, in Egypt; many of them were men of Anatolian origin initially recruited by the semi-autonomous governors of Tunis and Algiers, or the sons of such recruits. In local chronicles, these soldiers are sometimes portrayed as a socially disruptive force. The links between Egypt's grandees and those of Tunis and Algiers, meanwhile, remain virtually unexplored. In 1730, the colourful Egyptian grandee Cherkes ('Circassian') Mehmed Bey, in flight from Egypt, took refuge with the autonomous governor of Algiers before crossing the Mediterranean to the north-eastern Italian port of Trieste, whence he travelled to Vienna to seek the aid of the Habsburg emperor. Apart from this episode, connections among these provincial strongmen are obscure, although they certainly existed and must, in fact, have been rather well-developed.

Meanwhile, the Horn of Africa had ancient ties to Yemen, which lay just across the Red Sea. In fact, the ancient civilization of the southern Arabian peninsula was more closely related to that of Ethiopia than it was to that of the northern Arabian peninsula. During the Middle Ages, merchants and ulema crossed back and forth with great regularity between Yemen and the Muslim regions of Somalia and Jabart (today's Djibouti). Yemen, before, during and after its tenure as an Ottoman province, boasted numerous ulema surnamed Jabarti. The ancestors of the historian Abd al-Rahman al-Jabarti migrated from Jabart to Egypt, and it is clear from al-Jabarti's obituary of his father that even in the late eighteenth century the family still identified to some degree with Jabart and with the Amharic culture of the Horn of Africa. Al-Azhar contained a residential college for students from Jabart, which both al-Jabarti and his father headed, as well as separate colleges for students from a variety of regions in sub-Saharan Africa.

China

Ottoman relations with China's Ming (1368–1644) and Qing (1644–1911) empires were almost entirely commercial. Best-known in this context is the flow of Ming dynasty blue and white porcelain into Ottoman territory during the fifteenth and sixteenth centuries, which inspired the Ottomans' own distinctive porcelain. This trade continued under the Qing, whose kilns produced many items specifically designed for the Ottoman market. Descriptions of the possessions found in the homes of deceased provincial grandees in the eighteenth century occasionally mention Chinese porcelain, as well as other exotic goods from India and European countries.

Of all premodern empires, that of China's Qing dynasty is perhaps most directly comparable to the Ottoman Empire, yet only a few attempts have been made at systematic comparison. Manchus from north of the Ming territories, the Qing, like the Ottomans, were ethnically alien to most of the populations they ruled. Qing land tax administration was somewhat similar to the system of *emin*s which prevailed in Egypt during the sixteenth and part of the seventeenth centuries, with district magistrates in charge of collecting a basic land tax, usually in cash. Like the Ottoman government, that of the Qing went through cycles of centralization and decentralization. During periods of decentralization, the provincial scholar-gentry, a class combining elements of ulema and *ayan* whose status was determined by the imperial civil service exam, exercised extraordinary influence in their home provinces, despite the fact that they did not hold official office in these locales. Towards the end of the eighteenth century, however, Qing society suffered a crisis similar to that suffered by the Ottomans two hundred years earlier, featuring population pressure, inflation and widespread banditry. In these circumstances, local warlords, many of whom had used privately amassed wealth to purchase official ranks and build armies, wielded authority in the provinces. They often controlled the revenues of multiple villages in a process that resembled tax-farming. They thus filled a social niche and played economic and political roles similar to those of Ottoman provincial *ayan*.

The Habsburg and Russian empires

Finally, enough structural and institutional similarities exist between the Ottoman Empire and its two chief European adversaries, the Russian and Habsburg empires, to call into question the heavy emphasis on western Europe in comparative exercises. Both these polities were multi-ethnic land empires that faced similar problems of provincial integration. Their systems of land tenure were far more 'feudal' than the Ottoman land regime. In the Habsburg domains, old noble families owned most of the land, which was worked by peasant farmers who were nominally free but bound to the noble estates by a daunting array of obligations. In Russia, serfs, whose status was codified in a law of 1649, worked the land of the nobles who owned them. The westernizing reforms of Tsar Peter the Great (r. 1689–1725) did nothing to improve their lot; on the contrary, Peter expanded serfdom to encompass virtually all Russian peasants.

During the same period when the Ottomans were struggling to incorporate the newly conquered Arab provinces, the Russians were conquering independent Central Asian Turkic khanates and coming to terms with a growing population of Muslim subjects; meanwhile, the Spanish Habsburgs faced the challenge of integrating their new American colonies into their empire. The rulers of all three empires assumed the role of upholder of the true faith, with all the symbolism and ceremonial this entailed: the Ottoman sultan represented Sunni Islam, the Habsburg emperor Roman Catholicism, the Russian tsar Orthodox Christianity; indeed, the tsar had taken up the mantle of defender of the Eastern Church following the fall of Constantinople to the Ottomans, consciously seeking to fill the religious and geopolitical gap left by the collapse of the Byzantines. All this meant that relations between these rulers and the religious officials of their respective realms were highly charged and occasionally contentious.

The comparison between the Ottoman provinces and the Spanish American colonies is suggestive in the light of ongoing efforts to place the Ottoman Empire and transatlantic empires in a meaningful comparative framework. Although the Ottoman provinces were not settler colonies in the manner of Mexico and the South American countries, to say nothing of British and French North America, the societies established by western European settlers in the Americas were in some respects similar to those of the Ottoman provinces, notably in the emergence of colonial elites and their encounters with governors and other officials from the metropolis, the sub-cultures of soldiers and slaves, and colonial religious and intellectual cultures and their engagement with those of the mother countries. These sorts of considerations allow for meaningful comparisons between Ottoman and western European provincial societies while avoiding the pitfalls of the standard military and political comparisons.

Such comparisons and connections enable us to globalize the Ottoman Empire in the true sense of the word: to see it not as a Muslim monolith confronting an equally monolithic West but as one of a number of empires in premodern Europe and Asia which made different choices in response to the challenges confronting them during this volatile period. Broader contextualization of this sort puts Ottoman responses to these challenges in perspective, making them appear more rational and far-sighted than they might seem if compared solely with military and political decisions taken by western European states. It likewise helps to subvert the teleological narrative of a cumbersome, unmanageable and inherently inferior empire that was somehow destined to 'fall' to the more progressive western European powers. More generally, the exercise points up the fact that the Ottoman Empire was not unique among premodern empires in its structures, its functions or its responses to the transformations of the seventeenth and eighteenth centuries, including European commercial and military expansionism. In this context, the experience of the Ottoman Arab provinces ceases to be part of the narrative of Ottoman inferiority and decline.

Interprovincial comparisons

Wide-ranging comparisons with other Eurasian empires mean little if scholars of the Ottoman Arab provinces know nothing of what was transpiring in the non-Arab provinces of the empire during the premodern era. After all, the Anatolian and Balkan provinces were not simply neighbours of the Arab provinces; they enjoyed direct, sustained and active connections to the Arab lands on a number of levels. As noted above, soldiers and officials rotated among all these provinces. The demographics of the Arab provinces were permanently affected by population influxes from Anatolia and the Balkans, as witness, in a single example, the numerous residents of various Arab countries who bear the surname Bushnaq ('Bosnian'). Shipments of commodities such as wood and furs from these other provinces to the Arab lands were near-constant, while the Arab provinces reciprocated with grain, camels, transshipped textiles and spices and, of course, coffee. The *ayan* of eighteenth-century Anatolia and the Balkans are not only directly comparable to their counterparts in the Arab provinces; in some cases, they were aware of each other and established contact. And while Arabophone intellectual culture is conventionally depicted as hermetically sealed from the non-Arab parts of the Ottoman domains, Arabic may have functioned as a sort of intellectual *lingua franca* among provincial ulema throughout the empire, much as Ottoman Turkish did among soldiery and officials. Ulema in seventeenth-century Hungary, for example, composed advice manuals in Arabic. This sort of interprovincial purview is an urgent desideratum in Ottoman studies, for it holds the greatest promise of enabling scholars of the provinces to transcend the tenacious barriers that continue to consign Arab, Anatolian and Balkan studies to mutually exclusive fields. This was by no means the reality of the empire; it is rather the legacy of nineteenth- and twentieth-century nationalism.

The question of nationalist historiographies

This book has tried to present the period between 1516 and 1800 as one during which the Ottoman Empire changed and adapted in response to a variety of internal and external stimuli, from new military technologies to global fiscal crisis to reformist spiritual movements to changes in the societies of its allies and enemies. Transformations within the societies of the Arab provinces have deliberately been presented within this broader context. In adopting this approach, the present study differs consciously from traditional nationalist historiographies, Arab, Balkan and, to a large degree, Turkish, which depict the period of Ottoman rule as one of stagnation, at best, and unchecked decline, at worst, during which the progressive tendencies of the 'native' peoples in question were stifled. This kind of blatantly nationalist narrative, which portrays the Ottomans in unrelievedly negative terms, has become all but obsolete in professional scholarship on most of the provinces and successor states concerned. If anything, it has been more tenacious in the Balkans and Hungary than it has been in the Arab countries.

This does not, however, signify the triumph of a new historiography in which the Arab provinces are fully integrated into the narrative of Ottoman history. Nationalism is a tenacious and pervasive ideology which still exerts an inordinate influence on the writing of Ottoman history, both studies of the Ottoman centre and those focusing on particular provinces. In fact, this centre–periphery dichotomy within the Ottoman field is itself coloured by nationalism since 'centrist' studies are often the preserve of Turkish historians, as well as European and North American scholars with little background in provincial history, while scholars from the other successor states of the Ottoman Empire tend to concentrate on the history of the provinces that preceded the nations of which they are citizens.

Recently, an approach to Arab provincial history has emerged that we might call 'neo-nationalist'. Far more sophisticated than old-school nationalist historiography, this approach attempts to globalize the Ottoman Arab provinces by way of circumventing the Ottoman imperial context within which they functioned. Thus, rather than stressing, for example, Egypt's commercial links to other Ottoman provinces and to the imperial capital, a study employing this approach emphasizes trade between Egypt and western Europe – this despite the fact that the vast majority of the trade in which the Ottoman Empire participated was internal. By the same token, the Arab provinces' cultural and intellectual life is evaluated without reference to Istanbul or to non-Arab provinces of the empire, even though intellectual exchange among scholars throughout the empire is easily demonstrated. Ironically, however, the nation-state-specific framework within which such studies are produced often means that historians who adopt this approach even overlook exchanges and reciprocal influences among various Arab provinces.

A common refrain among such scholars is that historical sources produced at the imperial centre shed little light on provincial history apart from the activities of the governing elite, who, as 'Turks', have little relevance to the lives and experiences of the vast masses of 'the people', who are tacitly understood to be Arab. This, however, is a mischaracterization of imperial sources, such as sultanic decrees, tax registers and military pay lists, which actually include astonishing amounts of detail on both the elite and sub-elite populations of the various provinces precisely because they result from a dialogue between government functionaries in the imperial chancery, on the one hand, and provincial grandees and administrators, on the other. A truly integrative historiography would take both central and provincial sources into account, recognizing the dialogue between them through which the narrative of provincial history is constructed and debated.

The implication of neo-nationalist historiography is that the Ottoman context has little relevance for the populations of the Arab provinces, apart from a tiny military and administrative elite. Thus, neo-nationalist scholars exploit locally produced sources with little or no regard for what was occurring in the imperial capital or in other parts of the empire during the period of their purview. Their assumption that these local sources reflect a self-contained provincial reality leads them to misread or overlook key clues to the provincial population's ties to the imperial centre, such as references to imperial functionaries designated only by abbreviated titles. Historiographical devotion to the middle or lower classes or the minority populations of one of the provinces hardly justifies ignoring the general political, economic and institutional history of the Ottoman Empire, for this was the immediate context within which provincial developments occurred. Moreover, such an attitude denies agency to the 'indigenous' populations whom these authors claim to represent since it treats them as a passive, undifferentiated mass who were utterly unconnected to the political, economic and social networks that bound one province to another and all to the imperial centre.

As this book has attempted to demonstrate, these sorts of connections were pervasive in the Ottoman Arab provinces, routinely cutting across class, status and ethno-regional boundaries. Even if members of the provincial military and administrative elite had more frequent contact with officials of the central government in Istanbul, other social elements in the Arab provinces were integrated into the imperial system in different ways. Rank-and-file soldiers of a wide variety of ethnicities and regional provenances participated in rich, multifaceted regimental cultures which, in many cases, transcended geographical boundaries and even the boundary between troops from the imperial capital and localized provincial troops. In the case of the Janissaries, even though *kapı kulları* from Istanbul clashed with localized *yerliyye*, both sides, somewhat ironically, partook of ancient regimental customs, lore, insignia and uniforms. Meanwhile, merchants, urban craftsmen and peasants alike participated in commercial networks that linked them to larger regional, interprovincial and international markets. At the same time, they interacted with and occasionally reacted against imperial and local officials, as well as new regulations and administrative developments. The highest echelons of the provincial ulema had extraordinarily close ties to their counterparts in other provinces and in Istanbul, fostering a brisk exchange of religious texts of various kinds and resulting in an often astonishing degree of mobility within the empire. Lower-ranking scholars often travelled through the Arab provinces and even to Anatolia in search of instruction. At the same time, membership of Sufi orders broke down ethno-regional barriers among ulema and 'commoners' alike.

Neo-nationalist historiography also manifests certain pan-Arab influences in its tendency to treat residents of the various Arab provinces as if they shared a tacitly acknowledged common identity which set them in implicit opposition to the non-Arab Ottoman territories. While such a distinction might seem sensible on the surface, it tends to ignore the complex factors contributing to provincial identities. Damascene and North

African residents of Cairo, for instance, of whom there were many, were not regarded as 'natives', despite the fact that they spoke Arabic and might have been well integrated into the city's social fabric for generations. By the same token, Turcophone Anatolians living in the same city were not necessarily regarded as a completely alien presence who could not possibly have an impact on civic life. A major problem with much-touted 'bottom-up' studies focusing on the lower and middle classes is that they often assume this fundamental dichotomy between a Turkish elite and Arab 'masses' which overrides more subtle and complex modes of self-definition among various social groups. Lamentably, many of the scholars who carry out these otherwise valuable studies lack familiarity with underlying Ottoman structures, parallels in non-Arab provinces to developments in the Arab provinces, and even basic knowledge of Ottoman institutions; some are even antagonistic towards the Ottoman superstructure. They thus misrepresent the society of the Arab provinces as self-contained and even hermetically sealed, bearing little or no effects of centuries of incorporation into the Ottoman Empire.

This study, in contrast, has sought to emphasize the extraordinary impact incorporation into one of history's largest and longest-lived empires had on the Arab lands. Evidence of this impact survives to this day in the governmental institutions, laws, architecture, language and foods of the modern Arab nation-states. These reminders, as well as the influences described in the preceding chapters, should leave no doubt that the history of the Arab lands between 1516 and 1800 was Ottoman history.

Present-day relevance

More and more often, historians feel compelled to justify their scholarship in terms of its applicability to present-day problems, as if the present were all that mattered and we will not all one day be history. As an historian, I believe that the history of the Ottoman Arab provinces before 1800 has value in its own right and need not be justified in this fashion. At the same time, however, I strongly feel that it is impossible to understand the present-day Middle East without some knowledge of this history. Although the region's current national boundaries are largely the work of European imperialists, many territories whose status has been disputed in the recent past, from the Kurdish regions to Kuwait to the Alexandretta *sanjak*, the strip of land jutting out from south-eastern Anatolia which is claimed by both Syria and Turkey, have their roots in Ottoman administrative arrangements. Likewise, divisions within existing nation-states, such as the territorial fractures plaguing Iraq or the far more subtle distinctions between northern and southern

Syria, reflect Ottoman provincial and intraprovincial boundaries. The Ottoman past can even shed light on the Arab–Israeli dispute. Jewish immigration to Ottoman Palestine began under Sultan Abdülhamid II (r. 1876–1909), whose policies affected the pre-state Zionist enterprise, while the Palestinian society that the settlers encountered had been shaped by nearly four centuries of Ottoman rule. Israeli land laws are still largely Ottoman; thus, any peace settlement involving the exchange of lands would have to grapple with Ottoman land tenure. During the multilateral peace negotiations that followed the 1991 Madrid peace conference, for that reason, the Jordanian delegation included a well-known Jordanian Ottomanist historian, Professor Muhammad Adnan al-Bakhit. Meanwhile, the Iran-Iraq war of 1980–8 and the current turmoil in Iraq to some degree reflect the region's historical status as the zone of contention between the Ottoman and Safavid empires; by the same token, Iran and Turkey have succeeded the two empires as the region's chief geopolitical powers, difficult though it seems for some diplomats to recognize this fact.

In short, the history of the Ottoman Arab provinces before 1800 is not simply a quaint prelude to a gritty and often bloody present-day reality. On the contrary, it is an integral part of a larger historical whole which is still in process. Vestiges of the Ottoman past are everywhere evident in the Middle East today. Understanding this past and acknowledging its Ottoman character are thus part and parcel of coming to grips with the present realities of the region.

BIBLIOGRAPHICAL ESSAY

Abbreviations:

BSOAS *Bulletin of the School of Oriental and African Studies*
EI² *Encyclopaedia of Islam*, 2nd edition

Introduction: Rewriting Arab History, 1516–1800

Sources for the study of the Ottoman Arab lands

One of the earliest archival studies of an Ottoman Arab province is Stanford J. Shaw, *The Financial and Administrative Organization and Development of Ottoman Egypt, 1517–1798* (Princeton, NJ, 1962). Many of Shaw's findings corroborate the conclusions which P.M. Holt drew from Arabic narrative sources. A nationalistic study of Ottoman Egypt which summarily dismisses Ottoman Turkish sources in favour of 'authentic' Arabic sources is Nelly Hanna, *In Praise of Books: A Cultural History of Cairo's Middle Class, Sixteenth to the Eighteenth Century* (Syracuse, NY, 2003); see especially p. 20.

Otherwise, works related to the topics surveyed in the Introduction are cited under the chapters that treat those topics in detail.

Chapter 1: Lands and Peoples

A good historical overview of the geography of the Ottoman Empire during its phase of rapid expansion is Donald E. Pitcher, *An Historical Geography of the Ottoman Empire from Earliest Times to the End of the Sixteenth Century* (Leiden, 1972). Concise historical surveys of the Middle East's major population groups include Bernard Lewis, *The Arabs in History*, rev. edn (New York, 1966); Gene R. Garthwaite, *The Persians* (Malden, MA, 2005); Carter V. Findley, *The Turks in World History* (Oxford, 2005); Mehrdad R. Izady, *The Kurds: A Concise Handbook* (Washington, DC, 1992); Richard G. Hovannisian, ed., *The Armenian People from Ancient to Modern Times*, 2 vols (New York, 1997); and Michael Brett and Elizabeth Fentress, *The Berbers* (Oxford and Cambridge, MA, 1996). Overviews of the various religions of the region in the pre-Islamic period can be found in Richard C. Foltz, *Religions of the Silk Road: Overland Trade and Cultural Exchange from Antiquity to the Fifteenth Century* (New York, 1999), and John Julius Norwich's *Byzantium* trilogy (*The Early Centuries, The Apogee, The Decline and Fall*) (London, 1988, 1991, 1995), which provides solid coverage of the various Christian schisms. Further detail on the Copts and Nestorians is provided in Theodore Hall Partrick, *Traditional Egyptian Christianity: A History of the Coptic Orthodox Church* (Greensboro, NC, 1996), and David Wilmshurst, *The Ecclesiastical Organisation of the Church of the East, 1318–1913* (Leuven, 2000).

The emergence of the various sects of Islam is covered succinctly but comprehensively in Bertold Spuler, *History of the Muslim World*, I: *The Age of the Caliphs*, trans. F.R.C. Bagley (Leiden, 1960; reissue Princeton, NJ, 1995). Greater detail on Shiite subsects can be found in Wilferd Madelung, *Religious Trends in Early Islamic Iran* (New York, 1988). One of the few scholarly works on Twelver Shiites in Arab lands is Yitzhak Nakash, *The Shi'is of Iraq* (Princeton, NJ, 1994), although Heinz Halm offers an accessible general overview of the subsect in his *Shia Islam: From Religion to Revolution*, trans. Allison Brown (Princeton, NJ, 1997). Farhad Daftary provides an exhaustive history of the Ismaili subsect in *The Ismailis: Their History and Doctrines* (Cambridge, 1990); a less intimidating introduction is his *A Short History of the Ismailis: Traditions of a Muslim Community* (Princeton, NJ, 1998). Perhaps the least biased and most accessible description of the Yazidi religion can be found in Izady's *The Kurds*, pp. 153–8, while the Druze are treated in Robert Brenton Betts, *The Druze* (New Haven, CT, 1988), and the Alawis (a.k.a. Nusayris) in Meir M. Bar-Asher and Aryeh Kofsky, *The Nusayri-Alawi Religion: An Enquiry into Its Theology and Liturgy* (Leiden, 2002).

Chapter 2: The Ottoman Conquest of the Arab Lands

Claude Cahen offers comprehensive discussions of conditions in pre-Ottoman Anatolia in his *The Formation of Turkey – The Seljukid Sultanate of Rum: Eleventh to Fourteenth Century*, trans. and ed. P.M. Holt (Harlow, Essex, 2001). Two classic, though today contested, studies of Ottoman origins are Paul Wittek, *The Rise of the Ottoman Empire* (London, 1938; repr. 1971) and M. Fuad Köprülü, *The Origins of the Ottoman Empire*, trans. and ed. Gary Leiser (Albany, NY, 1992); more recent studies include Rudi P. Lindner, *Nomads and Ottomans in Medieval Anatolia* (Bloomington, IN, 1983), and Cemal Kafadar, *Between Two Worlds: The*

Construction of the Early Ottoman State (Berkeley, CA, 1995). Colin Heywood offers a novel explanation of Ottoman origins, positing a Mongol lineage, in 'Filling the Black Hole: The Emergence of the Bithynian Atamanates', in Kemal Çiçek, *et al.*, eds, *The Great Ottoman-Turkish Civilisation*, I: *Politics* (Ankara, 2000), pp. 107–15.

Early Ottoman expansion and the development of Ottoman institutions are covered in Halil Inalcik, *The Ottoman Empire: The Classical Age, 1300–1600*, trans. Norman Itzkowitz and Colin Imber (London, 1973). Inalcik offers a more recent treatment in 'The Ottoman State: Economy and Society, 1300–1600', part 1 of Inalcik, ed., with Donald Quataert, *An Economic and Social History of the Ottoman Empire* (Cambridge, 1994).

The most authoritative scholar of the Mamluk sultanate is the late David Ayalon, whose numerous articles are collected in four volumes: *Studies on the Mamluks of Egypt (1250–1517)* (London, 1977), *The Mamluk Military Society: Collected Studies* (London, 1979), *Outsiders in the Lands of Islam: Mamluks, Mongols, and Eunuchs* (London, 1988) and *Islam and the Abode of War: Military Slaves and Islamic Adversaries* (Aldershot and Brookfield, VT, 1994); see also his article 'Mamluk' in *EI*[2]. Robert Irwin offers a more concise overview of the early Mamluk sultanate in *The Middle East in the Middle Ages: The Early Mamluk Sultanate, 1250–1382* (London and Sydney, 1986).

Carl F. Petry addresses the series of wars between the Mamluks and the Ottomans in the late fifteenth century, as well as the decisive confrontation between Selim I and Qansuh al-Ghuri, in *Twilight of Majesty: The Reigns of the Mamluk Sultans al-Ashraf Qaytbay and Qansuh al-Ghawri in Egypt* (Seattle, WA, 1993). The authoritative study of the Mamluks' Dulkadiroğlu vassals is the Turkish scholar Refet Yinanç's *Dulkadir Beyliği* (*The Dulkadir Beylik*) (Ankara, 1989); a dated but useful English-language source is *EI*[2], s.v. 'Dhū'l-Ḳadr', by J.H. Mordtmann [V.L. Ménage].

The most authoritative study of the Akkoyunlu Turcoman dynasty is John E. Woods, *The Aqquyunlu: Clan, Confederation, Empire*, rev. and expanded edn (Salt Lake City, UT, 1999). As for the Safavids, their early struggle with the Ottomans is covered in Adel Allouche, *The Origins and Development of the Ottoman-Safavid Conflict, 906–962/1500–1555* (Berlin, 1983).

Ottoman confrontations with the Portuguese in the Indian Ocean and their implications for Ottoman policy towards the Arab lands are addressed in the collected articles of Salih Özbaran, *The Ottoman Response to European Expansion: Studies on Ottoman-Portuguese Relations in the Indian Ocean and Ottoman Administration in the Arab Lands during the Sixteenth Century* (Istanbul, 1994). A dated but still useful study along the same lines is George W.F. Stripling, *The Ottoman Turks and the Arabs, 1511–1574* (Urbana, IL, 1942). The circumstances of Yemen before the Ottoman conquest of 1538 are treated in Jane Hathaway, *A Tale of Two Factions: Myth, Memory, and Identity in Ottoman Egypt and Yemen* (Albany, NY, 2003), Ch. 4.

The Ottoman conquest of Egypt and its aftermath are re-examined in a valuable study by the architectural historian Doris Behrens-Abouseif: *Egypt's Adjustment to Ottoman Rule: Institutions, Waqf, and Architecture in Cairo (Sixteenth-Seventeenth Centuries)* (Leiden, 1994). The Egyptian chronicler Ibn Iyas' account of the Ottoman conquest has long been available in an English translation: Muhammad ibn Ahmad ibn Iyas, *An Account of the Ottoman Conquest of Egypt in the Year A.H. 922 (A.D. 1516)*, trans. W.H. Salmon (London, 1921).

Chapter 3: The Organization of the Ottoman Provincial Administration

Galal H. El-Nahal offers a key example of religio-legal administration in the Ottoman Arab provinces in *The Judicial Administration of Ottoman Egypt in the Seventeenth Century* (Minneapolis, MN, 1979) while Yemen's special circumstances are covered in Jane Hathaway, *A Tale of Two Factions* (Albany, NY, 2003), Ch. 4. Ottoman treatment of the Twelver Shiite populations in Iraq is touched on in Yitzhak Nakash, *The Shi'is of Iraq* (Princeton, NJ, 1994), Ch. 1, and Dina Rizk Khoury, *State and Provincial Society in the Ottoman Empire: Mosul, 1540–1834* (Cambridge, 1997), pp. 169, 203–4.

Halil Inalcik provides a thorough-going introduction to the Ottoman provincial administrative hierarchy of *vilayet*s and *sanjak*s in *The Ottoman Empire: The Classical Age* (London, 1973), Ch. 13. Households founded by viziers, which from the late sixteenth century onwards were a frequent source of provincial governors, are treated in two seminal works: Metin Kunt, *The Sultan's Servants: The Transformation of Ottoman Provincial Government, 1550–1650* (New York, 1983), and Rifaat A. Abou-El-Haj, 'The Ottoman Vezir and Pasha Households, 1683–1703: A Preliminary Report', *Journal of the American Oriental Society* 94 (1974), pp. 438–47. As for the provincial law codes known as *kanunname*s, many of which were promulgated during the reign of Süleyman I (1520–66), only a few have been translated into European languages: for example, those of Damascus, Aleppo and Tripoli, Lebanon, in Robert Mantran, *Règlements fiscaux ottomans: les provinces syriennes* (Beirut, 1951), and that of Lemnos in Heath W. Lowry, *Fifteenth-Century Ottoman Realities: Christian Peasant Life on the Aegean Island of Limnos* (Istanbul, 2002), pp. 182–4.

Halil Inalcik's works constitute almost without doubt the best secondary sources on Ottoman land tenure. The *timar* system is discussed in *The Ottoman Empire: The Classical Age*, Ch. 13. The evolution of Ottoman Egypt's land regime is discussed in Stanford J. Shaw's extremely detailed, if rather ponderous, *The Financial and Administrative Organization and Development of Ottoman Egypt, 1517–1798* (Princeton, NJ, 1962). On tax-farming in the Ottoman Empire, Gabriel Baer's article 'Iltizām' in *EI²* is quite informative.

The problematic question of Egypt's administrative status is addressed in Jane Hathaway, *The Politics of Households in Ottoman Egypt: The Rise of the Qazdağlıs* (Cambridge, 1997). Examples of the 'conventional wisdom' that Egypt represented a Mamluk regime in all but name can be found in Michael Winter, *Egyptian Society under Ottoman Rule, 1517–1798* (London, 1992), and even in P.M. Holt, *Egypt and the Fertile Crescent: A Political History, 1516–1922* (Ithaca, NY, 1966), Chs 5–6.

Challenges to Ottoman rule in Egypt and Syria during the years immediately following the conquest of the Arab lands are still best summarized in Holt's *Egypt and the Fertile Crescent*, Ch. 3. Holt provides additional background on Janım Bey al-Hamzawi, the nephew of Khayrbay who opposed the rebellious governor of Egypt Ahmed Pasha al-Kha'in, in 'A Notable in the Age of Transition: Janim Bey al-Hamzawi (d. 944/1538)', in Colin Heywood and Colin Imber, eds, *Studies in Ottoman History in Honour of Professor V.L. Ménage* (Istanbul, 1994), pp. 107–15.

The massive rebellion launched by the Zaydi imam al-Mutahhar ibn Sharaf al-Din in Yemen during the 1560s is summarized in Hathaway, *A Tale of Two Factions*, Ch. 4, as are Ottoman relations with Yemen's Zaydi and Ismaili populations in the ensuing decades. A translated primary source which describes sixteenth-century Yemen is Clive K. Smith, trans. and ed., *Lightning over Yemen: A History of the Ottoman Campaign (1569–71) – Being a Translation from the Arabic of Part III of al-Barq al-yamānī fī al-fatḥ al-ʿuthmānī by Quṭb al-Dīn al-Nahrawālī al-Makkī as Published by Ḥāmad al-Jāsir (1967)* (London and New York, 2002).

Chapter 4: Crisis and Change in the Seventeenth Century

The 'decline' paradigm

The standard description of Ottoman decline literature is Bernard Lewis, 'Ottoman Observers of Ottoman Decline', *Islamic Studies* 1 (1962), pp. 71–87; repr. in Lewis, *Islam in History* (New York, 1973), pp. 199–213. One fairly influential decline treatise of the classic 'Mirror for Princes' type was translated into English over fifty years ago: Walter Livingston Wright, ed. and trans., *Ottoman Statecraft: The Book of Counsel for Vezirs and Governors by Sarı Mehmed Paşa, Defterdar* (Princeton, NJ, 1953). Critiques of the 'decline' paradigm, on the other hand, have become numerous only in the past twenty years, as witness Cornell H. Fleischer, *Bureaucrat and Intellectual in the Ottoman Empire: The Historian Mustafa Ali (1541–1600)* (Princeton, NJ, 1986); Douglas A. Howard, 'Ottoman Historiography and the Literature of "Decline" of the Sixteenth and Seventeenth Centuries', *Journal of Asian History* 22 (1988), pp. 52–77; Linda T. Darling, *Revenue-Raising and Legitimacy: Tax Collection and Finance Administration in the Ottoman Empire, 1560–1660* (Leiden, 1996), Ch. 1; and Jane Hathaway, 'Problems of Periodization in Ottoman History: The Fifteenth through the Eighteenth Centuries', *Turkish Studies Association Bulletin* 20 (1996), pp. 25–31.

Descriptions of abuses by the Janissaries and other regiments of soldiery can be found in Andreas Tietze, ed. and trans., *Mustafa Ali's Description of Cairo of 1599: Text, Transliteration, Translation, Notes* (Vienna, 1975), *passim*.

The crisis of the seventeenth century

The classic work on the wave of inflation that afflicted Ottoman society in the late sixteenth century is Ömer Lütfi Barkan, 'The Price Revolution of the Sixteenth Century: A Turning Point in the Economic History of the Middle East', trans. Justin McCarthy, *International Journal of Middle East Studies* 6 (1975), pp. 3–28. While Barkan makes the standard connection between this inflation and the flow of Spanish American silver into Ottoman territory, Şevket Pamuk's pioneering *A Monetary History of the Ottoman Empire* (Cambridge, 2000), especially Ch. 7, suggests that the inflation predated the influx of silver.

Apart from inflation, the major purported causes of the crisis are population pressure and the proliferation of firearms among the peasantry as a result of the employment of peasant mercenaries during the Long War against the Habsburgs. The standard work on the former is M.A. Cook, *Population Pressure in Rural Anatolia, 1450–1600* (London and New York, 1972), and on the latter Halil Inalcik, 'The Socio-Political Effects of the Diffusion of Fire-Arms in the Middle East', in V.J. Parry and Malcolm Yapp, eds, *War, Technology, and Society in the Middle East* (London and New York, 1975), pp. 195–217; repr. in Inalcik, *The Ottoman Empire: Conquest, Organization, and Economy* (London, 1978).

The most comprehensive account in English of the Jelali rebellions, the wave of peasant lawlessness to which the crisis gave rise throughout

Anatolia, is still William J. Griswold, *The Great Anatolian Rebellion, 1000–1020/1591–1611* (Berlin, 1983). A revisionist view of *Kul Kıran* Mehmed Pasha can be found in Jane Hathaway, 'The "Mamluk Breaker" Who Was Really a *Kul* Breaker: A Reappraisal of *Kul Kıran* Mehmed Pasha, Governor of Egypt 1607–11', in Hathaway, ed., *The Arab Lands in the Ottoman Era: Papers in Honor of Caesar Farah* (Minneapolis, MN, forthcoming).

The problem of *kul*s in the imperial capital, which culminated in the 1622 assassination of Sultan Osman II, is treated in several recent revisionist works: Gabriel Piterberg, *An Ottoman Tragedy: History and Historiography at Play* (Berkeley, CA, 2003); idem, 'The Alleged Rebellion of Abaza Mehmed Pasha: Historiography and the Ottoman State in the Seventeenth Century', in Jane Hathaway, ed., *Mutiny and Rebellion in the Ottoman Empire* (Madison, WI, 2002), pp. 13–24; and Baki Tezcan, 'The Military Uprising in Istanbul in 1622: A Historiographical Journey', in the same volume, pp. 25–43. The sort of East–West antagonism reflected in the assassination, and the governors' rebellions to which it gave rise, is discussed in Metin Kunt, 'Ethno-Regional (*Cins*) Solidarity in the Seventeenth-Century Ottoman Establishment', *International Journal of Middle East Studies* 5 (1974), pp. 233–9, and Gyula Kaldy-Nágy, 'The "Strangers" (*Ecnebiler*) in the Sixteenth-Century Ottoman Military Organization', in György Kara, ed., *Between the Danube and the Caucasus: Oriental Sources on the History of the Peoples of Central and South-Eastern Europe* (Budapest, 1987), pp. 165–9.

Localized Janissaries, known as *yerliyye*, became a formidable political and economic force in the course of the seventeenth century. P.M. Holt's *Egypt and the Fertile Crescent* (Ithaca, NY, 1966) gives a reliable overview of this development, although the information the book provides is divided among chapters dealing with different provinces (Chs 5, 7, 10). Studies focusing on specific provinces include Hathaway, *The Politics of Households in Ottoman Egypt* (Cambridge, 1997), on the origin of the Kazdağlı household in Egypt's Janissary regiment, and Jean-Paul Pascual, 'The Janissaries and the Damascus Countryside at the Beginning of the Seventeenth Century according to the Archives of the City's Military Tribunal', in Tarif Khalidi, ed., *Land Tenure and Social Transformation in the Middle East* (Beirut, 1984), pp. 357–69.

Jelali governors

Like the Jelali rebels from whom they took their name, the so-called Jelali governors of the seventeenth century were predominantly an Anatolian phenomenon. Nonetheless, analogues to the Anatolian Jelali governors were fairly numerous in the Arab provinces during the same period. Regrettably, secondary studies of these figures are still scarce. Holt's summary accounts in *Egypt and the Fertile Crescent* (Chs 7–8) remain worthwhile overviews of the rebellions of Ali Pasha Janbulad in northern Syria and Fakhr al-Din Ma'n II in Lebanon. Nonetheless, at least one micro-study of the Janbulad clan has shed new light on its identity: Abdul-Rahim Abu-Husayn, 'The Junblats and the Janbulads: A Case of Mistaken Identity', in Markus Köhbach, Gisela Procházka-Eisl and Claudia Römer, eds, *Acta Viennensia Ottomanica: Proceedings of the 13th CIEPO Symposium* (Vienna, 1999), pp. 1–6. The origins of Egypt's Faqari and Qasimi factions, highlighting their connection to East–West tensions in the Arab provinces, and the rebellion of Mehmed Bey, the Faqari governor of the Upper Egyptian superprovince of Jirja, are covered in Jane Hathaway, *A Tale of Two Factions* (Albany, NY, 2003), as is the Ottoman loss of Yemen in the 1620s and 1630s.

The Köprülüs

As important as the Köprülü grand viziers are, there is no single coherent study in a European language of their activities and their legacy. They receive attention in Kunt, 'Ethno-Regional (*Cins*) Solidarity', and Piterberg, *An Ottoman Tragedy*.

Chapter 5: Provincial Notables in the Eighteenth Century

Albert Hourani's classic article 'Ottoman Reform and the Politics of Notables' first appeared in William R. Polk and Richard L. Chambers, eds, *Beginnings of Modernization in the Middle East: The Nineteenth Century* (Chicago, 1968), pp. 41–68. It was reprinted in Albert Hourani, *The Emergence of the Modern Middle East* (Berkeley, CA, 1981), pp. 36–66; and in Hourani, Philip S. Khoury and Mary C. Wilson, eds, *The Modern Middle East: A Reader* (London, 1993), pp. 83–109. Examples of old-school 'local notables' historiography, assuming a fairly static population of Arabized *ayan*, are Abdul-Karim Rafeq, *The Province of Damascus, 1723–1783* (Beirut, 1966); Michael Winter, *Egyptian Society under Ottoman Rule, 1517–1798* (London, 1992); and Stephen H. Longrigg, *Four Centuries of Modern Iraq* (Oxford, 1925; repr. Beirut, 1968), although this list is by no means exhaustive.

In the past quarter century or so, a growing body of scholarship has begun to focus on the processes that undergird *ayan* status, above all the network of patron–client ties and the household which coalesces when a patron has large numbers of clients. One of the most cogent articulations of the historiographical approach necessary for a meaningful study of households is Ehud R. Toledano, 'The Emergence of Ottoman-Local Elites (1700–1900): A Framework for Research', in Ilan Pappé and Moshe Maoz, eds, *Middle Eastern Politics and Ideas: A History from Within* (London, 1997), pp. 145–62. A discussion of the household with specific reference to Ottoman Egypt is Jane Hathaway, *The Politics of Households in Ottoman Egypt: The Rise of the Qazdağlıs* (Cambridge, 1997).

Studies of specific *ayan*

Along with revisionist studies of how to frame the process of *ayan* formation, numerous revisionist studies of specific *ayan* households have appeared in the past twenty-five years or so. The trajectory of Egypt's Kazdağlı household is analysed in Hathaway, *The Politics of Households in Ottoman Egypt*. The anachronistic notion that the later Kazdağlıs, and particularly Ali Bey al-Kabir, represented a revival of the Mamluk sultanate is addressed in idem, 'Mamluk "Revivals" and Mamluk Nostalgia in Ottoman Egypt', in Michael Winter and Amalia Levanoni, eds, *The Mamluks in Egyptian and Syrian Politics and Society* (Leiden, 2004), pp. 387–406. The conventional view of Ali Bey can be found in, among others, Daniel Crecelius, *The Roots of Modern Egypt: A Study of the Regimes of Ali Bey al-Kabir and Muhammad Bey Abu al-Dhahab, 1760–1775* (Minneapolis, MN, 1981), and John W. Livingston, 'The Rise of *Shaykh al-Balad* Ali Bey al-Kabir: A Study in the Accuracy of the Chronicle of al-Jabarti', *BSOAS* 33 (1970), pp. 283–94.

Conditions in the province of Damascus during the eighteenth century, and the rise of the Azms in this context, are analysed in Karl K. Barbir, *Ottoman Rule in Damascus, 1708–1758* (Princeton, NJ, 1980); a valuable supplement to his work is Linda S. Schilcher, *Families in Politics: Damascene Factions and Estates in the Eighteenth and Nineteenth Centuries* (Wiesbaden, 1985). Clues to the careers of modern-day Azms can be gleaned from David D. Commins, *Islamic Reform: Politics and Social Change in Ottoman Syria* (New York, 1990), and Philip S. Khoury, *Urban Notables and Arab Nationalism: The Politics of Damascus, 1860–1920* (Cambridge, 1983). Suraiya Faroqhi's *Pilgrims and Sultans: The Hajj under the Ottomans, 1517–1683* (London, 1994) is a useful supplement to these monographic studies in emphasizing the centrality of the annual pilgrimage to Mecca to the political and economic dominance of Damascene and Egyptian *ayan* during the sixteenth and seventeenth centuries.

So far as Ottoman Aleppo is concerned, the most comprehensive study of the factional struggles between Janissaries and *ashraf* remains

Herbert L. Bodman, Jr's *Political Factions in Aleppo, 1760–1806* (Chapel Hill, NC, 1963). It has been supplemented, however, by three more extensive studies of the social and economic contexts within which Aleppo functioned in the eighteenth century: Abraham Marcus, *The Middle East on the Eve of Modernity: Aleppo in the Eighteenth Century* (New York, 1989); Bruce Masters, *The Origins of Western Economic Dominance in the Middle East: Mercantilism and the Islamic Economy in Aleppo, 1600– 1750* (New York, 1988); and Margaret L. Meriwether, *The Kin Who Count: Family and Society in Ottoman Aleppo, 1770–1840* (Austin, TX, 1999). Charles L. Wilkins, meanwhile, has produced two studies, as yet unpublished, one of which examines the leader of Aleppo's *ashraf* while the other provides a sophisticated analysis of the seventeenth-century militarization of Aleppine society which laid the foundation for the rise of Janissary-*ashraf* factionalism in the city: 'Ahmad Efendi Tahazade: *'Alim* and Entrepreneur in Eighteenth-Century Aleppo', unpublished MA thesis, Ohio State University, 1996; and 'Households, Guilds, and Neighborhoods: Social Solidarities in Ottoman Aleppo, 1640–1700', unpublished PhD dissertation, Harvard University, 2005. A study of the astonishingly similar role of the *ashraf* in the south-eastern Anatolian city of Ayntab is being prepared by Hülya Canbakal; a précis of some of her conclusions is contained in her 'On the "Nobility" of Provincial Notables', in Antonis Anastasopoulos, ed., *Provincial Elites in the Ottoman Empire – Halcyon Days in Crete V: A Symposium Held in Rethymno, 10–12 January 2003* (Rethymno, 2005), pp. 39–50.

A study of Ottoman Mosul which places the rise of the Jalilis in an impressively broad context is Dina Rizk Khoury, *State and Provincial Society in the Ottoman Empire: The Province of Mosul, 1540–1834* (Cambridge, 1997). While Ottoman Mosul and Basra have been the subject of several English-language monographs published in the last decade, Ottoman Baghdad has remained relatively neglected, perhaps because of the near impossibility of conducting research in Baghdad itself and the relative lack of satisfactory supplementary archival sources (for Basra, in contrast, India Office records can fill part of the archival lacuna while studies of Mosul now routinely make use of Istanbul's Prime Ministry Archives). In consequence, Longrigg's *Four Centuries of Modern Iraq*, historiographically obsolete though it is, remains one of the few available secondary sources, along with Ch. 10 of Holt's *Egypt and the Fertile Crescent*.

Georgian mamluks

There is no shortage of published works in English on the mamluk grandees of Egypt in the seventeenth and eighteenth centuries. In addition to Crecelius' *Roots of Modern Egypt* and Winter's *Egyptian Society under Ottoman Rule*, one can cite P.M. Holt, 'The Beylicate in Ottoman Egypt during the Seventeenth Century', *BSOAS* 24 (1961), pp. 214–48; David Ayalon, 'Studies in al-Jabarti I: Notes on the Transformation of Mamluk Society in Egypt under the Ottomans', *Journal of the Economic and Social History of the Orient* 3 (1960), pp. 148–74, 275–325; Michael Winter, 'Ali Efendi's "Anatolian Campaign Book": A Defence of the Egyptian Army in the Seventeenth Century', *Turcica* 15 (1983), pp. 267–309; and Gabriel Piterberg, 'The Formation of an Ottoman Egyptian Elite in the Eighteenth Century', *International Journal of Middle East Studies* 22 (1990), pp. 275–89. The drawback to all these works, however, is that they insist on linking the usages current among Ottoman Egypt's military-administrative households to those of the Mamluk sultanate while neglecting possible links to household-based political cultures in other Ottoman provinces or in the imperial capital. Awareness of the novelty of the flood of Georgians into Ottoman territory during the eighteenth century is evident in Hathaway, 'Mamluk "Revivals" and Mamluk Nostalgia in Ottoman Egypt', and *The Politics of Households in Ottoman Egypt*, as well as Daniel Crecelius and Gotcha Djaparidze, 'Relations of the Georgian Mamluks of Egypt with Their Homeland in the Last Decades of the Eighteenth Century', *Journal of the Economic and Social History of the Orient* 45 (2002), pp. 320–411; and Daniel Crecelius, 'Russia's Relations with the Mamluk Beys of Egypt in the Late Eighteenth Century', in Farhad Kazemi and R.D. McChesney, eds, *A Way Prepared: Essays on Islamic Culture in Honor of Richard Bayly Winder* (New York, 1988), pp. 55–67. A translated primary source which attests to the Georgian hegemony in late eighteenth-century Egypt, although it is often misinterpreted as an affirmation of the 'continuity' of Mamluk sultanate traditions, is Stanford J. Shaw, ed. and trans., *Ottoman Egypt in the Eighteenth Century: The Nizâmnâme-i Mısır of Cezzâr Ahmed Pasha* (Cambridge, MA, 1962).

Women in *ayan* households

Just as the imperial harem in Topkapı Palace served as a template for harems in the households of provincial grandees, so Leslie Peirce's masterful *The Imperial Harem: Women and Sovereignty in the Ottoman Empire* (New York and Oxford, 1993) serves as a template for secondary studies of the role of women in these households. Province-specific studies of such women include, for Egypt, Jane Hathaway, 'Marriage Alliances among the Military Households of Ottoman Egypt', *Annales*

Islamologiques 29 (1995), pp. 133–49, and Ch. 6 of *The Politics of Households in Ottoman Egypt*, as well as Afaf Lutfi al-Sayyid Marsot, *Women and Men in Late Eighteenth-Century Egypt* (Austin, TX, 1995); for Aleppo, Margaret L. Meriwether, *The Kin Who Count*, especially Chs 3–5, and Abraham Marcus, *The Middle East on the Eve of Modernity*, pp. 195–212; and for Mosul, Dina Rizk Khoury, 'Slippers at the Entrance, or Behind Closed Doors: Domestic and Public Spaces for Mosuli Women', in Madeline C. Zilfi, ed., *Women in the Ottoman Empire: Middle Eastern Women in the Early Modern Era* (Leiden, 1997), pp. 105–27. Barbir, *Ottoman Rule in Damascus*, pp. 86–9, takes up the case of the sister of Fethi Efendi, the *defterdar* of Damascus, who was entrusted with his wealth after his execution. Mary Ann Fay's 'Women and *Waqf*: Property, Power, and the Domain of Gender in Eighteenth-Century Egypt', in Zilfi, ed., *Women in the Ottoman Empire*, pp. 28–47, should be used with caution as it belongs to the old-school historiography which insists that the institutions of the Mamluk sultanate were revived in eighteenth-century Egypt; an interesting comparison, in any case, is Margaret L. Meriwether, 'Women and *Waqf* Revisited: The Case of Aleppo, 1770–1840', pp. 128–52 of the same volume. Among published primary sources, the British physician Alexander Russell's (1715?–68) *The Natural History of Aleppo: Containing a Description of the City, and the Principal Natural Productions in Its Neighbourhood. Together with an Account of the Climate, Inhabitants, and Diseases; Particularly of the Plague*, 2 vols, 2nd edn (Hants, 1969), I, pp. 276–312, is a lengthy description of the harem based on Russell's experiences treating the women of the Ottoman governor's household.

Eunuchs in *ayan* households

Very little has been published in the way of either primary sources or secondary studies on the functions of eunuchs in the households of provincial grandees. Because of the importance of exiled harem eunuchs in Egypt, more secondary studies are available on that population, although few focus specifically on their participation in grandee households. One can mention Jane Hathaway, *The Politics of Households in Ottoman Egypt*, Ch. 8; idem, 'The Role of the Kızlar Ağası in 17th–18th Century Ottoman Egypt', *Studia Islamica* 75 (1992), pp. 141–58; and idem, *Beshir Agha, Chief Eunuch of the Ottoman Imperial Harem* (Oxford, 2006), Chs 3, 5.

Shaun E. Marmon's *Eunuchs and Sacred Boundaries in Islamic Society* (New York and Oxford, 1995) focuses on the eunuchs who guarded the Prophet Muhammad's tomb in Medina, while Hathaway, *Beshir*

Agha, Ch. 6, brings the Tomb Eunuchs up to the Ottoman era in the context of the future Chief Harem Eunuch el-Hajj Beshir Agha's (term 1717–46) stint as Chief Tomb Eunuch in roughly 1715–16. A nineteenth-century eyewitness account of these eunuchs is provided by Sir Richard Francis Burton in his *Personal Narrative of a Pilgrimage to al-Madinah and Mecca*, 2 vols, memorial edn (London, 1893; republished New York, 1964), I.

Ayan architecture

Perhaps because of the heavy influence of architectural history in the recent historiography of Ottoman Egypt, studies of *ayan* architecture in that province are far more plentiful than studies of provincial architecture elsewhere. Particularly valuable are the studies of Doris Behrens-Abouseif, notably *Egypt's Adjustment to Ottoman Rule: Institutions, Waqf, and Architecture (Sixteenth–Seventeenth Centuries)* (Leiden, 1994) and *Azbakiyya and Its Environs from Azbak to Ismail, 1476–1879* (Cairo, 1985). André Raymond traces the development of what he has christened the Abdurrahman Kethüda Style in *Le Caire des Janissaires: l'apogée de la ville ottomane sous Abd al-Rahman Kathuda* (Paris, 1995). General guides to monuments which contain useful detail on *ayan* architecture include Richard B. Parker and Robin Sabin, *Islamic Monuments in Cairo: A Practical Guide*, 3rd edn, revised and enlarged by Caroline Williams (Cairo, 1985), and Ross Burns, *Monuments of Syria: An Historical Guide* (New York, 1992). Dina Rizk Khoury describes the building projects of Mosul's Jalili and Umari families in *State and Provincial Society in the Ottoman Empire*, while Beshara Doumani gives some idea of *ayan* architecture in Ottoman Palestine in *Rediscovering Palestine: Merchants and Peasants in Jabal Nablus, 1700–1900* (Berkeley, CA, 1995).

Cairo's *sabil-kuttab*s, the distinctive combinations of Quran schools and public drinking fountains, are surprisingly well published. Hamza Abd al-Aziz Badr and Daniel Crecelius have published the foundation deed of the *sabil-kuttab* commissioned by the future Chief Harem Eunuch el-Hajj Beshir Agha in 'The *Awqāf* of al-Hajj Bashir Agha in Cairo', *Annales Islamologiques* 27 (1993), pp. 291–311. Sitt Nafisa's *sabil-kuttab* just outside Bab Zuwayla has been restored by an American Research Center in Egypt/Egyptian Supreme Council of Antiquities team under the supervision of Polish conservationist Agnieszka Dobrowolska, who discusses the structure and its founder in 'Lady Nafisa and Her *Sabil*', *Al-Ahram Weekly* No. 757 (25–31 August 2005), available online at http://weekly.ahram.org.eg/2005/757/heritage.htm.

Chapter 6: Religious and Intellectual Life

*Qadi*s

Halil Inalcik provides a succinct yet comprehensive discussion of the ulema hierarchy that prevailed in the Ottoman central lands, as well as the informal judicial hierarchy which governed the appointments of chief judges in the Arab provinces, in *The Ottoman Empire: The Classical Age* (London, 1973), Ch. 16. The article 'Ḳāḍī 'Askar' by Gyula Káldy-Nagy in *EI²* supplies valuable supplemental information on the functions of *qadi*s, as does Galal H. El-Nahal's *The Judicial Administration of Ottoman Egypt in the Seventeenth Century* (Minneapolis, MN, 1979), which also treats the phenomenon, unique to the Arab provinces, of non-Hanafi *sharia* courts. Non-*sharia* courts, above all those for military personnel which operated according to the sultanic *kanun*, are addressed by Uriel Heyd, '*Kanun* and *Sharia* in Old Ottoman Criminal Law', *Proceedings of the Israel Academy of Sciences and Humanities* 3 (1967), pp. 1–18.

Thanks to the wave of research in Muslim court records beginning in the 1970s, a number of studies published in the last thirty years provide detailed treatments of provincial judicial systems, as well as discussions of court buildings; the manner in which a court register was compiled; the status of non-Muslims, women and slaves as witnesses in a Muslim court; the 'permanent' witnesses known as *shuhud al-hal*; and the practice of 'playing the courts' to obtain the most favourable decision. Of particular note, in addition to El-Nahal's above-cited study, are Abraham Marcus, *The Middle East on the Eve of Modernity* (New York, 1989); Nelly Hanna, 'The Administration of Courts in Ottoman Cairo', in Hanna, ed., *The State and Its Servants: Administration in Egypt from Ottoman Times to the Present* (Cairo, 1995), pp. 44–59; Leslie Peirce, *Morality Tales: Law and Gender in the Ottoman Court of Aintab* (Berkeley, CA, 2003); Najwa al-Qattan, '*Dhimmi*s in the Muslim Court: Legal Autonomy and Religious Discrimination', *International Journal of Middle East Studies* 31 (1999), pp. 429–44; and Amnon Cohen, *Jewish Life under Islam: Jerusalem in the Sixteenth Century* (Cambridge, MA, 1984), especially Ch. 6.

*Mufti*s

In the last twenty years, several valuable studies of the role of *mufti*s in general and Ottoman *mufti*s in particular have appeared. An insightful general collection is Muhammad Khalid Masud, Brinkley Messick and David S. Powers, eds, *Islamic Legal Interpretation: Muftis and Their Fatwas*

(Cambridge, MA, 1996). Two Ottomanist studies which focus on the Ottoman chief *mufti*, or Shaykh al-Islam, and above all the towering figure of Ebusuud Efendi, are R.C. Repp, *The Mufti of Istanbul: A Study in the Development of the Ottoman Learned Hierarchy* (London and Atlantic Highlands, NJ, 1986), and Colin Imber, *Ebu's-su'ud: The Islamic Legal Tradition* (Stanford, CA, 1997). A landmark exploration of how *muftis'* *fatwa*s influenced law in seventeenth- and eighteenth-century Syria is Judith E. Tucker, *In the House of the Law: Gender and Islamic Law in Ottoman Syria and Palestine* (Berkeley, CA, 1998). In addition, Karl K. Barbir examines the Muradi family's monopoly of the post of *mufti* of Damascus in 'All in the Family: The Muradis of Damascus', in Heath W. Lowry and Ralph S. Hattox, eds, *Proceedings of the Third Congress on the Social and Economic History of Turkey* (Istanbul, 1990), pp. 327–55, while brief but informative sections on *mufti*s in Ayntab and Mosul can be found in, respectively, Leslie Peirce's *Morality Tales* and Dina Rizk Khoury's *State and Provincial Society in the Ottoman Empire* (Cambridge, 1997).

Madrasas

The hierarchy of elite *madrasa*s in the Ottoman central lands is detailed in Inalcik, *The Ottoman Empire: The Classical Age*, Ch. 16. Shiite and competing Sunni *madrasa*s in the shrine cities of Iraq are briefly discussed in Yitzhak Nakash, *The Shi'is of Iraq* (Princeton, NJ, 1994), which admittedly deals mainly with late Ottoman-era institutions.

Al-Azhar's founding, evolution and gradual emergence as Egypt's premier *madrasa* are discussed in Paul E. Walker, 'Fatimid Institutions of Learning', *Journal of the American Research Center in Egypt* 34 (1991), pp. 179–200; Michael Winter, *Egyptian Society under Ottoman Rule* (London, 1992); pp. 118–26; Daniel Crecelius, 'The Emergence of the Shaykh al-Azhar as the Pre-Eminent Religious Leader in Egypt', in *Colloque international sur l'histoire du Caire, 27 mars–5 avril 1969*, assembled under the auspices of the Ministry of Culture of the Arab Republic of Egypt (Cairo, 1972), pp. 109–23; and Afaf Lutfi al-Sayyid Marsot, 'The Ulama of Cairo in the Eighteenth and Nineteenth Centuries', in Nikki R. Keddie, ed., *Scholars, Saints, and Sufis: Muslim Religious Institutions since 1500* (Berkeley, CA, 1972), pp. 149–65, which, for all its other useful qualities, exemplifies the position that the *madrasa*s of the Arab provinces, and thus the ulema trained in them, did not belong to the Ottoman ulema hierarchy. Al-Azhar's distinctive system of *riwaq*s, or residential colleges, is described in J. Heyworth-Dunne, *An Introduction to the History of Education in Modern Egypt* (London, 1968), and

Bayard Dodge, *Al-Azhar: A Millennium of Muslim Learning*, memorial edn (Washington, DC, 1974).

Mosque preachers

The mosque preacher career is most cogently covered in Madeline C. Zilfi, *The Politics of Piety: The Ottoman Ulema in the Post-Classical Age (1600–1800)* (Minneapolis, MN, and Chicago, 1988), Ch. 4; and idem, 'The Kadızadelis: Discordant Revivalism in Seventeenth-Century Istanbul', *Journal of Near Eastern Studies* 45 (1986), pp. 251–74.

Sufism

On the Sufi orders and their various lineages, a venerable yet valuable work is J.S. Trimingham's *The Sufi Orders in Islam* (Oxford, 1971), which provides succinct, useful information on all major orders.

Naqshbandis

Recent scholarship has stressed the variety of practices that existed among different branches of the Naqshbandiyya in scattered locations. Dina Le Gall's *A Culture of Sufism: Naqshbandis in the Ottoman World, 1450–1700* (Albany, NY, 2005) explores the peculiarities of the order's exponents in Anatolia and the Ottoman central lands in the centuries both before and after the Indian reforms. Two edited collections reflecting this regional variety are Marc Gaborieau, Alexandre Popović and Thierry Zarcone, eds, *Naqshbandis: cheminements et situation actuelle d'un ordre mystique musulman – Actes de la table ronde de Sèvres, 2–4 mai 1985* (Istanbul, 1990), and Elisabeth Özdalga, ed., *Naqshbandis in Western and Central Asia: Change and Continuity – Papers Read at a Conference Held at the Swedish Institute in Istanbul, June 9–11, 1997* (Istanbul, 1999). In the Arab provinces, the Naqshbandi order attracted the largest number of adherents in Damascus, where the Muradi family enthusiastically promoted it, as described in Karl K. Barbir's 'All in the Family: The Muradis of Damascus', cited above.

Khalwatis

A useful overview of the widespread and highly influential Khalwati order is B.G. Martin, 'A Short History of the Khalwati Order of Dervishes', in Nikki R. Keddie, ed., *Scholars, Saints, and Sufis*, pp. 275–305; the order in Egypt is exhaustively covered in Ernst Bannerth's 'La Khalwatiyya en Égypte: quelques aspects de la vie d'une confrérie',

Mélange de l'Institut Dominicain d'Études Orientales 8 (1964–6), pp. 1–74, which is an important source for Martin's article.

The best studies on the puritanical Kadızadeli tendency in a western language are Madeline C. Zilfi's, cited under 'Mosque Preachers', which address the Kadızadelis' clashes with prominent ulema belonging to the Khalwati Sufi order.

The ulema in social protest

The secondary literature on the ulema's role in social disturbances is best developed in the case of Ottoman Egypt, although often analyses of this role are embedded in broader works. An early publication which focuses specifically on the topic is Gabriel Baer's 'Popular Revolt in Ottoman Cairo', *Der Islam* 54 (1977), pp. 213–42. Protests of the sort led by Shaykh al-Dardir are briefly broached in Marsot's 'Ulama of Cairo in the Eighteenth and Nineteenth Centuries', as well as different versions of this article, and in André Raymond's *Artisans et commerçants au Caire au XVIIIe siècle*, 2 vols, new edn (Cairo, 1999 [1973]), II, p. 432.

The ulema and intellectual life

The conventional view of the 'stagnation' of provincial intellectual life under the Ottomans is given in, for example, Gamal el-Din El-Shayyal, 'Some Aspects of Intellectual and Social Life in Eighteenth-Century Egypt', in P.M. Holt, ed., *Political and Social Change in Modern Egypt: Historical Studies from the Ottoman Conquest to the United Arab Republic* (Oxford, 1968), pp. 117–32. A sharply revisionist, and very welcome, view is provided by Khaled El-Rouayheb, 'Opening the Gate of Verification: The Forgotten Arab-Islamic Florescence of the Seventeenth Century', *International Journal of Middle East Studies* 38 (2006), pp. 263–81. Libraries endowed by prominent local notables receive attention in Daniel Crecelius, 'The *Waqf* of Muhammad Bey Abu al-Dhahab in Historical Perspective', *International Journal of Middle East Studies* 23 (1991), pp. 57–81, and Jane Hathaway, 'The Wealth and Influence of an Exiled Ottoman Eunuch in Egypt: The *Waqf* Inventory of Abbas Agha', *Journal of the Economic and Social History of the Orient* 37 (1994), pp. 298–317. Meanwhile, the gestation of Murtada al-Zabidi's famous dictionary is explored in Stefan Reichmuth, 'Islamic Scholarship between Imperial Center and Provinces in the Eighteenth Century: The Case of Murtada al-Zabidi (d. 1205/1791) and His Ottoman Contacts', in Kemal Çiçek, ed., *The Great Ottoman-Turkish Civilisation*, III: *Philosophy, Science, and Institutions* (Ankara, 2000), pp. 357–65.

So far as historical chronicles are concerned, the *Selimname* genre and Ibn Zunbul's contribution to it are discussed in Jane Hathaway, *A Tale of Two Factions* (Albany, NY, 2003), Ch. 8. The standard survey of later Arabophone provincial chroniclers for Ottoman Egypt remains P.M. Holt, 'Ottoman Egypt (1517–1798): An Account of Arabic Historical Sources', in Holt, ed., *Political and Social Change*, pp. 3–12, which has now been supplemented by the articles collected in Daniel Crecelius, ed., *Eighteenth Century Egypt: The Arabic Manuscript Sources* (Claremont, CA, 1990). The chronicling tradition of Ottoman-era Yemen is the subject of Jane Hathaway, 'The Egyptian-Yemeni Symbiosis as Reflected (or Unreflected) in Ottoman-Era Chronicles', in Hugh Kennedy, ed., *The Historiography of Islamic Egypt (c. 950–1800)* (Leiden, 2001), pp. 211–20.

The sources of al-Jabarti's historical chronicle have been the subject of numerous publications. Among the most recent and revisionist is Daniel Crecelius, 'Ahmad Shalabi ibn 'Abd al-Ghani and Ahmad Katkhuda 'Azaban al-Damurdashi: Two Sources for al-Jabarti's *'Ajā'ib al-āthār fī'l-tarājim wa'l-akhbār'*, in Crecelius, ed., *Eighteenth Century Egypt: The Arabic Manuscript Sources*, pp. 89–102. A more conventional yet equally valuable treatment is P.M. Holt, 'Al-Jabarti's Introduction to the History of Ottoman Egypt', *BSOAS* 25 (1962), pp. 38–51. David Ayalon's 'The Historian al-Jabarti and His Background', *BSOAS* 23 (1960), pp. 217–49, details the circumstances surrounding the chronicle's composition.

As for descriptions of Arab provinces by visitors from other lands, Mustafa Ali's *Description of Cairo of 1599* has long been available in an English translation by Andreas Tietze (Vienna, 1975). In *In Praise of Books: A Cultural History of Cairo's Middle Class, Sixteenth to the Eighteenth Century* (Syracuse, NY, 2003), Nelly Hanna describes Yusuf al-Maghribi's dictionary of colloquial Egyptian Arabic and al-Muhibbi's dictionary of non-Arabic words which had infiltrated Syrian Arabic (pp. 114–15, 128–33), although she does not comment on the implications of al-Maghribi's sobriquet. A new English translation of Volume 10 of Evliya Chelebi's *Book of Travels*, which describes Egypt and Sudan, is in preparation by Robert Dankoff and will soon be published in Istanbul.

Chapter 7: Urban Life and Trade

The 'Islamic city'

One of the earliest volumes to begin to challenge the essentialist generalizations which past generations of scholars made concerning the so-called 'Islamic city' is Albert Hourani and S.M. Stern, eds, *The*

Islamic City: A Colloquium (Oxford and Philadelphia, 1970), although this work retained many paradigms that were later called into question. The field has benefited in the years since the publication of *The Islamic City* from the influence of urban and architectural history. André Raymond's *Grandes villes arabes à l'époque ottomane* (Paris, 1985) and the more abbreviated *The Great Arab Cities in the Sixteenth–Eighteenth Centuries: An Introduction* (New York, 1984) helped to place what used to be called 'the Islamic city' in a broader geographical and cultural context. More recently, Irene A. Bierman, Rifaat A. Abou-El-Haj and Donald Preziosi, eds, *The Ottoman City and Its Parts* (New Rochelle, NY, 1991), has brought together studies which achieve a new appreciation of the subtleties of Ottoman urban strategies and a new integration of the Ottoman urban experience with that of contemporary European societies. Of these, Ülkü Bates' 'Façades in Ottoman Cairo' (pp. 129–72) modifies the misleading impression, maintained by, among others, Doris Behrens-Abouseif in *Egypt's Adjustment to Ottoman Rule* (Leiden, 1994), that the Ottoman role in the Arab cities was that of caretaker, preserving Mamluk remains while adding very little that was distinctively Ottoman.

So far as the individual elements of a premodern Ottoman provincial city are concerned, many of these are covered in Raymond's two volumes, cited above, which also provide an impressive amount of information on the activities that took place in the 'urban caravanserai' known as a *khan*, *bedestan* or *wakala*. The manner in which Ottoman cities tended to grow, through the foundation of *waqf*s which in turn spawned large markets whose revenues were endowed to the maintenance of mosques and other religious and charitable establishments, is explained by Halil Inalcik in 'The Hub of the City: The Bedestan of Istanbul', *International Journal of Turkish Studies* 1 (1980), pp. 1–17. Raymond almost single-handedly brought the tenement-like *rab'* to the attention of urban historians of the Middle East, as witness his article 'The *Rab'*: A Type of Collective Housing in Cairo during the Ottoman Period', in *Architecture as Symbol and Self-Identity: Agha Khan Award for Architecture, Seminar Four* (Cambridge, MA, 1980), pp. 55–62; repr. in Raymond, *Arab Cities in the Ottoman Period* (Aldershot and Burlington, VT, 2002).

The layout and composition of residential quarters, as well as the housing arrangements available to residents, are discussed in Raymond's above-cited works; these are supplemented by Abraham Marcus, *The Middle East on the Eve of Modernity* (New York, 1989), Ch. 9, and idem, 'Privacy in Eighteenth-Century Aleppo: The Limits of Cultural Ideals', *International Journal of Middle East Studies* 18 (1986), pp. 165–83.

Valuable studies of residential structures and material culture in Arab cities include Nelly Hanna, *Habiter au Caire: la maison moyenne et ses habitants aux XVIIe et XVIIIe siècles* (Cairo, 1991), and Jean-Paul Pascual, 'Meubles et objets domestiques quotidiens des intérieurs damascains du XVIIe siècle', *Revues des Mondes Musulmans et de la Méditerranée* 55–56 (1990), pp. 197–207.

Urban change

André Raymond was one of the first scholars to conclude that urban populations increased during the Ottoman period, as he points out in 'The Ottoman Conquest and the Development of the Great Arab Towns', *International Journal of Turkish Studies* 1 (1980), pp. 84–101; repr. in Raymond, *Arab Cities in the Ottoman Period*. While articles in the edited volume *The Ottoman City and Its Parts*, cited above, address widespread Ottoman modifications to the urban fabric of various cities, changes to specific religious structures are treated in more specialized works, such as Oleg Grabar, *The Dome of the Rock* (Cambridge, MA, 2006), which covers, among many other subjects, Süleyman's restoration of the structure. Ottoman modifications to Mecca and Medina, above all the restoration of the Kaba, the Great Mosque and the Prophet Muhammad's tomb, are noted in Suraiya Faroqhi, *Pilgrims and Sultans: The Hajj under the Ottomans* (London, 1994), Ch. 5. Sir Richard Francis Burton's classic *Personal Narrative of a Pilgrimage to al-Madinah and Meccah*, 2 vols, memorial edn (London, 1893; republished New York, 1964) provides extremely detailed descriptions of both cities and all their sacred structures during the 1850s, with some mention of what changes had been made recently. Meanwhile, Ottoman additions to the tomb of Abu Hanifa in Baghdad and the Shiite shrines in Najaf and Karbala are treated in *EI²*, s.v. 'Baghdad', by A.A. Duri; s.v. 'Karbala', by E. Honigmann; and s.v. 'al-Nadjaf', by E. Honigmann [C.E. Bosworth].

Market regulation and trade

Perspective can be gained on the functions of the market inspector known as the *muhtasib* from studies of the medieval period, notably Ira Lapidus, *Muslim Cities in the Middle Ages* (Cambridge, MA, 1967), which focuses on Mamluk Damascus, and Jonathan Berkey, 'The *Muhtasibs* of Cairo under the Mamluks: Toward the Understanding of an Islamic Institution', in Michael Winter and Amalia Levanoni, eds, *The Mamluks in Egyptian and Syrian Politics and Society* (Leiden, 2004), pp. 245–76.

Within the past thirty-five years, a number of monographs on individual Ottoman Arab cities, based largely on Muslim court records, have offered in-depth examination of market regulatory mechanisms, as well as guilds; the organization and conduct of long-distance trade, both maritime and overland, and the merchants who conducted it; and trade between and among Ottoman provinces. Worth mentioning in this regard are André Raymond, *Artisans et commerçants au Caire au XVIIIe siècle*, 2 vols, 2nd edn (Cairo, 1999 [1973]); Bruce Masters, *The Origins of Western Economic Dominance in the Middle East: Mercantilism and the Islamic Economy in Aleppo, 1600–1750* (New York, 1988); idem, 'Aleppo: The Ottoman Empire's Caravan City', in Edhem Eldem, Daniel Goffman and Bruce Masters, *The Ottoman City between East and West: Aleppo, Izmir, and Istanbul* (Cambridge, MA, 1999), pp. 17–78; Abraham Marcus, *The Middle East on the Eve of Modernity*; Amnon Cohen, *Jewish Life under Islam: Jerusalem in the Sixteenth Century* (Cambridge, MA, 1984); Thabit A.J. Abdullah, *Merchants, Mamluks, and Murder: The Political Economy of Trade in Eighteenth-Century Basra* (Albany, NY, 2001); and Hala Fattah, *The Politics of Regional Trade in Iraq, Arabia, and the Gulf, 1745–1900* (Albany, NY, 1997). These can be supplemented by Halil Inalcik, 'The Ottoman Economic Mind and Aspects of the Ottoman Economy', in M.A. Cook, ed., *Studies in the Economic History of the Middle East* (London and New York, 1979), pp. 207–18, repr. in Inalcik, *The Ottoman Empire: Conquest, Organization, and Economy* (London, 1978); Gabriel Baer, 'The Turkish Guilds: Administrative, Economic, and Social Functions', in Baer, *Fellah and Townsman in the Middle East: Studies in Social History* (London, 1982), pp. 149–74; Suraiya Faroqhi, 'Crisis and Change, 1590–1699', part 2 of Halil Inalcik, ed., with Donald Quataert, *An Economic and Social History of the Ottoman Empire* (Cambridge, 1994); idem, *The Ottoman Empire and the World Around It* (London, 2004); and Rudolph P. Matthee, *The Politics of Trade in Safavid Iran: Silk for Silver, 1600–1730* (Cambridge, 1999). A readable introduction to New World crops in the Middle East is Paul Lunde, 'New World Foods, Old World Diet', *Saudi Aramco World* 43 (1992), pp. 47–55.

The African slave trade, including routes and conditions, is examined in Ehud R. Toledano's *Slavery and Abolition in the Ottoman Middle East* (Seattle, WA, 1998), although, admittedly, this book's focus is the nineteenth century. Efforts by Mehmed Ali Pasha, the autonomous governor of Egypt, to fashion Sudanese slaves into a modern army are the subject of Khaled Fahmy's *All the Pasha's Men: Mehmed Ali, His Army, and the Making of Modern Egypt* (Cambridge, 1997).

Guilds

Craft guilds in Middle Eastern cities became a source of contention during the 1970s, after S.M. Stern published 'The Constitution of the Islamic City', in Hourani and Stern, eds, *The Islamic City*, which lambasted Louis Massignon's conception of guilds which were essentially mystical brotherhoods. So far as specifically Ottoman guilds are concerned, Gabriel Baer in effect furthered Stern's line of thought in 'Guilds in Middle Eastern History', in Cook, ed., *Studies in the Economic History of the Middle East*, pp. 11–30, which asserted that no craft guilds existed before the Ottoman period, when the Ottoman state imposed them as a means of controlling the artisanate. In contrast, Baer's 1982 'Ottoman Guilds: A Reassessment', in Baer, *Fellah and Townsman in the Middle East*, pp. 213–22, is informed by more recent studies pointing to wide regional and chronological divergence in guild autonomy and fiscal authority. Research conducted in the intervening years has confirmed this variation in guild function. For a single example, Charles L. Wilkins, in 'Households, Guilds, and Neighborhoods: Social Solidarities in Ottoman Aleppo, 1640–1700', unpublished PhD dissertation, Harvard University, 2005, points out the empowerment during a prolonged period of warfare in the seventeenth century of the guilds in Aleppo which supplied provisions to the Ottoman armies.

While Baer, like Stern, initially rejected the conventional position that *futuwwa* organizations gave rise to guilds, Halil Inalcik, in *The Ottoman Era: The Classical Age* (London, 1973), Ch. 15, appears to accept it to a somewhat greater degree, as does Raymond in *Artisans et commerçants au Caire*, II, Ch. 12. Certainly the initiation rites of many Ottoman-era guilds had heavily mystical components. The origins of these quasi-mystical artisan brotherhoods are explored in Speros Vryonis, Jr, 'Byzantine Circus Factions and Islamic *Futuwwa* Organizations (*Neaniai, Fityān, Aḥdāth*)', *Byzantinische Zeitschrift* 58 (1965), pp. 46–59; repr. in Vryonis, *Byzantium: Its Internal History and Relations with the Muslim World* (London, 1971). Evliya Chelebi describes these organizations in his *Narrative of Travels in Europe, Asia, and Africa*, trans. Josef von Hammer-Purgstall, 4 vols in 3 (London, 1834; repr. 1968), I, part 2, section 78.

The coffee trade

A succinct and readable account of the origins of coffee, the commerce in Yemeni coffee and the culture to which it gave rise is Ralph S. Hattox, *Coffee and Coffeehouses: The Origins of a Social Beverage in the Medieval*

Near East (Seattle, WA, 1985). Favourable opinions of the medicinal properties of coffee can be found among the accounts of European observers cited in this work, as well as in Israel M. Goldman, *The Life and Times of Rabbi David ibn Abi Zimra* (New York, 1970), pp. 140–1, although Goldman seems unaware that it is coffee that his source is describing. As for the trade in Yemeni coffee, it is well covered in André Raymond's work, particularly *Artisans et commerçants*, I, Ch. 3; Michel Tuchscherer, ed., *Le commerce du café avant l'ère des plantations coloniales: espaces, réseaux, sociétés (XVe–XIXe siècle)* (Cairo, 2001); and Jane Hathaway, 'The Ottoman Empire and the Red Sea Coffee Trade', in Ebru Boyar and Kate Fleet, eds, *The Ottomans and Trade*, special issue of *Oriente Moderno* new series 25 (2006), pp. 161–71. Thabit A.J. Abdullah briefly discusses the prominence of the Omani fleet in the coffee trade during the eighteenth century in *Merchants, Mamluks, and Murder*, pp. 63–7. Socio-political ramifications of the coffee trade in Egypt are addressed in Jane Hathaway, *The Politics of Households in Ottoman Egypt* (Cambridge, 1997), Ch. 7.

The coffeehouse and the communal culture to which coffee (and tobacco) gave rise are described most vividly and succinctly in Hattox's book, Chs 6–8, wherein a wide array of primary accounts are cited. Popular culture in the Arab provinces, with an emphasis on oral storytelling, is addressed in Nelly Hanna, 'Culture in Ottoman Egypt', in M.W. Daly, ed., *The Cambridge History of Egypt*, II: *Modern Egypt from 1517 to the End of the Twentieth Century* (Cambridge, 1998), pp. 87–112; and idem, 'The Chronicles of Ottoman Egypt: History or Entertainment?' in Hugh Kennedy, ed., *The Historiography of Islamic Egypt* (Leiden, 2001), pp. 237–50. The resonance of Baybars specifically is addressed in Jane Hathaway, 'Mamluk "Revivals" and Mamluk Nostalgia in Ottoman Egypt', in Levanoni and Winter, eds, *The Mamluks in Egyptian and Syrian Politics and Society*, pp. 387–406; and idem, *A Tale of Two Factions* (Albany, NY, 2003), Ch. 2, while the Turkish translation of the *Shahname* is the subject of Ananiasz Zajaczkowski, 'La plus ancienne traduction turque en vers du *Šâhnâme* de l'état mamelouk d'Égypte (XV–XVIe siècles)', *Belleten* 3 (1966), pp. 51–63.

Chapter 8: Rural Life

Land tenure

On Ottoman land tenure in general and on the foundations of Ottoman Egypt's land tenure system, see the references for Chapter 3. The *chifthane* system is introduced in Halil Inalcik, part 1 of Inalcik, ed., with

Donald Quataert, *An Economic and Social History of the Ottoman Empire* (Cambridge, 1994), Ch. 6. So far as tax-farming, or *iltizam*, is concerned, the urban variety, which appeared as early as the sixteenth century, is addressed in Mohsen Shuman, 'The Beginnings of Urban *Iltizam* in Egypt', in Nelly Hanna, ed., *The State and Its Servants: Administration in Egypt from Ottoman Times to the Present* (Cairo, 1995), pp. 17–31; rural *iltizam*, which became widespread in the seventeenth century, is described in the articles by A.A. Abd al-Rahim, Abdul-Rahim Abu Husayn, Kenneth M. Cuno and Abdul-Karim Rafeq in Tarif Khalidi, ed., *Land Tenure and Social Transformation in the Middle East* (Beirut, 1983). An incisive analysis of the effects of *malikane*, the life-tenure tax farm, is Ariel Salzmann, 'An Ancien Régime Revisited: "Privatization" and Political Economy in the Eighteenth-Century Ottoman Empire', *Politics and Society* 21 (1993), pp. 393–423.

Village life

The registers of village revenues known as *tapu tahrir defterleri* are discussed in Muhammad Adnan al-Bakhit, 'The Role of the Hanash Family and the Tasks Assigned to It in the Countryside of Dimashq al-Sham, 790/1388–976/1568: A Documentary Study', in Khalidi, ed., *Land Tenure and Social Transformation*, pp. 257–89. A useful appraisal of the methodological potential of this source is Amy Singer, '*Tapu Tahrir Defterleri* and *Kadı Sicilleri*: A Happy Marriage of Sources', *Tarih* 1 (1990), pp. 95–125. Pious endowment deeds, or *waqfiyyas*, are described in John R. Barnes, *An Introduction to Religious Foundations in the Ottoman Empire* (Leiden, 1987). As for Muslim court registers, masterful descriptions of their idiosyncrasies are provided in Amy Singer, *Palestinian Peasants and Ottoman Officials: Rural Administration around Sixteenth-Century Jerusalem* (Cambridge, 1994), and Leslie Peirce, *Morality Tales: Law and Gender in the Ottoman Court of Aintab* (Berkeley, CA, 2003).

Village leadership and the titles of village leaders are discussed in Singer, *Palestinian Peasants and Ottoman Officials*, pp. 32–45, which deals with the sixteenth century; later periods are addressed in Kenneth M. Cuno, 'Egypt's Wealthy Peasantry, 1740–1820', in Khalidi, ed., *Land Tenure and Social Transformation in the Middle East*, pp. 303–32; and Gabriel Baer, 'The Village Shaykh, 1800–1950', in Baer, *Studies in the Social History of Modern Egypt* (Chicago, 1969), pp. 30–61. Shirbini's unusual commentary, which sheds light on the conditions of peasant life, has been translated as *Brains Confounded by the Ode of Abu Shaduf Expounded*, ed. and trans. Humphrey T. Davies (Dudley, MA, 2005).

A number of the city monographs cited under Chapter 7 also provide valuable depictions of the rural hinterlands surrounding the cities they take as their subjects. This is particularly true of Abraham Marcus' *The Middle East on the Eve of Modernity* (New York, 1989). In addition, we may cite Dina Rizk Khoury, *State and Provincial Society in the Ottoman Empire* (Cambridge, 1997); Dror Ze'evi, *An Ottoman Century: The District of Jerusalem in the 1600s* (Albany, NY, 1996); and Beshara Doumani, *Rediscovering Palestine: Merchants and Peasants in Jabal Nablus, 1700–1900* (Berkeley, CA, 1995), all of which evoke the networks linking agricultural production to urban manufacturing, and thus peasants to merchants and artisans. Discussion of ulema migration is provided by Afaf Lutfi al-Sayyid Marsot, 'The Ulama of Cairo in the Eighteenth and Nineteenth Centuries', in Nikki R. Keddie, ed., *Scholars, Saints, and Sufis* (Berkeley, CA, 1972), pp. 149–65; and by Elizabeth Sirriyeh, *Sufi Visionary of Damascus: Abd al-Ghani al-Nabulsi, 1641–1731* (New York, 2004).

Tribes

Major tribal groupings in Egypt and Yemen during the Ottoman period are covered in Hathaway, *A Tale of Two Factions* (Albany, NY, 2003), Chs 3–4. In Greater Syria, the roles of the Hanash and Furaykh families are analysed by Muhammad Adnan al-Bakhit, 'The Role of the Hanash Family', in Khalidi, ed., *Land Tenure and Social Transformation*, pp. 257–89, which also notes Turcoman tribes living in the region before the Ottoman conquest; and Abdul-Rahim Abu-Husayn, 'The *Iltizam* of Mansur Furaykh: A Case Study of *Iltizam* in Sixteenth-Century Syria', in the same collection, pp. 249–56. Kurdish tribes in the territory that now comprises the border regions of Turkey, Iraq and Syria are treated in Hakan Özoğlu's *Kurdish Notables and the Ottoman State: Evolving Identities, Competing Loyalties, and Shifting Boundaries* (Albany, NY, 2004), Ch. 3.

Movement and change among the tribal populations of the Arab provinces during the Ottoman era are most often discussed in the context of broader provincial studies. The migration of the Anaza and their emergence as regional power brokers in Syria and Iraq are discussed in Dick Douwes, *The Ottomans in Syria: A History of Justice and Oppression* (London, 2000), and Karl K. Barbir, *Ottoman Rule in Damascus* (Princeton, NJ, 1980), which also notes Turcoman tribes settled by the Ottomans in Syria and Iraq (*EI*[2], s.v. 'Anaza', by E. Gräf, is a useful supplement). Hathaway's *A Tale of Two Factions*, Ch. 3, deals with Egypt's Sa'd-Haram factionalism and the rise of the enormous

Hawwara confederation. Tribal migrations in Iraq in response to the Wahhabi juggernaut are covered in Hala Fattah, *The Politics of Regional Trade in Iraq, Arabia, and the Gulf* (Albany, NY, 1997), and Thabit A.J. Abdullah, *Merchants, Mamluks, and Murder* (Albany, NY, 2001), both of which also provide glimpses of tribal custom. The emergence of the Uqayl or Agayl population of merchants-cum-caravan escorts is described in the article 'Uqayl', by H. Kindermann, in *EI²*.

Finally, the revisionist argument that the Ottoman Empire was not fullly incorporated into the so-called European world economy until the nineteenth century is made by Roger Owen, *The Middle East and the World Economy, 1800–1914* (London, 1981); Suraiya Faroqhi, part 2 of Halil Inalcik, ed., with Donald Quataert, *An Economic and Social History of the Ottoman Empire* (Cambridge, 1994); and idem, *The Ottoman Empire and the World Around It* (London, 2004). The corresponding argument that most agricultural trade was intra-imperial can be found in Donald Quataert, 'The Age of Reforms, 1812–1914', part 4 of Inalcik, ed., with Quataert, *An Economic and Social History of the Ottoman Empire*.

Chapter 9: Marginal Groups and Minority Populations

A vast secondary literature has been produced over the past forty years on minority religious populations under Islamic rule, treating the entire period from the establishment of the first Muslim community at Medina to the present. On the Pact of Umar, the foundational document for the treatment of these minorities, Mark R. Cohen's 'What Was the Pact of Umar?: A Literary-Historical Study', *Jerusalem Studies in Arabic and Islam* 23 (1999), pp. 100–57, provides a useful summary of the various versions of this problematic text, as well as scholarly opinion on it. Meanwhile, the *jizya*, or poll tax, and its implications are the subject of Daniel C. Dennett's still-classic *Conversion and the Poll Tax in Early Islam* (Cambridge, MA, 1950).

Communal leadership

The fluid boundaries of the early Ottoman polity, when Greek Christians served alongside Turkish tribesmen and even received *timar*s, are brilliantly evoked in Cemal Kafadar, *Between Two Worlds: The Construction of the Early Ottoman State* (Berkeley, CA, 1995), especially Chs 2–3. Lay leadership of minority communities, with specific reference to the Jewish community, is addressed in Amnon Cohen, *Jewish Life under Islam:*

Jerusalem in the Sixteenth Century (Cambridge, 1984), Ch. 3; Mark A. Epstein, 'The Leadership of the Ottoman Jews in the Fifteenth and Sixteenth Centuries', in Benjamin Braude and Bernard Lewis, eds, *Christians and Jews in the Ottoman Empire: The Functioning of a Plural Society*, 2 vols (New York and London, 1982), I, pp. 101–16; and Aryeh Shmuelovitz, *The Jews of the Ottoman Empire in the Late Fifteenth and the Sixteenth Century* (London, 1984).

Jews

A great deal has been written about the expulsion of Spain's Jews and the immigration of large numbers of them to Ottoman territory. A succinct and accessible summary is Jane S. Gerber, *The Jews of Spain: A History of the Sephardic Experience* (New York, 1992). Bernard Lewis, *The Jews of Islam* (Princeton, NJ, 1984), provides an even more compact overall survey of the experience of Jewish communities under Islamic rule; his account is particularly strong for the Ottoman period. A fairly recent collection of cutting-edge studies on Ottoman Jewry is Avigdor Levy, ed., *The Jews of the Ottoman Empire* (Princeton, NJ, 1994). The classic works on Doña Gracia and Don Joseph Nasi remain Cecil Roth, *The House of Nasi: Doña Gracia* (Philadelphia, 1947), and idem, *The House of Nasi: The Duke of Naxos* (Philadelphia, 1948). A venerable source on the Kabbalists of Ottoman Safed is Morris S. Goodblatt, *Jewish Life in Turkey in the Sixteenth Century as Reflected in the Legal Writings of Samuel de Medina* (New York, 1952). Collections of translated primary sources include Norman A. Stillman, *The Jews of Arab Lands: A History and Source Book* (Philadelphia, 1979), which also supplies an historical narrative of major developments, and the more problematic Bat Ye'or, *The Dhimmi: Jews and Christians under Islam*, preface by Jacques Ellul, trans. David Maisel, *et al.* (Rutherford, NJ, and London, 1985).

Arguably the most innovative studies of Ottoman *dhimmi*s to appear in recent years concern the crisis period of the seventeenth century. In an insightful analysis of the apparent growing intolerance of that time, Marc David Baer's *Conversion and Conquest in Ottoman Europe* (New York and Oxford, forthcoming) addresses the thorny question of how tolerance and persecution are defined and used as analytical categories. The career of Sabbatai Sevi has attracted new interest in recent years, resulting in a spate of new works; of note among these is Matt Goldish, *The Sabbatean Prophets* (Cambridge, MA, 2004). Effects of Sabbatai Sevi's movement in Egypt and Yemen are examined in Jane Hathaway, 'The Grand Vizier and the False Messiah: The Sabbatai Sevi Controversy and Ottoman Reform in Egypt', *Journal of the American Oriental*

Society 117 (1997), pp. 665–71, and idem, 'The Mawza' Exile at the Juncture of Zaydi and Ottoman Messianism', *Association for Jewish Studies Review* 29 (2005), pp. 111–28. Among the rare primary sources that describe Sabbatai Sevi and movements inspired by him in Ottoman territory are Paul Rycaut, *The History of the Turkish Empire from the Year 1623 to the Year 1677* (London, 1680), pp. 200–19; and P.S. van Koningsveld, J. Sadan and Q. al-Samarrai, trans. and commentary, *Yemenite Authorities and Jewish Messianism: Ahmad ibn Nasir al-Zaydi's Account of the Sabbathian Movement in Seventeenth-Century Yemen and Its Aftermath* (Leiden, 1990). Although a new literature has emerged in Turkish on the Sabbatians known as Dönmes, primarily with reference to the sect in modern Turkey, for factual information in English, Gershom Scholem's 'Doenmeh' article in the *Encyclopedia Judaica* remains seminal.

Syrian Catholics and non-Muslims in financial service

The experiences of non-Muslim merchants in the employ of European trading companies, and the Syrian Catholic phenomenon in particular, are treated in Robert Haddad, *Syrian Christians in Muslim Society: An Interpretation* (Princeton, NJ, 1970), and, in tandem with the phenomenon of Jewish merchants, in Bruce Masters, *Christians and Jews in the Ottoman Arab World: The Roots of Sectarianism* (Cambridge, 2001), Ch. 4, as well as idem, *The Origins of Western Economic Dominance in the Middle East* (New York, 1988). John W. Livingston provides a unique analysis of Ali Bey's shift in patronage from Jews to Orthodox Christians in 'Ali Bey al-Kabir and the Jews', *Middle Eastern Studies* 7 (1971), pp. 221–8, while Daniel Crecelius discusses the bey's finances and his reliance on a Coptic banker in *The Roots of Modern Egypt* (Minneapolis, MN, 1981), Ch. 3. Norman Stillman's *The Jews of Arab Lands*, p. 338, offers a European observer's account of Haim Farhi, the Jewish financial advisor to Ahmed Pasha al-Jazzar.

Twelver Shiites

Until recently, Twelver Shiites under Sunni Ottoman rule were, with a few exceptions, almost entirely unstudied. Within the past fifteen years, however, at least two studies in English have appeared of Shiites in the Arab provinces: Yitzhak Nakhash, *The Shi'is of Iraq* (Princeton, NJ, 1994), and Graham E. Fuller and Rend Rahim Francke, *The Arab Shi'a: The Forgotten Muslims* (New York, 1999). Regrettably, the first treats the period before 1900 in rather cursory fashion while the second is a policy study orientated towards present-day realities. The Matawila, Shiite peasants in southern Lebanon and northern Palestine, are noted in the eyewitness account of Mikhayil Mishaqa, *Murder, Mayhem, Pillage, and Plunder: The History of Lebanon in the Eighteenth and Nineteenth Centuries*, trans. Wheeler M. Thackston, Jr (Albany, NY, 1988). Meanwhile, the Italian scholar Marco Salati has published a study of the Zuhri family of Aleppo: *Ascesa e caduta di una famiglia di Ašrāf Sciiti di Aleppo: i Zuhrāwī o Zuhrī-zāda (1600–1700)* (Rome, 1992).

Non-elite slavery

Regrettably, there is very little in the way of secondary studies of non-elite slaves, most of whom were female East African house servants, before the nineteenth century. A useful overview of all types of Ottoman slavery, even given its nineteenth-century focus, is Ehud R. Toledano, *Slavery and Abolition in the Ottoman Middle East* (Seattle, WA, 1998).

Women

The secondary literature on women in Islamic societies has proliferated since the early 1970s. A solid general overview is Wiebke Walther, *Women in Islam from Medieval to Modern Times*, trans. C.S.V. Salt (Princeton, NJ, 1993; 2nd printing 1995). So far as women in the Ottoman Empire are concerned, venerable titles such as Fanny Davis' (1904–84) *The Ottoman Lady: A Social History from 1718 to 1918* (New York, 1986) have been supplemented in recent years by numerous studies of greater theoretical sophistication. Leslie Peirce's path-breaking *The Imperial Harem* (New York and Oxford, 1993) demystified the harem institution and the dynamics of reproductive politics. The 'parallel households' established by elite women in the Arab provinces are described in the sources cited under 'Women in *Ayan* Households' for Chapter 5. Broader studies of women in specific Arab provinces include Afaf Lutfi al-Sayyid Marsot, *Women and Men in Late Eighteenth-Century Egypt* (Austin, TX, 1995), and Dror Ze'evi, *An Ottoman Century: The District of Jerusalem in the 1600s* (Albany, NY, 1996), Ch. 7. The condition of Aleppine women within the context of the family, including marriage, divorce and inheritance, is described in Abraham Marcus, *The Middle East on the Eve of Modernity* (New York, 1989), Ch. 5. These subjects and more general concerns relating to women's use of Muslim law courts are discussed in Judith E. Tucker, *In the House of the Law: Gender and Islamic Law in Ottoman Syria and Palestine* (Berkeley, CA, 1998), and Leslie Peirce, *Morality Tales: Law and Gender in the Ottoman Court of Aintab*

(Berkeley, CA, 2003). How specific gender-related issues are framed in Islamic law is the subject of Judith E. Tucker, 'The Fullness of Affection: Mothering in the Islamic Law of Ottoman Syria and Palestine', in Madeline C. Zilfi, ed., *Women in the Ottoman Empire: Middle Eastern Women in the Early Modern Era* (Leiden, 1997), pp. 232–52; and Amira Sonbol, 'Rape and Law in Ottoman and Modern Egypt', in the same volume, pp. 214–31. The use of Muslim law courts by Christian women is treated in Najwa al-Qattan, '*Dhimmi*s in the Muslim Court: Legal Autonomy and Religious Discrimination', *International Journal of Middle East Studies* 31 (1999), pp. 429–44, especially pp. 432–7. Finally, Dina Rizk-Khoury discusses the effects of war on women in a frontier province in 'Slippers at the Entrance, or Behind Closed Doors: Domestic and Public Spaces for Mosuli Women', in Zilfi, ed., *Women in the Ottoman Empire*, pp. 105–27.

The poor and disabled

'Disability studies', as it is called, is quite a new field which has yet to make much of an impact on the historiography of the Middle East. A rare study of blindness, albeit in a medieval context, is Fedwa Malti-Douglas, '*Mentalités* and Marginality: Blindness and Mamluk Civilization', in C.E. Bosworth, *et al.*, eds, *The Islamic World from Classical to Modern Times: Essays in Honor of Bernard Lewis* (Princeton, NJ, 1989), pp. 211–37; two additional articles on blindness by the same author are cited in the notes.

Charitable institutions have become an important focus of research just in the past decade or so, as witness Michael Bonner, Mine Ener and Amy Singer, eds, *Poverty and Charity in Middle Eastern Contexts* (Albany, NY, 2003), and the monographic studies by two of the editors of this volume: Amy Singer, *Constructing Ottoman Benevolence: An Imperial Soup Kitchen in Jerusalem* (Albany, NY, 2002), and Mine Ener, *Managing Egypt's Poor and the Politics of Benevolence, 1800–1952* (Princeton, NJ, 2003). Cairo's nineteenth-century soup kitchens and homeless shelters are the subject of Mine Ener's 'Getting into the Shelter of Takiyat Tulun', in Eugene Rogan, ed., *Outside In: On the Margins of the Modern Middle East* (London, 2004), pp. 53–76. Otherwise, Abraham Marcus briefly examines charitable activities in Ottoman Aleppo in *The Middle East on the Eve of Modernity*, Ch. 5, while Mark R. Cohen addresses charitable activities among Middle Eastern Jewish communities, albeit for an earlier period, in *Poverty and Charity in the Jewish Community of Medieval Egypt (Jews, Christians, and Muslims from the Ancient to the Modern World)* (Princeton, NJ, 2005).

Chapter 10: Ideological and Political Changes in the Late Eighteenth Century

A revisionist, post-declinist view of the Ottoman Empire's economic recovery in the first half of the eighteenth century can be found in Şevket Pamuk, *A Monetary History of the Ottoman Empire* (Cambridge, 2000), Ch. 10. Meanwhile, the best account of the regularization of the Ottoman ulema during this period is Madeline C. Zilfi, *The Politics of Piety* (Minneapolis, MN, and Chicago, 1988), Ch. 5.

'Neo-Sufism'

The term 'neo-Sufism' was coined by the late Fazlur Rahman in a publication aimed at a broad audience: *Islam*, 2nd edn (Chicago, 1979 [1966]), pp. 205–6. He used it to describe what he saw as a new trend among Sufis of the late eighteenth century, characterized by rejection of Ibn Arabi's doctrine of 'unity of being', reduced emphasis on veneration of Sufi shaykhs in favour of veneration of the Prophet Muhammad and, correspondingly, increased study of the Prophet's sayings (*hadith*). While certain of these tendencies can arguably be observed among the post-Sirhindi Naqshbandis of India, Yemen, the Hijaz and Syria, other 'mainstream' Sufi orders persisted in their 'unorthodox' practices, as has been forcefully pointed out by R.S. O'Fahey and Bernd Radtke in 'Neo-Sufism Reconsidered', *Der Islam* 70 (1993), pp. 52–87.

The Mughal context in which the Naqshbandis flourished and in which Ahmad Sirhindi's reforms took shape is described in John F. Richards, *The Mughal Empire* (Cambridge, 1993). Arthur F. Buehler, *Sufi Heirs of the Prophet: The Indian Naqshbandiyya and the Rise of the Meditating Sufi Shaykh* (Columbia, SC, 1998), especially Ch. 3, briefly tracks the careers of Sirhindi and his spiritual descendant Shah Walliullah and gives the overall trajectory of the reformist movement. Meanwhile, the spread of the reformed Naqshbandi order into the Ottoman Arab provinces is described in Karl K. Barbir, 'All in the Family: The Muradis of Damascus', in Heath W. Lowry and Ralph S. Hattox, eds, *Proceedings of the Third Congress on the Social and Economic History of Turkey* (Istanbul, 1990), pp. 327–55; and John O. Voll, 'Linking Groups in the Networks of Eighteenth-Century Revivalist Scholars: The Mizjaji Family in Yemen', in Nehemia Levtzion and John O. Voll, eds, *Eighteenth-Century Renewal and Reform in Islam* (Syracuse, NY, 1987), pp. 69–92.

While B.G. Martin's 'A Short History of the Khalwati Order of Dervishes', in Nikki R. Keddie, ed., *Scholars, Saints, and Sufis* (Berkeley, CA, 1972), pp. 275–305, gives the standard narrative of Mustafa al-Bakri's reforming influence on Egyptian Khalwatism, al-Bakri's legacy is sharply questioned by Frederick de Jong in 'Mustafa Kamal al-Din al-Bakri (1688–1749): Revival and Reform of the Khalwatiyya Tradition?' in Levtzion and Voll, eds, *Eighteenth-Century Renewal and Reform in Islam*, pp. 117–32. Muhammad al-Hifni's mystical trajectory is described in Martin's article, as are African offshoots of the Khalwatis, which are also discussed in L. Carl Brown, 'The Religious Establishment in Husainid Tunisia', in Keddie, ed., *Scholars, Saints, and Sufis*, pp. 79–91; and in Nehemia Levtzion, 'The Eighteenth Century: Background to the Islamic Revolutions in West Africa', in Levtzion and Voll, eds, *Eighteenth Century Renewal and Reform in Islam*, pp. 21–38. The mobilization of these African offshoots against European encroachment is discussed in O'Fahey and Radtke, 'Neo-Sufism Reconsidered'.

As for the common ground between Sufism and the Kadızadeli tendency, the spiritual and intellectual legacy of Birgevi Mehmed Efendi is explored in Bernd Radtke, 'Birgiwis *Tariqa Muhammadiyya*: Einige Bemerkungen und Überlegungen', *Journal of Turkish Studies* 26 (2002), pp. 159–74.

Wahhabism

Too often, the development and spread of Wahhabism are addressed in the secondary literature as an adjunct of the rise of the Saudis, as in Alexei Vassiliev, *The History of Saudi Arabia* (London, 1997). In contrast, Wahhabism's theological underpinnings are the subject of Hamid Algar, *Wahhabism: A Critical Essay* (Oneonta, NY, 2002). Wahhabism's influence outside the Arabian peninsula during the nineteenth century has been studied by only a handful of scholars, e.g. Edgar Pröbster in 'Die Wahhabiten und der Magrib', *Islamica* 7 (1935), pp. 65–112. The Saudi-Wahhabi capture of Mecca and Medina and Mehmed Ali Pasha's reconquest of the Holy Cities are described in Afaf Lutfi al-Sayyid Marsot, *Egypt in the Reign of Muhammad Ali* (Cambridge, 1984).

The reign of Selim III

The standard work on Selim III's reign, highlighting his reforms, is Stanford J. Shaw, *Between Old and New: The Ottoman Empire under Selim III, 1789–1807* (Cambridge, MA, 1971). Virginia H. Aksan describes the disintegration of the Janissaries by the eighteenth century in 'Whatever Happened to the Janissaries? Mobilization for the 1768–1774 Russo-Ottoman War', *War in History* 5 (1998), pp. 23–36. Aksan is likewise the author of a book supplying excellent background to the 1768–74 war and the diplomatic context within which Ottoman statesmen of the time operated: *An Ottoman Statesman in War and Peace: Ahmed Resmi Efendi (1700–1783)* (Leiden, 1995). An insightful examination of Russian overtures to Ibrahim and Murad Beys is Daniel Crecelius, 'Russia's Relations with the Mamluk Beys of Egypt in the Eighteenth Century', in Farhad Kazemi and R.D. McChesney, eds, *A Way Prepared: Essays on Islamic Culture in Honor of Richard Bayly Winder* (New York, 1988), pp. 55–67.

The historian al-Jabarti's initial *History of the French Occupation* is available in English: Shmuel Moreh, trans., *Napoleon in Egypt: Al-Jabarti's Chronicle of the French Occupation, 1798*, expanded edn (Princeton, NJ, 2004). The sequence and motivations of al-Jabarti's writings are scrutinized by Lars Bjørneboe in *In Search of the True Political Position of the Ulema: An Analysis of the Aims and Perspectives of the Chronicles of Abd al-Rahman al-Jabarti (1753–1825)* (Aarhus, Denmark, 2007).

Conclusion

Languages in the Arab provinces

The languages spoken in the Ottoman Arab provinces, particularly Egypt, are still a contentious subject. For the conventional dichotomous 'Arabic-v.-Turkish' view, see, for example, Michael Winter, *Egyptian Society under Ottoman Rule* (London, 1992). Egyptian colloquial Arabic during the Ottoman period has been intensively studied by Madiha Doss, who unfortunately does not appear to have published a great deal on the subject; see, however, her 'Some Remarks on the Oral Factor in Arabic Linguistics', in *Dialectologia Arabica: A Collection of Articles in Honour of the Sixtieth Birthday of Professor Heikki Palva* (Helsinki, 1995), pp. 49–61. The persistence of Georgian language and culture among Egypt's late eighteenth-century mamluks is addressed in Daniel Crecelius, 'Russia's Relations with the Mamluk Beys of Egypt in the Eighteenth Century', in Farhad Kazemi and R.D. McChesney, eds, *A Way Prepared: Essays on Islamic Culture in Honor of Richard Bayly Winder* (New York, 1988), pp. 55–67; and Daniel Crecelius and Gotcha Djaparidze, 'Relations of the Georgian Mamluks of Egypt with Their Homeland in the Last Decades of the Eighteenth Century', *Journal of the Economic and Social History of the Orient* 45 (2002), pp. 320–411.

Westernizing reforms

Attempts at westernizing reform from the mid-eighteenth century to the Tanzimat, as well as the fiscal crisis of the 1870s and Ottoman exploitation by the European imperial powers, are summarized in Donald Quataert, part 4 of Inalcik, ed., with Quataert, *An Economic and Social History of the Ottoman Empire*, and idem, *The Ottoman Empire, 1700–1922* (Cambridge, 2000), Ch. 4, as well as Bernard Lewis, *The Emergence of Modern Turkey*, 3rd edn (Oxford, 2002 [1961, 1968]), Chs 3–4. The central Ottoman and Egyptian land laws are treated in Quataert, part 4, Ch. 33, and Kenneth M. Cuno, *The Pasha's Peasants: Land, Society, and Economy in Lower Egypt, 1740–1858* (Cambridge, 1992), while British abolitionist pressures are examined by Ehud R. Toledano in *Slavery and Abolition in the Ottoman Middle East* (Seattle, WA, 1998), Ch. 4.

The Ottomans and the world: India

The standard work on the history and institutions of the Mughal Empire is John F. Richards, *The Mughal Empire* (Cambridge, 1993). General Mughal patronage of the Naqshbandi Sufi order is analysed by Arthur F. Buehler in *Sufi Heirs of the Prophet* (Columbia, SC, 1998), Ch. 3. Various features of the Mughal land tenure system are addressed in EI^2, s.v. 'Mansabdar', by John F. Richards, and S. Nurul Hasan, 'Zamindars under the Mughals', in Muzaffar Alam and Sanjay Subrahmanyam, eds, *The Mughal State, 1526–1750* (New Delhi, 1998), pp. 284–98.

Africa

Sufism and the dissemination of Sufi orders constituted a key component of the relationship between the Ottoman Arab provinces and western Africa. Offshoots of the Khalwati order which took root in western Africa are covered in the sources listed for Chapter 10 under 'Neo-Sufism'. Abdul-Karim Rafeq discusses the North African soldiery known as Maghariba, with specific reference to their employment in Syria, in *The Province of Damascus* (Beirut, 1966); Ali Bey's Maghribi troops are mentioned in Daniel Crecelius, *The Roots of Modern Egypt* (Minneapolis, MN, 1981). Connections between Egypt's grandees and those of Ottoman North Africa are briefly discussed in Jane Hathaway, 'Çerkes Mehmed Bey: Rebel, Traitor, Hero?' *Turkish Studies Association Bulletin* 22 (1998), pp. 108–15.

China

Art historical studies have thus far shed the most light on Ottoman imports of Chinese porcelain, focusing chiefly on its influence on Ottoman porcelain manufacture and its appearance in Ottoman miniature paintings. A representative discussion appears in John Carswell, *Iznik Pottery* (London, 1998), Ch. 6. A rare publication which compares institutions in the Ottoman Empire and Qing China, albeit in the context of nineteenth-century social change, is Huri İslamoğlu-İnan, ed., *Constituting Modernity: Private Property in the East and West* (London, 2004). A classic source on Qing provincial administration is T'ung-Tsu Ch'ü, *Local Government in China under the Ch'ing* (Cambridge, MA, 1962). The rise of provincial warlords in response to the crisis of the late eighteenth century is covered in Philip A. Kuhn, *Rebellion and Its Enemies in Late Imperial China: Militarization and Social Structure, 1796–1864* (Cambridge, MA, 1970).

The Habsburg and Russian empires

As for the Habsburg and Russian empires, basic overviews of their respective institutions are Paula Sutter Fichtner, *The Habsburg Monarchy, 1490–1848: Attributes of Empire* (New York, 2003), and Nicholas V. Riasanovksy, *A History of Russia*, 6th edn (Oxford, 2000). Of the many studies of Spanish American society during the Habsburg period, two which address the tension between colony and mother country are Kenneth Andrien and Rolena Adorno, eds, *Transatlantic Encounters: Europeans and Andeans in the Sixteenth Century* (Berkeley, CA, 1991), and Irving A. Leonard, *Books of the Brave: Being an Account of Books and of Men in the Spanish Conquest and Settlement of the Sixteenth-Century New World* (Cambridge, MA, 1949; republished Berkeley, CA, 1992).

Interprovincial comparisons

It lies well beyond the scope of this work to provide a comprehensive list of even English-language secondary sources on the non-Arab provinces of the Ottoman Empire. What is sobering is that so few studies exist which compare two or more provinces, even Arab ones. Collections of studies whose scope encompasses Arab, Anatolian and Balkan provinces are, fortunately, becoming more common. Edhem Eldem, Daniel Goffman and Bruce Masters, eds, *The Ottoman City between East and West* (Cambridge, 1999) may be mentioned in this regard, as may Antonis Anastasopoulos, ed., *Provincial Elites in the Ottoman Empire – Halcyon Days in Crete V: A Symposium Held in Rethymno, 10–12 January 2003* (Rethymno, Crete, 2005), and Madeline C. Zilfi, ed., *Women in the Ottoman Empire* (Leiden, 1997). The use of Arabic among Balkan ulema is discussed in an as yet unpublished paper by Günhan Börekçi: 'When

Budin Falls: Military Defeat, Crisis and Ottoman Religio-Political Thought as Reflected in a Late Seventeenth-Century *Nasihâtnâme*', Ohio State University, 2004.

Nationalist historiographies

Old-school nationalist studies of Arab provinces include Abdul-Karim Rafeq, *The Province of Damascus* (Beirut, 1966); Stephen H. Longrigg, *Four Centuries of Modern Iraq* (Oxford, 1925; repr. Beirut, 1968); and P.J. Vatikiotis, *The History of Egypt*, 3rd edn (London, 1985 [1969]), which deals primarily with the nineteenth and twentieth centuries. A good example of neo-nationalist historiography in English is Nelly Hanna, *In Praise of Books: A Cultural History of Cairo's Middle Class, Sixteenth to the Eighteenth Century* (Syracuse, NY, 2003); otherwise, Michael Winter's *Egyptian Society under Ottoman Rule* appears to share certain attitudes towards Ottoman Egyptian society, notably an insistence on its quintessential 'Arabness', though Winter's book does not present comparisons between Ottoman Egypt and western Europe.

OTTOMAN SULTANS TO 1839

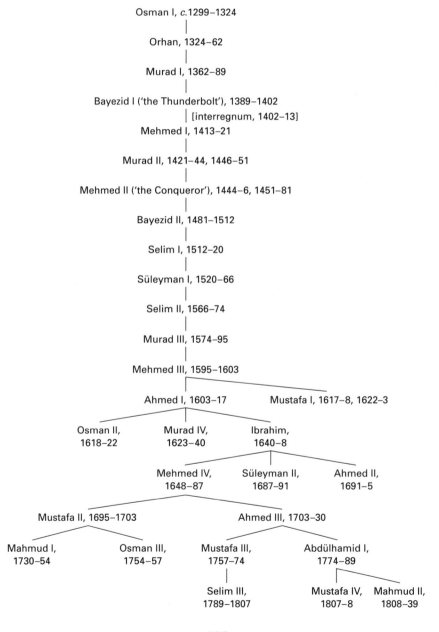

Osman I, c.1299–1324

Orhan, 1324–62

Murad I, 1362–89

Bayezid I ('the Thunderbolt'), 1389–1402
[interregnum, 1402–13]

Mehmed I, 1413–21

Murad II, 1421–44, 1446–51

Mehmed II ('the Conqueror'), 1444–6, 1451–81

Bayezid II, 1481–1512

Selim I, 1512–20

Süleyman I, 1520–66

Selim II, 1566–74

Murad III, 1574–95

Mehmed III, 1595–1603

Ahmed I, 1603–17   Mustafa I, 1617–8, 1622–3

Osman II,   Murad IV,   Ibrahim,
1618–22   1623–40   1640–8

Mehmed IV,   Süleyman II,   Ahmed II,
1648–87   1687–91   1691–5

Mustafa II, 1695–1703   Ahmed III, 1703–30

Mahmud I,   Osman III,   Mustafa III,   Abdülhamid I,
1730–54   1754–57   1757–74   1774–89

Selim III,   Mustafa IV,   Mahmud II,
1789–1807   1807–8   1808–39

POLITICAL CHRONOLOGY

Istanbul	Anatolia	Aleppo	Damascus	Iraq	Egypt	Yemen
1453: Ottoman conquest						
						1509–38: coastal region under control of Ottoman naval officers
	1514: Ottomans defeat Safavids at Chaldiran					
	1515: Ottomans conquer Dulkadiroğlu			1515: Ottoman conquest of Mosul		1515: nominal Mamluk rule along coast
		1516: Ottoman conquest	1516: Ottoman conquest			
					1517: Ottoman conquest	
			1522: Janbirdi al-Ghazali's rebellion			
					1523: rebellion of Janm and Inal	

Istanbul	Anatolia	Aleppo	Damascus	Iraq	Egypt	Yemen
					1523–4: Ahmed Pasha's rebellion	
					1525: Ibrahim Pasha issues *kanunname*	
				1534: Ottoman conquest of Baghdad and Basra		
			c.1568: end of power of Hanash family in Bekaa valley and adjacent regions			1538: Süleyman Pasha makes Yemen an Ottoman province
			c.1568–94: Furaykh family in Bekaa valley			1567–8: Imam al-Mutahhar's rebellion

c.1596–1607: Jelali rebellions	1602: Damascus Janissaries expelled by governor and Hüseyin Pasha Janbulad

1605–7: Ali Pasha Janbulad's rebellion | c.1598–1634 Fakhr al-Din Ma'n II dominates Lebanon | c.1596–1668: Afrasiyabs in control of Basra

1621: Bakr Subashi defeats Yusuf Pasha for control of Baghdad | 1605: Ibrahim Pasha murdered by cavalry troops

1609: cavalry rebellion crushed by Kul Kıran Mehmed Pasha |
| 1622: murder of Osman II | | | | |

Istanbul	Anatolia	Aleppo	Damascus	Iraq	Egypt	Yemen
	1623: Abaza Mehmed Pasha's rebellion			1623: Safavids occupy Baghdad		
						1630s: Qasimi imams oust Ottomans
c.1635–83: Kadızadelis influential						
				1638: Ottomans reconquer Baghdad		
					1640s: emergence of Faqari and Qasimi factions	
1656–76: Köprülü Mehmed and Fazıl Ahmed Pashas grand viziers	1658: Abaza Hasan Pasha's rebellion					

			1659: rebellion of Mehmed Bey al-Faqari, governor of Jirja	1679: Zaydi imam expels Jews
		1694: Muntafiq seize Basra c.1700: Anaza tribe moves into Euphrates valley 1704–1831: Georgian governors in Baghdad and Basra	1711: civil war between Faqaris/Janissaries and Qasimis/Azeban	
	c.1700: Anaza tribe moves into Euphrates valley			
1659: Abaza Hasan Pasha's rebellion defeated				
1665–7: Sabbatai Sevi episode				

Istanbul	Anatolia	Aleppo	Damascus	Iraq	Egypt	Yemen
			c.1725–1808: Azm governors dominate Damascus	1726–1834: Governors from Jalili family dominate Mosul		
					1730: Faqaris defeat Qasimis	
					1730s–69: Hawwara tribe dominates Upper Egypt	
				1733: Nadir Shah besieges Baghdad		
				1736: Nadir Shah besieges Mosul		
			1740: *kapı kulları* expelled from Damascus			
			1746: execution of Fethi the *defterdar*			

	1748–98: Kazdağlı household controls Egypt	1770: Ali Bey's rebellion
1746–75: Zahir al-Umar dominates northern Palestine	1757: Hüseyin ibn al-Makki presides over pilgrimage caravan disaster	1775–1804: Ahmed Pasha al-Jazzar dominates northern Palestine and southern Lebanon
c.1747–1808: *yerliyye* Janissaries v. *ashraf*, led by Tahazades		

Istanbul	Anatolia	Aleppo	Damascus	Iraq	Egypt	Yemen
1789–1807: reign of Selim III; Nizam-i Jedid						
			1799: Al-Jazzar defeats the French		1798: Bonaparte's invasion	
				c.1800: Shammar tribe dominates northern Iraq		
					1811: Mehmed Ali Pasha massacres Mamluks	
		1813: Jelal al-Din Pasha destroys *yerliyye* Janissaries				

GLOSSARY

Abbasids: Arab dynasty descended from the Prophet Muhammad's uncle Abbas. They held the caliphate from 750–1258 CE, ruling from Baghdad, the capital they founded in 762, although their military and political authority was severely compromised by provincial overlords and Iranian and Turkish invaders from the tenth century onwards.

Abkhazia: A region in the north-western Caucasus Mountains, on the north-eastern shore of the Black Sea; today the north-western portion of the Republic of Georgia. In the seventeenth century, it became an important pool of mamluks for the Ottoman palace and various provincial grandees.

agent of the harem (Arabic, *wakil Dar al-Saada*): The permanent representative in Egypt of the Ottoman Chief Harem Eunuch, usually a provincial grandee. He was responsible for ensuring that revenues and grains earmarked for the Holy Cities of Mecca and Medina were collected and delivered.

agha: A title held by (1) the highest officer in a military regiment, (2) a eunuch of the Ottoman palace.

akche: The Ottoman silver coin.

Akkoyunlu: 'White Sheep' Turcomans who ruled eastern Anatolia, northern Iraq, north-western Iran and parts of the Caucasus from the late fourteenth century to 1502. They were decisively defeated by the Ottomans in the late fifteenth century and by the Safavids in the early sixteenth century.

Alawis (Alevis; also called Nusayris): A religious sect found in north-western Syria, northern Lebanon and southern Anatolia. Although not doctrinally Shiite, they revere Ali ibn Abi Talib.

amin: See *emin*.

amir: See emir.

Anaza (Anayza) Bedouin: Nomadic population of desert Arabs, originally from the central Arabian peninsula. They migrated into Syria and Iraq in the late seventeenth century and during the eighteenth century served as escorts to the Damascus pilgrimage caravan. They became very influential in central and southern Iraq during the late eighteenth century.

ashraf (singular, *sharif*): The population of descendants and purported descendants of the Prophet Muhammad. They were a major political and military force in eighteenth-century Aleppo, Ayntab and Marash.

awlad al-Arab: Literally, 'sons of the Arabs', a broad, flexible term designating the local population of an Arab province, as opposed to the Rumis, populations from Anatolia and the Balkans. The term perhaps includes children of Bedouin nomads or even of sub-Saharan Africans.

ayan: Collective term for localized political elites in the Ottoman Arab provinces. The *ayan* included military-administrative personnel and, according to some definitions, ulema and wealthy merchants.

Azeban (singular, Azeb, Azab): An infantry regiment deployed as garrison troops in most of the Ottoman Arab provinces. They were usually less numerous than the Janissaries and were often political rivals to them, above all in Cairo and Baghdad.

bedestan: See *khan*.

Bedouin (singular or plural): Arab tribesman or tribesmen, often nomadic or semi-nomadic, who inhabited the countryside of most Arab provinces.

berat: An official government certificate, issued to confirm the bearer's status, e.g. as holder of a particular grant of revenue rights. In the eighteenth century, certain Christian and Jewish merchants in the Ottoman Arab provinces received *berat*s confirming their legal protection by the French or British government, or by the government of one of the Italian city-states; they were thus subject only to the laws of these countries. They were often called *beratlı*s, 'those with *berat*s'.

bey: A variation on the ancient Turkic title *beg*, 'lord', and an abbreviation of the Ottoman rank of *sanjak beyi*, the governor of a subprovincial district known as a *sanjak*. In Egypt, the title and rank also extended to the holders of certain provincial administrative positions such as *defterdar* and pilgrimage commander.

beylerbeyi: Literally, 'bey of beys', the governor of an Ottoman province.

cadastral survey: A government survey of all tax revenues in an Ottoman province, normally listing all districts in a province, all villages in a district, and all households in a village. These surveys were carried out in the Arab provinces during the sixteenth century but only rarely thereafter.

caliph: Anglicized form of the Arabic *khalifa*, 'successor'. The successor to the Prophet Muhammad as leader of the Muslim community. Sometime between the Ottoman conquest of the Arab lands and the late eighteenth century, the Ottoman sultan came to be recognized as the caliph of all Sunni Muslims.

caravanserai: See *khan*.

chelebi: An Ottoman title roughly equivalent to 'esquire', used by courtiers, some ulema and some Sufi leaders. By the eighteenth century, it had been largely displaced by the title *efendi*. In Ottoman Egypt, the governor's Jewish banker also held the title *chelebi*.

Chief Harem Eunuch: Also called Darüssaade Ağası ('Agha of the Abode of Felicity') or Kızlar Ağası ('Agha of the Girls'), the chief of the eunuchs who guarded the harem of Topkapı Palace. Ordinarily an East African, he supervised the Holy Cities Pious Foundations and exercised enormous political authority.

Chief Tomb Eunuch: See Shaykh al-Haram.

chifthane system: The agricultural regime dominant in the Ottoman Empire, whereby free peasants farmed *chiftlik*s.

chiftlik: A plot of land farmed by free peasants, equivalent to the amount that could be ploughed by a pair (Turkish, *chift*) of oxen.

Circassia: A region in the north-west Caucasus, north of Abkhazia; today a region in southern Russia. It was a major source of mamluks for the later Mamluk sultanate and for the Ottomans beginning in the late sixteenth century.

concubine: A slave girl who served as a sexual partner for the Ottoman sultan or for any wealthy personage.

Conservatives: During the reign of Selim III (1789–1807), the faction among the Ottoman administration, both central and provincial, who opposed Selim's reforms, particularly because of heavy French involvement in implementing them. They tended to be supported by Russia.

Copts: The indigenous Christian population of Egypt. They believe that Jesus has a single, inseparable nature, at once human and divine. During the Ottoman era, they were influential in Egypt's financial administration.

courtyard house: A type of middle- to upper-class residence common in the Mediterranean region, featuring two storeys of rooms arranged around a central courtyard. Living space was usually on the upper floor, kitchens and store-rooms on the ground floor.

Darüssaade Ağası: See Chief Harem Eunuch.

defterdar: The chief financial officer of the Ottoman Empire or of one of the Ottoman provinces.

devshirme: The Ottoman system of 'collecting' Christian boys from villages in the Balkans and Anatolia, converting them to Islam, and training them for service as palace pages or as Janissaries. It was instituted in the late fourteenth or early fifteenth century and abandoned during the seventeenth century.

dhikr (**Turkish**, *zikir*): Literally, 'remembrance', the signature vocal ritual of a Sufi order, designed to focus the members' attention on God. It was often performed just prior to or in conjunction with the *sama*.

dhimmi (**Turkish**, *zimmi*): Literally, 'protected one', a non-Muslim mono-theist living under Muslim rule, subject to the ruler's protection in return for the payment of a poll tax (*jizya*, Turkish *cizye*) and certain restrictions on public behaviour and clothing.

dhow: A ship heavily used in trade in the Indian Ocean and Red Sea, featuring a wooden (usually teak-wood) hull and lateen sails.

Dhu'l-Faqar (**Turkish**, **Zülfikar**): The double-bladed sword of Ali ibn Abi Talib, subject of numerous legends and claims to ownership. Anthropomorphic Ottoman-era depictions of the sword were emblazoned on battle flags, particularly those of the Janissaries. The sword was the namesake of Egypt's Faqari faction.

Diphysite: Referring to the belief, prevalent among most Christians today, that Jesus possessed two separate natures: one human, one divine. This position was opposed by Monophysites, including Copts and Jacobites.

divan: A governing council, such as the grand vizier's council or that of a provincial governor, consisting of several prominent government officials.

Dönmes: Popular name for adherents of a nominal sect of Islam consisting of followers of the Jewish messianic figure Sabbatai Sevi (1626–76). Dönmes do not adhere to normative Muslim or Jewish practice but follow their own mystical, post-messianic Jewish rites.

Druze: A religious sect descended from Ismaili missionaries in Lebanon and Syria who believed that the Fatimid caliph al-Hakim (r. 996–1021) was divine. The Druze became an influential population in Lebanon. Fakhr al-Din Ma'n II, who carved out an autonomous bailiwick in parts of Lebanon, Syria and Palestine in the early seventeenth century, was the most famous Druze personage of the Ottoman era.

Dulkadiroğlu: Rulers of a Turkish principality in south-eastern Anatolia who were vassals to the Mamluk sultanate. Their principality fell to the Ottomans in 1515, following the Ottoman victory at Chaldiran.

efendi: An Ottoman title held by government bureaucrats and ulema. Today, it is equivalent to 'sir' or 'madam'.

emin (**Arabic, *amin***): An official appointed from Istanbul to collect taxes in Egypt during the late sixteenth and early seventeenth centuries.

emir (**Arabic, *amir***): (1) A generic term for a non-Ottoman prince or chieftain, e.g. a Kurdish or Bedouin leader, who held autonomous or quasi-autonomous jurisdiction over his territory; (2) a generic term for a local or regional strong-man, such as a semi-autonomous subprovincial governor or regimental commander; (3) a high-ranking mamluk military-administrative official under the Mamluk sultanate.

Faqaris: One of two rival factions, the other being the Qasimis, who dominated Egyptian political and economic life from roughly 1640–1730. The faction's name derived from the image of Ali ibn Abi Talib's sword Dhu'l-Faqar, which was emblazoned on many Ottoman battle flags.

Fatimids: Ismaili Shiite dynasty who founded a counter-caliphate hostile to the Abbasids in the tenth century CE Starting from a base in Tunisia, they conquered Egypt, Syria and the Holy Cities from the Abbasids in 969 and founded a new capital, Cairo. Afterwards, they sent missionaries into Abbasid territory to undermine the Abbasid regime from within.

fatwa (**Turkish, *fetva***): A legal opinion on a point of Islamic law given by a *mufti*, usually in response to a formal query. A *fatwa* was not binding in a Muslim law court.

futuwwa: Code of 'young manhood' which gave rise to urban brotherhoods, usually specific to particular crafts. Although *futuwwa* organizations were long thought to have given rise to craft guilds, they contained a heavy mystical element and in many respects more closely resembled Sufi brotherhoods.

Geniza, Cairo: A collection of documents of all kinds generated by the Jewish community of Cairo between the ninth and nineteenth centuries. Because many of them contained the name of God, they were not destroyed but stored in a special chamber in the Ben Ezra Synagogue in Fustat, today a southern district of Cairo.

ghulam: A young male elite slave, similar to a mamluk but often somewhat younger. This term was used in lieu of 'mamluk' by the Seljuks of Rum and the Safavids.

grand vizier: The chief government minister of the Ottoman Empire and head of the Ottoman government. His authority came to rival that of the sultan beginning in the sixteenth century.

Habesh: The Ottoman province of Abyssinia, consisting of the coastal regions of present-day Ethiopia and much of present-day Sudan. It was conquered by Özdemir Pasha during the early 1550s.

hajj: The annual pilgrimage to Mecca which every Muslim is enjoined to make at least once during his or her lifetime if at all possible.

Halvetis: See Khalwatis.

Hanafis: Followers of the Sunni legal rite named for Abu Hanifa (699–767), initially characterized by its reliance on free reasoning as opposed to strict adherence to the Quran and traditions of the Prophet Muhammad. The Hanafi rite was the official legal rite of the Ottoman Empire.

Hanbalis: Followers of the Sunni legal rite named after Ahmad ibn Hanbal (780–855), characterized by its strict adherence to the Quran and the verifiable traditions of the Prophet Muhammad, and its mistrust of free reasoning in legal decision-making. Hanbalism was the rite of the Wahhabis and Saudis.

hara: A neighbourhood, often residential, in a Middle Eastern city; roughly synonymous with *mahalla*.

Haram: One of two rival Bedouin factions, the other being the Sa'd, which dominated the Egyptian countryside during the seventeenth and early eighteenth centuries. They were allied with the Qasimi faction.

harem: The portion of a residence set aside for the women of the family and off limits to males who are not family members.

harem house: A separate house for the women of a grandee's family, usually run by the grandee's wife.

hass: The largest grant of land revenue, larger than a *timar* or *zeamet*, usually assigned to a vizier or the governor of a province where the *timar* system predominated.

havass-i hümayun: 'Crown lands' set aside for the imperial family's use. Revenue collection rights to these lands were sometimes sold as tax farms to grandees, who delivered the revenues to the central treasury.

Hawwara: Semi-nomadic tribe, originally Berber, which migrated from present-day Algeria to Egypt during the Middle Ages. During the Ottoman period, they controlled most of Upper Egypt until the defeat of their leader by Ali Bey al-Kabir in 1769.

Head of the Jews: The religious and political head of Egypt's Jewish community from the late eleventh century until the Ottoman period. The Ottomans abolished the office, preferring to deal with secular representatives of the community.

Hijaz: The western coastal plain of the Arabian peninsula, including the cities of Mecca, Medina and Jidda.

himaya (**Turkish**, *himayet*): Literally, 'protection', the practice whereby Janissaries took over a shop in the bazaar, placing the shopkeeper under their 'protection'. The Janissaries claimed a portion of the shop's profits while the merchant was inscribed on the Janissary rolls and thus became exempt from taxation.

Holy Cities Pious Foundations (Awqaf al-Haramayn, Haremeyn Evkafı): The imperial pious foundations established by various Ottoman sultans and imperial women to provide grain and public services to the poor of Mecca and Medina, as well as pilgrims to those cities. Revenues for the foundations came from lands and properties throughout the Ottoman Empire, but above all from villages in Egypt. The foundations were supervised by the Chief Harem Eunuch.

ijaza: A certificate issued by a *madrasa* teacher or private instructor, declaring the student's mastery of a particular exegetical, theological or legal text and authorizing him to teach it.

ijtihad: Method of reaching a legal decision through independent rational thought, as opposed to reliance on the Quran, sayings of the Prophet, precedent or logical analogy. Ostensibly, Sunni jurists ceased to employ *ijtihad* in the ninth century, although some reformist movements of the eighteenth and nineteenth centuries proposed resurrecting it. Shiite ulema never abandoned *ijtihad*.

iltizam: See tax-farming.

imam: (1) The religious functionary who leads prayers and sometimes delivers the Friday noontime sermon in a mosque; (2) a descendant of the Prophet Muhammad recognized as caliph by one of the Shiite subsects; (3) the caliph recognized by the Kharijite sect.

Imamis: Twelver Shiites, the subsect who believe that the son of the eleventh Shiite *imam* went into occultation in 873 CE and will return at the end of time. This was the doctrine of Iran's Safavid empire.

Ismailis: The subsect of Shiites, sometimes called Seveners, who believe that the son of the seventh Shiite imam went into occultation towards the end of the seventh century CE, although different permutations of this belief began to appear during the ninth century. Ismailism was the doctrine of the Fatimid caliphate.

Jacobites: Monophysite Christians of Syria whose church was spearheaded by the resolutely Monophysite bishops of Antioch in the fifth century CE. Their church is also known as the Syrian Orthodox Church.

Janissaries: Ottoman elite infantry, probably founded in the late fourteenth century and until the seventeenth century recruited largely through the *devshirme*. The imperial Janissaries, based in Istanbul, were augmented by provincial garrison regiments who were often called Mustahfizan.

Jelali governors: Governors of Ottoman provinces during the seventeenth century who rebelled against the central government. Their name derives from the Jelali rebels.

Jelali Rebellions: Term for widespread unrest in the countryside of Anatolia and, to some extent, the Arab provinces during the late sixteenth and early seventeenth century; triggered by massive inflation and large numbers of armed peasant mercenaries.

jihaz (**Turkish,** *ceyiz*): Equivalent to a trousseau, the household goods, often consisting largely of textiles, which a bride brought to her marriage.

jizya (**Turkish,** *cizye*): The poll, or head, tax levied on non-Muslim monotheists living under Muslim rule.

Kabbalah: Body of mystical Jewish oral tradition compiled in thirteenth-century Spain. Rabbi Isaac Luria (1534–72), a resident of Ottoman Safed, developed a messianic interpretation of it that came to be known as Lurianic Kabbalah.

kadı: See *qadi*.

Kadızadelis: A puritanical trend, thought by some to be a coherent movement, among Hanafi ulema in seventeenth-century Istanbul and, to a lesser degree, the Ottoman provinces. The Kadızadelis opposed innovations to the Prophet Muhammad's practice and were particularly antagonistic towards Sufism.

kanunname: Literally, 'book of law', a code of sultanic law, supplemental to the *sharia*, for a particular Ottoman province, usually attached to that province's cadastral survey.

kapı kulları: Literally, 'slaves of the gate', soldiers, especially Janissaries, dispatched to the provinces from Istanbul, as opposed to entrenched local forces (*yerliyye*).

Kapudan Pasha: The supreme admiral of the Ottoman navy.

kazasker: See *qadi askar*.

kethüda, *kâhya*: A title held by (1) the second-highest officer in a military regiment, after the *agha*; (2) the lieutenant or steward of a high government official; (3) the secular representative of a non-Muslim community, particularly in Anatolia and the Balkans.

Khalwatis: Widespread Sufi order which originated in medieval Central Asia before spreading to Egypt, Anatolia and the Balkans. The order enjoyed great popularity in Istanbul during the seventeenth century and in the Arab provinces, above all Egypt, during the eighteenth century. It is characterized by its members' practice of occasionally retreating to cells (Arabic singular, *khalwa*) for solitary prayer and meditation.

khan (**Turkish,** *han*): A large, usually two-storey roofed building where long-distance merchants could store and sell their goods. The lower storey was ordinarily for pack animals, the upper storey for the merchants and their merchandise. While earlier Islamic regimes had built such structures in isolated spots along major trade routes, the Ottomans built them in major cities, where they functioned as major sites for the purchase and sale of specific goods. An urban *khan* often handled a single commodity, such as textiles, coffee or flax. In Egyptian cities, the *khan* was known as a *wakala* or *qaysariyya*, in Anatolian cities as a *bedestan*. Most westerners know the *khan* as a caravanserai.

Kharijites: A small sect of Islam which originated with followers of Ali ibn Abi Talib who rejected his claim to the caliphate when he agreed to arbitration at the Battle of Siffin in 657 CE Kharijites believe that any Muslim can be imam, or caliph, so long as he is unfailingly just. During the Ottoman era, Kharijites were found in Oman and in parts of what is now Algeria.

khatib: The official who delivers the sermon (*khutba*) in a mosque after Friday noontime prayers. An imam can also perform this function.

khutba: The sermon preached by a *khatib* in a mosque after Friday noontime prayers. The sultan's name was recited in the *khutba*.

Kızlar Ağası: See Chief Harem Eunuch.

Köprülüs: Albanian family of grand viziers who promoted a reforming military and political agenda during the late seventeenth and early eighteenth centuries.

Küchük Kaynarja, Treaty of: 1774 treaty which ended the Russo-Turkish war of 1768–74. Conceding defeat, the Ottoman Empire ceded the Crimea to Russia and allowed the Russian navy free passage from the Black Sea to the Mediterranean. This is the first international document in which the Ottoman sultan is acknowledged as caliph of the world's Sunni Muslims.

kul: One of the 'sultan's servants'. A term applied to any soldier or government functionary, but above all those recruited through the *devshirme*. Soldiers of *kul* origin formed a troublesome power elite in Istanbul and Egypt during the early seventeenth century. *Kul*s in Istanbul were responsible for the murder of Sultan Osman II (r. 1618–22).

lateen sail: A ship's sail which is triangular, as opposed to square. Indian Ocean ships used lateen sails, which gave their ships increased manoeuvrability. Ultimately, both the Ottomans and the European powers combined lateen and square sails on their ships.

Long War: A series of inconclusive battles between the Ottoman and Habsburg empires from 1593 to 1606. The Habsburgs' heavy use of gun-bearing infantry forced the Ottomans to hire gun-bearing peasant mercenaries to counter them. These mercenaries ultimately contributed to the Jelali Rebellions.

madrasa (**Turkish**, *medrese*):   An Islamic theological college that probably had its origins in the tenth century. The *madrasa* curriculum included Quranic exegesis, law, theology and sometimes mathematical sciences. Most Ottoman ulema and many government bureaucrats were trained in *madrasa*s. In the Ottoman central lands, *madrasa*s were ranked according to the salaries of the ulema who taught in them.

mahalla: A neighbourhood, often residential, in a Middle Eastern city; roughly synonymous with *hara*.

mahr: The dowry that a groom's family paid to his bride. Often, the bride received half at the time of marriage and the remaining half in case of divorce or her husband's death.

malikane: The life-tenure tax farm, introduced towards the end of the seventeenth century. It became a major source of sustainable wealth for eighteenth-century provincial *ayan*, who treated it as heritable wealth.

Malikis: Followers of the Sunni legal rite named after Malik ibn Anas (715–95), characterized by its emphasis on traditions of the Prophet Muhammad as the basis for legal decisions. Malikism is prevalent in Upper Egypt and North Africa.

mamluk: An elite military slave. Mamluks were widely used in the Muslim world from the mid-ninth to the early nineteenth century. Until the late thirteenth century, they were largely Central Asian Turks; after that date, more and more were imported from the Caucasus. From the late sixteenth century, the Ottomans made heavy use of mamluks at the imperial court and in the Arab provinces. During the eighteenth century, Georgian mamluks became particularly influential.

Maronites: Christian sect in Lebanon that takes its name from the fifth-century priest John Maron, who rejected the Monophysite beliefs of the bishops of Antioch. The Maronites named their own patriarch in the late seventh century but reaffiliated with the Vatican in 1182.

Matawila: Shiite peasant population of southern Lebanon and northern Palestine.

Mevlevis: Members of the Sufi order named after Mevlana Jelal al-Din Rumi (d. 1273), famous for its 'whirling' *sama*. The order was particularly popular at the Ottoman court.

millet: An Ottoman Turkish term for a coherent population or community. Before the nineteenth century, it was applied most commonly to the Muslim community as a whole and to non-Ottoman Christian communities. In the nineteenth century, it became the framework for administration of the various non-Muslim communities of the Ottoman Empire.

miri: Literally, 'belonging to the emir', an adjective referring to land owned by the Ottoman state, i.e. the vast majority of agricultural land in the Ottoman Empire.

Mirror for Princes: A genre of courtly advice literature dating back to the Sasanian empire, advising the ruler on how to rule justly and correct injustices. From the sixteenth century onwards, this genre became the major template for Ottoman 'decline' literature.

Monophysite: Referring to the belief that Jesus possessed one indivisible nature, at once human and divine. Monophysite doctrine prevails in the Coptic, Ethiopian and Jacobite churches. It is opposed by Diphysites, who form the vast majority of Christians today.

mufti: A Muslim jurisprudent authorized to give legal opinions, or *fatwas*, on specific points of law, usually in response to formal queries. A *mufti* could be appointed by the central Ottoman government or simply acknowledged as a judicial authority by his community.

muhtasib: The inspector of public markets in an Ottoman city whose duty was to ensure that all public behaviour conformed with the *sharia*. In Cairo, his duties were assumed by the Janissary *agha* during the seventeenth century; in Aleppo, the office of *muhtasib* was apparently subsumed by the craft guilds.

mülk: Land and other property that is privately owned, as opposed to *miri*.

muqataa: A grant of revenue. In Ottoman usage, it is more or less synonymous with a tax farm.

murid: A Sufi 'seeker' who becomes the disciple of a spiritual master (*murshid*) in a particular Sufi order.

murshid: Literally, 'guide', a spiritual master in a particular Sufi order, often the head of the order, who directs the mystical training of his disciples (*murids*).

Mustahfizan: Literally, 'protectors', a regiment of Janissaries who acted as garrison troops in a provincial capital.

Mustarabs: The Arabic-speaking Jews who comprised the vast majority of the Jewish population of the Ottoman Arab provinces before the influx of immigrants from Spain and Portugal in the late fifteenth and early sixteenth centuries.

nahiya: A judicial subdistrict within a *qada*, the territory under the judicial authority of a *qadi*. Judges at the *nahiya* level might belong to one of the non-Hanafi legal rites, depending on the population of the region.

na'ib: Literally, 'representative', a subordinate *qadi* who adjudicated at the *nahiya* level. While Hanafi *na'ibs* were often clients of a province's chief *qadi* and left office when he did, *na'ibs* of non-Hanafi rites were often members of prominent local families who served for life.

naqib al-ashraf: The head of the descendants of the Prophet Muhammad in an Ottoman province. Until the eighteenth century, the *naqib* was appointed from Istanbul by the imperial *naqib al-ashraf*; afterwards, he was usually a local notable.

Naqshbandis: Sufi order that originated in medieval Central Asia before spreading to India. In the seventeenth century, a reformist branch spread from India to Yemen, the Hijaz, Egypt and Syria, as well as the imperial capital. The reformist branch is known for its silent *dhikr*; the order as a whole is known for its doctrine of 'solitude in society', which encourages members to be socially and politically active.

narh: A policy of government price-fixing, widely used by the Ottomans, on essential commodities such as olive oil, grain and sugar. Set prices for such goods were registered in Muslim law courts and enforced by local *qadi*s.

Nestorians (also Assyrians): Christian sect that takes its name from the fifth-century Antioch monk John Nestorius, who was patriarch of Constantinople from 428–31. The sect represents an extreme version of Diphysitism, believing that Jesus possessed two entirely separate essences. Nestorian Christians were influential in Iraq and were patronized by the Sasanians and the Abbasids.

Nizam-i Jedid: Literally, 'the New Order', the programme of largely military reforms attempted by Selim III (r. 1789–1807) and revived by Mahmud II (r. 1808–39), centring on a new army trained and equipped in the European style. The army itself came to be known by the name Nizam-i Jedid.

Nusayris: See Alawis.

Pact of Umar: The document that served as a template for the treatment of non-Muslim monotheists living under Muslim rule. Supposedly the peace treaty between the second caliph, Umar ibn al-Khattab (r. 634–44), and the Christians of Jerusalem, it probably dates at least in part from a century or more later. The Pact pledges certain restrictions on non-Muslims' behaviour and appearance in return for the ruler's protection. Under the Ottomans, the provisions of the Pact of Umar were only sporadically enforced.

pasha: A title, originally Persian, given to Ottoman viziers and provincial governors.

provisionism: A term for the economic strategy long thought to have been followed by the Ottoman state, whereby the government encouraged imports,

discouraged exports of basic commodities, and selectively imposed price controls in order to ensure that all of the imperial domains were well provisioned.
This strategy arguably contributed to preparedness in wartime and limited competition for resources among different social strata, thus helping to preserve social
order.

qada: The administrative district within an Ottoman province that falls under
the jurisdiction of a *qadi*.

qadi: A judge who presided over a Muslim law court in a city or town. He
had the authority not only to rule on cases but to execute his rulings. In a smaller
city or town, he was the equivalent of a mayor.

qadi askar (**Turkish,** *kazasker*; also *qadi al-quda*):   (1) One of two supreme
judges of the Ottoman Empire, with jurisdiction over Rumelia or Anatolia. The
qadi askar of Anatolia appointed all judges in the Arab provinces, except for
the chief judge of each province, who by the sixteenth century was appointed
by the chief *mufti* of Istanbul; (2) the chief judge of Egypt, who received the
title as an honorific.

Qasimis: One of two rival factions, the other being the Faqaris, who dominated Egyptian political and economic life from roughly 1640–1730. The faction's name derived from Qasim Bey the Great, a grandee of Egypt in the early
seventeenth century, whose enormous household apparently provided the germ
of the faction.

Qays, Qaysi: One of two major divisions of Arabs whose origins date from
the pre-Islamic era and whose rivalry crystallized during the early Islamic conquests. Originally, Qays comprised the 'northern' Arabs, Yemen the 'southern'
Arabs; with the Islamic conquests, however, the ethno-geographical distinctions became meaningless as tribes from both populations spread throughout
the Islamic empire and non-Arabs became affiliated with the two blocs. During
the Ottoman period, the Qays–Yemen rivalry existed primarily in Lebanon and
Palestine.

qaysariyya: See *khan*.

qishr: A beverage popular in Yemen and the Horn of Africa, consisting of a
sweetened infusion of the husks of coffee beans.

rab':   A form of 'tenement' housing that dates back to the Roman era in Egypt
and the Mediterranean. It consisted of a two- to three-storey block of merchant
or working-class flats, often built over a *wakala*, with a shared staircase, well
and latrine.

Ramadan: The ninth month of the Islamic lunar calendar, occasion of a
sunrise-to-sunset fast.

Reformers: During the reign of Selim III (1789–1807), the faction among
the Ottoman administration, both central and provincial, who supported
Selim's reforms. They tended to be supported by France.

reisülkuttab: The chief scribe of the Ottoman chancery, responsible for correspondence with foreign rulers and their representatives and a major factor
in diplomatic negotiations from the late seventeenth century onwards. By the
mid-eighteenth century, he had become a proto-foreign minister.

Rifais: Sufi order named after the Baghdadi mystic Ahmad al-Rifai (1119–83), well represented in Ottoman Iraq, Syria and Egypt. They are known for a ritual in which they inflict physical torments upon themselves in order to demonstrate that their devotion to God prevents pain and injury.

riqaba (**Turkish,** *rekabet*): The Islamic legal principle whereby the ruler holds sovereign rights to the land and its natural resources.

riwaq: A residential college at al-Azhar university in Cairo. Most *riwaq*s were dedicated to students from particular regions, e.g. Upper Egypt, the Blue Nile and the province of Damascus, or ethnicities, e.g. Turks and Indians, although a few were non-region- or ethnicity-specific, and one was set aside for blind students.

Rum: historically, the territories formerly under Byzantine ('Roman') rule. Under the Ottomans, Rum referred to the Ottoman central lands, including Istanbul, western Anatolia and perhaps the easternmost parts of the Balkans.

sabil-kuttab (**Turkish,** *sebil-mekteb*): A Quran school (*kuttab*) above a public drinking fountain (*sabil*). It was a popular focus of pious foundations in late Mamluk and Ottoman Egypt. In the late Mamluk and early Ottoman eras, a *sabil-kuttab* was usually attached to a larger religious complex; by the eighteenth century, most were free-standing.

Sa'd: One of two rival Bedouin factions, the other being the Haram, which dominated the Egyptian countryside during the seventeenth and early eighteenth centuries. They were allied with the Faqari faction.

Saladin, Salah al-Din: Kurdish general (1138–93) most famous for expelling the Crusaders from Jerusalem. Although a Sunni loosely associated with the Seljuks, he served the Fatimids as a military commander against the Crusaders before abolishing the Fatimid caliphate and founding his own dynasty, the Ayyubids, who ruled Egypt, Syria and the Hijaz from 1171–1250.

sama (**Turkish,** *sema*): Literally, 'listening', the signature communal ritual of a Sufi order, usually consisting of set movements, often to music. It was designed to focus the members' attention on God and could lead to spiritual annihilation of the self in God. It was often performed immediately following or in conjunction with the *dhikr*.

sanjak: Literally, 'flag', an administrative district within an Ottoman province.

sanjak beyi: The official who administered a *sanjak*. In Ottoman Egypt, someone with this rank could also hold one of several key administrative positions, such as pilgrimage commander or *defterdar*.

sarraf: A money-lender, often also a merchant. Jews and Armenian Christians were overrepresented in this profession. Often the governor of an Ottoman province would have a personal *sarraf* who acted as a sort of financial consultant.

sekban: A mercenary soldier, usually from among the peasantry or urban population of Anatolia or the Balkans. *Sekban*s were initially hired during the Long War to supplement the Ottoman infantry. Afterwards, they became a major component of imperial armies and of the armies of provincial governors and grandees.

Sephardic: Refers to Jews from Spain and Portugal and their descendants. Following the 1492 expulsion of Jews from Spain, many Sephardic Jews emigrated to Ottoman territory, where they soon became the dominant Jewish population.

Shafiis: Followers of the Sunni legal rite named after Muhammad ibn Idris al-Shafii (767–820), who introduced the science of verification of Prophetic sayings. Shafiism is prevalent in Lower Egypt and parts of Syria and among Kurdish populations. It spread along the oceanic trade routes from Egypt to coastal Yemen, southern India, Malaysia and Indonesia.

shahbandar: Literally, 'king of the port', the chief of the informal organization of long-distance merchants in certain Ottoman Arab provincial capitals.

Shahname: Literally, (*Book of Kings*) the Persian national epic, spanning the period from the mythical first Iranian kings to the Sasanian dynasty and the Islamic conquest of Iran. The tales were rendered in verse by the Iranian poet Ferdowsi (935–c.1020).

Shammar tribe: Large Bedouin confederation of central Arabia who initially supported the Saudis in the late eighteenth century, then fell out with them and migrated into northern Iraq, where by the early nineteenth century they exercised regional hegemony.

sharia: Islamic law, comprising legal strictures from the Quran, the sayings of the Prophet Muhammad, and the legal decisions of the first few generations of ulema.

shaykh: A generic title for a leader, e.g. of a tribe, a village, a Sufi order or a religious or educational institution.

Shaykh al-Azhar: The rector of al-Azhar university in Cairo. The office emerged in the late seventeenth century.

shaykh al-balad: Originally, the headman of a village, particularly in Egypt. From about 1730, the same title was applied to a new office, equivalent to governor of Cairo, held by one of Egypt's beys.

Shaykh al-Haram: The chief of the corps of African eunuchs who guarded the Prophet Muhammad's tomb in Medina. From the late seventeenth century, he was often a former Chief Harem Eunuch.

Shaykh al-Islam (Turkish, *Şeyhülislam*): The chief *mufti* of Istanbul and, by extension, of the entire Ottoman Empire. Beginning in the sixteenth century, he appointed the chief judges of the Ottoman provinces.

Shiites: Adherents of the minority sect of Islam who believe that Muhammad designated Ali ibn Abi Talib to succeed him as leader of the Muslim community on his death and that subsequent caliphs, or imams, should be descendants of Ali and Muhammad's daughter Fatima. Major subsects are the Imamis, or Twelvers; Ismailis, or Seveners; and Zaydis.

shuhud al-hal: A body of 'permanent' witnesses, often from among the leading residents of a city or town, who made themselves available at a Muslim law court to ensure that cases followed proper Islamic legal procedure, to provide oral testimony in contentious cases, and to witness various transactions.

Shulhan Arukh: Literally, *The Set Table*, a brief, practical guide to Jewish law composed by the noted Sephardic rabbi Joseph Karo (1488–1575) in sixteenth-century Safed, Palestine.

silsila: The chain of mystical transmission from master to disciple that links the founder or reputed founder of a Sufi order to subsequent generations of leaders. The *silsila*s of many orders ultimately went back to one of the companions of the Prophet Muhammad, particularly Ali.

subashi (**also** *wali*):   Literally, 'head of the water', the chief of police in an Ottoman provincial city, often a localized Janissary.

Sufism: Islamic mysticism, characterized after the twelfth century CE by Sufi orders.

sunna: The tradition or 'custom' of the Prophet Muhammad and his companions, including the first four caliphs, consisting of their words and deeds.

Sunnis: Adherents of the majority sect of Islam who believe that the caliph should be chosen by community consensus, which is thought to be part of the *sunna*, or 'custom', of the Prophet Muhammad.

suq: A bazaar, usually open-air, in a Middle Eastern city; also, a market street devoted to a certain kind of good or craft.

Syrian Catholics: Orthodox Christians in Ottoman Syria who recognized the Vatican during the eighteenth century under pressure from the French, whom many of them served as commercial agents and from whom they received diplomatic protection.

Tanzimat: Literally, 'reorganizations', the programme of westernizing political reforms, including abolition of the *jizya*, land tenure reform, and moves towards consultative government, enacted by the central Ottoman authority between 1839 and 1876.

tapu tahrir defteri: Literally, 'register of title deeds', a government register resulting from a cadastral survey, listing all villages in a province and all households in each village, as well as unattached populations such as bachelors. Such registers yield information on revenue sources and population.

tariqa: Literally 'path', a Sufi order.

tax-farming: System of delegating revenue collection in which the tax farmer, usually a wealthy government official or grandee, purchased at auction the revenue-collection rights to a given territory or urban operation. Any revenue the tax farmer collected in excess of the purchase price became his profit. Tax-farming became widespread in the Ottoman Empire during the seventeenth century and was a major factor in the rise of provincial notables.

timar: A grant of land revenue collection rights assigned to a military commander in lieu of a salary. The timariot was expected to use the revenues to equip a certain number of horsemen for the sultan's army. In the Arab lands, the *timar* system was imposed in Syria and northern Iraq.

tujjar (**singular,** *tajir*):   Long-distance merchants who shipped goods overland and/or overseas.

Turcomans: Nomadic and semi-nomadic Turkic tribal populations who migrated from Central Asia into various parts of Iran, eastern Anatolia, northern Iraq, northern Syria and Lebanon in the wake of the Mongol invasions of the thirteenth century. The Karakoyunlu, Akkoyunlu and Safavid dynasties were of Turcoman origin. In addition, the Ottomans appear to have settled Turcomans in northern Syria and Iraq during the sixteenth century.

Twelver Shiites: See Imamis.

ulema: Literally, 'those having knowledge', a blanket term for Islamic scholar-officials, encompassing *qadis*, *muftis*, theologians and *madrasa* professors. An ulema hierarchy prevailed in the Ottoman central lands whereby top positions in the religious establishment were awarded to graduates of the most prestigious *madrasas*.

Umayyads: Arab dynasty, descended from a wealthy clan of Mecca, who held the Sunni caliphate from 661–750 CE. They are reviled by Shiites for usurping the caliphate from the descendants of Ali ibn Abi Talib and for ordering the death of Ali's son Husayn.

'unity of being': The mystical concept, articulated by the Spanish mystic Muhyi al-Din ibn Arabi (1165–1240), that all of creation is a part of God. Although this came to be a tenet of most Sufi orders, it was denounced by some conservative ulema as tantamount to pantheism.

Uqayl (also Agayl): Conglomerate of merchants and Bedouins of various tribes who came to control overland trade among Syria, Iraq and the Arabian peninsula during the eighteenth century. They served as agents for the merchants of Damascus and Baghdad, and escorted commercial caravans between the two cities, as well as pilgrimage caravans leaving the two cities for Mecca.

usufruct: The use of the land, as opposed to the land itself. Most land-holding rights in the Ottoman and earlier Islamic empires were to the land's usufruct: that is, to the crops that could be grown on the land and the revenue they produced.

vali **(also *wali*)**: The governor of an Ottoman province, synonymous with *beylerbeyi*: The term was most commonly used in the Arab provinces.

vilayet: The province a *vali* (*beylerbeyi*) administered.

vizier (also vezir, wazir): A government minister holding the rank of pasha. Most provincial governors and many members of the grand vizier's *divan* were viziers.

vizier and pasha household: A household, consisting of a network of patron–client ties, established by a vizier in the Ottoman central government or by a provincial governor. Such households played a pivotal role in the rebellions of the Jelali governors during the seventeenth century.

Wahhabis: Puritanical Sunni sect which emerged in the Arabian peninsula during the eighteenth century and allied with the Saudis against the Ottoman government. They opposed all innovations to the *sunna* of the Prophet Muhammad, including Sufism and using community consensus or logical analogy to reach a legal decision.

wakala: See *khan*.

wakil **(Turkish, *vekil*)**: An agent, usually a commercial or legal agent. A *wakil* could, for example, represent a woman in a Muslim law court or conduct business transactions on behalf of a long-distance merchant or Ottoman official. See also 'agent of the harem'.

wali: See *subashı* and *vali*.

waqf (**Turkish, vakıf**):   A pious foundation whereby revenues from selected lands and/or properties were endowed in perpetuity to the upkeep of a religious or charitable institution, such as a mosque, *madrasa*, soup kitchen, hospital, Quran school or public drinking fountain. *Waqf* could also be used to circumvent inheritance laws; in that case, the founder might name a family member superintendent of endowed family property.

waqfiyya (**Turkish, vakfiyye**):   The foundation deed of a *waqf*, stipulating the founder and superintendent, as well as all goods, services and salaries to be provided for the institution endowed.

Yazidis: Adherents of an ancient, Zoroastrian-influenced Kurdish religion, most widespread in northern Iraq, centring on the worship of powerful angels. Because one of these angels is named Iblis, a Muslim appellation for Satan, the religion has often been wrongly described and maligned as devil-worship.

Yemeni Arabs: See Qays, Qaysi.

yerliyye: Localized Janissaries, as opposed to the *kapı kulları* dispatched from Istanbul. Beginning in the late sixteenth century, *yerliyye* became especially influential in Damascus and Aleppo.

yeshiva: A Jewish theological college, analogous to a *madrasa*.

Zaydis: The smallest surviving subsect of Shiism. They do not recognize a set line of imams but believe that any descendant of Ali's son Hasan or Husayn can be imam if he is just and able to defend the community. The name derives from Ali's great-grandson Zayd, recognized as the fifth imam by early Zaydis, who rebelled against the Umayyads in 740.

zeamet: A large grant of land revenue collection rights, larger than a *timar* but smaller than a *hass* grant, usually assigned to senior military commanders in lieu of a cash salary.

INDEX